D1498863

YOUR SELF

YOUR SELF

An Introduction to Psychology

Miriam S. Grace
Philip T. Nicholson
Don R. Lipsitt, M. D.

Photography by Kenneth M. Bernstein

Drawings by Margery Frem,
Philip Nicholson,
and Jack Nicholson

HART PUBLISHING COMPANY, INC.
NEW YORK CITY

Contents

*Choosing a career and a spouse; the
pressures of work; the meaning of
love; "stages" of adulthood; the mid-
life crisis and the empty-nest syndrome; middle age to old age; what
the old teach the young.*

ulation of the brain; brain mapping;
the body's messenger system; chemi-
cal therapies; brain surgery; biofeed-
back: revealing the body to itself.

III. People in Groups

V. Thinking About Yourself

YOUR SELF

To Carmen P. Rinaldi
for his warmth, vitality, and concern
as an educator and as a person.

Acknowledgments

We would like to thank four people who have been our "silent co-authors" in this venture:

Anita Firestone, who has been our constant supporter, offering ideas and encouragement throughout the last two years;

Carmen Rinaldi, who commented on this text—often with humor—line by line, tried it out on his children, and reminded us that good grammar still exists;

Ethel Sadowsky, who watched over our "sexism," and more seriously, helped us with clarity, punctuation, and a parent's perspective;

Lillian Murdock, who offered excellent suggestions for each chapter, and literally captured the spirit of the book by verbalizing the final chapter.

We would also like to thank Paul Sullivan and Ralph Mosher, who wrote the chapter on "Moral Development"; Douglas Fulrath, who created the section on "psychological settings" in "Perception and Persuasion"; and Roger Aubrey, for his suggestions and support.

Kenneth Bernstein captured our own "family of man" (and woman) photographic essay for the book. Margery Frem, Janet Epstein, Jack Nicholson, and Myron Tupa did the excellent line drawings with a minimum of direction from us. We would like to thank Jules Feiffer and Random House for permission to use his cartoons.

Daniel Stein was our editorial consultant. We really appreciated his thoughtful guidance, humor, and enthusiasm. Special thanks also go to John Thorn, who worked so patiently with us.

This book was inspired by the openness of our students and their willingness to share their concerns and experiences. They taught us how to teach psychology in a meaningful way. Three students were especially helpful in the preparation of this book: Debby Fenn, Karen Goldrich, and Julie Wolfe.

Finally, we would like to thank our families and friends for their ideas, suggestions, encouragement, and patience: Beth Nicholson, Merna Lipsitt, Eric and Steven Lipsitt, Judy Grace, Mr. & Mrs. Joseph Grace, Robert Alexander, Brenda Anderson, Bernard Saslow, Jerry Summer, Robert Sperber, Barbara Rabinovitz, Sally Broudo, and Susan Flynn.

Introduction

Make it thy business to know thyself,
which is the most difficult lesson in the world.
CERVANTES, *Don Quixote*

Imagine for a moment that you could see your whole life unfold before your eyes, from birth through old age. What will you be like when you are twenty-five? Will you have a job or be in school? Will you be married? Will you still be living in the same city, or will you be located hundreds of miles away? Will your personality change and your values shift? Will you be more outgoing or more shy? More serious or more relaxed?

Picture yourself at forty. What will you look like? Vigorous and fit, or fighting the waistline bulge of middle age? Settled with three children, single, or divorced? Approaching the peak of your career, or working in a dead-end job? You may be happy or frustrated as you look back over your shoulder at the first half of your life. How will you view the years to come?

At age seventy, will you be working or retired? Living in your own home? In an apartment? With your children? In a residence for the elderly? Who and what will fill your days? Maybe you will be energetic and involved in life; or

if i knew all the questions i'd have all the answers.

perhaps you will be just marking time. Will you feel lonely, empty, regretful, and sad? Or will you be wiser and more content, with peace of mind from a life well-lived?

Although you can only guess at the answers to these questions, you probably know a lot more about your future than you realize. Most people do not radically change their personalities and values between seventeen and seventy. If you are relaxed and easy-going now, you will probably continue to be so. If you are serious and intense, you will most likely have the same drive and determination at forty. People *evolve* as they grow older, building and elaborating on their *basic* personalities. They usually make subtle and gradual shifts in one direction or another as they move through different life experiences.

However, basic behavior patterns are often repeated. The dependent child may become a dependent adult, searching for a spouse who will make all the decisions and provide security and protection. The adolescent who learns to be aggressive and outspoken in the classroom may continue to be assertive years later on the job and at home. It is therefore possible to predict a considerable amount about a person's future from studying his past and present behavior.[1]

A Common Thread

Psychologists have tried to chart the course of human development from birth to death. While we are all unique individuals, we nonetheless share basic life experiences. Psychologists have identified "stages" of development we all normally pass through and possible "crisis" points we are likely to encounter along the way.

Consider your uniqueness. You have a different personality from your brothers, sisters, and parents. You have different skills and aptitudes, likes and dislikes. No one else has the exact same experiences from day to day. Only you know what you are thinking.

Nonetheless, your friends share many of your thoughts, feelings, and problems. They also are anxious to leave home and be on their own. They are eager to decide on a job or a career and to develop a meaningful relationship with someone of the opposite sex. They, too, fear that they will love and be rejected. They have the same conflicting feelings as you: determined to be independent adults, yet sometimes longing for the security and protection of childhood. These conflicts are common in the "stage" of life called adolescence. Your experiences, while essentially unique, do have a common thread shared by others.

Individual Differences

In addition to tracing the normal course of human development, psychologists also try to explain the causes of individual differences. Why are two children in the same family so different? If the oldest child had been born third instead, would his or her personality still be the same? How much does gender account for differences in personality? Why does one person learn faster than another?

Why does one person argue in a heated way when angry, while another person in the same situation is silent and just walks away? What causes someone to develop an ulcer under stress, while another person experiences similar challenges and remains in good health? How does a person's behavior as a member of a group differ from his behavior as an individual? Do ethnic and racial groups have their own characteristics?

An Approach to Life

Psychology is an important part of everyday life. You probably use a "common-sense" *psychological approach* in a variety of situations, perhaps without realizing it. Sitting at the breakfast table you may wonder what would be *the best way* to ask your parents to give you the car for the evening. Passing a friend at school with whom you are angry, you wonder whether to confront or ignore him.

Which will be more effective and make you feel better?
When your teacher asks you why you are behind in your
work, what reasons will you give? How will you bargain
for extra time?

Which group of friends will you sit with at lunch?
What will you tell the others so they will not be offended?
As you walk to your job after school, you may be mulling
over the conversation you had with your girlfriend; you
wonder how you might have handled it differently.

As customers surround the shirt counter, how will you
keep them patient while you wait on one customer who
can't make up his mind? What "technique" will you use to
sell the shirts? When your younger brother announces at
dinner that you were the one who left the dirty dishes in
the sink, will you handle his disloyalty with a punch, a
bribe, a laugh, or a threat?

We all use a kind of amateur psychology in learning
how to deal more effectively with other people. We
decide how best to phrase a question, how to settle an
argument, how to correct someone tactfully. We also try
to understand our own feelings and behavior. Why do we
"deny" that we are hurt when someone forgets to invite us
to a party? Why might we blame others for a mistake we
made? How can we feel both happy and sad at the same
moment? What motivation do we sometimes have when
we just "forget" to do an errand? Why do we get
depressed? How can we help ourselves snap out of it?

As an amateur psychologist, you would probably
decide these issues by intuition and common sense. As you
begin to study psychology formally, you will gain a much
more factual and reliable approach to understanding
human behavior.

Psychology is the study of mental processes and

behavior: how people think, feel, and act. (More generally, it is the study of the behavior of organisms.) "Psyche" comes from the Greek word meaning "soul" or "mind," and "logy" means "theory" or "science." Psychology is an *organized body of knowledge* which is expanding rapidly. Many of its principles were learned from precise scientific experiments with animals, such as rats and monkeys, as well as with people. Several of its theories come from close observation of thousands of people over long periods of time. The study of psychology will provide insight into and understanding of every aspect of your life.

In this book, we focus on both the normal course of human development and the variety of factors which contribute to our individual differences in personality, intelligence, and character. We will ask you to apply many psychological principles to your own life. While no book will supply you with all the answers to the questions we have raised, we hope you will learn to understand yourself and others better by thinking about these common life experiences.

YOUR TIME LINE

Draw a line (in any shape) which best represents your life up to this point. Mark the important events in your life on it. Be specific. Ask your parents and grandparents for information about your childhood. Your friends might also help you with important experiences over the last five years.

Then continue the line (in a different color ink or with dashes) to reflect how you expect your life to progress through adulthood. Write in significant events in the order in which you expect them to occur.

1. *What does your time line tell you about yourself?*

    Why were these events important?

    How have they affected your life?

    How different would you be if you could have changed one or two events along your line?

    Was it difficult to ask people about yourself? If so, why?

2. *How flexible or fixed does your future seem to you?*

    How did you choose each future event? Explain the timing, conclusions, and assumptions about your life.

    What power do you have to change the course of your life?

FOOTNOTES

1. Regrettably, the English language does not offer a pronoun without gender, except for the frequently inappropriate "one." To fill this void, some people in recent years have advocated the use of "he/she," "s/he," and other rather awkward locutions. In this book, we generally use the traditional male pronouns because they present less stylistic difficulty. We hope that readers will understand that "she" could be substituted for "he" in most instances in this text.

I.

The Life Cycle

To every thing there is a season, and a time to every purpose under the heaven:

A time to be born, and a time to die; a time to plant, and a time to pluck up that which is planted; . . .

A time to get, and a time to lose; a time to keep, and a time to cast away;

ECCLESIASTES, *III, 1, 2, 6*

I.

The Past in Your Future: Childhood

For most people, childhood memories are special. We think back to those worlds of make-believe we shared with a friend; to our first day at school when we did (or did not) cry; to a neighborhood job that made us feel rich and independent. We think of those birthday parties to which we invited the whole class . . . and got twenty presents. We remember when we were picked for the baseball team . . . and when our first pet died.

Although we may remember only highlights of our childhood, psychologists tell us that those early years are *the most crucial in our lives*; they shape our intellectual growth, mold our personality, and establish our basic values and attitudes about life. Human development is not a haphazard process; it is an orderly sequence of events which builds on past experience.

Probably more research is being done in child development than in any other area of psychology, yet there are still many unanswered questions. To what extent are personality and intelligence inherited? To what extent are they influenced by our culture, environment, and experiences? Why are two children from the same family so different? How much does a newborn infant under-

Photo courtesy of Kenneth M. Bernstein

Childhood memories are very special.

stand? Is the oldest child really more likely to succeed? Is an only child inevitably spoiled? How does a child's self-image affect his schoolwork? In this chapter we explore the enormous impact of childhood experiences in shaping a person's life.

14

REMEMBERING WHEN

1. *What is your earliest memory in childhood?*

   How old were you at the time?

   Why do you think that you recall this as your first memory?

2. *Create a collage of your own childhood memories in a sequence of time. Explain the significance of each event or experience which stands out in your memory.*

3. *Ask your parents about their childhoods. How different were theirs from yours?*

   What caused the differences?

   What is your mother's or father's earliest memory?

In the Beginning

It is startling to think that so much of who we are and what we will become is settled in an instant. Yet all the physical characteristics we inherit from our parents are determined at the moment a male sperm penetrates a female egg and causes each to release 23 particles called *chromosomes.*

These 46 chromosomes in the fertilized egg contain much smaller particles called *genes*—genes are the "carriers" of all that we inherit. Except for identical twins, each child inherits a *different and unique* combination of his father's and mother's genes. That is why no two children in a family look exactly alike.

Within two weeks of conception, the fertilized egg is implanted in the mother's uterine wall. The fertilized egg divides and subdivides rapidly, producing thousands of cells which soon begin to take shape; some of these cells form organs. Within eight or nine weeks, the embryo is one inch long, with a visible face, mouth, eyes, arms, and legs. At the end of the third month, the fetus, now three inches, resembles a male or female human being. By sixteen weeks, the fetus begins to kick. The mother can now feel life within her. At twenty-eight weeks, the fetus would probably be able to live if born prematurely.

What do those genes, joined at conception, control? We know that a person's physical characteristics are influenced by heredity: height, skin tone, hair color and texture, eye color, the shape of the nose. Intellectual potential is also influenced by heredity.

Moreover, scientists believe that blood pressure, length of life, and certain personality characteristics may be partially under genetic control. For example, shyness may be in one's genes! Diseases like diabetes, glaucoma, hemophilia, sickle cell anemia, and Tay-Sachs may be passed from parent to child. Three out of every 100 children are born with a genetic defect which may cause a physical abnormality or mental retardation.

Since we know inheritance plays a major role in defining a child's future, it is now possible for parents to consult a genetic counselor who will take a family history and can predict genetic problems. Parents can be tested to see if they are carriers of any disease. Though we still have much to learn about the role of heredity, its tremendous significance in human development is undeniable.

The Prenatal Environment

Ninety-three percent of all babies in this country are born healthy and normal. Yet "environmental" factors affect the baby even *before it is born*. The mother's diet and nutritional reserves are essential to the developing fetus. This is a serious problem for some Americans, and it has grave implications for those countries plagued by famine and poverty.

Barbara Wyden points out: "Nutrition, or more precisely malnutrition, has a direct effect on the way the brain grows: if a fetus does not receive enough nourishment, the rate of brain cell division slows down. A seriously deprived fetus may have 20 percent fewer brain cells than normal. If a newborn is seriously undernourished during the six months after birth, cell division is also slowed down—again by as much as 20 percent. If an infant should have been malnourished both in *utero* and after birth, the arithmetic is tragic. The brain may be 60 percent smaller."[1] It is too late to remedy the situation later. Premature birth, physical defects, small size, and even death may result from serious malnutrition.

Nutritional reserves must be built up over a long period of time. A woman's body begins to prepare for childbirth as early as adolescence. Merrill Read of the National Institute of Child Health and Human Development notes, "Getting ready to be a mother during a woman's adolescence is almost as important as the actual time when she's a mature woman and pregnant."[2]

The mother's age and medical history are also important influences on the fetus. Psychological studies have shown that mothers under 20 or over 35 tend to have a higher proportion of retarded youngsters than mothers between 20 and 35 years of age. A doctor always asks a pregnant woman whether she has had the German measles. This disease could seriously damage the fetus if contracted in the first few months of pregnancy.

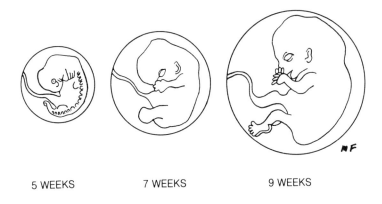

5 WEEKS   7 WEEKS   9 WEEKS

The Developing Embryo—"Environmental" factors affect the baby even before it is born. The mother's diet, age, and health are important medical concerns, as well as whether she smokes or takes drugs. Given all the possible prenatal influences, it is easy to understand why the study of child development must begin with conception rather than with birth.

Smoking can affect fetal development. Some studies show that when a mother smokes, there is an increase in the fetal heart rate. Smoking may also lead to premature birth. In Britain, a study covering a random sample of

15,000 children found that the death rate of infants born to mothers who had smoked during pregnancy was 26 percent higher than for infants born to non-smokers.[3]

Drugs may also harm the developing fetus. The tranquilizer thalidomide, once taken by many pregnant women in Europe, resulted in babies born with radically deformed limbs. Large doses of certain barbiturates cause brain damage in the fetus. Many other drugs are being studied for possible effects upon the fetus.

Emotional stress also produces a physiological reaction in the mother. For example, one researcher found that "bodily movements of fetuses increased several hundred percent while their mothers were undergoing emotional stress. If the mother's emotional upset lasted several weeks, fetal activity continued at an exaggerated level throughout the entire period."[4] Adrenalin and other chemical agents released into the mother's bloodstream may pass through the placenta and affect the developing fetus. Anxiety and tension may also cause a more difficult labor and delivery for the mother.

Another potential problem is Rh Factor incompatibility. This condition may develop when a mother has Rh negative blood and her husband has Rh positive blood—which occurs in 12 percent of all American marriages. If the developing fetus has Rh positive blood, some of its blood cells may leak into the mother's bloodstream, causing her to produce antibodies against the baby's blood. Although the first child is usually not affected, future babies could be. Until recently, the later babies were given transfusions, when necessary, to prevent damage. Now a new vaccine has been developed which can stop the Rh negative mother's production of antibodies so that the baby will not be harmed.[5]

IN THE BEGINNING

1. *What traits do you think you inherited from your mother? Your father?*

   Do your brothers and sisters share those traits?

   Are any diseases common to your family?

   What does your mother remember about being pregnant with you? With your siblings?

2. *Analyze your present diet. How nutritional is it?*

3. *Consult an obstetrician or family doctor. Find out:*

   How much weight is it reasonable for a pregnant woman to gain? Why?

   Are there any particular foods essential to her diet?

   How much exercise and sleep does she need?

   What questions will be asked when taking her medical history?

   Will she be allowed to smoke or take any drugs?

   What procedure will be followed in delivering the baby?

   What is post-partum depression?

4. *Suppose your friend asks you for help in finding a place where she can get good prenatal care. What*

> *agencies, hospitals, or clinics are there in your community to help her? What services does each provide?*

Given all these possible influences on the fetus, it is easy to see why the study of child development must begin with conception rather than with birth. Scientist Niko Tinbergen has accurately stated that "from the moment the egg cell is fertilized, the organism begins to interact with its environment."[6]

The Newborn

The average full-term baby weighs between six and eight pounds at birth and is about twenty inches long. A slap on the baby's buttocks causes the famous "birth cry," inflating the baby's lungs so that he can breathe unaided.

Within the first minute of birth, the baby is given the Apgar test which measures the baby's heart rate, breathing effort, muscle tone, reflex responses, and color. A high rating means the baby is normal and healthy.

What sense can the tiny infant make of the world? The newborn can hear, see, smell, and feel pressure and pain. He realizes when his position is changed. The only sense that lags behind temporarily is taste.

The infant is also born with certain *reflexes*, natural responses which he does not have to learn. For example, the placing of a nipple on the baby's lips starts him sucking. The baby grasps your finger if you touch his palm, a reflex which disappears by the fourth month. The baby cries when he feels discomfort or hunger. Crying is his principal method of communicating with the world.

Newborns sleep about 80 percent of the time, and spend their waking moments feeding and looking. As the baby physically matures and learns from interacting with his surroundings, he gradually develops the skills and capacities that make him seem more like a person.

The newborn child does not realize he is a separate individual. Until he is five or six months old, he does not differentiate between himself and the rest of the world. The baby depends completely on others for survival and for the physical warmth and affection which promote trust in the world.

The importance of "contact comfort" was demonstrated by psychologist Harry Harlow in his famous experiments with monkeys. Harlow exposed two groups of infant monkeys to "artificial mothers" made of either wire or terry cloth. For one group of monkeys, the terry cloth mother provided the milk from a bottle in its chest. For the other group, the wire mother did the feeding. Harlow wanted to see to which mother the infant monkeys would become attached when given a choice. He found that even when the wire mother did the feeding, the infant monkeys spent much more time with the cloth mother. Contact comfort is very important to the infant.

Is "Mother Love" Natural?

Most of us assume that the minute we see our newborn child we will love it. Two researchers found that love is not an instant emotion. Kenneth Robson of Tufts University School of Medicine and Howard Moss of the

National Institute of Mental Health studied a group of 54 bright young women and their first babies. They found that "34 percent of the mothers had no feelings at all for their babies when they first set eyes on them; 7 percent reported negative feelings—'I couldn't look at her,' 'I wanted them to take him away.' About half said they had positive feelings, but only seven women described these feelings as love."[7]

Most of the women reported that it took six to nine weeks before they felt love. Robson and Moss noted that "the emotion was triggered by very specific happenings" such as when the baby began smiling at the mother and responding to her. Since our culture expects a mother to love her baby, neutral or negative feelings may make the mother feel guilty or anxious. It is important to realize that love may be learned!

In other cultures, mother love may not even be expected. For example, in Aritama, an isolated community in Colombia, South America, " . . . neither men nor women desire children as objects of love. Men want children as economic resources, and women view childbearing and raising as an unpleasant duty to their husbands. . . . Frequently the baby is handled rather roughly. . . . He is handled like a dead weight, devoid of all feeling, and hardly any thought is given to his being comfortable and safe. . . . They handle him as if his only need were food."[8]

Infants: Happy, Shy, or Just Difficult?

How early do babies show their personalities? The New York Longitudinal Study suggests that most babies fall into three temperamental categories. The majority are "easy babies" with happy, pleasant dispositions. The second group are "slow-to-warm-up babies" who are cautious of people and new situations. One out of every ten babies is born "difficult." The difficult baby is intense. He may rage and cry, have irregular eating and sleeping habits, and adjust more slowly to new situations. Alexander Thomas of the New York University School of Medicine explains, "The baby will eventually adapt if the parents are consistent, firm, and loving." The parents "must learn to grit their teeth and sweat it out. They must learn it is wrong to do something, anything, to stop the crying. This only teaches baby he can get anything he wants by howling."[9]

Researchers do not yet know why some babies are born difficult, but as these babies grow older they usually learn to adapt and fit in. Thus babies show a distinct temperament even within the first few months of life!

Infancy is a crucial time of life. The baby grows rapidly, doubling his weight by four or five months. The range of his learning is greater than at any other stage of development. He will learn to crawl and to walk, to communicate with words and actions. He will "take in" the world. The infant will smile with delight and sense when to become anxious. At this stage, the baby's relationship with his mother is the most important factor in his life. She represents the whole world to him.

We began by stating that the earliest years of life have an extremely important influence on a person's later development. Let us see why this is true by examining the ideas of Sigmund Freud, Jean Piaget, and Erik Erikson. Their theories help to explain the social, emotional, and intellectual development of the young child.

Sigmund Freud: The Psychosexual Approach

At what age would you guess that your personality was pretty well set? At ten? At fifteen? At twenty? Sigmund Freud believed that your personality was basically defined within your first six years of life: Freud, a Viennese psychiatrist who lived from 1856 to 1939, startled the world with his theories about human development.

The Structure of Personality

Freud believed that the personality is made up of three interacting forces: the *id*, the *ego*, and the *superego*. Simply stated, the *id* consists of our *biological drives and instincts*: the energy directing our desire for food, for sex, for simple reflex actions like blinking and sneezing. The *id* is made up of all the impulses, wishes, and needs that are constantly pushing for expression, without regard for anyone else's convenience. When the baby is hungry, he wants to eat immediately! If he feels uncomfortable, he screams or thrashes about, even if his parents are disrupted in the middle of the night. If he must "go," it doesn't matter to him whether it's in his bed, or on the floor, or in his pants. Whenever tension builds up, expression and satisfaction are the goal—come what may!

Before long, social circumstances and the needs of others begin to have an impact. The child learns that he will not be allowed to impose *all* of his desires on others. To adapt, the child develops an *ego* which can observe, think, reason, and select appropriate behavior. The id says, "I am hungry," but the ego says, "Lunch isn't served for half an hour; I'll have to wait." The ego does the work of trying to satisfy our needs and desires in ways which will be reasonable and socially acceptable. Sometimes the ego may simply have to say "no" to a wish or desire pushing for expression or satisfaction.

While the ego can do a pretty good job of decision-making, it sometimes needs a little help. The *superego* is developed by the age of six to help distinguish right from wrong, good from bad, social from anti-social. The superego is the "moral" part of the personality, particularly our conscience. Someone once defined the conscience as "that which keeps us from doing what we shouldn't do even when no one is looking."[10] In other words, the superego is our built-in value system *learned from our parents and culture*. It makes us feel guilty when we do something of which others would not approve. It makes us feel proud of ourselves when we do what is "right." The ego must "try to integrate the often conflicting demands of the id, the superego, and the external world."[11] Too strong a superego makes us rigid and inhibited. Too weak a superego may lead us into conflicts with other people or cause a lack of ambition.

Usually the three forces of the personality "work together as a team."[12] The id, the ego, and the superego are just names for the psychological processes going on within us. As the child develops, he begins to work out a comfortable balance among these three processes. As a baby he is most responsive to his id impulses. By the time he is ready to start school, he has gained a superego from five years of life experience.

How does this happen? Freud believed that children pass through a series of distinct stages as they develop. He felt that the experiences we have in each stage shape our personality and determine what we will be like later in life. Therefore, the first six years are crucial in human development.

The Psychosexual Stages of Development

A baby enters the world helpless, totally dependent on others for survival. In the *oral* stage (the first year of life), the infant's main preoccupation is eating. But the baby "takes in" more than food. Nestled in a parent's arms, the baby views the world around him. The interaction between parent and child as the baby is being fed, changed, and held makes the child feel either comfortable and secure or tense and anxious. The tone of their relationship is established early. If the child's needs are consistently met, he begins to develop trust in the outside world.

Freud called this the oral stage because the major activity of an infant when awake is eating. The sensual pleasure of sucking is important to the infant. At a later point the child may suck his thumb when feeling insecure, perhaps wishing to be back at this protected oral stage.

Personality traits derived from patterns learned during the oral stage include gullibility (taking in whatever one is told), sarcasm (oral aggression), dependency, passivity, insecurity, and the desire to acquire things. Oral satisfaction may lead to friendliness, optimism and self-assurance. The "oral type" takes great pleasure in eating, drinking, and smoking.

In his second year, the infant moves into the *anal* stage of development. The child begins to learn bowel and bladder control. He is urged not to wet his pants but to wait and go to the toilet. He must learn how to delay immediate gratification of an impulse. The ego begins to take command. The impulses of the id are tempered.

If done in a gradual and relaxed manner, toilet training can give the child a sense of mastery and accomplishment. However, if started too early, before the child has the physical capacity to perform this task, the lesson he learns may be that he is helpless and frustrated when demands are made on him. If pushed too hard, even a child with physical control may decide to rebel against parental efforts to train him. When training is carried out carefully and sensitively, however, the child learns that he is not helpless or passive and that he can now exert some control over his life.

Parents and child specialists speak about "the terrible two's." At this age, struggles occur not only over toilet training but over many forms of behavior. The child is physically able to "take charge" by walking, climbing, and exploring. If his parents aren't ready for all this activity, the question of who is controlling whom becomes a major problem. Sometimes telling a two-year-old to stop a specific behavior gets the same response seen in adults when they read a "don't touch" sign—they simply *have* to do what they're told not to. Personality characteristics which originate during this stage of development may include stubbornness, stinginess, orderliness, punctuality, defiance, compulsiveness, creativity, and productivity.

The third stage, when the child is between three and five years old, is called the *phallic* or *Oedipal* stage. Children become more aware of their genital organs, enjoy the sensual pleasure of masturbation, and have fantasies involving love relationships with their parents.

Photo courtesy of Kenneth M. Bernstein

Every young child progresses through *stages* of development. In the oral stage, the infant is helpless and dependent on others for his care. During this first year of life, the
infant's main preoccupation is sucking and eating. But the
baby "takes in" more than food: nestled in a parent's arms,
the baby views the world around him. In his second year,
the baby moves into the anal stage of development, when
toilet-training takes place. The child begins to walk, climb,
and explore, and often his desires and behavior put him
into a contest with his parents!

Boys and girls become more aware of their parents as being *married* to each other, and there is great interest in and curiosity about this "new" discovery. Boys may daydream or fantasize about what it would be like to marry their mothers. (This is the commonly discussed *Oedipus complex*, named for the Greek king who killed his father and married his mother.) Girls desire to have their fathers all to themselves.

The child knows these wishes are unrealistic fantasies. The young boy pulls back, afraid his father will punish him for being a "rival." He gives up his wish to take his father's place, but tries instead to copy his father's style in hopes of one day finding a woman like his mother. He comes as close as possible to the fantasy of marriage by trying to identify with, or be like, his father. The girl's break with her father is more gradual than the boy's break with his mother. In our culture, it is more acceptable for fathers to continue to show affection for their daughters. Yet the young girl also begins to identify with her mother and hopes to marry a man like her father someday.

In the Oedipal stage, children learn to become more independent of their mothers. This is not easy. You may remember the many times you crawled into bed with your parents seeking security and protection from a frightening world! In "My Oedipus Complex," novelist Frank O'Connor describes this stage of life well:

> *Father was in the army all through the war—the first war, I mean—so, up to the age of five, I never saw much of him, and what I saw did not worry me. . . . In fact, I rather liked his visits, though it was an uncomfortable squeeze between Mother and him when I got into the big bed in the early morning. . . .*

One morning I got into the big bed, and there, sure enough, was Father in his usual Santa Claus manner, but later, instead of a uniform, he put on his best blue suit, and Mother was as pleased as anything. I saw nothing to be pleased about, because, out of uniform, Father was altogether less interesting, but she only beamed, and explained that our prayers had been answered and off we went to Mass to thank God for having brought Father safely home.

The irony of it! That very day when he came in to dinner he took off his boots and put on his slippers, donned the dirty old cap he wore about the house to save him from colds, crossed his legs, and began to talk gravely to Mother, who looked anxious. Naturally, I disliked her looking anxious, because it destroyed her good looks, so I interrupted him.

"Just a moment, Larry!" she said gently.

This was only what she said when we had boring visitors, so I attached no importance to it and went on talking.

"Do be quiet, Larry!" she said impatiently, "Don't you hear me talking to Daddy?"

This was the first time I had heard those ominous words, "talking to Daddy," and I couldn't help feeling that if this was how God answered prayers, he couldn't listen to them very attentively.

* * * * *

At teatime, "talking to Daddy" began again, complicated this time by the fact that he had an evening paper, and every few minutes he put it down and told Mother something new out of it. I felt this was foul play. Man for man, I was prepared to compete with him any time for Mother's attention, but when he had it all made up for him by other people it left me no chance. Several times I tried to change the subject without success.

"You must be quiet while Daddy is reading, Larry," Mother said impatiently.

It was clear that she either genuinely liked talking to Father better than talking to me, or else that he had some terrible hold on her which made her afraid to admit the truth.

"Mummy," I said that night when she was tucking me up, "do you think if I prayed hard God would send Daddy back to the war?"

✿ ✿ ✿ ✿ ✿

Father and I were enemies, open and avowed. We conducted a series of skirmishes against one another, he trying to steal my time with Mother and I his. When she was sitting on my bed, telling me a story, he took to looking for some pair of old boots which he alleged he had left behind him at the beginning of the war. While he talked to Mother I played loudly with my toys to show my lack of concern.

✿ ✿ ✿ ✿ ✿

But as time went on I saw more and more how he managed to alienate Mother and me. What made it worse was that I couldn't grasp his method or see what attraction he had for Mother. In every possible way he was less winning than I. He had a common accent and made noises at his tea. I thought for a while that it might be the newspapers which she was interested in, so I made up bits of news of my own to read to her. Then I thought it might be the smoking, which I personally thought attractive, and took his pipes and went round the house dribbling into them till he caught me. I even made noises at my tea, but Mother only told me I was disgusting. It all seemed to hinge round that unhealthy habit of sleeping together, so I made a point of dropping into their bedroom and nosing around, talking to myself, so that they wouldn't know I was watching them, but they were never up to anything that I could see. In the end it beat me. It seemed to depend on being grown-up and giving people rings, and I realized I'd have to wait.

But at the same time I wanted him to see that I was only waiting, not giving up the fight. One evening when he was particularly obnoxious, chattering away well above my head, I let him have it.

"Mummy," I said, "do you know what I'm going to do when I grow up?"

"No, dear," she replied. "What?"

"I'm going to marry you," I said quietly.

Father gave a great guffaw out of him, but he didn't take me in. I knew it must only be pretence. And Mother, in spite of everything, was pleased. I felt she was probably relieved to know that one day Father's hold on her would be broken.[13]

Are Freud's stages of development, such as the Oedipus complex, universal? In Israel, children who are raised in a kibbutz do not go through the Oedipal struggle with the same intensity as do children raised by their parents. Psychologist Bruno Bettelheim explains, "It is the economic and social dependency of the child, and the mutual emotions that arise between parents and child through their intimate living together, that makes for the Oedipal situation, and not the biological fact of parenthood."[14]

After the Oedipal stage, the child enters *latency*, a period in which his interests are focused outside the home—on school, peers, and activities. As his world expands, the child becomes less absorbed in seeking sensual gratification. Love and sex are submerged issues until adolescence.

Freud's psychosexual theory shows how the child learns to adjust his personal needs to the outside world and to develop a conscience and an understanding of acceptable behavior. The child learns to control his impulses and to delay gratifying his desires. He learns to *repress* (put out of his conscious mind) those thoughts which might make him feel anxious or guilty. The child learns behavior appropriate to his or her sex, and gradually assumes independence in venturing out into the world.

The infant begins life motivated by the desires and drives of the id for food and sensual pleasure (sucking, contact comfort, wetting his pants when the urge comes). As he progresses through the anal and Oedipal stages, the child's ego and superego become important and exert some control over the id. The child learns not to expect instant gratification, but rather to adjust to *other people's* rules and expectations, eating when they say to, going to the bathroom, and being "good." The child learns to *think* and to *reason* and thereby to adapt to his surroundings. In the first six years of life, a person develops from an id-controlled infant into a child with a more balanced personality (ego, superego, and id).

THOSE FIRST SIX YEARS

1. *Ask your parents what you were like as an infant: happy, shy, or difficult?*

   Were your brothers and sisters different? How?

2. *What "carryovers" from the oral and anal stages of development do you see in adult behavior?*

3. *Do you remember any specific incidents in your childhood which affected your developing a conscience? Describe them.*

4. *How would you describe the interplay of id, ego, and superego in your personality?*

The basic balance of the forces of your personality comes from the experiences of these formative years. You may emerge as impulsive and pleasure-oriented (strong id), moderate and rational (strong ego), or rigid, inhibited, and moralistic (strong superego). How would you describe yourself in these terms?

When we re-examine Freud's theories in more depth (in Chapter 4, "The Push and Pull of Inner Needs"), we will see how our unconscious childhood desires may be expressed, often indirectly, in adult life. Through psychoanalysis, the Freudian therapist helps to re-create a person's childhood memories in order to relate current behavior to past experience. All of us display personality traits we acquired during those first six years of life!

Jean Piaget: Learning Is Developmental

You probably do not remember how you first learned to talk, or to add and to multiply, or to reason out a problem. Most of us have forgotten the difficulties we had in making sense of the world. We tend to assume that our ability to use logic came naturally, and therefore that the major difference between an adult and a child is just in the amount of knowledge each has. Not so, says Jean Piaget, a Swiss psychologist famous for his theories about intellectual development.

Piaget maintains that a child reasons differently from an adult. Piaget believes that learning involves *creating*. The mind is not a camera which simply "records a pre-existing world of persons and things."[15] Instead, the mind functions like a creative artist who interprets the world as he sees it, perhaps quite differently from the way others see it. All of us, including the child, interpret reality from a personal point of view. Think of how many times several people have watched the same incident and have described it differently. Or look at an abstract painting and ask friends what they see in it: each will describe it in the light of his or her individual experience. We all see selectively, and interpret what we see. An adult views the world differently than a child does.

Piaget also believes that learning is developmental. Our ability to think evolves through a series of four stages. What and how we think is related to our stage of development. Everyone goes through these stages in the same order, using two processes to learn. A person *assimilates*, or absorbs the world from a subjective point of view. He also *accommodates*, or adjusts his perceptions to "conform with outer reality."

Stages in Intellectual Development

In the *sensorimotor stage* (from birth to about two), the child explores the world through the senses: looking, sucking, smelling, listening, touching. At the beginning of this stage, the child has no sense of self versus the rest of the world. Objects appear and disappear—nothing seems permanent or logical. "It is as if the child were on a train watching the world pass before him."[16]

As he grows, the baby begins to learn that his actions produce certain results. He repeats those actions which bring pleasant results. For example, each time the baby pulls a lever on the crib, music is produced. When he taps a toy it moves, so he taps it again. Gradually the baby realizes that he is a separate being from all these objects, and that he can control them.

Up to six or eight months, the baby will not cry when his mother leaves the room. If she is not visible, she does not exist! The baby relates only to what he can see. But soon the game of peek-a-boo delights the baby. He is surprised and amused to see a person disappear and then appear again. If you hide a toy under his pillow, the baby now looks for it. He also recognizes familiar people and objects. He becomes attached to his mother (or whoever is most prominent in his life) as the specific person who makes him feel secure. When strangers approach, he may become anxious and cry.

During his first two years, the baby learns to coordinate his arms and his legs, to turn over, and to crawl. He explores his surroundings, learning how to judge space, distance, and size. At times this may be frightening, and he may cling to a "security" blanket or animal. Watch how fast a baby reacts when this security object is taken away! In these first two years, physical growth combined with experience help the baby to develop his intelligence.

The ages from two to seven are the *preoperational* years. The child learns to use *words* to represent objects. He can point to his pet and say "dog." Through the use of language he can now interact much more fully with those around him, asking questions and making his desires known. Think of how often the young child asks, "What's that?" or "Why?" Because the child believes there is a *purpose* to everything, he may ask, "Why is the sky blue?"

Young children may confuse "names" with the objects themselves. They do not understand that names are just labels. A crayon is a crayon; no further definition seems required. As David Elkind explains: "The child at this point is like the old gentleman who, when asked why noodles are called noodles, replied that 'they are white like noodles, soft like noodles and taste like noodles so we call them noodles'."[17]

In this stage, the child also *assigns life to inanimate objects.* Many youngsters believe that "the sun and moon follow them when they are out for a walk . . . that anything which moves is alive . . . that dreams come in through the window at night."[18] Remember your favorite childhood stories and poems. Clouds could sing in *Winnie-the-Pooh.* Remember how you chanted, "Rain, rain, go away. Come again some other day," as if your wish could control the elements?

The child *imitates* parents and siblings. He plays make-believe. He may dress up like an older brother or mimic his mother. Yet his thinking is still limited. To the young child, seeing is believing. He is *egocentric*: he assumes that everyone perceives things the way he does and shares his feelings and wishes. If you and the child are

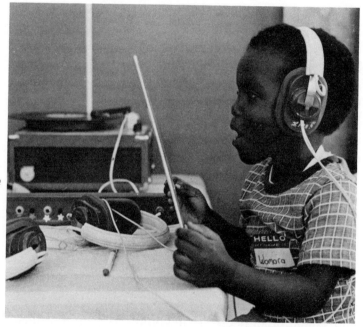

Piaget believes that children go through stages in their intellectual development. In the first two years, they explore the world through their senses. In the years from two to seven, they learn to use words, to ask questions, to try things out to see how they work. When children are seven or eight, they begin to reason in a logical way, and can therefore follow rules.

looking at the same object from opposite sides of the room, the child will not understand that it looks different to each of you.

At this age, children can sit side by side on the floor, yet be totally engrossed in their own daydreams. They are not really relating to each other; they are in their own worlds of make-believe. Yet they would get upset if their friends had to leave! Piaget calls this "parallel play."

In the third stage, from ages seven to eleven, the child learns to *reason* logically. This is called the *concrete-operational stage*. The child can now think things through "in his head," rather than having to see them before his eyes.[19] He can add and subtract mentally rather than having to count on his fingers. He can follow *rules*. Whether it is a card game at home, baseball in the neighborhood, or mathematics and reading in school, the child is constantly learning to follow rules at this age.

An understanding of physical laws also begins to develop. The child realizes that a certain quantity of an item remains the same regardless of the shape of its container. For example, a tall, thin glass of four ounces of milk is not any more than a short, fat glass of the same amount. Piaget calls this *conservation ability*.

At this stage, a child learns to *classify objects* into groups: cats and dogs are now also "animals." He can understand other people's viewpoints. He can coordinate two dimensions, such as height and width, in his mind. At the preoperational stage, the focus was on one *or* the other. Now. able to manipulate ideas and symbols, the child can think at a much more sophisticated level.

In the fourth stage, from adolescence on, the young person learns to *think abstractly*. This is the *formal operational stage.* "Reasoning about the 'possible,' about ideas and events which are in the past, the future, or the imagination, is now within the person's scope."[20] The young person can create and test hypotheses and make judgments about ideas and values. It is now possible to analyze political, scientific, and religious concepts.

How Should We Measure Intelligence?

Piaget's theories suggest that there is a different level and quality of thinking at each stage of development. Piaget believes that intelligence tests should measure not just whether an answer is right or wrong, but the *quality* of the answer given. Pinard and Sharp explain: "A child who says that a nail sinks to the bottom of a tank of water 'because it's tired' is obviously in a different stage of mental development from one who says that the nail sinks 'because it's made of iron.' Neither explanation is correct, of course, but to equate the two is decidedly unfair. Nevertheless, most conventional I.Q. tests, by failing to investigate what lies behind a child's mistakes, do in effect equate children who give answers as dissimilar as these."[21]

Pinard and Sharp describe a new kind of intelligence test being developed at the University of Montreal's Institute of Psychology. The Institute did a pilot study of 500 French-Canadian children ages four to twelve. Their subjects represented a cross-section of the population in age, sex, ability, socioeconomic status, and family size. They used twenty-five experiments adapted from Piaget's work to measure the "quality" of a child's thinking. Pinard and Sharp describe in detail the test about floating and sinking objects:

The child sits at a table with a small tank of water on it. The examiner picks up the nail, lets the child feel it if he wants to, and says, "If we put this nail in the water, will it go to the bottom, or will it remain on the water?" Whichever way the child answers, the examiner says, "Explain to me, why do you think it will?" (Always "why"—it is the child's reasons that are illuminating, not the number of correct predictions, some of which might come by chance.)

Then the child puts the nail in the water to see what it will do. It sinks, of course, to the bottom where there already are two marbles—put into the tank with these same questions. (A toy boat and a wooden bead, also put into the tank earlier, are floating.) If the child predicted that the nail would float, the examiner says, "Why does it go to the bottom, do you think?"

The child who said "because it's tired" was assigned to the stage of precausal explanations, since all of the reasons he gave were characterized by this. Other statements typical of this stage are "because it gave itself a push" or, if the object floats, "because it doesn't want to get wet." The median age for this group was four years, seven months.

The child who answered "because it's iron" was in the early part of the stage of physical explanations. Children in this stage commonly refer to the weight, size, material or shape of an object, but often use these factors in an erroneous or contradictory way. This group's median age was seven years, four months.

After this particular child correctly predicted the nail's behavior—but gave the wrong reason—the examiner showed him a wooden peg. He predicted that it, too, would go to the bottom "because it's

wood." Then he put the peg in the tank. Seeing that it
floated, he reversed himself and invoked the same
reason that he gave for his prediction that it would
sink: "Wood, it's not hard, it remains on the water."
(When he says "hard," he is thinking in terms of
weight, not density. Many of the expressions used by
children of this level are roundabout ways of
referring to weight.)

After a few more steps, the examiner asks the child:

"Have you ever seen a large boat?" The examiner
hands the child a marble. "Which is heavier, a large
boat or a marble like this? . . . Then why does a large
boat stay on top of the water, and a marble go to the
bottom?" Faced with an example that does not fit the
rule he has formulated from the earlier part of the
test—light objects float, heavy objects sink—the
child is naturally perplexed. Some give up and say, "I
don't know." Some fall back into precausal
thinking—the boat floats "to prevent people from
drowning." Some base their argument on the
presence of air in the boat or the fact that the amount
of water in the tank is small. In a large lake, the
marble would float, they think, "because there is
enough water."

Only two children hit upon the exact principle of
floating of bodies. One said, "a boat is not heavy for
its size and a marble is heavy and small." The other
one said, "because a large boat displaces much
water, and the small marble does not displace
enough water for its weight."[22]

Although not everyone agrees with his theories, Piaget's
impact has been growing. He has taught us to ask a child

"why" rather than just saying "right" or "wrong." He has shown us that intelligence is not simply a matter of accumulating knowledge!

Can Your I. Q. Be Raised?

Benjamin Bloom of the University of Chicago estimates that one half of a person's mature intelligence is developed by the age of four. Some Harvard researchers now say that the most crucial time in a child's intellectual development is from ten months to one and a half years. Why? Bloom feels "that the child's environment has a maximum impact on a developing characteristic during that characteristic's period of most rapid growth. Thus, since human intelligence grows most rapidly before the age of four, this is the time when the environment can influence it most easily. As time goes on . . . more and more powerful forces are required to produce a given amount of change in a child's intelligence, if it can be produced at all—and the emotional cost of this change is increasingly severe."[23]

Although every child must go through Piaget's stages of intellectual development, how *much* is learned at each stage depends on the environment. "The more new things a child has seen and heard, . . . the more he wants to see and hear. The greater variety of things a child has coped with, the greater his capacity for coping, and the more new methods he is able to invent by combining or recombining what he has learned before."[24]

Bloom's studies of identical twins who were separated at birth show that environment can account for a twenty-point difference in I. Q. between them.* He notes that in

---

* Refer to Glossary for an explanation of "I.Q." and other technical terms.

Israel, children raised at home by poor and illiterate Oriental Jews (from North Africa and Yemen) have very low I. Q.'s (an average of 85), compared with Jewish children of European background (average I. Q. 105). "When both kinds of children are raised in the same communal nurseries from birth on, however, both have an average I. Q. of 115—a jump of 30 points for the Oriental children. . . . [these] children had spent twenty-two hours a day in the kibbutz nursery for at least four years."[25]

In a similar study, Rich Heber of the University of Wisconsin organized an enrichment program for children from a poor area of Milwaukee. Children from this area typically had very low I. Q.'s, many in the retarded range. Working with newborn babies from this background, he showed that they could achieve an I. Q. of over 100 within three years.[26]

It is important to remember, however, that I. Q. tests only measure specific abilities needed to do well in school; they do *not* necessarily measure *general* intelligence. I. Q. tests are *culture-bound*: those from different cultures and backgrounds are less likely to do well on them. High I. Q.'s do not guarantee success, and low I. Q.'s do not inevitably lead to failure. Motivation plays a crucial part in academic success.

Eight Crucial Months

In 1965, Harvard researchers under the leadership of Burton White began a study to find out just what factors influenced a child's competence.[27] The results were startling. They found that the period between ten months and one and a half years is the most decisive in a child's intellectual development.

What happens in these eight months? The children

45

start to crawl around and explore their surroundings. They begin to understand others and to talk. Their environment becomes very important as a challenge to their curiosity.

Piaget maintains that a child reasons quite differently from an adult. *What* we think and *the way* we think are related to our stage of development.

In those homes where the parents (a) stimulate their children's curiosity by providing a rich variety of toys, (b) allow them to roam around and explore, and (c) answer their questions with careful explanations, the children gain important social and intellectual skills. The children learn that it is desirable to ask questions and that adults can be resources to help understand the world. The children's knowledge and confidence grow.

Parents who carefully "protect" both their children and their possessions do not allow their children this chance to understand and master their environment. Some parents do not act as consultants, helping their children to make sense out of the world. Their children become embarrassed to ask questions and reluctant to seek help.

The Harvard research group suggests that in these eight crucial months, children learn an approach to the world around them. They may become more curious, knowledgable, and confident, or hesitant and unsure of themselves. Parents play an important role in cultivating their children's interests and ability to succeed in the future.

What all these studies seem to show, then, is that the intelligence of young children is not fixed. Environment makes a difference. Nature sets the limits, but nurture determines the extent to which you fulfill your potential.

Jean Piaget has made an important impact on our understanding of human intelligence, just as Freud revolutionized the study of human behavior. There is still considerable controversy about the relative importance of "nature versus nurture," but Piaget has given us a framework which shows how intelligence develops.

YOUR SELF

TESTING PIAGET

1. *Bring an abstract art object to class. Have each member of the class write down what each object makes him think of. Compare everyone's perceptions. How different are they? Why is this so?*

2. *Send three people separately into a room where all sorts of activities are going on. Allow them to stay 5 seconds. Ask each to report to the class what he saw without hearing the description given by the other two.*

   How different were their reports?

   Why might each have focused on the particular things described?

Try this experiment with a room empty of people. Ask each to describe the furnishings in detail after a five second exposure.

   Did they notice different things?

   What does this tell you about the importance of point of view?

3. *Try some "conservation experiments" with young children (between 4-7).*

   Use different-shaped glasses; pour a fixed quantity of juice from one to the other and ask the child which has more.

48

Take two identical crackers; break one into pieces and let the other remain whole. Which is more?

Use playdough. Twist the same quantity into different shapes.

4. *Visit a supermarket and analyze how various products are packaged. How is optical illusion used to market goods?*

    How does this relate to "conservation ability?"

5. *Which fairy tales do you remember?*

    Why do you think they made such a strong impression on you?

    Can you remember any imaginary playmates you had?

6. *Knowing how early intelligence develops, what kinds of educational programs would you recommend for parents of young children? Investigate resource centers available in your community to help parents with young children.*

7. *Design an educational toy that will help a child learn a concept. Use inexpensive materials from your house. Be sure that you keep Piaget's stages in mind, so that your goal is realistic for a child at a specific age.*

Erik Erikson: The Eight Stages
of Emotional Development

How would you describe an emotionally healthy person? Are there specific characteristics of mental health, or is it just the absence of mental illness?

Most of us can describe behavior we consider abnormal, but we find it harder to pinpoint traits of the well-adjusted person. Erik Erikson of Harvard has proposed some guidelines of positive mental health by building on Freud's "psychosexual stages." Erikson believes that personality *continues to develop throughout life*. A different emotional issue is central to each of eight stages of development.[28] For example, gaining a basic trust in the world is every infant's first emotional hurdle. The child then concentrates on the second step, gaining a sense of "autonomy" or control over oneself and one's actions.

As one progresses from birth through old age, one builds on the foundation of previous personality accomplishments. With each stage, a new level of "social interaction" opens up. Yet while this sequence unfolds, it is still possible to go back and alter the emotional outcome of an earlier stage. For instance, a child abused by his parents as an infant may later gain trust and confidence with the help of a supportive first-grade teacher.

The first four stages of emotional development occur during childhood. The main issue in the first year of life is *Basic Trust vs. Basic Mistrust*. The infant is totally dependent on others for care. Whether the child sees the world as trustworthy therefore depends on how well and how consistently his needs are met. If held when crying, fed when hungry, changed when wet, and entertained

50

while awake, the child begins to feel secure. He gradually learns that although he is separate from his mother, he can count on her to appear when needed. Being held and fed is often what starts a baby smiling: the baby concentrates on the mother's face and begins to associate it with pleasure. His response to her may be a smile.

As he forms an attachment to his mother, the baby becomes more anxious when strangers approach, a reaction René Spitz calls "eight-month anxiety." Games like peek-a-boo are helpful to reassure the infant that his mother will return, though momentarily out of sight.

Erikson calls the second stage (from ages one through three) *Autonomy vs. Shame and Doubt*. With his developing motor and mental skills, the child realizes he can do things on his own. He is anxious to explore and exert some control over his surroundings. Parents who encourage the child to master what he is capable of doing help the child gain confidence and trust in himself. If they criticize or overprotect him, the child becomes unsure of himself and doubts his own capabilities. Toddlers are very mobile at this stage. They are into everything and require lots of attention. There is a delicate balance between encouraging a child to try new ventures and protecting him from dangerous or frustrating situations.

To develop a sense of autonomy, a child must "experience over and over again that he is a person who is permitted to make choices. He has to have the right to choose, for example, whether to sit or whether to stand, whether to approach a visitor or to lean against his mother's knee, whether to accept offered food or whether to reject it, whether to use the toilet or wet his pants. At the same time, he must learn some of the boundaries of self-determination. He inevitably finds that there are walls he

Photo courtesy of Kenneth M. Bernstein

With his developing motor and mental skills, the young child now realizes he can do things on his own. He is anxious to explore and exert some control over his surroundings. The toddler is *into everything!*

cannot climb, that there are objects out of reach, that, above all, there are innumerable commands enforced by powerful adults."[29]

The child at four and five years wrestles with the issue

of *Initiative vs. Guilt*. At this stage the child is very active. He can run around, play games, and communicate his thoughts, wishes, and fantasies. He can plan ahead, but he also knows the risks involved in his exploits. His parents should encourage him, taking his questions and efforts seriously. If they show no interest in his accomplishments, the child may become discouraged and become reluctant to try new activities. He may feel more like a nuisance than a person with worthwhile ideas and valued contributions. (This is also Freud's "Oedipal stage," when the child's conscience is emerging and when the child feels guilty if he oversteps his bounds.)

The last stage in childhood, from ages six to eleven, centers around *Industry vs. Inferiority*. The child spends most of his time in and around school, where he is involved in numerous learning situations. Tasks and projects must be completed, and there is pressure to keep up with schoolmates. He can either gain a sense of self-respect from doing well and being praised, or a feeling of inferiority because he cannot master important physical and mental skills. School is the first big test in the "real world." According to Erikson, "Many a child's development is disrupted when family life has failed to prepare him for school life or when school life fails to sustain the promises of earlier stages."[30]

A child's major emotional tasks, then, involve gaining trust in the world and in himself; gaining a sense of independence and self-sufficiency; learning to value his capabilities in exploring his surroundings; and achieving a sense of mastery and self-respect in important mental and physical skills. Erikson identifies other issues which become critical in adolescence and adulthood: the

53

achievement of a sense of personal identity; the ability to establish intimate personal relationships; a sense of feeling productive and useful, able to guide one's children; and a feeling of satisfaction in how one has lived one's life.

Erikson's stages provide a framework through which to consider how our life experiences continue to influence our personality development. All of us have to deal with these issues. It is how we resolve them that helps to determine the kind of people we become and the sort of lives we lead.

A Child's Self-Image

Emotional growth can be painful. A child must learn how to accept failure as well as success, guilt and anxiety as well as security. If he does poorly in school, will his parents still love him? If he hates his sister, is he an awful person? If he is not athletic, will the other kids still like him? To the child, these are often frightening thoughts.

A child must also learn how to express his feelings of jealousy and anger according to the "rules" of acceptable behavior. He must learn to talk rather than to hit, to share rather than to hoard. Most of all, he must learn how to accept and like himself as he is, with both his good and bad feelings, his accomplishments and limitations. The most important emotional achievement in childhood is establishing a strong self-image, a sense of worth and dignity.

How do we protect a child's self-image? A child learns to see himself as he thinks others see him. If he senses that his opinions are respected, his feelings are understood, and his activities are supported, he will gain confidence in

School is the first big test in the "real world." The child learns to master important physical and mental skills, and can gain a sense of self-respect from doing well and being praised.

himself. But if his parents are critical and demanding, harsh and unsympathetic, the child may decide that he is, in fact, inadequate. As Dr. Haim Ginott explains in his book *Between Parent and Child,* "There is no escape from the fact that a child learns what he lives. If he lives with criticism, he does not learn responsibility. He learns to condemn himself and to find fault with others. He learns to doubt his own judgment, to disparage his own ability, and to distrust the intention of others. And above all, he learns to live with continual expectation of impending doom."[31]

Parents' Anger, Children's Feelings

When children fight, spill milk on the rug, refuse to eat, or insult a relative, it is natural for a parent to become angry. A child can learn much from these minor crises if his parents focus their anger on the *incident* rather than on the child's personality and character. Dr. Ginott's approach is to say, "It makes me angry when you hit your sister," rather than, "You bad boy! All you ever do is cause trouble." The first statement does not attack or embarrass the child, leaving him with wounds long after the incident is over.

As Dr. Ginott states, "A parent must like his children, but he must not have an urgent need to be liked by them every minute of the day."[32] In other words, he must be able to set limits. Dr. Ginott believes that "a limit should be so stated that it tells the child clearly (a) what constitutes unacceptable conduct (b) what substitutes will be accepted."[33] A parent may tell the child, "I know you are angry. You should tell your brother why you are angry, but you may not hit him."

When parents are over-permissive and do not set limits, they cause their child anxiety by granting him too much freedom. A child feels secure when he knows what is expected of him. It frightens him to have more power than he can handle, more anger than he can control.

Discipline can be either love-oriented or power-oriented.[34] If the former, parents reason with their child; if the latter, they lay down the law and punish infringements. While power may be effective, reasoning encourages the child to exercise his judgment and shows respect for his opinions.

Anger and frustration are normal facts of life. Parents can be models in showing a child how to express anger and tolerate frustration. When anger is expressed constructively, a child will not have to feel guilty for his feelings or feel humiliated by his actions.

One of the most difficult problems for parents is how to deal with their child when he lies. Their natural reaction might be to explode or to preach, or both. Dr. Ginott suggests that children often lie when they feel the truth will not be accepted. "When punished for truth, children lie in self-defense. They also lie to give themselves in fantasy what they lack in reality. Lies tell truths about fears and hopes. They reveal what one would like to be or to do. . . . A mature reaction to a lie should reflect understanding of its meaning, rather than denial of its content or condemnation of its author. . . . When a child does lie, our reaction should be not hysterical and moralistic, but factual and realistic. We want our child to learn that there is no need to lie to us."[35]

Children have many fears, of which perhaps the greatest is being rejected and abandoned by their parents. Children need to know that no matter what they do, they will be loved and cared for. They also need to know that it is *normal* to have fears and anxieties, likes and dislikes. When parents listen to their child with sensitivity, they are reassuring him of this. As one child said in *Between Parent and Child*, "If my mixed-up feelings can be understood, they are not so mixed-up."[36]

Misplaced praise can be as detrimental as misguided criticism. Dr. Ginott suggests that praise, like criticism, should deal mainly with the child's accomplishments, not with his personality and character. For example, an adult should not tell a child, "You are *always* so good and thoughtful." While the child may not voice bad thoughts,

he knows that he often thinks them. Excessive praise will therefore make the child feel guilty: "It is embarrassing," Dr. Ginott writes, "for a person to be told that he is wonderful, angelic, generous, and humble. . . . He may not only reject the praise but may have some second thoughts about those who have praised him: 'If they find me so great, they cannot be so smart.'"[37] While parents must be supportive and encouraging, they must also be honest and realistic so that the child does not feel he must be perfect.

The childhood years are crucial in forming one's self-image. They are the years when one learns how to cope with guilt, anger, dislikes, and frustration. The child is

Copyright © 1974 by Jules Feiffer

rapidly developing a conscience, and he may be more critical of himself than others are of him. He therefore needs praise more than criticism, understanding more than punishment. A child high in self-esteem will expect to be liked and to be valued. He will have faith in his ability and judgment. A child with a poor self-image will often live in the shadow of others. He will not have the confidence to succeed or the self-assurance to be popular. A child's self-image is the emotional foundation for a lifetime.

Photo courtesy of Kenneth M. Bernstein

The child learns to see himself as others see him. A helpful adult will express an understanding of *all* the child's feelings, without making the child feel guilty or embarrassed. A child can accept advice and discipline far better when he knows he is still respected and loved, and it is only his *behavior* which must be changed.

YOU ARE THE PARENT

The child's view of himself is created by how he is treated, by the kind of responses he receives from others and by how his emotions, actions, statements, and observations are translated to him. The adult should realize that young children see everything as either black or white, with no shades of gray. He considers himself either naughty or nice, good or bad, lovable or awful. Adults also need to remember that to be human is to have all kinds of feelings—love and hate, compassion and competitiveness, courage and cowardice. Children, like the rest of us, are wrestling with this profound fact of life, trying to reconcile themselves to accepting all of it.

Thus we need to respond to children's emotions and social strivings so that the child can learn to like, accept, trust, and respect, that is, love himself. In communicating with a child, the messages should preserve his self-respect as well as the parent's, and statements of understanding should precede statements of advice or instruction. [38]

HELEN WESTLAKE

Directions: Eight incidents or situations are described below, adapted from an article by Eda LeShan.[39] Discuss each by:

A. Stating what your *immediate* or *natural* response would have been as the child's parent.

B. Explaining what a more *ideal* response would be in light of the above quotation. Often our quick, spontaneous response denies a child's feelings, makes him feel guilty or embarrassed, and diminishes his feelings of self-worth.

1. *Three-year-old is terrified of thunder.*

2. *Four-year-old screams and carries on in doctor's office while getting a shot.*

3. *Five-year-old wets his bed.*

4. *Four-year-old cries the first day of nursery school and won't let his mother leave.*

5. *Six-year-old won't share his toys when his friend comes to play.*

6. *Five-year-old starts to beat up a playmate.*

7. *Six-year-old lies about spilling juice on the rug.*

8. *Five-year-old says he hates his younger sister.*

Birth Order: A Measure of Your Personality?

Why are children in the same family so different? What would you be like if you were the first child rather than the third? If you were the middle child or the only child? Does your ordinal position among your siblings affect your personality, making you more outgoing or shy, more determined or relaxed? Psychologists agree that ordinal position *does* make a difference. It is one more environmental factor.

Family relationships change with the birth of each additional child. For example, parents usually focus more attention on their first child than on their third. What was a novelty with the oldest child—the first word, the first step—becomes expected and natural with the second and third. The family album often has many more pictures of the oldest child than of the youngest.

Being center stage does have its drawbacks, however. It may be particularly traumatic for the first-born when a second and third child come along. Suddenly *sharing* is expected. Suddenly the oldest child no longer has his parents' undivided attention. The oldest child may resent younger sisters and brothers and then may feel guilty about the resentment. After all, he is supposed to know better!

Younger children accept having to share because they never knew anything else. They can also justify their anger when abused by an older sibling: they do not have to feel guilty about self-defense.

There are many studies now in progress of how birth order affects personality, but the findings are not conclusive. The researchers recognize that many factors in addition to birth order must be considered: sex, ethnic and cultural background, socio-economic status, in-dividual differences, and role models.

The Gesell Institute, for example, has found that "first-born children are most likely to become eminent later on and, even as children, tend to be capable, strong-willed, effective persons. They tend to have a high sense of responsibility ... and to want to do things right. They have a high need for achievement and tend to be conscientious in their studies. They are, as a rule, not tremendously interested in others and like to be in positions where *they* are the leaders. Their relationship with parents tends to be close and successful. Also, they do have a tendency to become angry and irritable . . . first boys, especially, may be hard to raise but gratifying in their later accomplishments." They found that first-borns tended to make "responsible—though not necessarily comfortable—spouses" and "effective but not necessarily kind and tolerant parents."[40]

Why? Harvard's Jerome Kagan feels that since first-borns have only adults as role models, they tend to adopt adult standards of behavior. Younger children have less successful and less mature role models to follow in their brothers and sisters.[41]

What if you are number two? Gesell researchers predict that you may be less achievement-oriented than your older brother or sister, but more easy-going, tactful, adaptable, patient, and emotionally stable. You are probably more sociable and get along well with others. You are more likely to be a good spouse and a warm, affectionate parent.

As the youngest child, you are likely to be more passive, babyish, and withdrawn. As an adult you might be pleasant but somewhat reluctant to assume responsibility since you have always been looked after. While the Gesell researchers say the youngest feels "no great need to achieve," Kagan predicts the youngest will be "highly striving." This sharp difference of opinion reminds us that these ideas are more speculative than scientific.

Gesell researchers say that if you are the only child, you may be more self-confident and relaxed, because of a lack of competition and of jealousy. You may be a more private and less outgoing person and a more demanding spouse.

Birth order does *not* fix your personality but it seems to incline a person to certain traits. You may find that the description above fits your family. Maybe it does not. How do you think your ordinal position has affected you?

Sisters and Brothers: For Better or Worse?

Can there be any merit in having a younger brother or sister who follows you around and gets in the way? Or in having an older sibling with special privileges because of age, who punches you when your parents turn around? If you were an only child, might you be spoiled, or feel deprived? Would you be lonely, or overwhelmed with attention?

In quiet moments we can all list the advantages of having brothers and sisters. You have someone you can trust, someone who understands you, and an ally to protect you in the outside world. You have someone to be proud of and copy, a person who will also share in your success.

Yet after a family battle, you may wonder if the costs of sibling rivalry outweigh the benefits of brotherly love. One child psychiatrist, Richard Gardner, believes that sibling rivalry can be healthy and constructive.[42] He argues that siblings are the only "safe" target for a child's anger and frustration. The child feels that he cannot attack his parents without risking punishment and their withdrawal of love. He cannot alienate his neighborhood playmates because he fears loss of companionship and social isolation. So who is left? A sibling who cannot totally reject him despite these day-to-day skirmishes. Sibling rivalry provides one outlet for a child's anger.

Gardner believes "competition in moderation can be constructive." It can stimulate a child to achieve, to assert

"Please be good to your younger brother." Siblings are one "safe" target for a child's anger and frustration. Psychiatrist Richard Gardner explains that a child feels he cannot attack his parents without risking punishment and their withdrawal of love. He cannot alienate his neighborhood playmates because he fears loss of companionship and social isolation. So who is left and ever present? A sibling, who cannot totally reject the child despite these day-to-day skirmishes.

himself, to persevere. It can teach the necessity of team play, sharing, and compromise. The child learns how to lose as well as how to win. Parents may let a child beat them in a game. A sibling is unlikely to be so generous.

Siblings also "provide the child with important information about himself." Parents may overestimate their child; a brother or sister does not. Quick to criticize, siblings offer the child a different perspective.

Children can learn how to cope with frustration, jealousy, and anger through the lessons of sibling rivalry.

Brothers and sisters prepare a child for the less sheltered competition of the outside world.

Gardner admits some drawbacks. A child's self-image could be threatened. Intense jealousy or resentment could be destructive. For parents, the constant fighting can be nerve-wracking and draining. Nonetheless, Gardner maintains, sibling rivalry is a useful lesson in learning to live with others.

How can a parent ease the competition? According to Dr. Ginott, parents must focus on the individual needs of each child: In his book "Between Parent and Child" he says, "The effort entailed in measuring either emotional or material giving can make any person tired and angry. Children do not yearn for equal shares of love: they need to be loved uniquely, not uniformly. The emphasis is on quality, not equality. . ... The more vigilant we are to prevent apparent discrimination, the more alert each child becomes, in detecting instances of seeming inequality. . . . To each child, let us convey the uniqueness of our relationship, not its fairness or sameness."[43]

The Only Child

G. Stanley Hall, a famous American psychologist in the early 1900's, once said, "Being an only child is a disease in itself."[44] Some parents feel they have to have a second child for the benefit of the first. Current research shows this may not be true.

E. James Lieberman, a child psychiatrist, contends, "Parents can be just as tough on and expect just as much from an only child as they can with larger families. True, they are likely to spend more time with an only child, but this extra parental contact can mean an enrichment of the child's environment rather than an overindulgence of whims . . . parents who are older, better educated and established in life are more likely to be busy, active, creative people, less likely to have a need to live their lives through their children, which is probably better for the children in the long run."[45]

Studies have shown that first-born and only children are over-represented in the upper I.Q. group of our population. One study of "the dependency patterns in the behavior of nursery-schoolers—how well they integrated into the group, how many fights they had, how well they played with other children, how they behaved at meals—showed that the only children were less dependent, got along better with other children and were less clinging. The study suggested that children from larger families seek the maternal attention in the nursery which they fail to receive at home."[46] Only children were under-represented in another study of 1600 children visiting a psychiatric outpatient clinic for social and emotional problems; third and later-born children were over-represented.[47]

Michael Lewis of the Educational Testing Service believes that the absence of other children in the family does not automatically make a child spoiled. It is the parents' attitudes which determine the child's behavior. He cites Piaget's work on childhood egocentrism to show that, "It does no good to try to teach sharing too young."[48] Young children cannot see another's point of view anyway. They will be able to learn sharing in school.

Thus, only children are not doomed. Yet the size and make-up of your family do make a difference in your development. Such factors create a *specific environment for your emotional growth.*

WHICH NUMBER ARE YOU?

1. *How do you think your birth-order (ordinal) position in your family has affected you?*

   What specific advantages have you gained from your position?

   What have been the disadvantages?

   In what ways could parents counterbalance the effects of ordinal position on their children?

   In what ways does your sex make a difference in how you feel about being the oldest, the middle, or the youngest child?

2. *Does the Gesell description of personality traits fit the members of your family? In what ways?*

3. *Explain how sibling rivalry has affected you or members of your family.*

   How often do people compare you to your brothers and sisters? Do you like being compared? Why or why not?

   How do you feel about having a teacher who has taught one of your brothers or sisters?

4. *How would you judge the* quality *of a parent-child relationship?*

How important do you think *equality* is in the treatment of children?

How do your parents handle charges of favoritism in your family?

5. *How many children do you want to have? Why? How do you feel about the only child?*

Conclusion

A major argument in psychology is over which counts more, nature or nurture. Do our genes basically set the course for our life, or does our environment shape and mold us into the people we become? Skilled debaters could argue each viewpoint persuasively, but both factors are clearly important.

Photo courtesy of Kenneth M. Bernstein

Childhood memories are very special. We all think back to particular incidents, special accomplishments, even major disappointments. Yet we rarely stop to analyze how much we learned in those early years—how much our personality was shaped in such a short time.

In this chapter we have briefly outlined the social, intellectual, and emotional development of the child. The emphasis has been on *socialization:* the way in which a child learns "the values, attitudes, knowledge, skills, and techniques which a society possesses. . . . Socialization molds the child's biological potential into the pattern of functioning that we call human personality."[49]

We have focused on the family as the chief socializer in childhood. To a young child, the family *is the world.* It provides his ethnic background and religion, his values and tastes, his socioeconomic status and expectations. It is where the child learns curiosity, independence, responsibility, and self-confidence—or lack of them. Parents are role models for the child, defining the behavior appropriate to the child's sex. The family provides the child with an outlook on life and an attitude about himself. It helps him to think not only about what kind of person he wants to be, but also about what kind of person he does *not* want to be.

As the child begins to read, to watch television, and to go to school, a wider world opens up. Friends become important, offering the child other models to imitate and views to examine.

R. P. Smith describes what he learned from his friends in the "hut". You may recognize your own childhood in his description:

> It was a pitiful wreck of a tarpaper hut, and in it I learned the difference between boys and girls, I learned that all fathers did that, I learned to swear, to play with myself, to sleep in the afternoon. I learned that some people were Catholics, and some people were Protestants and some people were Jews, that

people come from different places. I learned that other kids wondered, too, who they would have been if their fathers had not married their mothers, wondered if you could dig a hole right to the center of the earth, wondered if you could kill yourself by holding your breath. (None of us could.)

I learned that with three people assembled, it was only for the briefest interludes that all three liked each other. Mitch and I were leagued against Simon. And then Simon and I against Mitch. And then—but you remember.[50]

Childhood memories *are* very special. We all think back to particular incidents, special accomplishments, even major disappointments. Yet we rarely stop to analyze *how much we learned* in those early years; how much our personality and future were shaped in such a short time.

Many years ago, the poet William Wordsworth wrote, "The child is father of the man." Modern research is proving that he was right.

AS A CHILD GROWS

Fill in the chart below with the major developmental issues of childhood described by Freud, Erikson, and Piaget.

How do they relate to each other?

AGE	FREUD	ERIKSON	PIAGET
1			
2			
3			
4			
5			
6			
7			
8			
9			
10			
11			
12			
13			

LOOKING BACKWARD

1. *Write a short story for children.*

   Explain the message you wish to convey and the reason for each character.

   Why do you think your story would catch a child's interest?

   What feelings and wishes does it express?

   How did you decide on your ending?

2. *Write about an incident or a theme from your childhood, relating the ideas of this chapter to your early life.*

3. *Gather a collection of children's books and games. Rate them according to the value you think they have. Explain your reasoning.*

   Which do children seem to like the most? Ask them why.

4. *If you had to give advice to a young parent, what would it be?*

5. *What kinds of services should the community provide for parents of young children? What services are available in your community?*

Suggested Reading

Bettelheim, Bruno, *Children of the Dream* (New York: Macmillan, 1969).

Brazelton, T.B., *Infants and Mothers: Individual Differences in Development* (New York: Delacorte, 1969).

Coles, Robert, *Children of Crisis: Migrants, Sharecroppers, and Mountaineers* (Boston: Little-Brown, 1971).

Coles, Robert, *Uprooted Children* (Pittsburgh: U. of Pittsburgh Press, 1970).

Erikson, Erik, *Childhood and Society* (New York: W.W. Norton, 1964).

Fraiberg, Selma, *The Magic Years* (New York: Charles Scribner's Sons, 1959).

Ginott, Dr. Haim, *Between Parent and Child* (New York: Macmillan, 1965).

Ginott, Dr. Haim, *Teacher and Child* (New York: Macmillan, 1972).

Harrison-Ross, Phyllis, and Barbara Wyden, *The Black Child— A Parents' Guide* (New York: Wyden, 1973).

Holt, John, *How Children Fail* (New York: Pitman, 1964).

Holt, John, *How Children Learn* (New York: Pitman, 1967).

Landau, Elliott, Sherrie Epstein, and Ann Stone, *Child Development Through Literature* (Englewood Cliffs, N.J.: Prentice-Hall, 1972).

LeShan, Eda, *How Do Your Children Grow* (New York: D. McKay, 1971).

Lidz, Theodore, *The Person: His Development Throughout the Life Cycle* (New York: Basic Books, 1968).

Neill, A.S., *Summerhill* (New York: Hart Publishing Co., 1960).

Pines, Maya, *Revolution in Learning: The Years From Birth to Six* (New York: Harper and Row, 1967).

Poussaint, Dr. Alvin; and Dr. James Comer, *Black Child Care* (New York: Simon and Schuster, 1975).

Spiro, Melford, *Children of the Kibbutz* (New York: Schocken, 1965).

Westlake, Helen, *Children, A Study in Individual Behavior* (Lexington, Mass.: Ginn and Company, 1973).

FOOTNOTES

1. Barbara Wyden, "Growth: 45 Crucial Months," *Life*, December 17, 1971. Copyright: Barbara Wyden for *Life*. © 1971 Time Inc.
2. *Ibid.*
3. *Time*, November 12, 1973.
4. Paul Mussen, John Conger, Jerome Kagan, *Child Development and Personality* (New York: Harper and Row, 1969), p. 85.
5. *Time*, September 24, 1973, p. 86.
6. Elizabeth Hall, "A Conversation with Nobel Prize Winner Niko Tinbergen," *Psychology Today*, March 1974, p. 70.
7. Barbara Wyden, "The Difficult Baby is Born That Way," *The New York Times Magazine*, March 21, 1971. © 1971 by The New York Times Company. Reprinted by permission.
8. Gerardo and Alicia Reichel-Dolmatoff, *The People of Aritama*, (Chicago: The University of Chicago Press, 1962).
9. Wyden, "The Difficult Baby," *op. cit.*
10. Ronald Johnson and C. R. Medinnus, *Child Psychology: Behavior and Development* (New York: John Wiley and Sons, 1965), p. 477.
11. Calvin Hall and Gardner Lindzey, *Theories of Personality* (New York: John Wiley and Sons, 1957), p. 34.
12. *Ibid.*, p. 35.
13. Copyright 1950 by Frank O'Connor. Reprinted from *The Stories of Frank O'Connor*, by permission of Alfred A. Knopf, Inc.
14. Bruno Bettelheim, *The Children of the Dream* (New York: Macmillan, 1969).
15. David Elkind, "The Continuing Influence of Jean Piaget," *Grade Teacher*, May/June 1971, p. 8.
16. Mussen, Conger, Kagan, *op. cit.*, p. 197.
17. David Elkind, "Giant in the Nursery—Jean Piaget," *The New York Times Magazine*, May 26, 1969.
18. *Ibid.*

19. *Ibid.*
20. Marilynne Adler, "Jean Piaget, School Organization, and Instruction," in *Educational Implications of Piaget's Theory,* edited by Irene J. Athey and Duane O. Rubadeau (Boston: Ginn and Company, 1970), p. 5.
21. Adrien Pinard and Evelyn Sharp, "I. Q. and Point of View." Reprinted from *Psychology Today,* June 1972. Copyright © 1972 Ziff-Davis Publishing Company. All rights reserved.
22. *Ibid.*
23. Maya Pines, "Why Some Three Year Olds Get A's and Some C's," *The New York Times Magazine,* July 6, 1969, p. 10. © 1969 by The New York Times Company. Reprinted by permission.
24. Maya Pines, *Revolution in Learning* (New York: Harper and Row, 1967).
25. Pines, *op. cit.,* 1969, p. 17.
26. Maya Pines, "A Child's Mind is Shaped Before Age Two," *Life,* December 17, 1971.
27. *Ibid.*
28. Erikson, Erik, *Childhood and Society* (New York: W. W. Norton, 1950).
29 Midcentury White House Conference on Children and Youth, *A Healthy Personality for Every Child—Fact Finding Report: A Digest* (Raleigh, N.C.: Health Publications Institute, 1951).
30. Erikson, *op. cit.,* p. 260.
31. Dr. Haim G. Ginott, author of *Between Parent and Child,* (New York: Macmillan, 1965); *Between Parent and Teenager* (Macmillan, 1969); *Teacher and Child* (Macmillan, 1972), p. 72.
32. Ginott, *Between Parent and Child,* p. 92.
33. *Ibid.,* p. 99.
34. Dorothy Rogers, *Child Psychology* (Monterey, California: Brooks/Cole, 1969).
35. Ginott, *op. cit.,* pp. 58-61.
36. *Ibid.,* p. 33.
37. *Ibid.,* p. 41.
38. From *Children—A Study in Individual Behavior* by Helen Gum Westlake. Copyright © 1973 by Ginn and Company (Xerox Corporation). Used with permission.
39. Adapted from Eda J. LeShan, "Are You Helping Your Child to Like Himself?" *Parade,* October 13, 1968.
40. Louise Bates Ames, "Oldest, Middle, Youngest and Only Child—

How Does It Affect Their Personality?" *Family Circle*, February, 1972.

41. Mussen, Conger, Kagan, *op. cit.*, p. 498.
42. Richard A. Gardner, M. D., "They Never Stop Fighting," *The New York Times Magazine*, November 28, 1971.
43. Ginott, *op. cit.*, pp. 132-133.
44. R. Kramer, "A Fresh Look at the Only Child," *The New York Times Magazine*, October 15, 1972. © 1972 by The New York Times Company. Reprinted by permission.
45. *Ibid.*
46. *Ibid.*
47. *Ibid.*
48. *Ibid.*
49. Gerald Leslie, *The Family in Social Context* (New York: Oxford University Press, 1967), p. 9.
50. Reprinted from *"Where Did You Go?" "Out." "What Did You Do?" "Nothing."* by Robert Paul Smith. By permission of W. W. Norton and Company, Inc. Copyright © 1957 by Robert Paul Smith.

2.

Time Caught Me Green and Growing: Adolescence

*Being myself includes taking risks with
myself, taking risks on new behavior, trying
new ways of "being myself," so that I can see
how it is I want to be.*

HUGH PRATHER, *Notes to Myself*[1]

Adolescence is a time to <u>experiment</u>: you try out many
different roles and images looking for the one that fits, the
one that is *really* you. It is a time for discovering emotions
and values that you never knew you had, for developing
deeper and more sensitive relationships. It is a time of
laughter and of joy. It is a time for accomplishments all
your own.

But adolescence is also a time of <u>painful self-
consciousness</u>, a time when you are sure everyone else is
happier and more confident than you are. It is a time of
<u>stress and anxiety</u>, a time when someone's passing remark
may hurt you deeply. You tend to <u>daydream</u> a lot and to
make ambitious plans which never quite get off the
ground. You may feel <u>impatient</u>, yet not be sure what
you're rushing to.

As you experience these <u>sudden shifts of mood</u> and
<u>mixed feelings</u>, you may start to wonder if something is

the matter with you. You assume that you are the only one feeling so mixed up. On the contrary, adolescence has its own description of what is "normal," as Anna Freud explains so well:

> *I take it that it is normal for an adolescent to behave for a considerable length of time in an inconsistent and unpredictable manner; to fight his impulses and to accept them; to ward them off successfully and to be overrun by them; to love his parents and to hate them; to revolt against them and to be dependent on them; to be deeply ashamed to acknowledge his mother before others and, unexpectedly, to desire heart-to-heart talks with her; to thrive on imitation of and identification with others while searching unceasingly for his own identity; to be more idealistic, artistic, generous, and unselfish than he will ever be again, but also the opposite: self-centered, egotistic, calculating. Such fluctuations between extreme opposites would be deemed highly abnormal at any other time of life.*[2]

When you are depressed and confused, it may be hard to accept the fact that all your feelings are normal and that others face the same problems.

From Childhood to Adulthood

Adolescence comes from the Latin word meaning "to grow up." In primitive societies, such as Samoa, anthropologists have found that there is no special word for growing up. Puberty (sexual maturity) may be marked by a special ceremony, after which you are treated as an adult. Since life is relatively simple, you grow up knowing

Every adolescent at some point faces what Erik Erikson has called an "identity crisis." This is the time when you struggle to define who you are and what you want out of life. Finding your identity does not mean you become a static, finished product; it means you achieve a *basic* sense of self, a sense of direction and purpose. It means you accept yourself as you are; that you are comfortable in making your own decisions; that you have established a basic set of values and ideals; and that you feel secure in dealing with others.

what job you will have. Often your marriage is arranged for you. Since an individual has few choices to make, primitive societies do not need an intermediate stage between childhood and adulthood for a person to define his direction in life.

Until the beginning of the twentieth century, the transition from childhood to adulthood was relatively easy in most small communities throughout the world.

Few young people ever faced an "identity crisis." Tevye, from the Broadway show "Fiddler on the Roof," explains life in nineteenth-century Russia:

> *Because of our traditions we've kept our balance for many years. Here in Anatevka we have our traditions for everything—how to eat, how to sleep, how to work, even how to wear clothes. . . . Because of our traditions, everyone here knows* who he is *and what* God expects him to do.[3]

Modern society, by contrast, offers a dazzling array of choices . . . and pressures. You must *decide* on an education, a career, a marital partner, a style of life. There is no distinct route to follow. Your experiences in adolescence may differ dramatically depending upon whether you grow up in the inner city, the suburbs, or a rural community. Television, radio, movies, and newspapers remind you constantly of your many options in work or travel and heighten your expectations.

There are also many different timetables which determine when you are an adult. You must be eighteen to vote in most states, yet you are an "adult" at twelve when you have to pay for a movie. Thirteen is the age of confirmations, sixteen is the driving age, eighteen the drinking age, and twenty-one the time of inheritance. Robert Havighurst, an educator and sociologist, says that you are an adult when you become self-supporting. By his measurement, a factory worker becomes an adult long before a medical student. You may reach physical maturity at one age, mental maturity at a different age, and social maturity at still a different time!

ADOLESCENCE: YOUR VIEW

1. *In what ways has your personality changed in the last five years?*

2. *What are the best things about being a teenager? The worst?*

3. *What does Hugh Prather (see quotation on first page of chapter) mean when he says that it is important to take risks with yourself? Do you agree?*

4. *Erik Erikson says that adolescence may be viewed as a "moratorium"—a breathing space between childhood and the demands of adulthood when a person is socially encouraged to explore his/her goals, values, and identity before making long-term commitments. The adolescent experiments with different ways of doing things and with various life styles in order to discover more about his/her personal needs.*

    What are the most important decisions you will have to make in the next few years? In what ways will the adolescent experience help you to make them?

    Do you think adolescence is a necessary bridge between childhood and adulthood? Do you think it is too long a period of time, or too short, or is it just right?

5. *Edgar Friedenberg has said of adolescents:*

> *They can be extravagantly generous and extravagantly cruel, but rarely petty or conniving. Their virtues are courage and loyalty; while the necessity for even a moderate degree of compromise humiliates them greatly. They tend to be pugnacious and quarrelsome about what they believe to be their rights, but naive and reckless in defending them. They are shy, but not modest. If they become very anxious they are likely to behave eccentrically, to withdraw, or to attack with some brutality; they are less likely to blend themselves innocuously into the environment with an apologetic smile. They are honest on occasions when even a stupid adult could have better sense.*[4]

Do you agree with his position? Why or why not?

Can you think of experiences you have had which prove his point?

Adolescence is the result of a complex society. It is a state of limbo between childhood and adulthood when you struggle to define who you are in our culture and what you will become. Adults may tell you these are the "best years of your life." But you also know these are difficult years, years of change.

Puberty: The Biological Age of Adulthood

Your body begins to change dramatically as you reach adolescence. You experience a spurt in physical growth and an increase in energy. Hormones are activated which stimulate your sexual development. Your body becomes more shapely and mature. You even begin to *feel* different. You may reach puberty, or biological adulthood, as early as eleven or as late as fourteen. There is no "set" age, and both extremes are normal.

Girls usually reach physical maturity before boys. They are often taller at this age and as much as two years ahead of boys in sexual development. As a girl's breasts begin to enlarge and her hips to widen, her body proportions change. Her ovaries develop and pubic hair appears. When menstruation begins, it is a dramatic signal to a girl that she has become a young woman.

Although boys get a later start than girls, at maturity boys average 6 to 8 percent taller than girls and 10 to 17 percent heavier. Boys develop rapidly between the ages of fourteen and nineteen. Their shoulders broaden, their genital organs increase in size, and pubic hair appears. They become stronger and better coordinated. Their voices deepen.

Most adolescents worry about their height, weight, and sexual development. *Growth is an uneven process,* beyond the control of the individual. The fifth-grade girl whose breasts are developed or who towers above her friends may feel awkward and self-conscious. Often those features which would bring pride later in life are embarrassing at an early age.

Since every person has both male and female

85

hormones, sometimes physical characteristics of the opposite sex temporarily appear. For example, a boy's breasts might slightly enlarge, causing embarrassment and concern. He may feel his penis is small, and therefore believe himself odd or different from his friends. Many boys will cut gym classes to avoid undressing and showering in front of their classmates.

Masturbation is common during adolescence. It is one way most boys and many girls release sexual tension. There are many myths about the results of masturbation. Some adolescents fear that it will affect their intelligence or eyesight, or give them acne. A boy may worry that he may use up his seminal fluid or damage his penis. Girls fear they may permanently harm their genital organs. Masturbation does *none* of these things. It has no harmful physical effects. Yet, if you worry about it, you may suffer embarrassment, self-consciousness, and guilt feelings. That is why it is important to remember that masturbation is a *normal* response to your increasing sexual drives.

Most adolescents have fantasies about sex. They may daydream about their wishes, read pornographic magazines, and meet with their friends to discuss sex. The more experienced sometimes brag, exaggerating their "conquests"; the less experienced may feel envious, yet not ready for an intimate relationship. Sexual "readiness" is a very personal matter, not guided by a timetable.

Some parents are uncomfortable discussing sex with their children. They may have mixed emotions about sex themselves, or find it too personal a topic to share their inner feelings. Other parents may display a more open expression of affection at home. They may be more

Adolescence is a time for discovering emotions and values that you never knew you had, a time for developing deeper and more sensitive relationships. In seeking love, affection, and approval, you must be willing to risk the possibility of rejection, hurt, and disappointment.

relaxed and direct about their views. If sex is a taboo subject, an adolescent may feel guilty about his desires and worry about his preoccupation with his body. An understanding parent, who is willing to listen and to offer information and advice, can give the adolescent a greater confidence in his sexual identity.

Development of Relationships

Children are basically self-centered. Their emotional attachment to the few people in their life is one-sided. A child views his parents as satellites of himself; he is too young to be interested in his parents or teachers as individuals with lives of their own. It is in adolescence that you start to become genuinely interested in other people.

The first sign of such emotional growth comes around the ages of ten to twelve. You probably remember picking a close friend of the same sex with whom to share your inner thoughts and concerns. You learned to trust and to care about him or her. Psychiatrist Harry Sullivan calls this the stage of "chumships." You may have also developed a crush on a teacher, or tagged along after an older brother or sister.

As your body begins to change rapidly, you need to explore your new physical identity. You may remember your first parties when you began to awkwardly experiment with sex. This is the age when one dares a friend to kiss or "make out" with a girl. It is the time when a girl blushes and giggles a lot. Physical appearance becomes important. You become more interested in clothes and styles. Yet the young adolescent is too preoccupied with testing his own image and feelings to be able to offer love to another person.

Personal Decisions

Today, boy-girl relationships start earlier and are more casual than ever before. Young people are more sophisticated than in earlier times and society is more tolerant. Most adolescents view this freedom with mixed feelings. They may be pleased with their greater mobility, privacy, and independence. Yet they may also be frightened by the need to make important personal decisions.

What decisions do you face? How do you feel about dating, love, sex? Should you be in love before you have an intimate sexual relationship with someone? Should you live with a person for a year or two to test compatibility for marriage? Should you honor your parents' views on dating? Should you try communal living? Your family upbringing, religious beliefs, emotional maturity, and present environment all influence your answers to these questions.

In the past, adolescents were shielded from such decisions. They generally followed the etiquette and custom of the day which frowned upon sexual intimacy before marriage. A large percentage of people still hold these values and provide their children with good reasons not to rush into sexual relationships. A girl may complain about her strict parents and yet be inwardly relieved that she must be home by twelve. A boy may be pleased that his date has a curfew so that he does not have to prove his masculinity.

Those who favor premarital intercourse argue that "teenagers are biologically, psychologically, and socially ready for sexual intercourse and moreover need this experience to consolidate their sexual identity, sense of self, and pattern of relationships with others."[5] Since unwanted pregnancies can be prevented, these advocates think that premarital sexual intimacy allows for more honest and total relationships, and that it helps one choose a marital partner more wisely.

Those who oppose premarital intercourse believe sexual intimacy should evolve from a relationship based on love and a binding commitment. They say giving in to sexual desires does not guarantee emotional growth and may allow a person to avoid the responsibilities of a more total relationship. They also argue that because of cultural and religious beliefs, an adolescent who indulges in premarital intercourse may develop feelings of guilt and anxiety.[6]

Movies, television, and magazines would lead you to believe that everyone is part of the "new morality." This belief puts pressure on you if you do not feel ready for sexual intimacy—you may feel anxious, insecure, and different. As one teenager said, "It's like nobody wants to be a kid anymore."[7]

It is important to feel comfortable with whatever decisions you make. If you just follow the lead of others, you may have nagging doubts later. As you progress from adolescence to adulthood, you must decide what is "right" for *you*.

In adolescence·your self-image is fragile. In seeking love, affection, and approval, you must be willing to risk the possibility of rejection, hurt, and disappointment. Finding a comfortable balance between your sexual desires and emotional needs is not easy. This is one of the most important tasks of adolescence.

Achieving Your Own Identity

As a child, your life was organized and predictable—your world was small and your tasks limited. You probably felt relatively secure. An action-oriented person, you lived

BARBARA'S THOUGHTS AT SEVENTEEN

People say times have changed; there isn't nearly as much pressure to date during high school as there used to be. This may be so but I personally feel the pressure. I hate it when people ask me if I have a boyfriend. I feel they are judging me by my answer. If I do have a boyfriend then I must be O.K.; if not, then just Oh. I don't have a boyfriend at the moment and when I have had them in the past my relationships haven't lasted very long. To describe my social life would be to say it's very boring. There just do not seem to be enough guys around, none to whom I appeal and none who appeal to me. People don't consider this; they judge you popular or unpopular. I'd like to have a boyfriend. A date would be a sure thing and there wouldn't be week-ends at clubs or just feeling sorry for myself. It's a feeling of being wanted and liked, which is most important along with the companionship. A boyfriend is a boost to the ego, someone to love and be loved by.

I often feel very lonesome and depressed because of what I feel I am missing. I hate the way girls have to sit home and wait for a guy to call, the first time at least. I know it doesn't *have* to be this way but I've grown up that way, and that's the way it is with me. Whenever I go to some social affair—a family gathering, a wedding of a dear friend of the family—I hate the questions: Do you have a boyfriend? Even worse: Why don't you have a boyfriend? I often think what is wrong with me, why don't I have a boyfriend, or that many dates? I hate thinking and feeling that way, but it's very hard to change the way one's been conditioned to think. Being dateless and boyfriendless makes me feel something is lacking in me.

I find nothing wrong with sex before marriage in the people around me. If two people love each other and understand themselves and what they want out of life, I would approve of their having a sexual relationship (not that my opinion would make a difference!). But being only 17 and thinking about sex at age 17, I feel much too young. I believe that sex and love go together; in order to have sex I will have to love the guy very much. I've been brought up with the thought that love, marriage, sex, and children all belong in the same category. My opinions and feelings towards sex stem from those early learnings. My parents would be crushed if they found out that I had a sexual relationship before marriage. They would blame themselves for something I had done which they would consider horrible. I respect them and their opinions a great deal, and I would never want to hurt them knowingly.

I have a feeling my opinions will change as I do some growing up. I need a good many years to find out who I am, what love is all about, and what I want in a relationship. I am very inexperienced. My opinions, though they are feelings, may be invalid because I have never really loved a guy enough to consider having a sexual relationship with him. People have told me that if I find a guy and fall in love, my views will change. I do not feel pressured by these people or by such a thought. My values are part of me and I stick to them. Not only do my morals oppose sex at my age, but I am also scared of it. Personally I have a long way to go before I consider sex.

- Barbara is an attractive, vivacious girl. How typical do you think her feelings are?

- Do boys face the same conflicts? Different problems? Explain.

- What assumptions do you make about people who date often? Who date rarely? Who go steady?

- Should girls feel free to ask boys out?

- Barbara discusses sex in relation to [a] age and readiness for an intimate relationship [b] desire for parental approval [c] love [d] morality. How do you feel about each of these issues?

only for the present—you did not worry very much about the future.

In adolescence, this "organization" breaks down. That sense of security fades away. The outside world looms very large and the future is very real. As the pressures to become independent mount, you must make many decisions.

Adolescence is a time for introspection. It is a time to test the many facets of your personality—to see what works . . . and what feels comfortable. Out of this period of disorganization and experimentation, you emerge with a new identity, a more permanent self.

Self-Esteem

We judge ourselves by what we feel capable of doing,
While others judge us by what we have already done.

LONGFELLOW

One of the most important tasks of adolescence is to achieve a sense of self-respect, a feeling of personal

SOME PERSONAL DECISIONS

1. *How important are the following factors in your willingness to "date" someone? Rank them in order of importance from a high of one to a low of twelve. Compare your order with that of your fellow students.*

    _____ *physical appearance*   _____ *personality*

    _____ *religion*   _____ *popularity*

    _____ *parents' preferences*   _____ *views on sex*

    _____ *race*   _____ *political views*

    _____ *intelligence*   _____ *character*

    _____ *future goals*   _____ *money*

What conclusions can you draw from the order you decided on?

2. *Think back to when you first started to notice signs of puberty—what feelings and anxieties did you have about your physical development?*

3. *How did you first learn about sex? What is the best way for an adolescent to learn about sex? From parents? From teachers? From peers? From books, television, or movies?*

4. *Alice and Mark are 17. They have been dating for a few months and like each other quite a bit. Mark*

decides they should become more sexually involved as a way of getting to know each other better, thus strengthening their relationship. Alice feels her parents would not approve, and she also feels she is not ready. She asks Mark to be patient. Mark feels Alice is being unfair and feels their relationship cannot progress. He stops dating her.

If you are a girl, take Alice's side and react to this situation.

If you are a boy, pretend you are Mark—how would you have reacted?

What do you think is the relationship between love and sex?

5. Diane and Jim like each other but are not in love. They have a sexual relationship and Diane becomes pregnant. She feels Jim should marry her. Jim says they both knew the risks involved, and he does not want to get married. He feels he is too young, and not in love. Diane feels he should marry her for the child's sake, and that they would learn to love each other.

Have seven people in class choose the following names from a hat:

Diane	Diane's father
Jim	Jim's mother
Diane's mother	Jim's father
a clergyman or counselor	

Then send the parents and counselor out of the room. Have Diane and Jim role-play the dilemma. After they have discussed the situation thoroughly, invite one set of parents in. Diane and Jim should present the dilemma to them for their reaction and advice. Next ask the other set of parents in and see how they react. Finally call in the counselor and have all seven discuss the matter.

After they finish the role-playing, the rest of the class should react to all the views presented.

What would you do if you were Diane or Jim in this situation?

Adolescence is probably the period in life when you are most self-critical. It is difficult to live up to your own standards, and also to the expectations of parents, teachers, and other adults.

worth. Yet, there is probably no other time in life when you are so self-critical and feel so inadequate. It is difficult to live up to your own standards and also to the expectations of parents, teachers, and other adults.

Anne Frank, in her famous diary, expressed this well:

> *I can watch myself and my actions, just like an outsider. The Anne of every day I can face entirely without prejudice, without making excuses for her, and watch what's good and what's bad about her. This "self-consciousness" haunts me, and every time I open my mouth I know as soon as I've spoken whether "that ought to have been different" or "that was right as it was." There are so many things about myself that I condemn: I couldn't begin to name them all.*[8]

An adolescent is sensitive to every challenge and remark made to him. He may interpret suggestions as criticism and worry that the criticism is valid—that, in fact, he is an unworthy person. It is hard to rebound from a challenge or be objective when you are so unsure of yourself. It is natural to feel anxious, resentful, and frightened.

Because the adolescent has had limited experience in interacting with others, he tends to magnify the reactions people have to him and to dwell on the unfavorable ones. In his book, *Peace of Mind,* Joshua Liebman discusses the achievement of self-esteem:

> *There are many temptations to self-contempt and self-destruction along the route that the ego takes to*

97

Photo courtesy of Kenneth M. Bernstein

In adolescence, it is important to be accepted and liked *as you are*, and for what you hope to be. Usually a close friend knows the "real" you, with all your hopes and fears, better than anyone else does.

maturity. As a matter of fact, one reason why man can be more continuously cruel to himself than to anyone else is that he is always available to himself as an object of attack. Other people are intermittently present as objects of our aggression, but our own ego is always there, even in sleep, as a citadel to be stormed, a fortress to be smashed, an enemy to be destroyed . . .

In our exalted moods we are afraid to admit guilt, hatred, and shame as elements of our personality;

98

and in our depressed moods we are afraid to credit ourselves with the goodness and the achievement which really are ours . . .

＊＊＊＊＊

We are relative, and not absolute, creatures; everything we do is tinged with imperfection . . . It will help us to make peace with ourselves if we realize that in this battle for self-discovery we need not emerge either a genius or a saint.[9]

Each person lives with his own doubts and insecurities, thinking everyone else is confident and secure. He assumes that only he is confused, anxious, and suffering inside. It is a painful process before you finally realize others share this same insecurity and self-doubt. Then you no longer feel so alone. It is at this point you may learn to accept yourself and *to value the person you are.*

The Inferiority Complex

Most adolescents are quick to recognize the term "inferiority complex." Alfred Adler, a Viennese psychiatrist, was the first to use this phrase in describing a person's feelings of inadequacy.

As a doctor, Adler became interested in how the body tries to repair its own weaknesses. For example, when one kidney fails, the other healthy kidney may take over and function for it. The healthy kidney works harder and grows stronger. It *compensates,* or makes up for the weak kidney.

99

SELF-ESTEEM: LOOKING AT YOURSELF

1. *If you had to pick just eight words which describe you best, what would they be?*

   How would the following people describe you:

Your Teachers	Your Parents	Your Friends	Your Employer

   Compare the descriptions. Who knows you best? Why?

2. *Describe four activities you do well. They can be related to school, sports, clubs, a job, etc.*

   List all the qualities required to do these things well. Did you consider these qualities as your strengths before? If not, why not?

3. *Pretend that you are applying for a job of your choice. The employer asks why he should hire you for the position. Write a recommendation for yourself, giving at least five strong reasons why you should be chosen.*

Sometimes people concentrate on their weaknesses and overcome them. Theodore Roosevelt's life proves that training and exercise can often transform a weak body into a healthy and strong one. The great orator Demosthenes stuttered as a child.

Adler reasoned that just as people could overcome physical weaknesses, they could also compensate for psychological weaknesses. *He believed that inferiority feelings were healthy and normal: they motivated people to improve themselves.* If a person is too easily satisfied with himself, he does not try to change. If he feels incomplete, he will strive for greater perfection. Adler realized that feelings of inferiority may be painful, yet he maintained that they help a person fulfill his potential.

Most people compensate in one way or another for their weaknesses. A poor athlete may put all his or her energies into becoming a top student, or vice versa. A quiet, withdrawn person may become a superior artist, channeling his or her emotions into expressive work. Napoleon is a good example of the little man who makes up for his size by tremendous self-confidence and drive.

The next time you have pangs of self-doubt and inferiority, remember Alfred Adler. Your doubts may be the first step to self-improvement!

Independence

As an adolescent, you want to feel independent. You need to feel you have the judgment and competence to manage your own life. You want people to take you seriously and to respect your opinions. In fact, you may sometimes express a desire for greater independence than you really want, just to make your point.

Ironically, just when you most need support and encouragement from those who love you, you are least able to accept their help. Increased knowledge, exposure, and sophistication lead you to question all the values, opinions, and assumptions you had previously taken for granted. You do not want easy answers or advice from your parents.

During this "reassessment," both you and your family may become tense and anxious. You may want to assert yourself at one moment, and may long for support and affection the next. This *ambivalence*—your conflicting feelings toward the same person or situation—may confuse your parents.

Sometimes you may feel relieved when your parents come up with a good solution to one of your problems, yet you may also feel angry with them for trying to help. Irene Josselyn explains why an adolescent may feel this way:

> He sees himself as having returned to childhood and having abandoned his struggle to become adult. This is a real blow to his pride. He resents his dependency because it has threatened his confidence in himself as a potential adult. In order to maintain his own self-respect, he must protest against this flight into childhood. To protest against himself is to acknowledge his own weakness, which he wishes to deny. . . . He chooses for his attack those who were cognizant of his defeat—his parents or other adults. He protests angrily that they will not let him grow up; they treat him as a child. He has chosen to be angry at his parents as a means of denying his own weakness and in order to shelter himself from his own self-contempt.[10]

Parents are also ambivalent—they want you to grow up, and yet they need to be needed! They are accustomed to being an important part of your life. It is hard for parents to watch their teenager wrestle with a problem they know they could solve for him. Sometimes they may offer help too quickly, and thus deny their son or daughter the chance to master the problem alone and thereby gain self-respect.

Wise parents encourage your independence and show confidence in your ability to make the right decision. They avoid lecturing or labeling you. Most adolescents resent it when a parent says: "When I was your age, I . . ." or "Why can't you be like . . ." or "It's your decision, but if I were you, I would . . . . " It is hard for a parent to resist giving advice or offering "constructive" criticism.

Parents have visions for their children. They want you to succeed where they failed, to become what they never became. Frequently, their definition of success differs from yours. Many parents live parts of their lives through their children. You may resent this burden of having to live up to *their* expectations and their dreams, even if you secretly share them. You may worry about disappointing your parents.

As you become more independent, your parents become aware that *they* are growing older. Parents may feel out of touch with what is "in"—styles and customs change rapidly. They may feel threatened by what you symbolize: an emerging adult who will replace them and their world.

It is not helpful for parents to try to bridge the generation gap by adopting the dress, language, and interests of the adolescent. Despite their admirable motives, they may really be encroaching on your sacred territory. Bernard Yudowitz notes:

> *Teenagers desperately need to be different from their parents. They have friends their own age to share their interests. Parents serve a much more important purpose in their lives. They are adult models—the people who show what it's like to be grown up. These are the years when children need to learn adult ways—not more childish ways—and parents are their chief reference point.[11]*

TRY TO SEE IT **MY** WAY. I **AM** NEARLY TWENTY AND IF I WAS **EVER** GOING TO MAKE THE BREAK **NOW** WAS THE TIME TO DO IT IMAGINE, HALF MY GIRL FRIENDS WERE ALREADY SEPARATED FROM THEIR HUSBANDS AND HERE I WAS STILL LIVING AT **HOME!**

SO I TOLD MY PARENTS I WAS MOVING OUT.

YOU CAN'T **IMAGINE** THE YELLING AND SCREAMING. MY FATHER SAID- "YOU'RE BREAKING YOUR MOTHER'S HEART!" MY MOTHER SAID- "WHAT WAS MY CRIME? WHAT WAS MY **TERRIBLE** CRIME?"

AND BEFORE I KNEW IT WE WERE IN THE MIDDLE OF A BIG ARGUMENT AND I TOLD THEM THEY BOTH NEEDED ANALYSIS AND THEY TOLD ME I HAD A FILTHY MOUTH AND SUDDENLY I WAS OUT ON THE STREET WITH MY RAINCOAT, MY SUITCASE AND MY TENNIS RACKET BUT I HAD NO PLACE TO **MOVE!**

SO I LOOKED AROUND DOWNTOWN AND EVERYTHING WAS TOO EXPENSIVE AND EVENING CAME AND ALL MY GIRL FRIENDS HAD RECONCILED WITH THEIR HUSBANDS SO THERE WAS ABSOLUTELY NO PLACE I COULD SPEND THE NIGHT.

WELL, **FRANKLY**, WHAT ON EARTH COULD I **DO**? I WAITED TILL IT WAS **WAY** PAST MY PARENTS BEDTIME - THEN I **SNEAKED** BACK INTO THE HOUSE AND SET THE ALARM IN MY BEDROOM FOR SIX THE NEXT MORNING.

THEN I SLEPT ON TOP OF THE BED SO I WOULDN'T WRINKLE ANY SHEETS, SNEAKED SOME BREAKFAST IN THE MORNING AND GOT OUT BEFORE ANYONE WAS UP.

I'VE BEEN LIVING THAT WAY FOR TWO MONTHS NOW.

EVERY NIGHT AFTER MIDNIGHT I SNEAK INTO MY BEDROOM, SLEEP ON TOP OF THE BED TILL SIX THE NEXT MORNING, HAVE BREAKFAST AND SNEAK OUT.

AND EVERY DAY I CALL UP MY PARENTS FROM THE DOWNSTAIRS DRUGSTORE AND THEY YELL AND CRY AT ME TO COME BACK. BUT, OF COURSE, I ALWAYS TELL THEM NO.

I'LL **NEVER** GIVE UP MY INDEPENDENCE.

INDEPENDENCE: WHO DECIDES?

1. *Lois is a sophomore in high school. Relaxed and easy-going, she is popular with several different groups of kids. One day, her parents start to complain that they don't like some of her friends. They have heard that these kids are wild and rude and not interested in doing well in school. Her parents ask Lois to stop going out with them. They tell her not to bring them to the house.*

   Lois gets upset. She says these kids are fun to be with and the rumors are untrue. She tells them she should have the right to choose her own friends.

   What should Lois do? How would you settle her disagreement with her parents?

   Would you feel differently if Lois were in the eighth grade or a senior in high school? How would age influence your decision?

   To what extent should parents get involved in:

   a. Your choice of friends
   b. How you spend your money
   c. Whom you date
   d. Your clothes and appearance
   e. The way you keep your room
   f. The grades you earn
   g. Your future educational/vocational plans

   Rate each issue on a continuum from 1 to 5. Place

the letter of each issue on the continuum wherever you think it belongs.

1	2	3	4	5
YOUR DECISION ALONE			YOUR PARENTS SHOULD HAVE A STRONG INFLUENCE	

Explain your reasoning for each.

Ask several adults what their views are on these issues.

2. *John is 16. His parents have told him that he cannot drink until he is 18 and on his own. They say he is too young now and it is bad for his health. John argues that they drink, and so he should be allowed to. Besides, all his friends have permission to drink. His parents tell him that the fact that they drink does not make it right, and they are doing what is best for him.*

Should parents impose standards on their children which they themselves do not follow?

When does one have the right to decide what is in one's best interest?

Does age make a difference in whether one drinks?

John goes to a party. Everyone is drinking and he joins in. When he gets home his mother is waiting up and asks if he has been drinking. What should he say?

3. *Barbara, age 16, tells her parents that she is going to a party Friday night. They ask her to be in at 12:30 a.m.*

since they cannot fall asleep until they know she is back safely. Barbara feels it would be embarrassing to have a curfew when her friends do not, and she argues that she can take care of herself. She feels her parents should trust her. She does not want anyone to leave the party early just to take her home. Her parents say that she must come in by 12:30 or she cannot go to the party at all.

Who is right? Why?

How would you settle the conflict?

Should there be different curfews for boys than for girls?

The struggle for independence is difficult for both you and your parents. But when you finally feel secure in your independence, you will be able to ask for advice and help when you need it . . . and your parents will talk to you as an adult.

Idealism

Eugene was not quite sixteen years old when he was sent away to the university . . . . He was a child when he went away: he was a child who had looked on much pain and evil, and remained a fantasist of the Ideal. Walled up in his great city of visions, his tongue had learned to mock, his lips to sneer, but the harsh rasp of the world had worn no grooving in the secret life . . . . He was not a child when he reflected,

*but when he dreamt, he was; and it was the child and
dreamer that governed his belief . . . . He believed in
brave, heroic lives. He believed in the fine flowers of
tenderness and gentleness he had little known. He
believed in beauty and in order, and that he would
wreak out their mighty forms upon the distressful
chaos of his life. He believed in love, and in the
goodness and glory of women. He believed in
valiance, and he hoped that, like Socrates, he would
do nothing mean or common in the hour of danger.
He exulted in his youth, and he believed that he could
never die.*[12]

THOMAS WOLFE, *Look Homeward, Angel*

Youth is a time of idealism. It is a time when you desperately need to believe that what is good and genuine in the world, and in yourself, can prevail.

You have been drilled with the concepts of justice, equality, and fair play since grade school. Your parents have talked of "character" and your church of "morality." In adolescence, you realize these are just concepts—the best man does *not* always win, the best candidate is not always elected. But it is also in adolescence that your commitment to the values and ideals you have set for yourself becomes all the more important. Youth is a time for reaching out to others, sharing their concerns and championing their causes.

By investing your energy in a cause, you can make your voice heard and your action productive. This is crucial—for adolescence is the time in life when you feel least able to influence others and to effect change. Fighting for your beliefs gives an immediate purpose and meaning to your life. Not everything is in the distant future.

Idealism may be an expression of one's growing "urge to love." Commitment to a cause may reflect a need to be needed and a desire to give of yourself—just as love does.

Progress has always depended on the idealism and energy of youth. The adolescent brings a new perspective to each problem. He is impatient and demands action. He is the conscience of adults, reminding them through his righteous indignation of their generation's shortcomings. He is the voice and instrument of change.

Usually, it is easier to identify a problem than to solve it. The frustration, apathy, and hostility you may encounter in working for change is a lesson already well-learned by most adults. But, fresh and unafraid, you may have the vigor to pursue an issue your parents have learned to accept and live with.

Idealism is a healthy and normal part of adolescence. It is important to dream your dreams, and cherish your beliefs. It would be difficult to incorporate such values as honesty, integrity, and social concern into your own personality if you could not believe that they were real and "workable" in the outside world.

The Peer Group

A friend is somebody who knows all about you, but likes you anyways.

ORSON WELLES

Everyone has the need to belong. Alfred Adler believed that every person is *born* with a *social* instinct which is later cultivated by his family and society. During

IDEALISM IN ACTION

1. *Before she and her family were killed by the Nazis, a young girl recorded these thoughts in her diary:*

It's really a wonder that I haven't dropped all my ideals, because they seem so absurd and impossible to carry out. Yet I keep them, because in spite of everything I still believe that people are really good at heart. I simply can't build up my hopes on a foundation consisting of confusion, misery, and death. I see the world gradually being turned into a wilderness, I hear the ever approaching thunder, which will destroy us too, I can feel the sufferings of millions and yet, if I look up into the heavens, I think that it will all come right, that this cruelty too will end, and that peace and tranquillity will return again.[13]

ANNE FRANK, *July, 1944*

Do you think that in her situation idealism was foolish or necessary? Why?

Do you believe that people are basically "good at heart"? Explain your view.

When is idealism *not* justified?

2. *What factors determine your ideals?*

3. *Have you given up or gained certain ideals in the last few years? Which ideals? Why?*

4. *What ideals would you be willing to fight for?*

5. *Can you give some examples of youthful idealism in action? What role have young people played in revolutions, anti-war demonstrations, religious movements, civil rights groups, etc.?*

6. *The rainbow is more beautiful than the pot at the end of it, because the rainbow is now. And the pot never turns out to be quite what I expected.*[14]

   HUGH PRATHER, *Notes to Myself*

   Do you agree? React to this statement from personal experience.

7. *Spend some time working on an issue or cause which interests you. Some suggestions are listed below. Then discuss with the class the problems of pursuing the group's goals and the feelings of the people involved. What reactions did you have to your experience, and what conclusions did you reach?*

   Interracial understanding.
   A political cause.
   The plight of the elderly.
   The situation of the unemployed.
   The situation of the welfare recipient.
   Religious tolerance.
   Abortion.
   Neighborhood improvement.
   Children's legal rights.

8. *Examine discipline procedures in your high school.
Are they fair and just? Can you propose alternative
ways of handling discipline which would be more
ideal?*

adolescence, when you feel insecure about your own
image, acceptance by your peer group is vital. It reassures
you that you are a worthy person, that some people like
you *as you are.*

Ralph Waldo Emerson once said, "A friend is a person
with whom I may be sincere. Before him I may think
aloud." Usually a close friend knows the "real" you, with
all your hopes and fears, better than anyone else does. It is
sometimes less threatening to share your concerns with a
friend having the same or similar experiences than with an
adult. Friends seem to understand when parents or
teachers may not.

You select an image when you choose your friends.
Their dress, their interests, and their attitudes become
yours. You are seen by others as a member of a group, or
as a certain "type." Every school has its athletes, its science
brains, its hippies, its ivy leaguers, its black-leather-jacket
types, and so forth. You can describe what each group is
like without personally knowing the students in the group.

Membership in a group brings certain privileges. You
are automatically invited to parties and other activities.
Your friends back you when you are faced with a serious
problem. You can exercise more power as a member of a
group than as an individual. Parents often feel defeated
when their son argues that he is the only one in his group

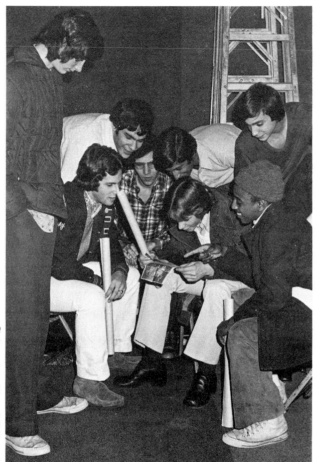

Photo courtesy of Kenneth M. Bernstein

As an adolescent, your self-image depends to a large extent on your acceptance by others. You need trusted friends on whom you can test your ideas and who reassure you in your decisions. You tend to use your peer group for much of the support you used to get from your family.

114

who is not allowed to have a car, or when their daughter says she is the only one among her friends with a midnight curfew.

Peer group pressure may also become a problem in adolescence. When you will not join your friends in smoking pot or in skipping a class, you may feel like an outsider. What do you do when a friend asks to copy your homework? Your loyalty is constantly on the line.

Often one has to "earn" his admission into a group. Fraternities formerly had "hazing" rites to test courage and loyalty. These often resembled the rites of puberty in more primitive cultures. The tests were sometimes dangerous, yet the need to belong overruled one's fear. The novel, *A Separate Peace*, describes jumping from a tree as the initiation test at one prep school:

> *I never got inured to the jumping. At every meeting the limb seemed higher, thinner, the deeper water harder to reach. Every time, when I got myself into a position to jump, I felt a flash of disbelief that I was doing anything so perilous. But I always jumped. Otherwise I would have lost face with Phineas, and that would have been unthinkable.*[15]

Initiations are less frequent and usually less dramatic today. There is more tolerance now for diversity and individuality.

However, the need to belong, to have some identifiable friends, is still strong. As an adolescent your self-image depends to a large extent on your acceptance by others. You need trusted friends to test out your ideas and reassure you in your decisions. Your peer group provides much of the support you used to get from your family.

YOUR PEER GROUP

1. *A sociogram is a diagram describing and outlining interpersonal relationships in a particular group. Draw a sociogram of your friends—closest friends nearest to you, acquaintances further away.*

What qualities and values do your friends have in common?

As you go further out from the center, does the list of qualities and values you share diminish?

2. *What kinds of things would you rather discuss with your friends than with your parents? Explain why.*

3. *What do you think the image of your group is to those outside your group? What factors account for this image: interests, clothes, grades, ethnic or socioeconomic group, long range plans, personality characteristics, others?*

4. *Paul is one of your closest friends. He is bright and he wants to go on to college. He is worried that his parents will not be able to afford the tuition. A local*

labor group has offered a large scholarship to the senior in your high school who does the best on their labor history exam. Several people take it—Paul gets the highest grade. He tells you afterwards that he brought notes with him and cheated.

Do you have a greater responsibility to turn Paul in or to keep his confidence?

Would it matter that two of your other close friends also took the exam? Would it matter if *you* took the exam?

Does it matter that Paul is bright and might have won anyway?

Does it matter that he needs the money as much as anyone who took the exam?

What kinds of issues would force you to put aside friendship?

5. *Words can mean that I want to make you into a friend, and silence can mean that I accept your already being one.*[16]

HUGH PRATHER, *Notes to Myself*

How is silence a form of communication?

Identity

Very early in the morning she would sometimes go out into the yard and stand for a long time looking at

*the sunrise sky. And it was as though a question came
into her heart, and the sky did not answer. Things she
had never noticed much before began to hurt her:
home lights watched from the evening sidewalks, an
unknown voice from an alley. She would stare at the
lights and listen to the voice, and something inside
her stiffened and waited. But the lights would
darken, the voice fall silent, and though she waited,
that was all. She was afraid of these things that made
her suddenly wonder who she was, and what she was
going to be in the world, and why she was standing at
that minute, seeing a light, or listening, or staring up
into the sky: alone. She was afraid, and there was a
queer tightness in her chest.[17]*

CARSON MC CULLERS,
The Member of the Wedding

Every adolescent at some point faces what Erik Erikson
has called an "identity crisis." This is the time when you
struggle to define who you are and what you want out of
life. It is a lonely and frightening experience. Only you can
make the decisions which will shape your future. It is easy
to become preoccupied with this soul-searching, and you
may find it hard to concentrate on your daily routine.
Achieving a sense of identity is the prime task of
adolescence—once attained, you are psychologically
ready to become an adult.

It is not easy to develop a sense of your own unique
identity. Carl Rogers, in a book entitled *On Becoming a
Person*, discusses the identity crisis of a typical psychiatric
client:

*Often he discovers that he exists only in response to
the demands of others, that he seems to have no self*

*of his own, that he is only trying to think, and feel and
behave in the way that others believe he ought to
think and feel and behave . . .* [18]

This helps to explain why an adolescent must rebel,
why he must challenge his parents' values and set new
ones for himself. It is important to achieve your *own*
identity.

Sometimes a young person will choose a respected
adult as a "role model" to pattern his personality after.
Seeing this adult as successful in relating to people or in his
career, he may try to emulate his personality and style.
Think of how many different careers you have considered
because you have liked specific people who held these
jobs and occupations.

During adolescence you wear many masks and play
many roles—this is normal and continues throughout life.
Everyone's personality changes according to his situation
at a particular moment. You may be outgoing and
talkative with your friends in the halls, yet shy and passive
in class discussion. You may be sarcastic with a younger
brother, argue with your mother, and be polite and poised
with your employer. Which is the real you? Probably all of
them! Everyone experiences temporary shifts in mood
and style around a "core" personality.

Finding your identity, then, does not mean you
become a static, finished product. It means you achieve a
basic sense of self, a sense of direction and purpose. It
means you accept yourself as you are; that you are
comfortable in making your own decisions; that you have
established a basic set of values and ideals; and that you
feel secure in dealing with others.

Conclusion

Someone once asked Sigmund Freud "what he thought a normal person should be able to do well." Expecting a lengthy reply, the person was surprised by Freud's concise answer: "To love and to work."[19]

Love, in its broadest sense, means: to value oneself, and to be able to extend love to a mate, to one's parents and children, to one's fellow man. It means you can give of yourself, you can accept love from others, and you can be honest in your relationships.

Photo courtesy of Kenneth M. Bernstein

Adolescence is a time for introspection. It is a time to test the many facets of your personality—to see what works . . . . and what feels comfortable. Out of this period of disorganization and experimentation, you emerge with a new identity, a more permanent self.

To work well, you must enjoy the work you have chosen. You must be able to grow through it, and benefit others by it. You must find it meaningful and rewarding. Work can mean having a hobby, or exploring an interest, as well as having a job.

Love and work cover almost all the important facets of your life. Freud's answer was not so simple after all. Adolescence is the time when you learn to love and to work.

Although adolescence is the period of greatest upheaval in your life, you will continue to change and adapt your personality throughout your adult years. You will face other times when you must re-evaluate your life and make difficult choices and adjustments. Adolescence is a most complicated time because you face so many changes all at once: changes in body, personality, values, and self-image.

It is important to remember that all the conflicting feelings of adolescence are part of this "normal" growth pattern. Love and hurt, joy and pain, success and disappointment all help to shape and define the person you are to become. It is a long and complicated route one travels to adulthood. As Joshua Liebman noted:

The human self is not a gift; it is an achievement.[20]

EXPERIENCING ADOLESCENCE

1. *How many different "roles" do you play in the course of a day? Describe your personality in each situation. For example, are you serious and intense in class but relaxed and easy-going with your friends?*

    When do you feel you are most natural, your "real" self?

2. *Create a collage that best represents the different facets of your personality. Have the class interpret it.*

3. *Here are some typical comments from adolescents. Choose three and role-play a situation in class that illustrates each. Then decide how each situation should be resolved.*

    My mother makes me do all the work at home because I'm the oldest.

    My parents are overprotective.

    My parents criticize me for bad grades even though I've tried my best.

    I'm always compared to my older brother.

    My parents only see things their way—they don't try to understand me.

    My parents have double standards—they can do things which I am not allowed to do.

4. Which do you think are the "best" years of life and which the "worst"? Why?

childhood   young adulthood

adolescence   middle age

old age

5. How might the adolescent experience be different in (a) the inner city; (b) the suburbs; (c) a rural area?

6. What advice would you give to a younger brother or sister about coping with the problems of adolescence?

7. Read a novel which deals with adolescence. In what ways do the characters portray some of the common themes of adolescence (identity crisis, independence, self-esteem, idealism, peer relations, concerns of puberty)?

Suggested Reading

Caplan, Gerald, and Serge Lebovici, *Adolescence: Psychosocial Perspectives* (New York: Basic Books, 1969).

Cole, Luella, and Irma Hall, *Psychology of Adolescence* (New York: Holt, Rinehart and Winston, 1970).

Esman, Aaron, *The Psychology of Adolescence* (New York: International Universities Press, 1975).

Frank, Anne, *The Diary of a Young Girl* (Garden City, N.Y.: Doubleday, 1967).

Ginott, Dr. Haim, *Between Parent and Teenager* (New York: Macmillan, 1969).

Group for the Advancement of Psychiatry, Committee on Adolescence, *Normal Adolescence* (New York: Charles Scribner's Sons, 1968).

Horrocks, John, *The Psychology of Adolescence* (Boston: Houghton Mifflin, 1969).

Kagan, Jerome, and Robert Coles, *Twelve to Sixteen: Early Adolescence* (New York: W.W. Norton and Company, 1972).

FICTION

Braithwaite, Edward, *To Sir With Love* (Englewood Cliffs, N.J.: Prentice-Hall, 1960).

Brown, Claude, *Manchild in the Promised Land* (New York: Macmillan, 1965).

Crane, Stephen, *The Red Badge of Courage* (New York: Random House, 1951).

Gaines, Ernest, *The Autobiography of Miss Jane Pittman* (New York: Dial Press, 1971).

Goldman, William, *The Temple of Gold* (New York: Knopf, 1957).

Hesse, Hermann, *Siddartha* (New York: New Directions, 1951).

Holland, Isabelle, *The Man Without a Face* (Philadelphia: Lippincott, 1972).

Knowles, John, *A Separate Peace* (New York: Macmillan, 1959).

McCluskey, John, *Look What They Done to My Song* (New York: Random House, 1974).

McCullers, Carson, *The Heart is a Lonely Hunter* (Boston: Houghton Mifflin, 1940).

McCullers, Carson, *The Member of the Wedding* (Boston: Houghton Mifflin, 1946).

Moody, Anne, *Coming of Age in Mississippi* (New York: The Dial Press, 1968).

Morrison, Toni, *Sula* (New York: Knopf, 1974).

Potok, Chaim, *The Chosen* (New York: Simon and Schuster, 1967).

Salinger, J.D., *The Catcher in the Rye* (Boston: Little Brown, 1951).

Sillitoe, Alan, *The Loneliness of the Long Distance Runner* (New York: Knopf, 1972).

Smith, Betty, *A Tree Grows in Brooklyn* (New York: Harper and Row, 1947).

Wiesel, Elie, trans. by Stella Rodway, *Night* (New York: Hill and Wang, 1960).

Wolfe, Thomas, *Look Homeward, Angel* (New York: Charles Scribner's Sons, 1929).

Wright, Richard, *Native Son* (New York: Harper and Row, 1940).

FOOTNOTES

1. Hugh Prather, *Notes to Myself* (Moab, Utah: Real People Press, 1970).
2. Anna Freud, *Psychoanalytic Study of the Child* (New York: International Universities Press, 1958).
3. *Fiddler on the Roof* (New York: Crown Publishers, 1965).
4. Copyright © 1959, 1964 by Edgar Z. Friedenberg, *The Vanishing Adolescent*, p. 10. Reprinted by permission of Beacon Press, Boston.

5. Committee on Adolescence, *Normal Adolescence* (New York: Charles Scribner's Sons, 1968), p. 86.
6. *Ibid*, p. 86.
7. Thomas Cottle, "Four Studies," *The New York Times Magazine,* November 26, 1972, p. 104.
8. Anne Frank, *The Diary of a Young Girl* (Garden City, New York: Doubleday and Company, © 1952, © 1967), p. 283.
9. Joshua Liebman, *Peace of Mind* (New York: Simon and Schuster, 1946), pp. 46, 53-4, 58.
10. Irene M. Josselyn, *The Adolescent and His World* (New York: Family Service Association of America, 1952), pp. 50-51.
11. Bernard S. Yudowitz, M.D., with Jean Pascoe, "Three Cheers for the Generation Gap," *Woman's Day,* 1972.
12. Thomas Wolfe, *Look Homeward Angel* (New York: Charles Scribner's Sons, 1957, p. 325.
13. Frank, *op. cit.*, p. 287.
14. Prather, *op. cit.*
15. John Knowles, *A Separate Peace* (New York: Macmillan, 1959).
16. Prather, *op. cit.*
17. Carson McCullers, *The Member of the Wedding* (Boston: Houghton Mifflin, 1946), p. 20.
18. Carl Rogers, *On Becoming A Person* (Boston: Houghton Mifflin, 1961), p. 110.
19. Erik Erikson, *Childhood and Society* (New York: W. W. Norton, 1950), p. 265.
20. Liebman, *op. cit.*, p. 41.

3.

"To Love and to Work": Adulthood and Aging

When you are sixteen, it seems as if you are the only one changing and in motion, while the rest of the world stands relatively still. It is hard to say what "thirty" is and what "forty" is. Often the difference is noted only in terms of graying hair and an expanding waistline. Everything seems so settled: marriage, a family, a career. Those years all look alike.

Psychologists have only recently begun to study how people change as they grow older. We continue to "evolve" all of our lives—and we must. We are constantly challenged by new situations and new options. Both good fortune and tragedy can change our lives overnight. Our satisfaction lies in our ability to adapt to life and to shape it.

In each of the case studies mentioned here (and discussed more fully on the following pages), an adult faces an identity crisis:

LISA AND JACK ANDREWS, both 24, seem happily married, until Jack loses his job. Suddenly he must begin all over again to find the "right" position. With his nagging self-doubts and Lisa's disappointment, the marriage becomes strained.

KENNETH ROGERS, age 42, is in a rut. Psychologists believe that most people go through a similar "mid-life crisis" when they question the value of their lives, realizing they may not accomplish all their goals. It is a time of new frustrations and fears: fear of losing one's youth and fear of facing death. Yet often it is in this mid-life re-evaluation that people like Kenneth Rogers gain a new perspective on life and a better sense of the value and satisfactions of being forty.

BARBARA BENSON must change at sixty-seven. Now that she is retired, she must find new interests and make new friends. Older people can change, but it is not easy. Barbara Benson must decide how she is going to give meaning to her new life.

Life never stops moving. You never stop changing and adapting. You will be a different person at twenty-five than you are today; and different again at forty-five. So it is important to look at adulthood and aging as *dynamic* years of life: years of achievement and stability, but also years of challenge and of increasing wisdom and potential.

Case #1: Lisa and Jack Andrews

Lisa and Jack Andrews had known each other since their sophomore year in high school. Friends used to kid them that they were the perfect match. Jack found a promising job as an assistant merchandiser in a discount house soon after graduation. If things worked out, he was to become the buyer of menswear. Lisa enrolled in a two-year program at the community college. By the time they were twenty-two, they had saved enough money to get married.

For the first two years everything was ideal. They both worked hard, but were happy. They treasured the few hours they could relax together in the evenings. On weekends, friends and family streamed in and out.

In the last six months, though, everything seemed to be changing. First, Jack's boss told him that business was very bad and he would have to lay Jack off. He knew he should look for a new job, but with the economy in a recession, where could he begin? Should he take odd jobs until he found the "right" position?

In addition, Lisa wanted to start a family. She tried to cheer Jack up and insisted she would continue working, but he knew she was disappointed. She seemed irritable and moody. Was he making her that way? He knew he was hard to live with: he felt insecure and restless. They found themselves barking at each other over little things. He felt like being alone so often now, away from all the pressures.

They began to wonder what had happened to their relationship. They could not seem to communicate.

Case #2: Kenneth Rogers

Kenneth Rogers tossed and turned but could not fall asleep. He had gone to bed at eleven; it was now one a.m. He stared at the ceiling and reviewed his day. It had started out badly. His wife told him over breakfast that she had accepted a dinner invitation for them for Friday night. He did not want to spend time with the Fishers: they were dull. Then his son Jeffrey started to nag him about getting the car for Saturday night. He read the morning newspaper as he sipped his coffee. An old high school acquaintance had died suddenly.

When he arrived at the office he could not concentrate. Telephone calls broke the monotony of a routine morning—and they were mostly complaints. He watched his secretary come and go. She was still young and attractive, in her mid-twenties. He wondered what *she* was going to be doing on Friday night, who she would be with. *But what was the use of daydreaming,* he said to himself, *he was forty-two and graying.* When he looked into the mirror, he felt very old. She was looking ahead to life, and he could only seem to look back.

During the afternoon sales meeting, his mind wandered. The new business recruit was making a presentation. He was articulate. Ken might have been impressed were he not envious. The boy had poise and self-assurance. He had a good future with the company. Ken had already peaked. Not that being a district manager was so bad. It just wasn't his dream. As he rode home that night, he wondered what he had done that was important that day. Not much.

He was irritable when he walked in the door. He poured himself a drink. After dinner he could have gone bowling, but instead he sat in front of the television. His back was bothering him. He would have to have it checked. He did not feel like talking to his wife. She would not understand. He wanted to catch his life and hold it in his grasp—but it was slipping through his fingers. Kenneth Rogers was "feeling forty."

Case #3: Barbara Benson
Barbara Benson had been looking forward to retirement

with mixed feelings. She was sixty-seven, and it had been getting more and more difficult to keep up with the fast pace of the office. People had told her at the retirement party how lucky she was. She could now do whatever she had always wanted to. Some of them really believed that, but she was not so sure. After all, what would she do? For the last twenty years the office had been her life. Her children were now married and had families of their own. No one was waiting for her at home.

When her husband died twenty years ago, she decided to take his place as a stockbroker. He had loyal clients and she knew the business well. She remembered how important it was to her at the time, like a new lease on life. Her children no longer needed her constant attention, and so work had kept her busy during the day. It provided the financial security she wanted. She liked the fast pace *then*—it was exciting. Besides, friends felt less sorry for her because she seemed so self-sufficient.

Now she could sleep late. It was hard to adjust to such leisure. Time seemed heavy and unstructured. The hours dragged. She daydreamed a lot. She wondered if the office missed her at all, if friends would continue to call her. She knew she could read or go to a museum, but that seemed unproductive. Her daughters called regularly, but they lived too far away for casual visiting. And she would not live with them: *this* was her home.

It was uncomfortable to live in the past, yet she had no plans for the future. She was a bright, alert woman, yet she felt useless. She was bored and lonely.

Early Adulthood

A major challenge of adolescence is decision-making. You have the final responsibility to choose your courses and

YOU ARE THE COUNSELOR

Pretend that Lisa and Jack Andrews, Kenneth Rogers, and Barbara Benson all come to you for help.

1. *How would you help Lisa and Jack Andrews?*

   Describe how each of them feels.

   What should Jack do about a job?

   How might their relationship be improved?

   Role-play in class a session between a marriage counselor and Lisa and Jack Andrews.

2. *How could Kenneth Rogers get out of his rut?*

   What changes could he make in his life?

   How could his wife and son help him?

3. *What hope can you give to Barbara Benson?*

   What do you think are her major concerns?

   How can she make her life meaningful?

   How would you feel in her situation?

   Keep each of these cases in mind during the discussion of the different stages of adulthood in this chapter.

Your Own Timetable

If you could plan your own timetable of development in adulthood, what would it be?

When would you complete your formal education?

When would you marry?

When would you have children?

When would you change jobs?

When would you retire?

curriculum, your activities and friends, and to do well or to fail. Your family, your environment, your experiences, and your values will influence the decisions you make.

Should you take a vocational program which will train you for a skilled job when you graduate from high school? Or should you prepare for college? And if you go to college, should it be for specific career training, or for a liberal arts background? How serious is it if you do not know at eighteen in what direction you wish to move? When *should* you know?

Should you leave home after high school for a dormitory or apartment? At what age can you be sure that you are ready to marry and settle down? What are the demands of love and intimacy? What are the satisfactions?

As you make the transition from adolescence to young adulthood, you find yourself concentrating on what

Freud described as the two major goals of adult development: to love and to work. (See conclusion of Chapter 2.) Let us look at each.

To Work

There are over 20,000 different kinds of jobs available in the United States today. No wonder most people become anxious about making the right choice. Since you have a minimum of work exposure and experience at age eighteen, it is a frightening as well as an exciting prospect.

Actually, you have more information with which to make your choice than you probably realize. When you think about your personality, your abilities, your values, and the opportunities available to you, you have already begun to narrow the field.

A major goal of early adulthood is to move from a period of exploration and decision-making to a period of stability and commitment: it is a time to chart the course of your life.

Career development begins in childhood. Remember how you played at being a teacher, a fireman, a doctor? Children *identify* with people in *visible* occupations, occupations which are part of their small world. They mimic the roles and personalities they see. Children also become interested in the jobs of those adults whom they admire personally. Their logic is: If I like Uncle Robert, and he is an engineer, then maybe I should be an engineer too.

Parents and other adults play an important role in shaping your attitude toward work. Is work an exciting opportunity, a creative experience, or a dull necessity? Is it a meaningful process, or the best short-cut to a goal? Is it a source of self-esteem, status, power, and fulfillment, or a source of discouragement, conformity, and boredom? As a child you form many opinions and attitudes about the world of work.

As you move through school, you learn important work habits: organization of time, problem-solving, perseverance, responsibility. You test your skills and abilities and form judgments about your own potential. You have experiences which bring you satisfaction: honors and prizes, the lead role in a play, an interesting part-time job. Someone may encourage you to pursue a talent, or may build your confidence to try some new direction. All these experiences may be important factors influencing your eventual career choice.

By the time you are in high school, you are making course choices which limit and define your options for the future. You may need Spanish and biology to go to college, but not to qualify as a printer's apprentice. And if you take all vocational courses, you cannot decide as a senior to apply to a liberal arts college. As you approach your graduation then, you have already made many decisions and have learned a lot about yourself and your values through this decision-making process.

You may be ready to choose an occupation and begin job training after high school. Or you may decide to work or travel for a year to "think things through." College and the military offer a bridge to adulthood: they give you the time to explore various fields before you finally make a career choice. They provide a temporary shelter from the demands of the working world.

Not everyone will know at eighteen or at twenty-two what occupation or career to pursue. Jack Andrews' case is not unusual. Although this may make you feel anxious, such "confusion" early in life can prove to be a positive factor. It may mean that you are not closing your options too early, that you need more time to test out different careers. By the time you do make your choice, you will feel that it was based on knowledge and experience of a wide range of possibilities and will be the best match for your abilities and goals. Erich Fromm notes, "most people make a decision about their careers at an age when they do not have the experience and judgment to know what activity is most congenial to them. Perhaps in their mid-thirties they wake up to the fact that it is too late to start that activity which they now know would have been the right choice."[1] Sometimes people choose too early out of a need for security, without knowing all the available possibilities. Everyone must find his or her *own* "right time" to settle on a job or a career. There is no prescribed timetable.

People usually choose occupations which fit their personalities. If you are shy, you would not choose politics or advertising. If you are outgoing, you may not want a desk job. You may choose public relations or business instead. If you enjoy the outdoors, you might consider a construction or recreational job.

Your career choice also reflects your values. If you wish to make a lot of money, you probably will not want to be a clergyman, social worker, or policeman. Yet if helping others is important to you, you may select one of those careers.

An occupation provides you with an identity and an image. It will shape and mold you and determine your life style. The hours you work, the people with whom you associate, the satisfactions you gain, the money you earn, the attitudes you form, are all determined by career choice. A career becomes more than just a job. It is a "purposeful life pattern."

People often change their occupations as they move through adulthood. Most people can do several types of jobs well. They may progress within their field or switch to a totally new career. Jack Andrews will probably find a satisfying position in the business world, although it may be quite different from the one with which he began. Leisure activities frequently provide an outlet to develop new interests and tap unused talents.

Work will assume as much importance in your life as you wish. If it becomes an all-consuming passion, other parts of your life may suffer. The "workaholic," obsessed with getting ahead, lets family and friends fade into the background. Sometimes work can be an escape when your life seems empty or family relationships are strained. On the other hand, you may view work as just a boring way to earn a check. That, too, is unfortunate.

The more work challenges you, fulfills your potential, and seems productive and important, the happier you will be. Work will probably consume at least one-half of your waking hours five days a week or more.

Choosing an occupation is a major task of early adulthood. It may take you one year or it may take several to finally make the right choice.

Work will assume as much importance in your life as you wish. The more work challenges you, fulfills your potential, and seems productive and important, the happier you will be.

THE CLASSIC WORKAHOLIC
ELLEN GOODMAN, *The Boston Globe*

He worked himself to death finally and precisely at 3 a.m. Sunday morning.

The obituary didn't say that, of course. It said that he died of a coronary thrombosis. I think that was it, but every one of his friends and acquaintances knew it instantly. He was a perfect Type A, a workaholic, a classic, they said to each other and shook their heads, and thought for five or ten minutes about the ways they lived.

This man who worked himself to death finally and precisely at 3 a.m. Sunday morning—on his day off— was 51 years old and he was a vice president. He was, however, one of six vice presidents, and one of three who might conceivably—if the president died or retired soon enough—have moved to the top spot. Phil knew that.

He worked six days a week, five of them until 8 or 9 at night, during a time when his own company had begun talking about the four day week for everyone but the executives. He worked like the Important People who are listed in this week's *New York* magazine along with their obsessive hours quotas: Gerald Lefcort, lawyer, 90 hours; Milton Greene, photographer, 81 hours; Robert Abrams, Borough President, 102 hours, per week. He had no outside "extracurricular" interests, unless, of course, you think about a monthly golf game that way. To Phil, it was work. He always ate egg salad sandwiches at his desk. He was, of course, overweight by 20 or 25 pounds. He thought it was okay though because he didn't smoke.

On Saturdays Phil wore a sports jacket to the office instead of a suit, because it was the weekend.

He had a lot of people working for him, maybe 60, and most of them liked him most of the time. Three of them will be seriously considered for his job. The obituary didn't mention that.

But it did list his "survivors," quite accurately. He is survived by his wife, Helen, 48 years old, a good woman of no particular marketable skills who worked in an office before marrying and mothering.

She had, according to her daughter, given up trying to compete with his work years ago when the children were small. A company friend said, "I know how much you will miss him," and she answered to no one in particular, "I already have."

In "missing him" all these years she must have given up the part of herself which had cared too much for the man. She would be "well taken care of."

His "dearly beloved" eldest of the "dearly beloved" children was a hard-working young executive in a manufacturing firm down South. In the day and a half before the funeral he went around the neighborhood researching his father, asking the neighbors what he was like. They were embarrassed.

Phil's second child was a girl who is now 24 and newly married. She lives near her mother and they are close, but whenever she was alone with her father, in a car driving somewhere, they had nothing to say to each other.

The youngest is 20, a boy, a high school graduate who has spent the last couple of years, like a lot of his friends, doing enough odd jobs to stay in grass and food. He was the one who tried to grab at his father and tried to mean enough to him to keep the man at home. He was

140

his father's favorite and over the last two years Phil stayed up nights worrying about the boy.

The boy once said, "My father and I only board here."

At the funeral, the 60-year-old company president told the 48-year-old widow that the 51-year-old deceased meant much to the company and would be missed and would be hard to replace. The widow didn't look him in the eye. She was afraid he would read her bitterness and, after all, she would need him to help her straighten out the finances, the stock options and all that.

Phil was overweight and nervous and worked too hard. If he wasn't at the office, he was worrying about it. Phil was a Type A, a heart attack natural. You could have picked him out in a minute, out of a line-up.

So he finally worked himself to death at precisely 3 a.m. Sunday morning. No one was really surprised.

By 5 p.m. on the afternoon of the funeral, the company president had begun, discreetly, of course, with care and taste, to make inquiries about his replacement. One of three men. He asked around: Who's been working the hardest?[2]

As you move from adolescence to young adulthood, you find yourself concentrating on what Freud described as the two major goals of adult development: to love and to work. You face choices and commitments in both these facets of your life.

Photo courtesy of Kenneth M. Bernstein

CHOOSING YOUR CAREER

1. *What is the "image" which comes to mind when you first think of people in the following careers? Play a game of "word association" in class, calling out your reactions to each occupational identity. Then analyze the reasons for the stereotype.*

accountant	doctor
lawyer	writer
secretary	policeman
psychiatrist	rock singer
actor/actress	advertiser
dancer	artist/decorator
banker	truck driver
gambler	model
researcher	clergyman
farmer	teacher
carpenter	politician

Would the stereotyped image of any particular occupation discourage you from considering it? Why?

Rank the above occupations according to "status." Explain your reasoning. How important is status to you in choosing an occupation?

What kinds of personality types might best fit each of the above occupations? Why?

2. *List all the questions you would ask about an occupation to determine whether it suits you.*

3. *Trace your own developmental history in relation to career choice. What phases did you go through? What were the influences on you at the time? What do you currently think you would like to do? Is it important to you to know at this time exactly what career you want to pursue?*

4. *Ask five different people what occupation or career they could see you involved in ten years from now, based on what they know of your personality, ability, values, and interests. Is there any consistency in their responses? Does their analysis agree with your own?*

5. *How would you feel about changing occupations when you are thirty? Forty? Fifty?*

6. *Do you have a responsibility to live up to your full potential? Why or why not?*

7. *What kinds of issues might be more important to you than whether you enjoyed your job?*

8. *Interview your parents and three other adults. How did each choose an occupation? If they had it to do over again, what would their choice be? Why? What advice would they give you about choosing a career?*

9. *How much should work be considered a "creative act" (an end in itself), rather than just a way to earn money?*

10. *Pretend that one of you is the personnel manager of a large hospital. You must hire people for the following jobs:*

> *nurse*
> *receptionist*
> *orderly*
> *surgical aide*
> *recreation leader*
> *telephone operator*

Have other class members play each of the "applicants."

What questions would you ask the applicant?

After each interview, what observations could you make about the applicant which would influence your choice?

Applicants: Did the interviewer put you at ease so that you could represent yourself the way you wished to?

To Love

> Love is a feeling of tenderness and devotion towards someone, so profound that to share that individual's joys, anticipations, sorrows and pain is the very essence of living.[3]

ALEXANDER MAGOUN

When you were a child, you wanted the warmth and security of love. You received love much more than you gave it. As an adolescent, you have romance and infatuation: a physical and emotional attraction to others. Childhood affection and adolescent romance prepare you for the development of mature love.

What is mature love? It rests in the capacity to give as well as to receive. It is based on a mutual exchange not always found between parent and child. It has an enduring quality and a spiritual depth not common in adolescence. It is both the result of, and the beginning of, a growth process.

Erich Fromm writes, "Infantile love follows the

A major goal in early adulthood is to find that level of intimacy and understanding which is the basis of mature love. Childhood affection and adolescent romance prepare you for the development of mature love.

Photo courtesy of Beth Nicholson

principle: 'I love because I am loved.' Mature love follows the principle: 'I am loved because I love.' Immature love says, 'I love you because I need you.' Mature love says: 'I need you because I love you.'"[4]

A major goal in early adulthood is to find that level of intimacy and understanding which is the basis of mature love. To love requires confidence in your own worth and willingness to accept another person's individuality. It requires compromise and trust. As Fromm notes, "Happiness is an achievement brought about by man's inner productiveness and not a gift of the gods."[5]

Children grow up with romantic fantasies about love and marriage. Prince Charming is handsome and rich; the Fairy Princess is warm and beautiful. In adolescence, the search is for the perfect person. There are still dreams about love at first sight. When you outgrow such expectations you are more ready to experience mature love.

It is important for you to follow your own timetable in deciding if and when you are ready for the commitment and responsibility of marriage. Today, many people have decided to remain single in order to devote themselves exclusively to a career, or to preserve their freedom, privacy, and independence. Whether or not you marry and whom you marry are among the most important decisions of your life. "The choice," writes Theodore Lidz, "is basically not of one person from among the inhabitants of the world but from the relatively small number of persons met under favorable circumstances at a very specific time in life."[6]

People marry for a variety of reasons, not always the right ones. Some people are looking for the security they feel marriage will provide. Some seek status or wealth. Others wish to replace a mother or father figure. They may have grown from dependent children into dependent adults, longing for the same kind of attention their parents used to shower on them.

There are women and men who marry to have children. Their children become their lives, and the parents barely relate to each other. Some people marry simply for companionship, as an escape from loneliness. They may be tired of eating by themselves, spending evenings alone, and constantly looking for *someone* to do *something* with. As Theodore Lidz notes, there are also "hostile marriages" to spite a parent or former lover, and "rescue marriages" to help a person out of a difficult situation. None of these marriages is based on mature love. Therefore, it is crucial to understand your *motivation* if you plan to marry.

In a healthy marriage, there is mutual respect and *interdependence*. One partner does not dominate the other. The richness of the marriage is based on preserving each other's individuality. In such a marriage both people continue to grow and develop, satisfying their diverse interests. For example, a mother with young children may need to do community work or have a part-time job to get out of the house and see other adults during the week. A husband and wife may decide to share housework and child-rearing responsibilities. If one spouse leaves the other behind, either socially or intellectually, there may be tension and resentment. Many marriages break up because one person's needs and desires have changed while the other person wishes to "keep things the way they were."

There is a lot of give and take, compromise, and adjustment in a good marriage. One woman remarked that she learned what it meant to be flexible when she got married. Her husband wanted an older and darker apartment with charm and atmosphere; she wanted something light and bright, with all the modern conveniences. He wanted to live in the city and she preferred the suburbs. They compromised and now live in a modern apartment in the city. Generally, the more compatible two people are in values, interests, backgrounds, and temperament, the more likely it is that their marriage will be happy.

The number of divorces doubled in this country between 1962 and 1972. Nationally, two out of every five marriages now break up. The most common complaints are: lack of communication, constant arguments, unfulfilled emotional needs, financial problems, sexual problems and infidelity, drinking, gambling, lack of

B. Weber

"You'd overlook my selfishness, stubbornness, stupidity, and lack of ambition if you really loved me."

interest in home life, cruelty, and in-law trouble. It is important to consider the possibility of these problems *before* you decide to marry. Remember the case of Lisa and Jack Andrews: do you think they were prepared for the hard times in their marriage?

Children: A Larger Commitment

An important decision in marriage is whether to have children, and if so, how many. Some couples today have decided not to have children. Both husband and wife may want to pursue their careers full-time, or they may want freedom for social activities and travel. Often, they may just feel they are not temperamentally suited to raising young children.

Most couples do feel a special sense of fulfillment in the act of creating another human being. A woman may feel more feminine by becoming a mother; a man's masculinity is reaffirmed by becoming a father. Parents relive their own childhoods as they watch their children grow. They feel needed and important. Children also provide parents with a vital "link to the future." Raising children well gives a new meaning and purpose to one's life. Parents live on through the impact they make on their children.

Children can unify or divide a couple depending on the parents' needs and maturity. If one parent showers so much attention on the child that the other parent is neglected, resentment and jealousy may occur. If the child is difficult and constantly cries, the parents may begin to feel inadequate and blame themselves for a situation out of their control. They may become angry with the child, and then feel guilty for their anger. It may

149

also be difficult to adjust to a new life style, staying home more and waking up for three o'clock feedings! Learning to be a parent is a major challenge of adulthood.

Parents must be the *center* of the family to provide their children with a sense of security. A child looks to the parents as role models and to their style of living for his style. The warmth and respect they show for each other reassures the child. The parents' "happiness as individuals, and as a couple, is just as important as anything they may be able to do for a child or they can give him."[7] It would be a burden on the child to make him the focus of attention, setting up expectations he cannot fulfill. If parents live only for their child, without goals and satisfactions of their own, the child may feel guilty that he is letting them down and may resent the pressure to "succeed."

Parents may assume complementary roles in providing their children with the love and guidance which they need. For example, Erich Fromm believes that there is a natural difference between maternal and paternal love: "Motherly love by its very nature is unconditional. Mother loves the newborn infant because it is her child, not because the child has fulfilled any specific condition, or lived up to any specific expectation. . . . Fatherly love is conditional love. Its principle is 'I love you because you fulfill my expectations, because you do your duty, because you are like me.' . . . In conditional fatherly love we find, as with unconditional motherly love, a negative and a positive aspect. The negative aspect is the fact that fatherly love has to be deserved, that it can be lost if one does not do what is expected. . . . The positive side is equally important. Since his love is conditioned, I can do something to acquire it, I can work for it; his love is not

Photo courtesy of Kenneth M. Bernstein

Parents relive their own childhoods as they watch their children grow. Children also provide parents with a "link to the future." Raising children well gives a new meaning and purpose to one's life.

outside my control as motherly love is."[8] Fromm considers both kinds of love essential: one provides emotional security, the other helps the child to learn and to grow.

Love, in all its dimensions, becomes a major focus in early adulthood. In self-love, you preserve your identity and uniqueness. In mature love, you transcend your own concerns, sharing another person's joys and disappointments. As a parent, you bestow a gift of love, gaining a new purpose and meaning for your life.

To love and to work: the foundations of adulthood.

ON LOVE

1. *How do you know when you are in love? What expectations do you have of love?*

2. *What effect does self-love have on love for another? Can you love someone else if you do not love yourself?*

3. *What characteristics are most important to you in choosing a husband or wife? Least important?*

4. *Ask your parents:*

   What they expected of love and marriage when they were your age.

   How they knew they were in love.

   How their ideas on love and marriage have changed through the years.

5. *Does the age at which you marry matter? When do you think you will feel "stabilized" and ready to make a wise choice?*

   Should there be a minimum age for marriage?

   Should there be a legal waiting period between filing for marriage and getting married?

6. *Should people live together before they decide to get married? Why or why not?*

7. *Should marriage be "forever," or should the marriage license be in the form of a renewable contract? Why?*

8. *Are marriage "contracts" (written agreements between husband and wife concerning specific issues in the marriage) worthwhile? If you were to write a marriage contract with your spouse, what kinds of things would you put in it?*

9. *How do you view the place of children in marriage? How many children would you like to have? Why?*

10. *Do you agree with Erich Fromm that maternal love is unconditional and paternal love is conditional? Explain your view.*

11. *Parents sometimes live vicariously through their children. What goals and standards do parents have the right to expect from their children? What kinds of expectations are unreasonable?*

12. *Should there be "no-fault" (i.e., not assigning blame to either partner) divorce? What criteria should be used to decide which parent gains custody of the children?*

13. *Analyze some songs which are popular now. What do they tell you about love?*

The Dimension of Time

Daniel Levinson and his colleagues at Yale University have been doing a study of "The Psychosocial Development of Men in Early Adulthood and the Mid-Life Transition."[9] The concept of developmental periods which they describe provides a useful framework with which to view young adulthood.

They call the period between the ages of sixteen and twenty-four "Leaving the Family." It is a time for developing a new "home base," and for gaining financial, social, and emotional independence. There are many routes to independence: college, work, the military, travel, marriage.

The period of the twenties is labeled "Getting Into the Adult World." The authors characterize this period as "a time of exploration and provisional commitment to adult roles, memberships, responsibilities, relationships. The young man tries to establish an occupation or an occupational direction, consistent with his interests, values and sense of self. He begins to engage in more adult friendships and sexual relationships, and to work on what Erikson has termed the ego stage of Intimacy versus Aloneness."

The thirties are a time for "Settling Down," a time for deeper commitments to work and family. "The man establishes his niche in society, digs in, builds a nest, and pursues his interests. . . ." He is ambitious, "having an inner timetable that contains major goals and way stations and ages by which they must be reached." By his mid to late thirties, he is looking for "that crucial promotion or other recognition." It is a time for "Becoming One's Own Man," for new independence and authority. It is the time for realizing one's goals, and often for questioning the value and meaning of one's life.

Many women proceed through stages similar to those defined for men in the Yale study. Career women may also have "inner timetables" guiding their progress and defining their goals. They, too, look for that "crucial promotion."

Married women in their twenties who work may wish to start a family by the time they are thirty. Some women take only a brief period off when they have children, and rapidly pick up on their careers.

The woman who has devoted her twenties to raising children may view her thirties and forties as a time to return to work or to school. She may be eager to re-establish an identity outside of the home and to utilize other skills and talents.

Everyone's timetable for social and vocational development differs. Some people may feel "late" if they have not married by twenty-one. Others may want to be free from commitments for a few years before they settle down. Your upbringing, social class, goals, and obligations will help to define your pace. The major goal of early adulthood is to move from a period of exploration and decision-making to a period of stability and commitment. It is the time to chart the course of your life.

Middle Age

Making youth the pivot of existence devalues the rest of life and prevents a view of the whole. Older people have nothing to live for, younger people nothing to grow up for.[10]

ANNE SIMON

Adolescents ask, "Who am I? Where am I going?" The middle-aged tend to reverse that question and ask, "Who am I? What have I done?" So begins the "mid-life crisis," a transitional period of restlessness and self-examination.

Kenneth Rogers (Case #2) is typical.

First, he is anxious about his health, his vigor, and his youthful appeal. He daydreams about his secretary, envies the young business school graduate, and looks in

Photo courtesy of Kenneth M. Bernstein

In adolescence, you ask the questions, "Who am I? Where am I going?" In middle age, you ask, "Who am I? Where have I been?"

156

the mirror for signs of aging in himself. As the father of a teenage son, he can no longer delude himself about being young.

Second, he reviews what he has accomplished. It is hard to live up to the dreams of youth. At forty you may realize that you will never be the company president. Rogers expresses the frustration and disappointment of unfulfilled dreams. Work controls him: he feels powerless, insignificant, unproductive, and bored.

Third, Rogers is totally absorbed in his problems. He has lost the detachment and perspective which would help him to see what is positive in his life. He has set up a barrier against those who could help him: his wife, his son, and his friends. He has allowed his life to become mechanical and dull, rather than assuming the responsibility for making it meaningful and challenging.

Author Barbara Fried looks whimsically at the symptoms of "middlescent forty":

> *Forty is a noticeably restless, introspective, morose, moody, peevish, and melancholy person. Thirty is sunny, cheerful, hard-working, and obedient to the demands of daily routines. . . . When asked to describe his life, Forty will reply vaguely that it is "awful," "boring," "dull," or "depressing," without being able to say exactly why. Thirty is satisfied with familiar surroundings. . . . Not so Forty, who instead is continually on the lookout for greener pastures and who spends much time daydreaming about running away with someone who will really appreciate him. Forty tends to be morbidly convinced that he is actually very sick (brain cancer and heart trouble are two especially favored self-diagnoses), and to grieve*

over the degeneration, both real and imagined, of his physical and mental capacities. It is not too much to say that Forty manages to make life miserable for those who must live with him, possibly because he seems unable to live with himself.[11]

For most people, the mid-life crisis will probably not be as dramatic as Fried describes. Yet there will be certain consistent themes: (a) a longing for youth, a fear of death, and a feeling that time is running out; (b) an assessment of goals and accomplishments—the value of one's life; (c) feelings of restlessness and stagnation.

The transition from young adulthood to middle age is not always smooth and easy. It calls for re-adjustments in our thinking and behavior, perhaps a new self-image. More keenly aware of the passage of time, the middle-aged person may refocus his energies on those tasks and those people most important to him.

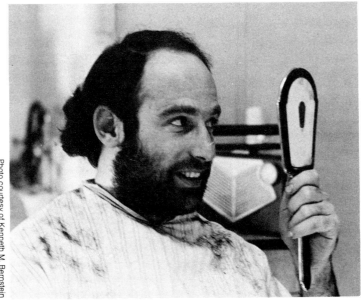

Photo courtesy of Kenneth M. Bernstein

For housewives in their late thirties and early forties, the problem may center on the "empty-nest syndrome." As their children grow up and leave home, middle-aged women may look to work, organizations, or school to fill the days they used to spend at home. They may feel a new sense of freedom and opportunity for self-fulfillment. However, they may also suffer from a lack of confidence in their unused abilities and skills, from anxiety about possible failure in the world of competitive work, and from a loss of feeling needed and essential.

The transition from young adulthood to middle age is not always smooth and easy. It requires readjustments in thinking and behavior. The mid-life crisis may lead to depression, withdrawal, or regressive behavior. Hopefully, and more likely, it gives a new sense of direction in life: the forty-year-old will decide to look forward to the satisfactions of the future rather than backward to the loss of his past. As Herbert Klemme of the Menninger Foundation explains, "The problem is not whether we will be engaged in the crisis, for we all are, were, or will be, but in how we will cope with it."[12]

Just as in adolescence, this middle age "identity crisis" may help a person to reassess his priorities in life. More aware of the passage of time, he may refocus his energies on those tasks and those people most important to him. The transition from one stage of life to another always involves the giving up of some pleasures and satisfactions. Ideally, a person can find *new* gratifications in the next phase of his life to replace those that have been lost.

From Forty to Sixty

There *are* new freedoms and satisfactions in middle age. Career pressures may start to decrease because there

159

is no longer a need to "prove yourself." You now become an advisor to those younger women and men who are still striving to establish themselves. You can rely more on your experience and reputation. Young adults have neither to fall back on. Financial rewards and security are greater in middle age. There is usually more recognition of your accomplishments, and you receive more challenging, "select" responsibilities.

As your children grow up, you have more time and more freedom to do what you want to do. You can return to old hobbies and talents, join organizations, and travel. You have the time to test your potential in many directions.

You also worry less about your children depending on you for guidance and support. When they leave home, you have to assume they can manage their own lives. As one mother explained, "I feel my job with them is done . . . I don't have to discipline them anymore. It's their problem . . . I hope I can always be a mother, but we'll treat each other as adults. I have a more relaxed feeling now."[13]

In middle age, you have more confidence in yourself than at any other time in life. It is a time when you feel secure about your abilities and skills and comfortable in relating to the people around you. Elizabeth Janeway writes:

> The likelihood of disastrous mistakes and horrible surprises diminishes. We know enough to tear up the letters that shouldn't be sent. Most of the time we bite back the unforgivable words. Shyness, strangeness, and self-consciousness fade. It's possible to see strangers simply as other people, and not as challenging competitors; to talk to them instead of

trying to top them. Oddly enough, this smaller world is also bigger because it is easier to move outside oneself, easier to enjoy new experiences.[14]

When sociologist Bernice Neugarten interviewed a group of middle-aged adults, she found that few of them wished to be young again!

There are physical and psychological adjustments necessary as you move from forty to sixty. As your physical stamina decreases, your body proportions change, your hormone balance shifts, and your skin begins to wrinkle and sag, you cannot help but acknowledge a new self-image. Aging may be a particularly sensitive issue for those who have depended largely on their physical appearance for self-esteem.

Women in their late forties and early fifties face *menopause*, the time when their reproductive potential ends. A decline in the estrogen hormone may make some women moody, depressed, and fatigued. With the loss of both their youth and their fertility, many women feel less feminine and less secure. In menopause, women psychologically begin a new stage in their lives. Although masculine hormones decrease more gradually, many men also report symptoms of depression and anxiety at this stage in life.

The concept of time is also different when you are in your forties and fifties. As Neugarten explains, "Life is restructured in terms of time-left-to-live rather than time-since-birth. Not only the reversal in directionality but the awareness that time is finite is a particularly conspicuous feature of middle age."[15] As an adolescent, you rarely read the obituary page. Your parents probably read this page regularly. As their friends and parents begin to die, they

HOW WILL YOU FEEL
AT FORTY-FIVE?

Roger Gould, a U.C.L.A. psychiatrist, has done a study of 524 women and men which suggests that adults pass through seven different developmental stages or "time-zones" as they mature.[16] There are special issues, concerns, and priorities at each stage. The adult personality evolves as one confronts and deals with the concerns at each stage.

Can you match the following age groups to the feelings typical at each stage?

AGE GROUPS

[1] 16-18

[2] 18-22

[3] 22-28

[4] 29-34

[5] 35-43

[6] 43-50

[7] 50+

(a) "What is done is done; the die is cast." "Too late to make any major change in my career." "Children previously cherished as extensions of oneself are now to be respected as individuals as they become young adults." "Life settles down."

(b) The "now" generation: "Now (is) the time to live, and now (is) the time to build for the future, both professionally and personally. These people concentrate their energies and will power on becoming competent in the real world, and as they develop self-reliance they make less use of their friends as a substitute for the family."

AGE GROUPS

[1] 16-18

[2] 18-22

[3] 22-28

[4] 29-34

[5] 35-43

[6] 43-50

[7] 50+

(c) The predominant theme: escape from parental dominance, despite underlying feelings of anxiety and dependence.

(d) A sense of "quiet urgency." Time is finite and pressing. One must hurry to make one's dreams come true. A time of tension with spouse, parents, and children.

(e) A "mellowing of feelings and relationships. Children are a satisfaction, and parents are no longer the cause of one's personality problems." People are "more eager to have 'human' experiences, such as sharing the joys, sorrows, confusions and triumphs of everyday life rather than searching for the glamor, the glitter, the power, or the abstract." The quality and meaning of life are important issues; one's health is a concern: "I can't do things as well as I used to. . . . "

(f) A time for "questioning what they (are) doing and why they (are) doing it." A time for self-reflection and recognition of

AGE GROUPS
[1] 16-18
[2] 18-22
[3] 22-28
[4] 29-34
[5] 35-43
[6] 43-50
[7] 50+

"deeper strivings that had been put aside. . . . "

(g) Substitution of friends for family; a growing independence—a time for leaving home for school, work, an apartment; a time to try making it on one's own.

Gould believes that most people progress through these seven stages, changing as they mature. "It's what you face, not how you face it, that is the common denominator." He also thinks that as people grow older, they become more accepting of themselves. They realize they cannot live up to the idealized image of adults which they once had as children; they cannot keep trying to "satisfy the magical expectations of a child's world." Too often people "hold themselves accountable for being perfect even when . . . conditions of a particular situation made the 'perfect' act inappropriate, unwise, unnecessary or impossible." While they may realize that they could not have done things differently, they nonetheless feel, "Somehow I should have been able to do it better." By dealing with the issues, attitudes, and feelings of each stage of adulthood, one gradually learns to update his childlike expectations of what he should be. He (or she) learns self-tolerance, the ability to live more comfortably with oneself.

KEY: *1-c; 2-g; 3-b; 4-f; 5-d; 6-a; 7-e*

are more conscious of their own mortality. Many women try to prepare themselves mentally for the possibility of widowhood. There were about 10 million widows in the United States in 1973; their average age was fifty-six.

In middle age, your sense of family responsibility also shifts. Your children have grown up, but your parents have grown old. It is your parents who now need your attention and care.

Most people tend to become more conservative as they grow older. They feel more comfortable doing things the way they always have, rather than trying new ideas and taking risks.

All of these changes are related to age and stage in life. Every period in life has its limitations, but every period also has its potential. In middle age, you are in the best position ever to be productive and creative. You have authority and security. With your children grown, you have freedom of time and freedom from responsibility. You can do many things you never had the chance to do before. Forty to sixty can be dynamic years of life.

Old Age

> *Every man desires to live long;*
> *but no man would be old.*
>
> JONATHAN SWIFT

It is not easy to grow old in the land of the young. In our society the accent is on good looks, vigor, and pleasure rather than wisdom, experience, and respect. Think about your own reaction to old age. What feelings and thoughts do you have when you see an elderly person on the street or in a market? Do you get impatient with his slowness?

CHANGING ATTITUDES:
CAN YOU EXPLAIN WHY?

Roger Gould has found the following patterns in people's attitudes and feelings.[17] Can you suggest some reasons for the patterns?

	AGE	20	30	40	50	60
I don't make enough money to do what I want.	RELATIVE RANKING OF QUESTION — LOW / HIGH					
It's too late to make any major changes in my career.						
There's still plenty of time to do most of the things I want to do.						
My personality is pretty well set.						
Life doesn't change much from year to year.						
My greatest concern is my health.						

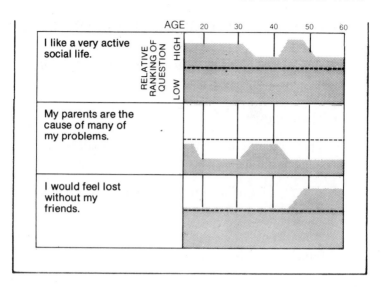

Do you feel sorry for him? Can you imagine *yourself* at seventy-five? How will *you* react to old age?

Most people have learned to fear old age as much as they fear death. This is a tragedy, not only for the old but for the young as well. Old age does not *have* to be sad. In treating the old as a burden, we are wasting them as a resource and we are trying to deny a major part of our lives. Simone de Beauvoir says, "the whole meaning of our life is in question in the future that is waiting for us. If we do not know what we are going to be, we cannot know what we are: let us recognize ourselves in this old man or in that old woman. It must be done if we are to take upon ourselves the entirety of our human state."[18]

What does growing old mean? It means, first of all, a decline in physical health. Four out of five people over sixty-five have at least one long-term illness. Symptoms of aging are obvious: failing eyesight, poor hearing, wrinkled skin, an arched spine, white hair, and slow

MIDDLE AGE: A PERSPECTIVE ON TIME

Interview several people between the ages of forty and sixty-five. Find out:

- Their ages.
- Their chief concerns and preoccupations at this stage in their lives.
- What goals and accomplishments they are working toward.
- How they view the future in relation to their families, work, retirement, hobbies, travel.

How does life change between forty and sixty-five? What consistent "themes" did you notice for people in their forties, their fifties, and their sixties?

methodical movement. Yet, when sociologist Bernice Neugarten studied over 2,000 people in their seventies, she found that the majority remained mentally healthy and able to function well. Many older people throughout history have continued to make important contributions despite their age: artist Pablo Picasso, Supreme Court Justice William Douglas, Israeli Prime Minister Golda Meir, cellist Pablo Casals, historian W. E. B. Dubois, Chinese leader Mao Tse-tung, to name a few.

Growing old means learning to live on a fixed income. Old people are among the first to suffer as prices rise. More than one fourth of the elderly presently live in sub-

168

standard housing with a limited budget for food and clothing. This directly affects their health and morale.

Growing old may also mean a return to financial, social, or emotional dependency. A widow may move in with her daughter's family to save money and escape loneliness. An older person may focus on his declining health as a way of saying, "Pay attention to me, care for me." Concentrating on illness may also be a way for the retired man to avoid facing what is really bothering him: his loss of identity and self-respect now that he feels unneeded and unproductive. As their circle of friends

It is not easy to grow old in the land of the young. In our society, the accent is on good looks, vigor, and pleasure rather than wisdom, experience, and respect. Most people have learned to fear old age as much as they fear death. This is a tragedy, not only for the old, but for the young as well.

grows smaller, the elderly depend on their children much more for their social contacts. Often the old feel guilty or embarrassed to lean on their children. Their children may resent having to assume responsibility for their parents. Nursing homes and retirement communities sometimes provide an alternative, now that the extended family, which includes three generations, is less common in the United States.

Older people fear loneliness and boredom more than anything else. Barbara Benson (Case #3) is typical. She allowed work to be her total preoccupation. Once she retired, she found herself without friends, hobbies, or interests with which to fill the vacuum. It is depressing to feel that you have nothing to wake up for and no one to live for. The best preparation for old age is living a rich, diversified life when you are younger, so that you have activities and interests to sustain you when you are older. Everyone needs to feel that there is a meaning to his life. Involvement with people and with projects not only keeps one busy but also makes one feel significant and useful.

There is nothing wrong with looking back when you are 75: an old person can be secure in the accomplishments and satisfactions of his life. No one can ever take them away. While a young person faces an uncertain future, the old person faces a certain past; and it brings inner peace and contentment to know he has lived well.

Photo courtesy of Kenneth M. Bernstein

Freud's "measure" of the normal, well-functioning person is again appropriate: a person who retains the capacity to love and to work can best cope with old age.

Habits tend to become more fixed as you grow older. Old people fear that they will not be able to adapt to change and therefore they cling to the routines they know well. Living by habit prevents anxiety. There are no surprises to face. If the old do not stay actively involved with life, the past represents their identity both to themselves and to others. That is one reason old people tend to reminisce a lot. Their past is rich in living; their future is limited. De Beauvoir notes, "The reason why the emotional memories that restore childhood are so treasured is that for a fleeting instant they give us back a boundless future."[19] Memories are, in a sense, dreams looking backwards.

There is nothing wrong with looking back when you are seventy-five. An old person can be secure in the accomplishments and satisfactions of his life. No one can ever take them away. While a young person faces an uncertain future, the old person faces a certain past. It brings inner peace and contentment to know he has lived well. Old age does not have to be sad.

Robert Peck has defined three developmental tasks for old age. First, one must maintain a "vital interest in living" through involvement in a variety of activities. One must learn to see oneself as a "worthwhile person" even though one may no longer have a work identity. The older person must have self-respect for the kind of person he is, and for the many roles he can still perform.

Second, an older person must learn to cope with physical decline, shifting the source of his happiness to "satisfying human relationships, or creative activities of a mental nature." While an older person may not move so fast, he retains his intellectual ability and the capacity for a rich emotional life.

Third, an older person must find the meaning of his life through "ego transcendence" rather than "ego preoccupation." Peck states:

> The constructive way of living the late years might be defined in this way: To live so generously and unselfishly that the prospect of personal death . . . looks and feels less important than the secure knowledge that one has built for a broader, longer future than any one ego ever could encompass. Through children, through contributions to the culture, through friendships—these are ways in which human beings can achieve enduring significance for their actions which goes beyond the limit of their own . . . lives. It may, indeed, be the only knowable kind of self-perpetuation after death . . . it requires deep, active effort to make life more secure, more meaningful, or happier for the people who will go on after one dies. . . . . Such a person would be experiencing a vital, gratifying absorption in the future.[20]

GRANDPARENTS: A PERSONAL VIEW

What can the old teach the young in an age when everything changes so quickly? Sharon Curtin, author of *Nobody Ever Died of Old Age*, wrote the following:

My grandparents were natural teachers. Most old people are. They had a tolerance based on experience that my parents, caught up in the day-to-day hassle of raising seven children, lacked. I remember one time my sister and I were about to receive "the worst beating ever" because we had stolen the last six-pack of beer. Worse, we had finished off every bottle. I was eight, my sister thirteen. We stood in the dust, bawling as loud as newly branded calves, as my father struggled to take off his belt. My head was spinning with fright and beer. My father seemed huge against the sky. I could smell his sweat and hear the wet leather being pulled through the loops of his Levis.

Then my grandfather began to laugh. He leaned against the fence, pointed a finger at my father, and said, "Hey, Pete, remember the time you and Tad and Tom raided that still belonging to old man Charles? You boys came home falling-down drunk. Your mother was crying and you all were sick in the privy. The old man came riding after you with a gun. It took a bottle of real liquor to calm the old fellow down. You boys took the pledge, promised your mother you'd never touch another drop. Seems like all the Curtins start early." And everyone laughed.

Laughed because for a minute we were all the same age. My father put his belt back on and I ran to my grandfather. It wasn't being saved from a beating that made me grateful. Sometimes I felt as if I were the worst person who ever lived. I think my grandfather understood this, and tried to make me see that I was human, my parents were human, we all made mistakes. It was a lesson in humility.

Because of my family, I have always been acutely aware of the importance of being related to other human beings, not only biologically, but in the way one life touches another through time. A walk or a smell or a particular color reminds me of someone, just as it did my grandparents in our long talks of "remember when." People were at the center of their teaching. People with peculiar ways, or special skills, or sad histories were used to teach all of us about life. It was being a grandchild that taught me about being an adult. I resented my parents because, somehow, being their child kept me childish. No matter how I loved and valued my parents, our relationship was stuck in the present. But my grandparents carried none of the guilt and anxiety and responsibility that weighed on my parents. They were able to transcend the years. It was almost as if my parents were the common enemy, and we—child and grandparents— formed an alliance for mutual protection.

It was an alliance filled with laughter and love. Filled with words most of all, with communication. My grandparents told me many stories, about war and politics, about my parents as children, about all the things they had seen and learned. I cannot imagine a life spent without old people around to give a perspective free from the pressures of the present.

✦✦✦✦✦

. . . . I suppose I simply feel you cannot have respect for and knowledge of all the stages of human life in the abstract; I believe contact with living representatives of the past and the future is necessary. Otherwise it is too easy to dismiss the past as meaningless and regard the future as something that never happens.[21]

"My grandparents told me many stories about war and politics, about my parents as children, about all the things they had seen and learned. I cannot imagine a life spent without old people around to give a perspective free from the pressures of the present."   SHARON CURTIN

Photo courtesy of Kenneth M. Bernstein

Conclusion

We grant goal and purpose to the ascent of life, why not to the descent?

CARL JUNG

The sun setting is no less beautiful than the sun rising.

PAUL GREEN

Too often, people dwell on opportunities missed in youth, rather than on the challenges of the present and the potential for the future. It is easier to assume that we are stuck with a script already written for our lives. We then do not have to feel so responsible to ourselves for continued change and growth and self-direction.

The second half of our lives rests on the foundation of our early years. Yet if we view our lives as static and dull after forty, we cut short the progress of our journey through life. We pass up the satisfactions of age, wisdom, understanding, and accomplishment. It is therefore important to accept life in all its fullness: every stage has its rewards as well as its frustrations and regrets. If each stage truly builds on the last, then as Archibald MacLeish notes, old age is "the farthest human journey, the journey toward the meaning of our lives."[22]

OLD AGE: LOOKING AHEAD

1. *Ask your grandparents to tell you what your parents were like as they grew up. What memorable incidents did they have in adolescence and young adulthood?*

2. *What are the problems old people face in your community? Visit a senior citizens' agency and find out what services are provided for the old.*

3. *How could older, retired people be used as resources in your community?*

4. *To what extent should children feel obliged to take care of their parents as they grow older? Why?*

   How do you feel about nursing homes? Retirement communities?

5. *Are old people better off living with their peers or within the extended family? Why?*

6. *Consider the case of Barbara Benson again. Do you have any new thoughts on how you would help her?*

Suggested Reading

Curtin, Sharon, *Nobody Ever Died of Old Age* (Boston: Little, Brown, 1972).

DeBeauvoir, Simone, *The Coming of Age* (New York: G.P. Putnam's Sons, 1972).

Epstein, Joseph, *Divorced in America: Marriage in an Age of Possibility* (New York: E. P. Dutton, 1974).

Fried, Barbara, *The Middle-Age Crisis* (New York: Harper and Row, 1967).

Gordon, Thomas, *Parent Effectiveness Training* (New York: Wyden, 1970).

Gould, Roger, "Adult Life Stages: Growth Toward Self-Tolerance," *Psychology Today,* Feb. 1975.

Kimmel, Douglas, *Adulthood and Aging* (New York: Wiley, 1974).

LeShan, Eda, *The Wonderful Crisis of Middle Age* (New York: D. McKay, 1973).

Lidz, Theodore, *The Person: His Development Throughout the Life Cycle* (New York: Basic Books, 1968).

Sheehy, Gail, "Catch-30 and Other Predictable Crises of Growing Up Adult," *New York,* February 18, 1974.

Young, Leontine, *The Fractured Family* (New York: McGraw-Hill, 1973).

FICTION, DRAMA

Bóntly, Thomas, *The Competitor* (New York: Charles Scribner's Sons, 1966).

Hemingway, Ernest, *The Old Man and the Sea* (New York: Charles Scribner's Sons, 1961).

Hesse, Hermann, *Rosshalde* (New York: Farrar, Straus and Giroux, 1970).

Hilton, James, *Lost Horizon* (New York: William Morrow, 1936).

Miller, Arthur, *A View from the Bridge,* in *Collected Plays* (New York: Vintage, 1957).

Miller, Arthur, *All My Sons,* in *Collected Plays* (New York: Viking Press, 1957).

Miller, Arthur, *Death of a Salesman* (New York: Viking Press, 1949).

O'Neill, Eugene, *Long Day's Journey into Night* (New Haven: Yale U. Press, 1956).

Spark, Muriel, *The Prime of Miss Jean Brodie* (Philadelphia: Lippincott, 1962).

Wharton, Edith, *Ethan Frome* (New York: Charles Scribner's Sons, 1911).

Williams, Tennessee, *The Glass Menagerie* (New York: New Directions, 1949).

Wright, Richard, *Native Son* (New York: Harper and Row, 1969).

FOOTNOTES

1. Erich Fromm, *The Revolution of Hope* (New York: Harper and Row, 1968), pp. 125-126.
2. Ellen Goodman, "The Classic Workaholic," *The Boston Globe,* November 22, 1974, p. 20. Courtesy of *The Boston Globe.*
3. Rabbi Roland Gittelsohn, *My Beloved is Mine, Judaism and Marriage* (New York: Union of American Hebrew Congregations, 1969), p. 8.
4. Erich Fromm, *The Art of Loving* (New York: Harper and Row, 1956), p. 40.
5. Erich Fromm, *Man For Himself* (New York: Holt, Rinehart and Winston, 1947), p. 189.
6. Theodore Lidz, *The Person* (New York: Basic Books, Inc., 1968), p. 397.
7. *Ibid.,* p. 454.
8. Erich Fromm, *The Art of Loving,* pp. 41, 43.

9. Daniel J. Levinson, et al., "The Psychosocial Development of Men in Early Adulthood and the Mid-Life Transition" (Unpublished).
10. Anne Simon, *The New Years—A New Middle Age* (New York: Alfred A. Knopf, 1968), pp. 33-34.
11. Barbara Fried, *The Middle-Age Crisis*, pp. 11-12. Reprinted by permission of the author and her agent, James Brown Associates, Inc. Copyright © 1967 by Barbara Fried.
12. Herbert Klemme, "Man: His Adulthood-Flame-Outs and Late Bloomers," 1969 (unpublished).
13. "Most Parents Feel Relief When Last Child Leaves Home," *The Boston Globe*, January 11, 1972.
14. Elizabeth Janeway, "In Praise of Middle Age," *McCall's*, October, 1971, p. 174.
15. Bernice Neugarten, *Middle Age and Aging* (Chicago: The University of Chicago Press, 1968), p. 97.
16. Adapted from: Roger Gould, "Adult Life Stages: Growth Toward Self-Tolerance." Reprinted from *Psychology Today*, February 1975. Copyright © 1975 Ziff-Davis Publishing Company. All rights reserved.
17. *Ibid.*, pp. 76-77.
18. Simone de Beauvoir, *The Coming of Age* (New York: G. P. Putnam's Sons, 1972), p. 5.
19. *Ibid.*, p. 376.
20. Neugarten, *op. cit.*, p. 91.
21. Sharon Curtin, "Grandparents," *The New York Times Magazine*, December 2, 1973 © 1973 by The New York Times Company. Reprinted by permission.
22. Archibald MacLeish, "The Age of Adolescence," *The Boston Globe*, December 19, 1973.
23. Robert Weber, *Parade Magazine*, October 20, 1974.

II.

The Complexities of Human Behavior

4.

Three Psychological Perspectives: An Introduction

Why do you behave as you do? How did you acquire the special style of thinking, feeling, and acting that you call your "personality"? Is it possible to change what you don't like about yourself? If so, how?

Psychologists respond to such questions with *theories* rather than firm answers. A theory is an attempt to tie many different observations together into an integrated group of general principles. Because human behavior is so complicated and psychology so young a science, there are many competing theories to explain why you behave as you do. Which theory you accept will sharply influence your ideas about how your personality evolved and how it can be changed.

Most psychologists approach the study of human behavior from within the framework of one of three separate perspectives. Some believe that one approach will eventually dominate the study of psychology, while others believe that the different perspectives will be gradually integrated to form a single, coherent theory of human behavior. In either case, it is important to realize that psychology is expanding rapidly and simultaneously along three separate paths. In this section, we will explore each path through the theories of influential psychologists who accept that point of view.

The Push and Pull of Inner Needs

First, we will discuss in more detail the ideas of Sigmund Freud, the pioneering explorer of the unconscious mind. By teaching himself to analyze dreams and other behavior, he developed a technique called *psychoanalysis* to help people with their problems. Freud also proposed a general theory of personality to explain our inner conflicts, feelings, and desires. We will then study Abraham Maslow's distinction between our "higher" and "lower" needs, together with Carl Rogers' method for encouraging personal growth. Finally, we will explore William Glasser's reality therapy and Viktor Frankl's theory that men and women need "meaning" in their lives.

Although these psychologists differ in many other ways, they all agree that your personality is best understood as the *outward* expression of *inner* needs, thoughts, and emotions.

B. F. Skinner and Behaviorism

Second, in Chapter 6, we will read about B. F. Skinner, a psychologist who believes that your personality is shaped by *rewards* from your environment rather than by inner thoughts and feelings. Skinner and his followers use terms which refer to *observable* behavior. They suggest that your behavior changes in highly predictable ways when the reward pattern in your environment changes. Animals and people both respond to behavioral *conditioning*. That is why Skinner says, "Pigeons aren't people, but it's only a matter of complexity."

Behaviorists are often accused unfairly of ignoring inner feelings. Actually, they are just as concerned with people's feelings as other investigators, but behaviorists believe that feelings are conditioned by the reward pattern of environment. Instead of seeking to understand feelings in order to understand behavior, they try to change behavior first, believing that this will influence inner feelings. The difference is a matter of emphasis.

The Electrical-Chemical You

Third, in Chapter 7, we will introduce a group of psychologists who explain behavior as the product of physical and chemical processes inside the body. José Delgado, William Dement, Barbara Brown, and Vernon Mark illustrate the *physiological* approach to psychology. They produce dramatic changes in behavior by electrical stimulation of the brain, chemical therapies, psychosurgery, and biofeedback, among other methods. Their aim is to understand the complex connections between our inner experience and specific combinations of electrical and chemical processes in our body.

Causes and Cures

Our primary purpose in this section is to explore how psychologists explain the *causes* of our behavior from three different theoretical perspectives. However, many ideas about the formation of personality are based on work with people who have mental or emotional problems. As a result, ideas about the *causes* of behavior are often connected with theories about *changing* or *"curing"* that behavior. We will therefore review different methods of changing behavior, called *therapies*, as we explore theories about causation.

Each of the next three chapters is designed to convince you that its approach is indeed the best way to analyze human behavior. If, after reading all three chapters, you feel that your own views of personality and behavior are pulled simultaneously in three different directions, you will have experienced some of the excitement that psychologists feel as they pursue their challenging profession.

5.

The Push and Pull of Inner Needs: Freud and Psychoanalysis

A month has passed since your accident on the stairs. Your superficial cuts have healed but your arm and hand remain paralyzed. A thorough medical examination establishes that there is no physical reason why you have no sensation or movement in the arm. You become upset when you learn that some people have suggested that you are merely pretending injury in order to avoid work. Your doctor advises rest, massage, and mineral baths. He suggests that you also contact another physician named Dr. Freud.

You are a young mother unable to breast-feed your firstborn child. You are extremely nervous, racked with nausea, and unable to sleep at night; you are a physical and emotional wreck. The baby must be breast-fed because no other source of purified milk is available. A friend refers you to Dr. Freud.

Discovery of the Unconscious

When Sigmund Freud began practicing medicine in Vienna, Austria, in the early 1890s, patients with symptoms like these often came to his office. At that time, there was no effective treatment for such "nervous disorders" which lacked apparent physical cause.

Hypnosis—The First Clue

Freud, however, had a strategy that he hoped would work. During his medical training in France, he learned a new technique called hypnosis. By this technique, some people could be placed in a trance-like state markedly different from their normal "level" of consciousness. The hypnotist could implant instructions in this strange new level of the patient's mind which continued to affect the person's behavior after the trance was removed—even though the person was unaware that his or her behavior was motivated by these instructions. Freud's teacher once demonstrated that even such symptoms as unexplained paralysis could be temporarily relieved through hypnotic suggestion. The reverse was also possible: hypnotic suggestion could *produce* symptoms resembling paralysis even in otherwise healthy persons!

Freud met patients at regular intervals, hypnotized them, and gave them instructions designed to remove whatever behavior bothered them. In 1892, he reported in a medical journal that the woman who previously could not breastfeed had been cured of her symptoms through two sessions of hypnosis.[1]

Unfortunately, the technique did not prove as effective as Freud had hoped. Some persons could not be easily hypnotized. Furthermore, the hypnotic suggestion seemed to work only as long as the patient continued in treatment with him. For example, the same young mother mentioned above returned to Freud after her second baby was born: the woman experienced the same inability to breastfeed that brought her to Freud in the first place. Another two sessions of hypnosis removed the problem, but the frequency of incidents like this led Freud to

Freud was a pioneer in explaining how "the push and pull of inner needs" controls our behavior. Sometimes our biological needs and drives (the id) are in conflict with what we know is possible and reasonable (the ego), or "right" (the superego). At other times, our conscience may bear down too hard on us, causing us guilt and anxiety. We are constantly trying to harmonize all our needs and desires.

suspect that patients obeyed the hypnotic instructions because they wanted to please him and not because of the power of such instructions. Freud decided to experiment with another method.

Free Association—A New Route to the Unconscious

From a medical colleague, Freud learned about a treatment called the "talking cure" or "chimney-sweeping." Actually, this method was invented by a patient named Anna O., who began telling her doctor about all the unpleasant and frightening events that happened to her each day when the symptoms of severe mental problems seized control of her. Talking brought her some relief. One of her symptoms actually disappeared after she told her doctor what was happening when it had *first* appeared. Perhaps, the doctor suggested to Freud, all patients would experience an *emotional release* or *catharsis* if they discussed the earliest onset of their illness. Freud took this hint, modified it, and applied it to treat a new patient named Fraulein Elisabeth who could not be hypnotized. Here is an account of Freud's earliest use of "free association," the key that enabled him to unlock the world of unconscious thoughts.

> *This was the method. The patient, lying down with closed eyes, was asked to concentrate her attention on a particular symptom and try to recall any memories that might throw light on its origin. When no progress was being made Freud would press her forehead with his hand and assure her that then some thoughts or memories would indubitably come to her. Sometimes in spite of that, nothing would seem to happen even when the pressure of the hand was*

repeated. Then, perhaps on the fourth attempt, the patient would bring out what had occurred to her mind, but with the comment: "I could have told you that the first time, but I didn't think it was what you wanted." Such experiences confirmed his confidence in the device, which indeed seemed to him to be infallible. They also made him give the strict injunction to ignore all censorship and to express every thought even if they considered it to be irrelevant, unimportant, or too unpleasant. This was the first step toward the later free association method.

Freud was still given to urging, pressing, and questioning, which he felt to be hard but necessary work. On one historic occasion, however, the patient, Fraulein Elisabeth, reproved him for interrupting her flow of thought by his questions. He took the hint, and thus made another step toward free association.[2]

By trial and error, Freud learned that he gathered more evidence, and obtained a clearer picture of his patient's inner thoughts and feelings, if he interfered as little as possible in the natural chain of events. Therefore, he stopped interrupting with questions or pressing his hand on the forehead of the patient.

As his patients allowed their thoughts to flow more and more freely, they often brought up the subject of dreams along with the chain of associations stimulated by a particular dream. Freud was himself a frequent dreamer, so he decided to make a systematic study by carefully recording his own dreams and his associations to them. This was the first step of his long and difficult self-analysis. Freud was a pioneer, with few friends to help

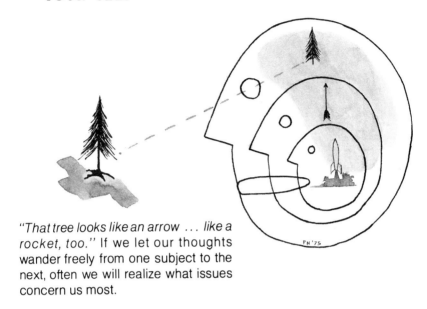

"That tree looks like an arrow ... like a rocket, too." If we let our thoughts wander freely from one subject to the next, often we will realize what issues concern us most.

him cope with the disturbing ideas and emotions he often uncovered in himself. Most of his medical colleagues were shocked by his work.

The Interpretation of Dreams

If you were to tell your dream or daydream to someone without giving him any background information, could he understand what happened in the dream? It might be difficult, since the people, places, and things in a dream often appear and disappear as if in a magical world or an animated film. Time, distance, and social customs do not limit the events taking place in the dream as they do in the waking world. Familiar items may appear in strange combinations. With all this confusion in the content of a typical dream, how can anyone discover the meaning or purpose of the dream?

192

WHAT DO YOU DREAM ABOUT?
A SHORT RESEARCH PROJECT

Freud and more recent sleep researchers tell us that we dream frequently during a typical night, even if we do not remember the dreams upon waking. Prepare yourself for capturing a dream by the following steps. First, place paper, pencil, and flashlight next to your bed. Second, set your alarm slightly earlier than you usually wake, or, if your parents wake you, resolve that you will force yourself to get out of bed the moment they arrive in the morning. Third, before you go to sleep the night before, tell yourself very firmly that you *will* remember whatever dream you are having when you wake. Needless to say, when morning arrives, be quick about getting up and writing down everything you remember, no matter how confusing it appears.

If you are less ambitious, there are two alternatives to capturing a fresh dream. You may already recall a particularly vivid past dream, in which case you should describe it. If this won't work, find a comfortable place where you won't be disturbed and let your mind drift wherever it will. In other words, "daydream." This type of fantasy often has a structure similar to night dreams. Write down everything that happens in your daydream.

Now think about the events that happened in the dream, and on a separate piece of paper record your "free associations" to the dream content.

Do you think that your dream has a *meaning* or *purpose*? If so, what is it?

Freud believed that the dreamers could interpret the meaning of their own dreams if they knew how to use his free association method. However confusing his patient's dreams appeared at first, he found that it was possible to trace a continuous linkage of ideas until the dream finally yielded an understandable pattern of thoughts. Freud wrote:

> We should divide the dream into its elements and start a separate inquiry into each element. . . . When the dreamer is questioned about the separate elements of the dream he may reply that nothing occurs to him. . . . We contradict him; we bring urgent pressure to bear on him, we insist that something must occur to him—and we turn out to be right.
>
> He will produce an idea—some idea, it is a matter of indifference to us which. He will give us certain pieces of information, which may be described as "historical" with particular ease. He may say: "That's something that happened yesterday," . . . or: "That reminds me of something that happened a short time ago."—and we shall discover in this way that dreams are connected with impressions of the last day or two much more often than we thought to begin with.
>
> And finally he will also recall, starting from the dream, events from further back and even perhaps from the far distant past.[3]

Freud found that the original thought underlying almost all dreams was a wish that the dreamer was unable to satisfy in his or her waking life. This basic wish might involve unacceptable sexual or aggressive behavior or some other strong but disturbing purpose. The dream is a

The dream is a magical fantasy in which our wishes are fulfilled. Even if we use symbols in our dreams, they can be interpreted. Freud was a pioneer in relating the world of dreams to our everyday desires and behavior.

magical fantasy in which the wish is fulfilled. Thus, the purpose of the dream, Freud reasoned, must be to release some of the frustration that accumulates when a wish is unfulfilled in our normal waking life. Here is a short dream quoted by Freud from a medical student's letter to him that illustrates this:

> *"July 13, 1910. Towards morning I had this dream: I was bicycling down the street in Tubingen when a brown dachshund rushed up behind me and seized me by the heel. After a little while I got off, sat down*

195

on a step, and began to hit at the beast, which had bitten firm hold of me. (I had no disagreeable feelings either from the bite or from the scene as a whole.) Some elderly ladies were sitting opposite me and grinning at me. Then I woke up and, as has often happened before, at the moment of transition to waking, the whole dream was clear to me."

... The dreamer reported: "I have recently fallen in love with a girl, but only from seeing her in the street, and I have had no means of getting in contact with her. The dachshund might have been the pleasantest way of doing so, especially as I am a great animal-lover and I liked this same characteristic in the girl." He added that he had repeatedly intervened in furious dog-fights with great skill and often to the astonishment of on-lookers.

We learn then that the girl he was attracted by was always to be seen in the company of this particular dog. As far as the manifest dream was concerned, however, the girl was omitted and only the dog associated with her was left. The elderly ladies who grinned at him may perhaps have taken the girl's place. His further remarks threw no adequate light on this point. The fact that he was bicycling in the dream is a direct repetition of the remembered situation. He never met the girl with the dog except when he was on his bicycle.[4]

This student's wish, to win the affections of a girl, was frustrated by his shyness and the social customs of that time. The unfulfilled wish provoked this dream. Why, then, was the most important person, the girl, omitted from the dream? Although only the dreamer can provide the detailed associations to give a complete answer, we can trace a likely chain of ideas that might lead to such a result.

Perhaps the student's wish involved sexual feelings that he would have found embarrassing if he were awake and in full control of his thoughts. How could the student's conscience be protected and, at the same time, the wish be expressed? In the dream, this problem is solved by distorting some of the original material. Although the observer in the dream was still female, the number of women present was increased and their age was raised so that sexual attraction was not appropriate. By this substitution, the unacceptable feelings were expressed through a special code.

This analysis of distortion in dream content implies that there are at least two types of mental forces, both of which operate unconsciously. The unsatisfied wish provides one force, but there is also another force that "censors" the wish. The censor judges the original wish to be too threatening to the person's self-image and prevents its expression until the unacceptable content is removed.

In proposing this idea of opposing forces in the mind, Freud was probably strongly influenced by his earlier experience with hypnosis. Unfulfilled wishes, like the hypnotist's instructions, are powerful sources of motivation, even though they operate outside our normal range of consciousness. Might a similar process be the underlying cause of our waking behavior as well as of our dreaming? How much of what we think and do during the day is *not* the result of deliberate choice, as we commonly believe, but is forced from within us by unconscious processes that operate like a hypnotist's instructions?

The Meaning of Everyday Mistakes

As Freud searched for more evidence to support his theory of unconscious conflicts, he decided to study those little mistakes that everyone makes but considers merely coincidental. Have you ever started to say one thing but let some embarrassing thought slip out? Have you ever forgotten the name of a person or place that you know well? Have you ever tried to submerge your anger at someone during a group discussion only to find yourself constantly making "objective" criticisms of that person's actions in the group? Have you ever forgotten an errand for your parents that you didn't want to do? Freud applied his free association technique to these everyday mistakes because he believed that every human action, no matter how seemingly insignificant, has a specific—even if hidden—cause.

He concluded that persons who make slips of the tongue or misplace items or forget things do so because they have at least two conflicting purposes that they are attempting to carry out at the same time. When the person chooses to express one of the competing purposes, he tries to "push" the other one "out of his mind." However, the submerged purpose fights back, either by interfering with its rival or by forcing a compromise in which both purposes are expressed together. This conflict may be wholly unconscious, so that the person himself may not be aware that one purpose has been hidden.

For example, when Freud asked someone why she persisted in using the maiden name of a friend who was married, the woman admitted that she disliked the friend's husband and disapproved of the marriage. Her unconscious hostility was interfering with the woman's conscious attempt to remember her friend's proper name.

In this simple example, the woman easily recognized the presence of an inner conflict after the mistake was brought to her attention. In more complex cases, one purpose may be "pushed out of mind" so thoroughly that it can be retrieved only by extended free association. For example, few people who hurt themselves in accidents will admit that their injury may have been partially motivated by an unconscious desire to punish themselves.

The process of "pushing" some idea or desire out of awareness and "holding" it in this unconscious limbo was called *repression* by Freud. As long as a repressed wish remains unsatisfied, it is a continuing source of mental tension. This frustrated energy reacts to repression by seeking *substitute* ways to express itself in behavior, by diverting itself into new channels. Freud believed that repression and rechanneling are basic psychological processes that occur in everyone, and provide the building blocks of personality structure.

While one set of mental forces—the basic drives and wishes of the person—push for expression in behavior, an opposing set of mental forces pushes back to repress those urges. The battle is on. When a repression successfully blocks a wish from achieving its goal, the energy of the frustrated wish is redirected toward fulfilling a substitute goal. If the repressing forces censor this second choice, then another rechanneling occurs, and perhaps others, until the original wish has assumed a form that no longer threatens the repressing forces.

In other words, the idea or desire that eventually reaches our consciousness is the last of an undetermined number of substitutions. Yet even though the original object desired has undergone many substitutions during the process of rechanneling, *the original wish has retained the same goal,* namely, to be expressed in conscious behavior. The wish still gets its power from the same source in the unconscious mind.

Many of your present preferences and habits may be the result of the repression and rechanneling of basic desires. When you were a baby you learned how pleasurable it could be to lie in your mother's arms, basking in her affection, and having all your needs met. The sense of contentment and well-being became associated in your mind with the taking-in of food. As a young child, you probably tried to preserve these feelings by sucking your thumb, by rubbing a soft blanket on your lips, or by sucking on a lollipop. Even in adult life, the desire to give up your independence and return to an earlier stage where your mother met your needs continues as a repressed wish. Repression of this infantile desire is necessary if you are to meet the demands that our society imposes on adults.

Nonetheless, you can still get at least a substitute satisfaction of this infantile desire if you put *something* into your mouth. In the past, eating was associated with love, warmth, and security. Your present substitute of gum, cigarettes, or overeating at lunch helps to bring back those same warm feelings to combat your disappointment.

If the *personal* wish of an individual is rechanneled into *other* fields—intellectual, humanitarian, artistic, etc.—the redirection of the original desire is called *sublimation*. Leonardo da Vinci's preference for painting warm and beautiful female figures, for example, could be explained as a sublimation of his desire to recapture and memorialize his feelings for his mother, from whom he was separated at an early age.

FREUDIAN CONFLICTS IN YOUR EVERYDAY LIFE

1. *Freud believed that we fulfill our wishes in our dreams. Can you remember specific dreams you have had after which you have felt pleased or happy? Describe such a dream and explain the wish you believe motivated it.*

2. *What is the meaning of the term "Freudian slip?" Can you describe any such slips or other "everyday mistakes" that have happened to you?*

   What kind of inner conflict might have motivated the mistake?

   How would you go about investigating whether or not an unconscious conflict underlay the apparent mistake?

3. *Freud thought that accidents were often the sign of a person's inner conflict. Can you recall any accidents you have had (such as dropping a dish or bumping into something) when you were angry with someone? Can you see how this accident supports Freud's point?*

4. *Might competitive sports events be considered examples of sublimation?*

   What basic drives are involved?

> How are these drives modified by the process of repression?
>
> Does this particular form of sublimation serve any important function?

The Forces of Personality

Thus far, we have mentioned repressing forces, censors, wishes, and drives without explaining (a) how they originate and (b) what purposes these forces seek to carry out. As Freud learned more about how the opposing mental forces battled among themselves, he distinguished three different types of forces. This distinction helped him to explain the origins and aims of mental functions.

Id—Reservoir of the Basic Drives

The id comprises all the basic drives of the human animal, such as sex, hunger, aggression, elimination of body wastes, and other powerful urges. In Latin, id means "it," which seems an appropriate name given the impersonal nature of biological urges. The id has only one goal: discharge of these basic drives. The individual experiences this discharge as pleasure. Mental processes in the id resemble those of a dream: disorganized, nonlogical, distorted, or disguised, and always pressing for immediate wish-fulfillment in fantasy if not in reality.

A closer examination of one basic drive will illustrate how the id works. The hunger drive is both physiological and mental. When the physiological need for food reaches a certain level, you become aware of the sensation of hunger, the mental "tension" that motivates your search for food. The aim of the hunger drive (as with id impulses in general) is *to discharge itself* by securing food; this results in a comfortable and "tension-free" state of mind and body, at least temporarily. Because the basic drives like hunger recur periodically, they provide a source of motivation that continues throughout a person's life.

However, the id is not well designed for finding food (or objects to satisfy its other urges). It can generate the desire for a certain object, but cannot obtain it without help. The behavior of infants is the clearest illustration of id impulses: when they feel a pressing need, they can only cry to let the world know how terrible they feel. Other people must come to their rescue and satisfy their needs. As the child grows older, his knowledge about how to manage reality for himself increases. By imitating his parents and by experimenting, he builds a new mental capacity, the *ego*.

Ego—The Force of Reality

To direct and discipline the search for gratification, the id must rely on a reality-oriented mental process called the *ego*, which in Latin means "I" or "self." From the hundreds of events occurring each day, ego processes select those which are important for you to see, hear, touch, taste, or think about. They calculate how to get you from one location to another, how much food you can buy with the money you have, how loudly you must speak to be heard. Ego processes warn of impending danger by making you anxious or fearful, thereby helping you to avoid a serious or harmful predicament.

When ego processes are permitted to work unimpeded, they accurately identify what is happening in your world and devise realistic and appropriate methods to satisfy the urges of your id. However, pressure on the ego from other parts of the personality may distort your perceptions and lead to mistaken interpretations of reality. This occurs because, in addition to its role as the reality-oriented part of the personality, the ego acts as a "moderator" between the insistent id impulses and other forces working against these wishes and drives. These restricting forces are directed by the third part of the personality, the *superego*.

Superego—The Force of Morality and Personal Ideals

As a child grows, he is forced to adapt his behavior to standards set by his parents (or parental substitutes). There is a "right" way to behave, which the parents reward, and a "wrong" way, which they punish. Gradually, the child adopts the parent's moral code as his own in the form of a "conscience." Once this happens, a person can judge his or her own behavior against certain internalized standards. If he violates these standards, he may feel guilty. Also, the child stores away an image of the kind of person he or she would like to become. This personal ideal provides another standard against which a person's behavior can be judged. In effect, the superego makes us feel good about what we do "right" and makes us feel guilty about what we do "wrong."

These superego processes are not concerned with manipulating reality, as the ego processes are. Instead, they apply moral standards learned in the past to judge present behavior. The superego imposes restrictions on the expression of id impulses, and it puts pressure on the ego to find ways to gratify the id that do not violate these

204

"Superego? Id? I don't believe in anything that can't be seen." Sometimes we do not realize that we have conflicting needs and drives, all pushing for expression and satisfaction. This conflict may make us feel anxious and tense.

restrictions. Because these mental forces *supervise* the ego's activity, Freud called them, collectively, the superego.

To sum up: Freud, using a method of "free association," learned that our *conscious* thoughts and emotions are *linked* by a continuous chain of ideas with other mental processes that are unconscious. A new link is added to the chain each time that repressing forces rechannel the original wish.

205

BOB'S CASE—THE ID, EGO, AND SUPEREGO IN ACTION

This story illustrates how all three types of mental processes contribute to a simple behavioral sequence. These processes usually operate unconsciously, so that we are aware only of the results of their functioning.

A curse bubbled up in Bob's throat and vented itself in a disgusted snort. *'I can't stand a minute longer in this stuffy classroom. Mr. Frimpton is the world's worst bore. Why,* he wondered, *do all these show-offs play along with him?'* Outside, the sun was headed west, the long shadows revealing that the best part of the afternoon was already over.

Crazy thoughts tugged at Bob. *'I could jump up right now, slam my books on the floor, dump over this worthless desk, tell all these idiots exactly what I think of them and of the school in general, and then stamp out of class!'* Bob's muscles tensed in anticipation, and he could barely contain his urge to walk out. He rocked back and forth nervously in his hard seat.

'But,' he reminded himself— there always seemed to be something wrong with his best ideas—*'I've got myself to protect.'* There would be a big hassle, like last time, and the

ID: impulse to seek immediate gratification, to reject the restrictions of an authority figure, and to express hostility toward him.

EGO: in its role as moderator between id and superego, the ego, by producing anxiety, warns Bob of the danger of his actions.

EGO: Bob sees that realistically it will not be to his advantage to give in to the id impulses. An alternative interpretation is that Bob's

206

principal wouldn't hesitate to kick him out of school since he'd been warned. *'I'm not afraid of the principal, or Mr. Frimpton, or anyone else; it's just that it's my last semester. If I make it through this one I'm free forever. Otherwise, it's a summer course for sure!'* Bob stopped rocking in his chair and slumped down with his legs pushed out in front of him.

'Then there's also Mom to consider. She's got enough trouble now dealing with her new job and with Janie's problems. It's not right for me to add more.' It made Bob sad to think of the troubles at home.

He was distracted by a bird that flew by the class window. He pulled himself out of his slump in a long, slow stretch that ended in a half-growl, half-yawn. Mr. Frimpton stopped in mid-sentence to stare at him, and smiles tugged at the corners of everyone's mouths. "Gee, am I sorry, Sir!" Bob said with a hint of mockery in his voice. "It just slipped out before I could catch it."

Bob was pleased to see that Mr. Frimpton could not recover his momentum in the last few minutes of class. He leapt to his feet at the first sound of the bell, feeling satisfied at having revenged a small part of the wrongs done him.

thoughts are merely a rationalization he uses to explain his actions to himself; the real force preventing his leaving is his superego. Under either interpretation, the outcome is that the impulses are repressed.

SUPEREGO: He will feel guilty if he adds to his mother's problems. This strengthens the repressing forces.

BEHAVIORIAL OUT-COME: The original urge is blocked by the repressing forces of the ego and the superego. The bottled-up anger and frustration is rechanneled from its direct expression to a less risky substitute, namely, a bit of disrespectful clowning. Bob derives some release of tension from this indirect expression, but some of the anger remains.

The value of separating mental processes into Freud's three categories is that it enables you to explain *why* Bob felt and acted as he did. Usually, we are not aware of these different processes at work. We are simply aware that we feel a certain emotion or that we reached a certain decision. However, if your emotions or your decisions often make you unhappy or get you into trouble with other people, then it becomes important to find out how your own mental processes contribute to your problems. In this search, Freud's three categories of id, ego, and superego can help you to separate a tangled mass of ideas, attitudes, and feelings and to analyze how they interact to produce your behavior.

Freud found it helpful to think of these forces in three categories: basic drives (id), forces that make realistic calculations (ego), and forces that reward "good" behavior and punish "bad" behavior (superego). These forces conflict with each other because considerations of reality or morality often require that the id impulses be repressed. However, when the id processes are denied direct gratification, they adapt by shifting to substitute objects to relieve their frustrated energy. The resulting series of repressions and redirections builds up a longer and longer chain of ideas until the last link of the chain escapes repression and *reaches our consciousness*. The free association technique retraces the chain, link by link, from the conscious thoughts or symptoms back to the basic wishes and drives that motivate behavior.

Hidden Problems

Have you ever had an unpleasant, tense feeling, perhaps accompanied by a dry mouth, rapid pulse, sweaty palms, or a tightness in your stomach or muscles? Of course you have; you probably recognize these symptoms as reactions to fear.

Free Floating Anxiety—A Special Kind of Fear

Have you ever felt a similar unpleasant tension when there seemed to be nothing in your environment to fear? Freud called this kind of diffuse, undirected, apparently causeless fear *free-floating anxiety*. He reasoned that it must be a reaction to some threat that comes from *inside* yourself. This does not mean that free-floating anxiety is not "real." You can be "paralyzed with anxiety" just as you can be "paralyzed with fear"; one fairly common type of emotional disturbance is termed an "anxiety attack" or a "panic."

Anxiety is a by-product of conflict among the three different mental processes. Our attempt to be "adult" and to deal realistically with the world—that is, to keep ego processes in control of our personality—is constantly threatened by the two other mental forces. When the id impulses get very strong, they threaten to overwhelm our better judgment. When the superego processes become

ID, EGO, SUPEREGO:
SEEING THEM IN YOURSELF

1. *Imagine that you are just waking up on the day of final exams. The weather is terrible. You're not prepared, and you're feeling very depressed. Write a short story of several paragraphs which describes what you would do, think, and feel that morning. If you wish, substitute a similar situation that you have in mind. Write only on the left half of the page, so that you leave enough space to return, after you finish the story, to note where id, ego, and superego processes are at work. Be prepared to read your story in class and to compare the different ways your classmates handle a similar problem.*

2. *Freud believed that id, ego, and superego processes worked in harmonious balance in the healthy person. Describe what might result if one aspect of the personality dominated the others. If you wish, refer to the short story you have just written.*

unreasonable in their moralistic demands, they threaten to punish us with heavy loads of guilt. When either happens, the three parts of the personality are not working harmoniously. Anxieties are the "sparks" thrown off as the parts clash with one another.

When anxiety builds up inside you, it can interfere with your ability to function effectively in daily life. Your ego—that is, your realistic self—works in self-defense to reduce the level of anxiety. The unconscious mental tricks that the ego uses are called *defense mechanisms*. The stories that follow illustrate some of the methods—usually unconscious—we all use to defend ourselves against anxiety.

Displacing an Emotion From One Object to Another

STU EVANS felt the disappointment stinging in his eyes, but by the time he and Andrew reached their street, self-pity had turned to anger.

"Don't take it too hard," Andrew said as he started up the steps to his house, "What can you do? It'll all be forgotten by tomorrow."

Stu nodded and continued down the sidewalk. A big plastic trash container loomed ahead. Any passerby would be forced to detour. It was still full. Somebody obviously hadn't gotten his garbage out in time to be picked up. Stu wasn't going to move out of the way for a lousy trash barrel! He felt the anger grab hold of him, and he placed a forceful kick at exactly the right spot. Papers and fruit peelings sprayed across the street and sidewalk. Coffee grounds stained the snow under the overturned barrel.

Defeating the trash container made Stu feel even angrier. He remembered how the gym teacher had humiliated him. "Evans," he had said, "if you can't play ball, at least keep your mouth shut so the real players can hear what I'm saying." In front of the whole class he said that!

As Stu opened the door to his house, he heard a friendly bark and saw the dog bounding across the room. "Get away," he screamed, "Leave me alone, Woofer!" He

Often we *displace* or redirect the expression of our emotions onto "safe" targets. When we are angry with a teacher or coach, we may hold that anger until we get home, and then vent it on our parents, siblings, or the family dog.

took another swipe with his foot, but this time he didn't connect. Woofer was a more elusive target than the trash can.

"Stu, you ought to be ashamed of yourself! Kicking a poor, friendly dog who is happy you're home!" Virginia, his younger sister, had seen everything. He blushed.

"Yeah. You're right, Virginia," he said sheepishly. "I don't know what got a hold of me." He bent over to give Woofer an apologetic pat.

We have already discussed how wishes and drives can become rechanneled if repression prevents them from obtaining their original object. A similar process of redirection takes place in the defense mechanism called *displacement.* Stu's anger at the coach would have gotten him into even more trouble if he had expressed it directly, so he turned it inward during the gym class. As he walked home, the repressed anger grew harder and harder to contain. It finally broke out, not against the coach who first caused it, but against such substitute objects as the trash barrel and the family dog. It is this process we describe when we say that the anger is *displaced* from the coach to the trash barrel and the family dog.

Displacement is a common defense mechanism which allows people to "let off steam." Positive emotions can also be displaced. For example, a person who receives a promotion and lavish praise from his or her boss may feel friendly and generous toward *everyone* until the glow wears off.

Displacement may be used in combination with other defense mechanisms or strategies for relieving anxiety. The ego uses all the resources available to it, often employing more than one mechanism at the same time. One of the reasons it is so difficult to analyze behavior is that a single thought or action may have several meanings for the person involved.

Denying Your Feelings and
Projecting Them onto Another Person

MIKE dragged the covers back and shot an irritated glance at the alarm clock. It was already eight-thirty! Who had turned off the alarm buzzer without waking him? His body was yearning to slip back into the warm cave. An ache along the back of his head reminded him how much booze he had consumed at the Friday night dance. Cold water felt good on his face, and two aspirins followed a glass of juice down to his stomach.

Well, now it was very clear how he stood with Carol. He'd been right when he told her that she was acting differently, more distant, like she was uneasy having him around. His big mistake was believing all her excuses—she was "tired," or "worried about her test," or some other cop-out. After a whole year of doing everything he could for her, of keeping her as his one and only girl, she'd picked this way to pay him back—humiliating him right in the middle of a dance and in front of the whole school.

"Mike? Mi-i-ke?? You're going to be late for work, dear!" He heard the high-pitched, accusing voice of his mother drift up from the kitchen. "Mike, what are we going to do with you?" The voice was coming down the hall now. "Your father was just livid this morning when he saw the way you banged up his fender, and there was all that loud noise at three in the morning. The neighbors probably heard it too. I just don't think you've been yourself since you started seeing that Carol Hanson . . ."

Mike felt a twinge in his stomach. "How do you think *I* felt when that crazy driver ran into me?" flashed in his mind, but he said nothing and pushed past her into the hall, down the stairs, and out the front door.

Even though he caught a bus without having to wait, Mike was over an hour late. Bill had already put out the fresh fruit and was stamping prices on some soup cans. No one said anything, so Mike put on his store jacket and began sorting cartons in the back room. It was almost noon before Bill walked up to him.

"Hey, Mike, I'm not sure the boss wants this stuff

uncrated," he observed, "Maybe you should check that out first?"

Mike felt a clamp in his chest, felt the pounding of everyone's mistakes that were being piled on his head. The whole week had been one long kick at him, and now Bill was rubbing in his recent promotion to supervisor by making Mike look careless.

"Why don't you just get off my back, Bill?" he exploded. "I've been around here just as long as you, so don't play supervisor to me! You think you're so big now, poking around to find something, anything, to complain about. I'm not going to put up with that garbage very long!"

"Hey, Mike, wait a minute, just ho-o-old up." Bill looked taken aback. "I wasn't criticizing what you were doing. I was just thinking out loud to myself. I was trying to save you some time and effort, since I think I overheard someone say earlier this morning that there would be a change in that shipment you're handling. Say, you're really touchy today, man. What's the matter with you?"

It is easy to see that things are not going well for Mike and that he is angry from the moment he wakes. Notice how he handles his anger. When something goes wrong, his reaction is always: "I'm not to blame for that. You are accusing me unfairly, and I am justified in being angry at you because you are attacking me without reason." Mike blames someone else for not waking him up on time, for breaking up his romance, for bumping his father's car, and for the fight with Bill. He *denies* that he is in any way responsible, that there is any reason to be angry with himself instead of others.

215

Mike can justify his anger to himself only by interpreting other peoples' behavior as an attack, at the same time denying that he gave them any reason to attack him. This unconscious trick of (a) denying that a strong emotion is bottled up inside you, ever ready to explode, and (b) perceiving that same emotion in someone else is called *denial and projection*. Everyone uses this defense mechanism to some extent, but some people—like Mike—adopt it as their primary way of dealing with problems.

The danger of relying on denial and projection in your relations with other people is that you will make many mistakes in interpreting their statements and actions. In the story, for example, when Bill asks Mike a reasonable question that is emotionally neutral, Mike reacts as if he were under a direct attack. Not only is Mike angry, but the amount of anger is wholly out of proportion to the magnitude of Bill's "offense," if we accept Mike's mistaken analysis of Bill's remark.

If the mechanism of denial and projection is so thoroughly in control of someone's personality that *everything* seems threatening, a psychologist would describe that person as *paranoid*. A paranoid person may not feel any anxiety, for he is "successfully" denying that the troubles he encounters are partly his fault. The paranoid person considers his fears and suspicions to be a natural reaction to a threatening world. While this mechanism may allow him to feel less internal tension, he sacrifices his ability to perceive reality accurately.

Another possible interpretation of Mike's behavior in the story is that it involves *displacement* of anger caused by his parents onto a substitute person, namely his girlfriend Carol. Or, the anger might initially have been caused by *both* the parents and Carol and then been displaced onto Bill.

However, the additional element that makes Mike's behavior more than a simple displacement of anger is his feeling that he is *justified* in being angry, that other people are *provoking him purposely*. This additional element signals that denial and projection are at work. Although a person does not need an excuse to displace his anger from one object to another, an "excuse" makes the person feel justified in his actions. This case illustrates how several defense mechanisms can combine so effectively that it is difficult to identify them separately.

Reaction Formation Against Unwanted Feelings

CAROL and Wendy walked across the playing field. "What a scene last weekend," Wendy ventured. "You were always hanging onto Mike everywhere you went. When you and I were talking last week, he was the best of the best. The break-up was so abrupt; I just don't understand."

After a short silence, Carol began softly, "I think we had to have a big, dramatic fight to put a definite end to it. When we first started seeing each other, there were no problems at all. We always preferred to do things together instead of in the group. But then it seemed like there were times when I was missing out; everyone else was having a great time, and Mike and I were sitting back watching. I certainly couldn't tell him that I would rather be doing something else than be with him, and he probably felt the same way and didn't tell me. Do you see what I mean? It got to be that more and more you had to cover up what you really felt, to fake things, and that makes you feel angry and depressed."

"Carol, nobody even suspected that you felt that way. You and Mike looked so in love; you were always being affectionate in the halls. I heard some girls say that they thought the two of you were showing-off—that's how well you had everyone fooled."

"Well, that's right. That's what we were doing in a way: showing off. You *have* to play-act if people expect you to behave in a certain way all the time, because sometimes you don't *really* feel that way. I just did what I thought people did when they are in love, but when I began to feel less and less that way toward Mike, I got angrier and angrier with myself for being such a hypocrite. I kept going by just pushing that out of my mind and concentrating on my "performance"!

"Couldn't Mike tell that something was wrong?"

"No. He is really dense when it comes to people's feelings. Mike has no idea of what goes on inside himself, either. And his idea of how men should behave—wow! You'd have to be around him as much as I was to be able to believe it! You know how he always swaggers around school, and how he speeds up and down the street when his father lets him use the car. He's always having to prove himself to be the big man, tough, hard. I think he actually prides himself on the amount of trouble he gets into. At least then people have to take him seriously. It was always: 'My folks are hassling me.' Or, 'The principal is just waiting for me to make one more mistake, because he wants to get rid of me.' Or, 'I don't know why I didn't get the supervisor job at the grocery store instead of Bill.' You know what I mean, always complaining that someone was doing something to poor, exploited Mike. 'But just wait,' he'd always say, 'I'll get even.' Wow, just talking about that scene makes me feel great to have broken out of it."

"Well, Carol, after all, you were playing a pretty convincing part yourself. I can't count how many times I heard you purring about how *feminine* you felt being around such a *strong* man.'" Wendy couldn't withhold a touch of sarcasm. "Sometimes you left some bad feelings among the other girls with that bit."

Carol laughed as she agreed: "Yes, it was a great act, Wendy, and that was the heart of the problem. A relationship like Mike's and mine won't work unless both people keep on playing the expected roles. He played the big, tough hero, and that forced me to play the soft, clinging admirer. Don't you see? If we ever stopped the play-acting, then we'd have to be real with each other, and that meant . . . that meant there would be a fight, just like last Friday night. That was one of the few times Mike and I were really honest about how we felt about each other."

Mike and Carol were unable to expand their initial romance into a deep and mutually satisfying relationship, one that adapted naturally to shifts of emotion and to changing circumstances. They both felt constant pressure to display their affection by the most extravagant means possible, as if the exaggeration of one emotion would push out of their awareness any contrary emotions they might also feel, such as irritation, sadness, independence, or weakness. At first, this emotional strait-jacket was unconscious, but then Carol began to resent being forced to express what she really didn't feel at the time. The more she became aware of the natural shifts in her inner feelings, the more energy and strain it required to maintain the outer pretense of constant affection for and dependence on Mike.

Some people believe that certain natural feelings are "bad," so they try to shut out any awareness that such feelings exist by forcing a display of the *opposite* feeling. To fight off sadness or depression, they will continually pretend to be light-hearted and happy. To suppress their natural needs to trust and depend on someone else, they aggressively assert their independence, even if that is inappropriate behavior for their situation. For this defense to work, it must be constantly in operation, because if the person ever stopped play-acting, the feared feelings might surface.

In this defense mechanism, called a *reaction formation*, the adult and realistic part of the personality (ego) has surrendered control to the superego's moral judgments. Like other defense mechanisms, reaction formations tend to distort the person's perceptions of the real world, and to require a great deal of mental energy to keep up with the pretense.

Both Mike and Carol tried to pretend that their relationship was not cooling by exaggerating their outward display of affection. By provoking a fight with Mike, Carol was eventually able to break the hold of this particular reaction formation. This blow-up was a useful, public "justification" for her giving up the affectionate and dependent role that others had learned to expect from her.

Another type of reaction formation is illustrated by Mike's ideal of masculine behavior. Like many men, he is afraid to reveal any tenderness or weakness, feeling that these traits are suitable only for women. A man must be strong, aggressive, and competitive, he would say. The demands of reality, however, are much more complex than in this stereotyped "sexist" view.

Many feelings and behaviors fall into natural pairs that co-exist in everyone, male or female: love-hate, compliance-rebellion, strong-weak, independent-dependent, active-passive, happy-sad, and so on. By using defense mechanisms, a person can suppress the unwanted feelings, but only at the cost of limiting his or her own capacity to experience life.

Separation Anxiety, Fixation, and Regression

MARIA, a high school senior, longed for the opportunity to get a job, rent her own apartment, meet new friends, and live her own life as a young adult. For nearly four whole years, she had thought how romantic and satisfying independence would be, compared to her present situation—sharing a room with a younger sister, having to spend many nights at home babysitting for her brother, washing dishes . . . . Once she had her own apartment, she would always use paper plates and plastic silverware!

All that would be behind her now; Maria was getting her wish. In just a matter of hours, she would walk onto the high school stage, reach out for her diploma, shake hands with the principal, and walk out into a changed life.

The house was bustling this morning as the rest of the family made last-minute preparations to attend graduation . . . dressing the baby, ironing a white shirt for Dad.

How long will it really take me to find a job? she wondered to herself. *I wish the guidance counselor could*

*have found something already. The government employ-
ment office hasn't called, either.* The shift in Maria's mood
had been abrupt. Suddenly she sensed a hint of panic
buried somewhere deep inside her, and she didn't like to
think about it. *It'll be just great to get out of school,* she
insisted to herself. *I'll keep up with Carmen and Sue and
Pete, even though I won't see them every day; we agreed
to meet once a week for a while.* Of course, Joe, who had
also joined in the agreement, had already dropped out of
school to enter the Army. It was hard to control what
happened to people, Maria thought; she doubted that she
and her three best friends would stay together once they
each had different jobs in different areas of the city and
were meeting new people.

Maria knew just how she would decorate the
apartment. A smile tugged at her lips as she pictured her
new freedom. No more Mother always giving you work to
do; no more Father to embarrass you in front of the boys
by insisting that you can't do this or that. Both parents
were making final adjustments in the next room. Maria
loved them both very much. *What are they feeling now,*
she wondered. It was hard to imagine what things would
be like around here after she was gone. *Will my parents
still love me as much as they do now? Will they be hurt
when I tell them that I want to get my own apartment?
When I come home from work, who will I talk to? Who
will I share my life with once I leave them?* There it was
again: the gray underside of her emotions, swirling up and
trying to ruin this happy day. Sometimes it seemed that
whenever she had good luck, it flipped over at the last
minute and showed a spoiled side underneath.

"It's time to go," Father yelled from the street, "Let's
get moving!" Maria bounced down the stairs behind

everyone else and slipped into the car. As they pulled away from the curve, Father put his arm around Maria's shoulder. "Maria, it's your big day," he said gaily. Maria fought back a sudden wish to cry.

Maria is grappling with *separation anxiety*, the fear of leaving a familiar life style for a new and uncertain future. Fear of failing, of letting yourself and other people down, of not meeting the standards you set for yourself—these can build up tension even if you have no reason to be so anxious. In some people, the ego processes are not prepared to manage this kind of tension. Rather than accepting the normality of experiencing anxiety about losing familiar and comfortable supports, they try to

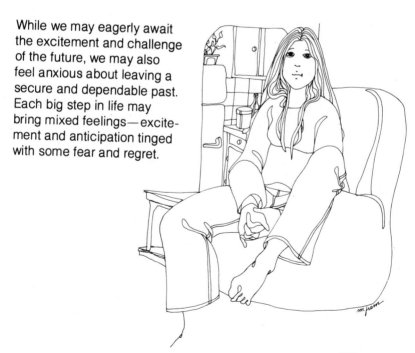

While we may eagerly await the excitement and challenge of the future, we may also feel anxious about leaving a secure and dependable past. Each big step in life may bring mixed feelings—excitement and anticipation tinged with some fear and regret.

YOUR SELF

avoid the painful feelings by rejecting the new opportunity for personal development and psychological growth.

If the person merely refuses to progress beyond his current developmental stage, this defense is called *fixation.* If the person becomes so upset that he or she goes back to an even earlier stage of development—for example, to childlike dependence on the parents—then the defense is called *regression.*

Maria is an adolescent striving to become independent from her family by setting up a new life, a new home, and new friends. At the same time, she is worried that her parents, whom she loves, may resent her leaving, and that she is leaving them too early, since she does not "feel like an adult." It is a big risk to cut yourself away from the constant love and support of your parents when you do not have a guarantee of a compensating love and support from the new persons who will populate your life. In such situations, it is normal to feel anxious and experience sudden shifts of mood like those that troubled Maria.

In our competitive and highly mobile society, separation anxiety—and the risk of fixation or regression to defend against that anxiety—is a problem everyone faces regularly. People are always moving to new areas of the city or nation, or becoming parents, or losing friends and family through illness and death; in countless ways, everyone is compelled to deal with rapid change in his or her life.

Avoidance

FRED sat rigidly upright in his chair, looking straight forward. This was the class he liked least; the teacher was always asking students what they felt about this or that.

Although he'd read his assignment thoroughly the night before, he knew his mind would go blank if he were called on. That's what always happened. The girl across the room was staring . . . what's wrong? Then he noticed he was jiggling his feet nervously and biting at his lip, just as Dad had told him not to do. Relief surged through his body when the bell rang, allowing him to escape from that room.

Stacking his books neatly in his locker, he didn't see George walk up behind him. He was surprised by the booming voice: "Hey, Fred, you've got the cleanest locker in the school!" Fred smiled. "Can I talk to you for a minute?" George asked, and Fred nodded. "The dance committee needs someone to be in charge of refreshments this week, and Pat mentioned that you might be willing to do it. What do you think?"

Fred was flattered that someone had recommended him for something important to the school, but that pleasant glow was short-lived. He knew he would have to get the materials, which meant pleading with someone to give him a ride to and from the store, and , worse yet, he would have to show up at the dance to serve the punch. Fred usually avoided the dances altogether, and when he did go, he always sat in a corner and had a miserable time. The churning sensation that hit his stomach whenever a group of people crowded around him flashed briefly through his mind.

"Well, George," he mumbled, "I really wish I could help you out, but my parents and I were planning a short trip this weekend, and . . . ah . . . I'm afraid I can't. Maybe some other time." Fred felt terrible when he lied. Now he'd committed himself to staying inside his house for a whole weekend. Why was it so hard for him to do what everyone else did without even thinking about it?

"Okay, another time," George said as he moved toward the stairs.

Fred feels extremely anxious about events that are happening all around him. His response is to withdraw from them. Although he is initially pleased about the offer of a responsible class job, his fear of having to engage in spontaneous relationships with other people threatens the limited and narrow world into which he tries to retreat. His extensive repressions of his own feelings might be weakened if he reaches out for something new, so Fred sacrifices the opportunity for personal growth to defend against his anxieties. He acts like the person who ducks into a store to avoid meeting someone he dislikes who is approaching him on the sidewalk.

Fred's defense against anxiety is known as *avoidance*. This defense mechanism occurs because free-floating anxiety is associated with a particular person or situation. Once this mental connection is established, a person may adopt an elaborate series of restrictions on his behavior which are designed to avoid any contact with the feared person or situation. People who rely extensively on avoidance to defend themselves against anxiety may gradually increase the *number* of thoughts or acts they repress as well as increasing the *strength* of the repressions. These repressed persons want to create a world that is predictable and orderly so that their elaborate system of defenses will not be challenged. Outwardly, they appear tense and restricted in body movements and speech, and they limit their contacts with the chaotic stream of life as much as possible.

226

Avoidance occurs because anxiety is associated with a particular person or situation. Once this mental connection is established, a person may adopt an elaborate series of restrictions on his behavior. These restrictions are designed to avoid any contact with the feared person or situation.

Is Change Possible?

Anxiety, that peculiar form of free-floating fear that occurs when your realistic and adult self (ego) is threatened by strong inner processes, can unconsciously worsen your problems. Excessively rigid use of defense mechanisms like displacement, denial and projection, reaction formation, fixation, regression, or avoidance can cause you to misinterpret reality and thereby to create difficulties for yourself.

If you recognize some pattern of behavior that seems to consistently cause problems in your relations with other people, what can you do about it? How can you discover—and change—the unconscious motivations that might be limiting your personal growth? How can you protect your mental and emotional health? These are the questions we are about to discuss.

Psychoanalysis and Problem-Solving

Freud believed that your personality is shaped during the first six years of life. (This subject is also discussed in Chapter 1.) By interacting with your environment—especially with your parents—you learn the basic patterns for dealing with your inner drives, with frustration, and with authority figures. How you interpret reality and respond to life's challenges in the future will reflect the habits you learned in the past. In other words, the past gets "transferred" into the present and future. Thus, if your ego and your superego have developed in such a way that they cannot work harmoniously with your instinctual drives (id), you may carry the same problems of inner tension and anxiety throughout your life.

To relieve these feelings, you are likely to overuse one of the defense mechanisms which gets rid of the anxiety but also distorts your perception of reality. As a result, the same type of mistakes are likely to be repeated again and again in different life situations.

PERCEIVING YOUR WORLD:
THE ROLE OF DEFENSE MECHANISMS

1. *Make up a conversational sentence that illustrates each of the listed defense mechanisms. For example, a reaction formation might be illustrated by the comment, "You say I look sad, but I have never been unhappy in all my life!"*

   Displacement

   Denial and Projection

   Reaction Formation

   Fixation

   Regression

   Avoidance

2. *Since defense mechanisms are usually employed unconsciously, how can you recognize if one is influencing your behavior? What are the indirect signs that the defense mechanisms noted above are in operation?*

3. *Which story about defense mechanisms reminded you most of your own behavior? Can you describe an instance where that kind of defensive thinking or acting influenced you for better or worse?*

4. *What role might defense mechanisms play in prejudice?*

Developmental Stages—
A Pattern for Future Problem-Solving

To break away from these nonproductive, repetitive patterns, it is helpful to understand how the three types of mental forces were originally created. Freud believed that our ability to deal with reality (ego processes) and our internal moral code (superego processes) are learned in three stages.

Ego processes start to develop in the first year of life as the baby distinguishes his own body from the outside world. Mother cannot always instantly deliver what the baby wants, but the infant soon learns that by his own actions—a smile or cry—he can attract attention and lessen his frustration. An ego develops as the baby learns how to gain what he or she wants in the real world.

Many of the interactions between mother and child concern feeding or affectionate handling. Since feeding is the focus for learning experiences in the first year, this period is called the oral stage. In later life, when you feel the need to "take in" something like food, affection, support, ideas, or whatever, you are likely to approach the situation with the same *general* methods you learned in your first year.

In the second and third years, feeding and affection assume a familiar pattern, but a new issue arises that focuses the child's attention on self-control. That issue is toilet-training, so the name assigned this period is the *anal* stage. To earn the parents' praise, the child must delay the pleasant release of tension that accompanies the passing of body wastes. He or she learns that some behaviors are "bad" and others are "good." Since one of the "good" behaviors is obeying the parents' requests, the child also learns at this stage how to deal with authority figures.

As you learn to obey your parents' standards of conduct, you acquire the superego processes that follow you throughout life. When your parents are no longer present to reward or punish, you administer the rewards and punishments yourself, using their moral code which you have internalized as part of your personality. In later life, when you are involved in situations that require "giving things up," "making things," "self-control," "cleanliness," or "moral decision-making," you are likely to approach such situations with the same *general* methods you learned in the second or third year of life.

In the *Oedipal* stage, the ego and superego processes continue to develop. At four or five years, the child discovers that the genitals are a source of pleasure. The difference between male and female sex organs becomes a matter for puzzlement, and then concern. At the same time, the parents begin to treat these differences as important, insisting that the child behave "like a boy" or "like a girl." The child senses that in some vague way he or she is in "competition" with the parent of the same sex for the time and attention of the other parent. Although these childish feelings are obviously not realistic, they are nonetheless very strong. The male child wants an exclusive relationship with his mother while the female child wants her father for herself.

Imagine how distressing this triangle is for the child. He or she is competing with someone much more powerful and skilled, someone both loved and resented. The frustration of this unfulfilled wish, and the fear of retaliation by the parent-competitor, are painful feelings that the child must somehow resolve. The usual solution is to give up the original love-object and to select as the next best alternative someone who resembles the loved parent and can take his or her place.

You will recognize this device as a form of repression and rechanneling of the forbidden wishes onto a substitute object. The child decides to imitate the behavior of the parent-competitor in the hope of attracting a similar person. In the process of *imitation*, more parental standards are stored in the superego. A popular song of past years illustrates the Oedipal compromise: "I want a girl just like the girl who married Dear Old Dad!"

Psychoanalytic Therapy: Freeing Your Present from Your Past

The memories and lessons of the first six years are retained in your unconscious mental life. As we observed earlier, unconscious forces have the power to influence your perceptions, thoughts, feelings, and behavior outside of your awareness. Thus, if you find that your behavior often makes you unhappy or that you keep getting into the same kinds of trouble with other people, it is important to find out if habits you learned in your earliest years are contributing to your problems. Experiences from your past may be transferred onto present situations where they aren't appropriate. Hans Strupp, writing in *Psychology Today*, describes this *transference* in more detail:

> *Most of us have "unfinished business" with the parent figures of our childhood. Our unfinished business is not with the parents as they actually were,*

but as we experienced and distorted them as children. Indeed, the more unresolved struggles we have with our parents, the more we remain embroiled, entangled and dependent on them, and the more severe our emotional difficulties are likely to become when we reach adulthood.

The exact nature of these struggles is deeply buried, because their full realization would be too painful. In psychoanalytic terms, they are repressed and defended against. As adults, we are driven continually to re-enact these problems with contemporary figures who become significant to us emotionally. However, since the original circumstances, the people, and the patient's own situation have changed, there is no possible way of working out the original conflict, which continues unabated on an unconscious level and often is aggravated by repeated frustrations. Psychoanalysts call this tendency to repeat troublesome patterns the transference *and they diagnose individuals afflicted by this tendency as suffering from a transference neurosis. . . .* [5]

Is there any way to undo the past, to free your future life from the self-defeating habits acquired in your earliest years? Freud argued that the basic personality pattern could not be altered, but he also believed that a person could at least learn to recognize the unconscious forces which distort his perception of reality. If you can indirectly detect the self-defeating, unconscious processes at work, then you can control their effects by compensating with the more rational parts of your personality.

In psychoanalysis, one looks back into his past to understand how childhood experiences have influenced his
present feelings and behavior. Often, habits learned in our
earliest years contribute to our problems.

The aim of psychotherapy, Freud believed, was the
strengthening of the realistic ego processes by exposing
the person to his or her hidden wishes (id) and
prohibitions (superego). When asked what the goal of
psychoanalysis was, Freud once replied, "Where id was,
there ego shall be."

If a therapist helps people with problems by using the
"pure" psychoanalytic technique, the course of treatment
goes something like this: the person comes several times a

week to the psychoanalyst's office and talks about every aspect of his or her life. The therapist occasionally asks the person to 'free-associate' to selected topics that come up.

Just as someone's characteristic style of dealing with problems is "transferred" from his past to his present interactions in daily life, there is a similar transference of past feelings about parents onto the therapist. If, for example, the individual had difficulties as a child with a nagging parent, he or she may mistakenly interpret the therapist's comments as nagging or criticism. If the person always longed for a closer relationship with a parent, he or she may try to entice the therapist to fill this need. Such unreasonable expectations increase as the person gradually feels more trust in the therapist and reveals the deepest secrets of his or her personality.

Meanwhile, the therapist is extremely careful to remain neutral. This neutrality becomes very important when the person tries to distinguish reality from the distortions and misinterpretations that get him or her into trouble. At this point, the therapist can point out that the person's strong emotions towards him are the person's own creations, imported from the past. The therapist can also draw parallels between distortions that take place in the therapy situation and similar distortions the person makes in the outside world.

The natural tendency to transfer habits of the past into the present is first intensified in psychoanalytic therapy, then used by the therapist to teach the person about his unconscious mental processes. This teaching process, as it pulls up unresolved problems from the past and submits them to a new and more rational analysis, eventually gives the person a tremendous sense of relief. A new awareness of their own inner workings gives people an increased ability to harmonize the interactions of id, ego, and superego processes. This results in a chain reaction: fewer threats to the ego mean less anxiety. This in turn permits a relaxation of defense mechanisms and more spontaneous responses. A successful psychoanalysis, Freud believed, will lead to a more comfortable and productive life.

Traditional psychoanalytic therapy is expensive and

"I have the strong feeling you disapprove, Doc." Sometimes a person will "transfer" his former ways of dealing with important people to the therapy session. If, for example, the individual had difficulties as a child with a nagging parent, he may mistakenly interpret the therapist's comments as criticism.

time-consuming, but Freud's basic ideas have also been used in other ways. Some followers devised methods for providing short-term support during temporary emotional crises. Others accelerated therapy by confronting patients more actively with their inconsistencies and evasions.[6]

Freud also stimulated new theories about personality which were quite different from psychoanalysis. We will devote the remainder of this chapter to an exploration of these innovations.

Can Personality Be Changed?

Did Leonardo da Vinci paint because of an unfulfilled childhood wish? Might his painting be an unconscious attempt in adult life to "bring back" his lost mother and to "recapture" the pleasure of her care and attention? If we apply Freud's ideas strictly, we would examine Leonardo's experiences in his first six years to explain his later behavior. If you investigate thoroughly, Freud might say, you will always find that behavior is motivated by a need to find pleasure and to avoid frustration. Leonardo's painting is simply a highly *sublimated* expression of this basic principle of motivation.

Many of Freud's followers disagreed with this explanation of behavior. Why is it necessary, they asked, to believe that the only sources of motivation are basic physiological drives like hunger, aggression, and sex? Perhaps people have many different needs or drives that unfold at different stages of their development. Life can be more, these followers maintained, than a continuous repetition of personality patterns learned in one's first six years. It can also be described as a continuous process of

THE INFLUENCE OF YOUR PAST

1. *What are some examples of personal characteristics that might be acquired at each stage of development—oral, anal, and Oedipal?*

   What sort of parental behavior would be likely to instill these lessons in a child?

2. *What does it mean to say of someone that he is a "father figure" or that she is a "mother figure"?*

   Can you explain in Freudian terms why someone might seek out a mother figure or father figure?

3. *Invite a local psychotherapist to class. Ask what he or she does in a typical therapy situation. Does he use Freudian concepts? If so, how does his style differ from traditional psychoanalysis? If a local therapist is not available, an interesting dramatization of an initial therapy session entitled "What Do You Want Me To Say" is available from CRM Educational Films.*

4. *To illustrate the Freudian principle that a person's perception is influenced by past habits (transference) and present feelings (e.g. displacement, projection), try this experiment. Make a simple inkblot and privately ask five different people what they "see." Record their responses but not their names. How different are the responses? How do you account for the differences, since the stimulus is the same for*

everyone? The Rorschach Inkblot Test and the Thematic Apperception Test use this approach for psychological diagnosis; you can find more information about this subject under those topics in your local library.

growth, of becoming whatever one can be, of realizing one's inner potentialities through action.

Just as a tiny acorn has the potential to become a giant oak if its natural growth is not blocked by circumstances, a child will grow into a happy and productive person if his or her natural development is not stunted by other people or the environment. In this view, Leonardo painted because he had a need to fulfill that creative capacity stored inside himself.

This approach is reminiscent of the developmental theories of Erik Erikson discussed in Chapter 1. Erikson says that there is a regular series of critical issues that everyone must face at different times in life, and there is a growth and deepening of the personality ·as each challenge is faced and resolved. Erikson, then, is one of many followers of Freud who modified Freud's original theories in the direction of *continuous* personal development.

Under what conditions will you be able to realize your inner potential? What ingredients are essential for growth to take place? A psychologist named Abraham Maslow provided a fascinating response to that question.

Maslow's Hierarchy of Needs—What You "Need" Depends on What You Already Have!

Maslow suggested that instead of a single need to seek pleasure through discharge of basic physical drives, there are several groups of needs. One satisfies these groups of needs as one might ascend a staircase, step by step. The group of needs with first priority—the first "step"—must be at least partially satisfied before any mental energy can be devoted to satisfying the needs of the second priority. Once a need is satisfied, it no longer motivates the person, so his or her attention is focused on the higher levels of need that remain unsatisfied.

Maslow believed that there are five groups of needs. In order of priority, they are:

1. Basic physiological needs—hunger, sex, sleep, etc.

2. Needs for safety—security, stability, dependency, protection, freedom from fear, anxiety, chaos, etc.

3. Needs for love, affection, and belongingness.

4. Needs for esteem—self-respect, respect from others, competence, achievement, etc.

5. Needs for self-actualization—"What a man *can* be, he *must* be."

The following diagram illustrates· the process of shifting from one set of needs to another. Each pitcher represents one group of needs. The amount of liquid in each pitcher represents the amount of "satisfaction" that is present.

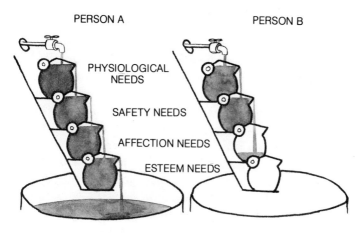

PERSON A   PERSON B

PHYSIOLOGICAL NEEDS

SAFETY NEEDS

AFFECTION NEEDS

ESTEEM NEEDS

SELF-ACTUALIZATION NEEDS

Abraham Maslow has suggested that people satisfy their various needs in an established order of priority. The group of needs with first priority must be at least partially satisfied before there is any energy left over to devote to satisfying the needs with the second priority. As we satisfy each group of needs, we move closer to self-actualization—the fulfillment of our *total* potential.

Maslow suggested that a common mistake psychologists make is to assume that humans are always motivated by the "lower" needs they share with the rest of the animal world. In our modern society, most people have the physiological and safety needs at least partially satisfied. Under these conditions, it is no longer accurate to view all human behavior as motivated by the "lower" drives like hunger and sex, as Freud tended to do. Maslow wrote:

> *Obviously a good way to obscure the higher motivations, and to get a lopsided view of human*

> *capacities and human nature, is to make the organism extremely and chronically hungry or thirsty. Anyone who attempts to make an emergency picture into a typical one, and who will measure all of man's goals and desires by his behavior during extreme physiological deprivation is certainly being blind to many things. It is quite true that man lives by bread alone—when there is no bread. But what happens to a man's desires when there is plenty of bread and when his belly is chronically filled?*
>
> *At once other (and higher) needs emerge and these, rather than physiological hungers, dominate the organism. And when these in turn are satisfied, again new (and still higher) needs emerge, and so on. This is what we mean by saying that the basic human needs are organized into a hierarchy of relative prepotency.*[7]

Maslow believed that too many psychological theories are based on studies of people who are suffering from mental and emotional problems. In his hierarchy of needs, these persons are still operating at the lower or middle levels. He tried to correct this imbalance by studying persons whose needs for safety, belongingness, love, and esteem had already been adequately satisfied.

> *Even if all these needs are satisfied, we may still often (if not always) expect that a new discontent and restlessness will soon develop, unless the individual is doing what he, individually, is fitted for. A musician must make music, an artist must paint, a poet must write, if he is to be ultimately at peace with himself. What a man can be, he must be. This need we may call self-actualization.*

The specific form that these [self-actualization] needs will take will, of course, vary greatly from person to person. In one individual it may take the form of the desire to be an ideal mother, in another it may be expressed athletically, and in still another it may be expressed in painting pictures or in inventions. At this level, individual differences are greatest.[8]

In his studies of self-actualizing people, Maslow found that they tend to see reality more accurately because they have no motives to distort it in self-defense. They accept human nature in themselves and in others and show more naturalness in their behavior than most people. Being alone does not frighten them. They have a quality of detachment and independence that frees them from worries about social expectations. They tend to focus on problems in the external world rather than to be worried about their own personal feelings. They are not afraid of the unknown and preserve an openness to new experiences.

Having a strong empathy with other human beings, self-actualizers are able to form very deep friendships with a few persons, and at the same time respect the dignity and equality of all people. Even their sense of humor is different from most people's. They seldom make jokes that are hostile or based on someone else's inferiority. Above all, self-actualizing people are creative. They express their inner nature in whatever they choose to do.

Maslow believed that we could all be self-actualizing persons if our growth were not limited by unfortunate circumstances.

Rogers' Nondirective Therapy:
Removing Obstacles to Personal Growth

People sometimes become overly concerned with surface appearances, with "oughts" and "shoulds," with pleasing others, and with meeting the expectations of others. What they outwardly say and do is not accurately matched with what they inwardly feel and think. In the words of psychologist Carl Rogers, their public selves are not *congruent* with their inner selves; they are "defensively organized."[9]

To help people release these inner restrictions on their natural process of growth, Rogers developed *client-centered therapy*. Its aim is to help a person "get in touch with the self that underlies surface behavior."[10] Because the needs and capacities of each individual are different, the therapist does not lead the client in any special direction. Instead, he builds a supportive atmosphere based on empathy with the client's situation and attentive listening to the feelings behind the client's behavior. Feelings are reflected back to the person: "You look very sad now," or "You must find it very difficult to choose among all those possibilities." Rogers' *nondirective* therapy focuses on the person's present life rather than on systematic reconstruction of the past, as in psychoanalysis.

In this warm and understanding environment, a client feels secure enough to examine his or her life and to *experiment* with honesty and openness as a way of relating to self and to others. As the defensive orientation breaks down, natural processes of growth take over. An openness to experience, a trust in oneself, an internal code to guide value judgments, and a willingness to regard

A POTENTIAL FOR GROWTH

1. *Can you find examples from news reports of people who are living at each level of Maslow's hierarchy of needs?*

2. *Can you think of anyone you know who is "self-actualizing"? What aspects of that person's life make you think this?*

3. *Imagine that you are thirty years old, living whatever you believe would be a "self-actualizing" life for you. Write a paragraph describing the important features of your imagined life. Whom do you associate with? What do you do? What are your goals?*

4. *Role-play a situation in which a friend comes to you with a personal problem and you use Rogers' nondirective approach. Try to be* empathetic *and* reflect back *your friend's feelings as accurately as you can. What is the value of this approach? Does it have any drawbacks?*

one's personality as an ever changing process—these are characteristics that Rogers notes as marks of mental health and maturity.[11]

The Search for a Meaning in Life

Viktor Frankl is a psychotherapist who survived the Nazi concentration camps during World War II. He believes that your attitude toward the future is as important a factor in your behavior as those influences from the past emphasized by Freud.

The Need for a Future

If you lose your hope for the future, you also lose your sense of the meaningfulness of life itself. This loss can impose severe mental and emotional difficulties, and in extreme cases, can even be fatal:

> The prisoner who had lost faith in the future—his future—was doomed. With his loss of belief in the future, he also lost his spiritual hold; he let himself decline and became subject to mental and physical decay. Usually this happened quite suddenly in the form of a crisis, the symptoms of which were familiar to the experienced camp inmate. We all feared this moment—not for ourselves, which would have been pointless, but for our friends. Usually it began with the prisoner refusing one morning to get dressed and wash or to go out on the parade ground. No entreaties, no blows, no threats had any effect. He just lay there, hardly moving. If this crisis was brought about by an illness, he refused to be taken to the sickbay or to do anything to help himself. He simply gave up. There he remained, lying in his own excreta, and nothing bothered him anymore.
>
> Those who know how close the connection is between the state of mind of a man—his courage and hope, or lack of them—and the state of immunity of

> *his body will understand that the sudden loss of hope*
> *and courage can have a deadly effect. . . .*
>
> *The death rate in the week between Christmas,*
> *1944, and New Year's, 1945, increased in camp*
> *beyond all previous experience . . . the explanation*
> *for this increase did not lie in the harder working*
> *conditions or the deterioration of our food supplies*
> *or a change of weather or new epidemics. It was*
> *simply that the majority of the prisoners had lived in*
> *the naive hope that they would be home again by*
> *Christmas. As the time drew nearer and there was no*
> *encouraging news, the prisoners lost courage and*
> *disappointment overcame them. This had a*
> *dangerous influence on their powers of resistance*
> *and a great number of them died.*
>
> *As we said before, any attempt to restore a man's*
> *inner strength in the camp had first to succeed in*
> *showing him some future goal. . . . "He who has a*
> why *to live for can bear with almost any* how."[12]

Frankl suggests that the lessons learned in prison are relevant for men and women who feel that their lives are basically empty. Problems of despair and boredom bring many people to psychological counselors.

What Gives Meaning to Life?

What makes life meaningful is a very personal question that must be answered by referring to the specific life circumstances of an individual:

> *The meaning of life differs from man to man, from*
> *day to day and from hour to hour. What matters,*
> *therefore, is not the meaning of life in general but*
> *rather the specific meaning of a person's life at a*

> given moment. *To put the question in general terms would be comparable to the question posed by the chess champion, "Tell me, Master, what is the best move in the world?" There simply is no such thing as the best or even a good move apart from a particular situation in a game and the particular personality of one's opponent. The same holds for human existence. One should not search for an abstract meaning of life. Everyone has his own specific vocation or mission in life; everyone must carry out a concrete assignment that demands fulfillment. Therein he cannot be replaced, nor can his life be repeated. Thus, everyone's task is as unique as is his specific opportunity to implement it. . . .*
>
> *The question of the meaning of life may actually be reversed. Ultimately, man should not ask what the meaning of his life is, but rather must recognize that it is he who is asked. In a word, each man is questioned by life; and he can only answer to life by* answering for *his own life; to life he can only respond by being responsible.*[13]

Psychologists who, like Frankl, insist that you are always free to choose your own attitude toward life are often called *existentialists*. Meaning cannot be given to you by others, the existentialists say, and if you want to find meaning in life, you must accept the responsibility to *create* a meaning through your own hopes, plans, actions, and relationships with others.

There are at least three ways a person can give meaning to his or her life, Frankl concludes. First, people can set goals for themselves and work to achieve them through action—"doing deeds," as Frankl calls it.

Second, people can "experience values" directly by

relating to a beautiful work of art, a magnificent natural environment, a religious ceremony, or by loving another person. A very intense experience of this sort might suddenly make everything in a person's past seem important and meaningful in retrospect, however unfortunate life had been up to that point. He or she then sees the earlier disappointments as preparation for this moment. Loving another person is a particularly meaningful experience, since it gives the person who loves the capacity to see potentialities in the loved one and to help the loved one become what he or she can be.

Third, even for people who must face an unpleasant but unavoidable fate, there can be meaning in suffering. Frankl cites two cases to illustrate this point: an elderly man who was severely depressed after the death of his wife and a middle-aged woman who attempted suicide after her healthy son died at eleven years of age, leaving her with one other son who was paralyzed. Frankl suggested to the elderly man that his suffering was a *sacrifice* for the benefit of his deceased wife: his survival spared her the pain of grief she would have felt had he died first. In a group therapy situation, the despairing mother heard another woman tell how much she suffered because she missed her opportunity to have and to love children. Suddenly the mother saw that making life better for her crippled son was an important contribution, that there was a reason she should continue to endure her grief for the lost son. The suffering of both persons became bearable once they saw a meaning in it.

One of these three ways of creating values and giving meaning to life is always available to each of us, Frankl observes: "... everything can be taken from a man but one thing: the last of the human freedoms—to choose one's attitude in any given set of circumstances, to choose one's own way."[14]

Learning To Choose Well: Glasser's Reality Therapy

Psychiatrist William Glasser also emphasizes the importance of value choices for achieving and maintaining mental health. He suggests that people with mental and emotional problems often drift into a "failure identity." They are unable to become involved in satisfying and productive relationships with other people.

To relieve the pain of their loneliness and demoralization, they are likely to withdraw or to provoke others by acting hostile and aggressive. This further isolates them from meaningful involvements with other people. A therapist must be careful not to encourage this self-preoccupation.

> *Talking at length about a patient's problems and his feelings about them focuses upon his self-involvement and consequently gives his failure value. Long discussions about a patient's problems are a common and serious error in psychotherapy. They increase rather than decrease his self-involvement and his misery. . . . It is tempting to listen to his many complaints because they seem so urgent. Doing so may reduce his pain and make him feel better for a while as he basks in the attention his complaints have gained him. If he does nothing to change his behavior, however, his pain will return and he will grow disillusioned with therapy.*[15]

Instead, the therapist should aim for a warm, personal relationship with the patient that models a more positive way of relating to the world. He should focus on the present and future rather than on the past.

While feelings are important, ultimately it is a person's *behavior* toward others that will determine whether or not he feels good about himself and others. Therefore, the therapist should encourage patients to examine how their own behavior contributes to their problems. Glasser writes:

> A person often comes to my office complaining of how bad she feels. She is depressed, upset, worried, and miserable. Believing she should tell me about these feelings in great detail (in fact, she wants to), she is surprised when I, a psychiatrist, a person supposed to be keenly attuned to misery, cut her rather short and say: "I believe you. You have convinced me that you are depressed and I appreciate that you are upset. But what are you doing?
>
> ...I must get her behavior out on the table so she can become aware of it. Unless we become aware of our behavior, we cannot learn to behave more competently.
>
> . . . To help the patient see his behavior and choose new behavior that will lead to involvement with others, we continually ask, "What are you doing? What are you doing now? What did you do yesterday? What did you do the day before yesterday? What did you do last week?"[16]

As the patient becomes increasingly aware of his or her behavior patterns, therapy focuses on evaluative questions. Is this behavior good for me? Is it good for other people I care about or whom I want to care about me? Will it be tolerated by my community?[17]

Once a person decides that certain values are important to him, the Reality Therapist helps him to develop realistic plans for accomplishing those goals and to make a personal commitment to carry out the plans. If a person commits himself to a goal which he himself has chosen and creates a realistic plan of action for achieving that goal, then no excuses are accepted if the commitment is not met. As long as the person values the same goal, he is responsible for taking those steps that promise to lead to its fulfillment.[18]

> *The therapist must insist that a commitment made is worth keeping. The only commitments many failures [patients] have made are to their irresponsibilities, their emotions, and their involvement with themselves. These commitments have mired them deeply in failure. The therapist cannot help unless he and the patient are both willing to re-examine the plan continually and make a mutual decision either to renew the commitment, if the plan is valid, or to give it up, if it is not. The therapist must say to the patient, "If you are not going to do it, say so, but don't say you are and then give excuses when you fail." Excuses are bad in almost all situations, whether between husband and wife, parent and child, or teacher and student. Excuses, rationalizations, and intellectualizations can become the death knell of any successful relationship . . . .*
>
> ✿ ✿ ✿ ✿
>
> *To do Reality Therapy well requires the ability not to accept excuses, not to probe for fault, not to be*

*a detective to find out Why. Reality Therapy
assumes that a commitment, according to a
reasonable plan, can always be fulfilled. A good
therapist never gives up. His tenacity helps the
patient gain the experience of fulfilling a commitment to a responsible plan, possibly for the first time
in his life.*[19]

Both Glasser and Frankl insist that it is the patient's
responsibility to make the important decisions in his or her
life. A past filled with failure, unhappiness, and repression
does not dictate how the present and future must be lived.
The role of a therapist is not to choose for the patient but
to assist him in clarifying his own values and in acquiring
the skills necessary to achieve his ends.

Conclusion

With Frankl and Glasser, who believe that every man and
woman has the freedom to give meaning to his or her own
life, we have shifted our perspective a considerable
distance from Freud, who believed that our every act,
thought, and feeling is determined by specific causal
factors from the past. While Frankl and Glasser state that
we can exercise our will and make authentic choices,
Freud argues that all our choices are controlled by the
unconscious dynamics of the id, ego, and superego, and
that the "will" itself is the product of these interacting
forces. Maslow and Rogers provide a third interpretation
of personality: humans have a natural pattern of growth
stored inside them that will blossom under the right
conditions.

CHOOSING FOR YOURSELF

1. *Frankl suggests that you can give meaning to your life by "doing deeds," by "experiencing" love or beauty or other values, or, finally, by suffering. What makes your life meaningful to you now? What would make it meaningful in the future?*

2. *Make your own chart like that below and fill in information about each of the psychotherapies we have studied. In class, compare the different theories about behavior change.*

	How do problems originate?	What is the motivating force behind the behavior?
FREUD		
ROGERS & MASLOW		
FRANKL & GLASSER		

254

IN THERAPY SESSIONS . . .

	What is the therapist's role?	What is the time period emphasized?	What is the sequence of behavior change?
FREUD			
ROGERS & MASLOW			
FRANKL & GLASSER			

All of these psychologists, however much they differ among themselves, remain firmly committed to one common principle: *human behavior is best explained by analyzing the inner mental states of men and women and by understanding how these inner states get translated into behavior.*

In the next two chapters, we will explore the ideas of psychologists who follow a very different approach. The *behaviorists* believe that we can predict and change behavior more effectively if we concentrate on observable behavior and *ignore* inner thoughts and feelings. Another group of scientists believes that behavior is best explained by electrical and chemical (physiological) processes in the body.

255

Suggested Readings

Faraday, Ann, *Dream Power* (New York: Coward, McCann, 1972).

Frankl, Viktor, *Man's Search for Meaning* (Boston: Beacon Press, 1962).

Freeman, Lucy, *The Story of Anna O* (New York: Walker, 1972).

Freud, Sigmund, *Interpretation of Dreams* (New York: Modern Library, 1950).

Freud, Sigmund, *New Introductory Lectures on Psychoanalysis* (New York: W. W. Norton, 1933, 1965).

Freud, Sigmund, *Psychopathology of Everyday Life* (New York: W. W. Norton, 1965).

Friedman, Lawrence, *Psychoanalysis: Uses and Abuses* (New York: Paul Eriksson, 1968).

Glasser, William, *The Identity Society* (New York: Harper and Row, 1972).

Glasser, William, *Reality Therapy* (New York: Harper and Row, 1965).

Hall, Calvin, *A Primer of Freudian Psychology* (New York: World, 1954).

Jones, Ernest, *The Life and Work of Sigmund Freud* (New York: Basic Books, 1961).

Maslow, Abraham, *The Farther Reaches of Human Nature* (New York: Viking, 1971).

Rogers, Carl, *On Becoming a Person* (Boston: Houghton Mifflin, 1961).

Stone, Irving, *Passions of the Mind* (New York: Doubleday, 1971).

Wilson, Colin, *New Pathways in Psychology: Maslow and the Post-Freudian Revolution* (New York: Taplinger, 1972).

FOOTNOTES

1. James Strachey, ed., *Standard Edition of the Complete Psychological Works of Sigmund Freud* (London: Hogarth Press, 1966), Vol. 1, p. 115.
2. *The Life and Work of Sigmund Freud* (edited and abridged in one volume by Lionel Trilling and Steven Marcus), by Ernest Jones, © 1961 by Basic Books, Inc., Publishers, New York.
3. Reprinted from *Complete Introductory Lectures on Psychoanalysis* by Sigmund Freud. Translated and edited by James Strachey. By permission of W.W. Norton and Company, Inc. copyright © 1920, 1935 by Edward L. Bernays. Copyright © 1933 by Sigmund Freud. Copyright renewed 1961 by W.J.H. Sprott. Copyright © 1965, 1964, 1963 by James Strachey. Copyright © 1966 by W.W. Norton and Company, Inc.
4. *Ibid;* p. 187.
5. Hans Strupp, "Freudian Analysis Today." Reprinted from *Psychology Today*, July 1972, p. 38. Copyright © 1972, Ziff-Davis Publishing Company. All rights reserved.
6. Peter Sifneos, *Short-term Psychotherapy and Emotional Crisis* (Cambridge: Harvard University Press, 1972), pp. 44-46, 75-88.
7. Abraham H. Maslow, *Motivation and Personality*, 2nd Edition (New York: Harper & Row, 1970), p. 38. [See also: Maslow, *The Farther Reaches of Human Nature* (New York: Viking, 1971), pp. 43, 318, 322.]
8. *Ibid.*, pp. 45-51.
9. Carl R. Rogers, *On Becoming a Person* (Boston: Houghton-Mifflin, 1961), pp. 166-171.
10. *Ibid.*, p. 108.
11. *Ibid.*, pp. 115-125.
12. Viktor E. Frankl, *Man's Search For Meaning* (Boston: Beacon Press, Copyright © 1959, 1962 by Victor Frankl), pp. 117-118. Reprinted by permission of Beacon Press.
13. *Ibid.*, pp. 171-172.
14. *Ibid.*, p. 104.
15. William Glasser, *The Identity Society* (New York: Harper & Row, 1972), p. 111.
16. *Ibid.*, pp. 115-116.
17. *Ibid.*, p. 118.
18. *Ibid.*, p. 123.
19. *Ibid.*, pp. 128-129.

6.

"Pigeons Aren't People, But It's Only a Matter of Complexity": B.F. Skinner and Behaviorism

STEPHEN B. is in danger of being expelled from school.[1] He is always exceeding the acceptable limits of classroom behavior. He habitually arrives late; he gets out of his seat without permission; he talks or is otherwise disruptive while other students are speaking. The teachers, the school principal, and his parents have all tried to change Steve's disruptive behavior, first by providing counseling and then by imposing penalties. Neither strategy worked, so Steve and his parents decide to try psychotherapy.

If you were the therapist, and had a Freudian approach, how could you help Steve? What questions would you ask him? Even if you don't have enough information to give specific answers, you remember the general method: you would focus on the "push and pull of inner needs," on how Steve "sees" things, on how he "feels" about them, on what he hopes to achieve by his behavior. You would search for unconscious motivations underlying the objectionable behavior, and you would try to lead Steve to an understanding of how these forces influence his actions. You might conclude, for example, that Steve has "unresolved hostile feelings toward authority figures," or that he is "so insecure that he needs constant attention even if it takes the form of punishment." Unfortunately, although the therapy sessions produce some meaningful communication between you and Steve, the classroom disruptions continue.

The Behaviorist Approach to Steve's Case

After heated discussion, the principal and Steve's teachers agree to exclude him from school unless a last resort works. This alternative was proposed to them by a *behavioral* psychologist:

"We will draw up a 'contract' in which each person involved—Steve, his parents, his teachers, and the principal—agrees to act in specific ways. Steve can do as he pleases.

"All the teachers must agree to send Steve home immediately as soon as he breaks any rule they have asked the class to observe. For example, he may not cause a disruption while another student is talking or walk around the room when he feels like it. Teachers will agree to avoid any attempt to influence or change Steve's behavior in any way. They will not speak with him about present or past misbehavior.

"Steve's parents must agree not to talk with him about school at all and not to punish him for any school-related behavior.

"Finally, the principal agrees to take charge once Steve leaves the class, to insure that he leaves the school and goes home. He agrees not to initiate any discussions with Steve about his school behavior.

"In other words, everyone agrees that if a certain event takes place—namely, Steve's disruption of the class—a series of actions will automatically follow without any discussion about those actions."

The psychologist predicts that if everyone behaves according to the agreed schedule, Steve's disruptions will stop and he will want to learn like the rest of the students. What do you predict will happen? If you were the principal, would you agree to try this method? If you were Steve's parents, would you agree, realizing that Steve might use this arrangement to drop out of school?

The method that the behavioral psychologist proposed is very different from the approach of Freudian psychologists. The focus of attention in the "contract" plan is not on Steve directly but rather on Steve's *environment*—the persons, places, and things with which he interacts. The behavioral psychologist plans to restructure the environment that Steve lives in. For each act that Steve performs, the consequence or reaction will be different from that of the previous environment.

Compare the consequences of disrupting a class under the old system with those under the new one. Before, Steve was *rewarded* whenever he misbehaved. Everyone, including his fellow students, his teachers, the principal, and his parents, paid attention to him. When people don't get attention for their good behaviors, it sometimes seems better to cause a disturbance than to be ignored. Under the new "contract," a disruption by Steve brings little or no attention; its only result is exclusion from the company of his schoolmates. There is no reward for disruptive behavior. But as always, rewards are still available for learning and for interacting with the other students. Will Steve's behavior change simply as a result of this new environment?

The first day, Steve lasts five minutes. He gets up out of his seat, his teacher sees him and immediately gives the signal to leave. He reports to the office and goes home. His mother says nothing to him about it. The next day he stays for ten minutes. This time he leans back in his seat too far so that the chair falls with a loud clatter. His teacher merely signals him to leave. His mother does not discuss it with him when he gets home. However, she becomes very upset and calls the psychologist. The psychologist reassures her that this is precisely what should happen and that he is very pleased with the teacher's cooperation. He predicts that Steve will last fifteen minutes the next day and cautions her not to discuss school with Steve even if Steve tries to draw her into a conversation about it. This pattern continues.

Mother has to be reassured twice more that things are going well and that it is important that Steve actually be sent home on each occasion that he exceeds a specified limit. Father threatens to [beat] . . .him for his misdeeds, even though he has acknowledged that previous attempts to use [force] have ended in obvious failure and even worsening of misbehavior. The teacher admits that when Steve is not there the whole class is calmer, more productive. The other children wonder what's going on. They begin to feel sorry for Steve because he is sent home for such trivial offenses.

Finally, on the ninth day after the contract was

made, Steve stays all day. He proudly announces this to the principal. The principal is surprised and says so. For the rest of the year, with only two exceptions, Steve remains in class without a single disruptive act. He soon begins to do his work. Parents and teacher remark that "he is not the same child." The other children like him now and play with him. He is more relaxed. . . .

The teacher and the parents want the contract discontinued now that he is controlling himself. This is done. His chronic misbehavior returns immediately and with renewed vigor. The contract is installed again. The misbehavior disappears instantly. The same contract is used the following year. The third year it is used only during the last semester. The following year it is not used at all—Steve is in charge of himself.[2]

In Steve's restructured environment at home and school, there is no pay-off, no reward, for being disruptive. Scientists who believe in a "behaviorist" approach to psychology explain the resulting change in Steve as follows:

As with any behavior, a person or animal is more likely to repeat that behavior if he is rewarded for it. The tendency to behave similarly in the future is strengthened or *reinforced* as long as the circumstances of the environment continue to reward it. Conditions in our environment, then, control what behavior we learn, and shape what behavior is maintained over time. A behavioral psychologist summarizes this theory by stating that behavior is *conditioned* by the consequences it produces in an environment. To change behavior, change the environment: this will condition a new set of behaviors that is designed to obtain rewards from the new structure.

Will Steve's improved behavior persist once the specially structured environment is removed? Why don't old behaviors reappear in response to old environmental conditions? In Steve's case, relapses did occur several times when he was allowed to function in the class without a contract. The behaviorist would say, however, that even though Steve initially works and learns solely to avoid being separated from his friends, he will eventually learn that working and understanding events in the world can *themselves* be rewarding. Once this shift occurs, the contract can be removed in gradual steps because the person has learned to find rewards in the old environment where he could not find any before.

Training Animals and Birds to Work

To understand how the conditioning process works with people, it is useful to look at simpler cases than Steve's. B. F. Skinner, the psychologist who made behaviorist methods as important and popular as they are today, started by experimenting with animals and birds.

Suppose you are given a small white rat and a specially-designed box (a "Skinner box") similar to that in the picture on page 264. There is a lever beside a small eating cup. If the rat bumps the lever, a piece of food will drop into the cup. The rat has never experienced such a device before. What do you predict will happen?

When you place the rat in the box, it runs around as it would in any new environment. Accidentally, it brushes past the lever and—surprise! A piece of food appears.

The behavior of this rat is shaped by rewards it receives in the unusual environment of a "Skinner box." Food pellets drop into the feeding cup whenever the rat performs a behavior which the experimenter wants to reinforce. Behaviorist psychologists evolved a general theory of learning (applicable to people as well as to rats) from many experiments of this type.

After more running and a few more accidental bumps, the rat begins to *associate* its behavior—bumping the lever— with a reward from the environment, namely, food. From then on, it repeatedly presses the lever when hungry.

When Skinner and other behaviorists describe what happened with the rat, every statement is about a *fact that can be directly observed*. There are no statements at all about the rat's inner feelings or motivations.

264

SHOULD STEVE BE CONDITIONED?

1. *How would you have responded to Steve's behavior if you were:*

   The teacher?

   The principal?

   His parents?

2. *Do you think this method of behavioral conditioning is "good" for Steve or for use with other persons? Why or why not?*

3. *Does it matter that this method does not attempt to discover what Steve feels or thinks about his problems?*

4. *Should this method be used for people of all ages? Are there any restrictions you would place on its use? What if Steve did not consent to the contract—should it be used anyway?*

Fact A: The rat exhibits an initial behavior: running around the box.

Fact B: One particular action, hitting the lever, is followed by a consequence: food.

Fact C: Since the rat gobbles up the food, the food

> can be regarded as a positive consequence
> or *reward*.

Fact D: The rat frequently pushes the lever to obtain food and continues to do so as long as environmental conditions remain the same.

Using these facts, we can make the following predictions: An initial behavior is more likely to occur in the future if it is *reinforced* by a positive consequence from the environment. In addition, all behavior is shaped or *conditioned* by the *structure of the environment*. These statements are the basic principles of behaviorism. Behaviorist psychologists believe that their theories are better explanations of behavior than the "push and pull of inner needs," and that patterns of behavior can be predicted and even changed using behaviorist principles alone without considering the subjective point of view of the person or animal who is behaving.

Do you agree that Skinner may be right about rats, but wonder if it is fair or reasonable to compare humans with rats? The behaviorists are prepared to answer your challenge! It is possible to teach pigeons, porpoises, and all sorts of birds and animals to perform very complex tasks using conditioning techniques. As Skinner puts it, "Pigeons aren't people, but it's only a matter of complexity," not a difference in basic principles! Let's look at pigeons first, then people.

Pigeons Threaten to Replace People!

IT WAS LEARNED TODAY through reputable sources that Union Local 101 has submitted a formal objection to the Wonder Widget Electronic Company's policy of hiring

Can pigeons do some jobs more effectively than people? Psychologists have found that it is possible to teach pigeons, porpoises, and many other kinds of birds and animals to perform complex tasks by using conditioning techniques. Behaviorists have gained much of their scientific knowledge by working with animals in these learning experiments. This knowledge may then be applied to the understanding of human behavior.

pigeons to do a man's job. An experimenter using behavioral conditioning techniques trained pigeons to recognize defects in small electronic parts passing on a mock assembly line. When placed in position on the real assembly line, these birds inspected almost one thousand parts per hour for four hours straight. Believe it or not, the birds showed no fatigue; indeed, the longer they worked, the better they performed. The only limit on the birds' effectiveness was that the human operators who were checking the pigeons' work were unable to keep up! Sources from Local 101 indicate that Wonder Widget executives were known to have discussed the comparative advantages of adding pigeons to the regular staff

267

because, in addition to working more effectively, they cost little (under $5.00), eat "chicken feed," require little sleep, and have been known to work continuously for days. The prospect of lay-offs in a time of rising unemployment prompted union officials to submit the complaint. Company spokesmen indicate that union requests will be respected. Thus, Wonder Widget will continue "to send men to do a pigeon's job."[3]

A funny story, but it is based on a real experiment! How is it possible to teach a pigeon such a complex task? The same conditioning principles that teach *simple* behavior to a *rat* will teach *complicated* behavior to a *pigeon or a person.* The major difference is that a complex task must be broken down into a chain of separate steps, with each successive step being a closer approximation to the target behavior. (Hence the name for this technique— "shaping behavior by reinforcement of successive approximations.")

Let's say you are in charge of training one pigeon to perform the first part of its inspection job: to approach an electronic widget and peck at it. (You'll teach it to recognize defects at a later stage of training.) Can you identify a set of target actions that guide the pigeon towards your goal step by step?

To begin with, the pigeon has a natural behavior of cocking its head and looking in different directions. An obvious first step, then, is to reward the pigeon if and only if it looks in the direction of the widget you put on the wall of the cage. Once you condition the bird to look frequently at the widget, you change your reinforcement schedule: now you reward the pigeon if and only if it looks

Pigeons have been taught to perform complicated tasks by a conditioning process called "reinforcement of successive approximations." The complex task is divided into separate steps, and the pigeon is conditioned to perform first one step, then another, until the whole task is mastered. Pigeons trained in this manner can perform some jobs as well as or better than men or machines!

Photo courtesy of Will Rapport

at the widget and then steps in that direction. Once the pigeon will consistently walk up to the widget, you again change your reinforcement schedule. This time, you reward the pigeon if it pecks at the object. Within a relatively short time, you have trained the pigeon to look for a widget, walk up to it, and peck at it. You need only continue the same step-by-step procedure to teach the other elements in the overall task, such as distinguishing normal widgets from defective ones.

Shaping Your Behavior: Reward vs. Punishment

Diana, a baby still unable to walk, is holding herself up by grabbing the seat of a chair. Mother smiles and speaks encouragingly, then moves to a point just beyond her daughter's reach. The little girl hesitates, then takes a single, unsteady step into her mother's arms, where she is patted and kissed. "Try again," Mother says, holding the child steady for a minute, then backing another step away, "Come again to Mother." Another step. All the while, this little girl is learning that she can influence Mother to give rewards if she behaves in certain ways.[4]

Do you see any similarities between this type of teaching and the conditioning of a pigeon by rewarding its "successive approximations" to a desired behavior? The initial behavior here—the child's having pulled herself up, using a chair as a crutch—may be reinforced by two different types of rewards. From her mother, she receives the social reward of praise and affection; she also acquires the skill of walking which enables her to satisfy many of her own needs. Mother is encouraging the child's curiosity and independence. If this encouragement is consistently applied by the mother, these characteristics are likely to persist in the child's later life.

BILL was always a problem for his mother. Even before he learned to walk, he was always in the way around the apartment. His mother had to spank him regularly to keep him on the rug in the front room while he played. Bill learned to walk later than most children, but when he started he was even more rambunctious—he just got into everything. It was useless to tell him not to do something simply because it was dangerous. All Bill understood was a slap across the wrist. When he was allowed to play with other children on the sidewalk or playground, he would invariably be filthy when he returned. This meant a spanking, and then more work to argue him into the bath.

When he went off to school, Bill's mother thought that she would finally get some relief. But now the teachers are telling her that Bill always seems nervous at school, that he is afraid to ask about things in the lesson that he doesn't understand, and that he won't join in the playground games voluntarily.

Can you explain how Bill's behavior at school was conditioned by his earlier experiences? Bill's case illustrates how parents can sometimes teach a child the wrong lessons—or the right lessons but in a wrong way. These conditioned behaviors, like those learned by Diana, also tend to persist in later life, even though they don't help the person to obtain the responses he or she wants from the environment. Bill's mother was relying on *punishment* as a tool for changing his behavior rather than providing *positive rewards* that would pull him in the direction in which she wanted him to go. Skinner believes strongly that punishment (or "aversive conditioning," as he calls it) is less effective for shaping behavior.

Skinner is opposed to punishment on several grounds. First, his research shows that someone who is punished for a behavior may nonetheless repeat it in the future. When the environment changes (for example, if the punisher leaves temporarily) the forbidden behavior will return. A child punished for sex play does not lose his or her inclination to experiment. A teenager put in reform school for vandalism does not necessarily lose the inclination to destroy things.

Second, punishment may condition someone to feel

opposing emotions simultaneously, a conflict which produces emotional distress. For example, a child punished for sex play may later be unable to form satisfactory relationships because of a feeling that sex is pleasurable but "bad." The delinquent teenager's inclination to flee when discovered in some antisocial act may develop into a more dangerous and unpredictable conflict between flight, on the one hand, and an attack against those who want to punish him, on the other.

Third, punishment may have another bad side-effect. Skinner writes:

> . . . a person may subsequently behave "in order to avoid punishment." He can avoid it by not behaving in punishable ways, but there are other possibilities. Some of these are disruptive and maladaptive or neurotic, and as a result they have been closely studied. The so-called "dynamisms" [or ego defenses] of Freud are said to be ways in which repressed wishes evade the censor and find expression, but they can be interpreted simply as ways in which people avoid punishment. *Thus, a person may behave in ways that will not be punished because they cannot be seen, as by* fantasying *or* dreaming. *He may* sublimate *by engaging in behavior which has rather similar reinforcing effects but is not punished. He may* displace *punishable behavior by directing it toward objects which cannot punish—for example, he may be aggressive toward physical objects, children, or small animals. He may watch or read about others who engage in punishable behavior,* identifying *himself with them, or interpret the behavior of others as punishable, projecting his own tendencies. He may* rationalize *his behavior by*

giving reasons, either to himself or others, which make it nonpunishable.[5] [Emphasis added.]

Even though punishment doesn't work as well as a system of *positive* reinforcement, our society still relies heavily on this less effective tool to control our behavior. Behaviorists argue that we could achieve dramatic results throughout our society if we were to change from punishment to reward as a means of conditioning target behaviors.

In several kindergarten rooms in St. Louis, for example, children were paid to learn.[6] If Susan or Sam would be yanking at the sleeves of other children, or messing up their drawings, or would be engaged in some other undesirable behavior, instead of scolding, the teacher would ignore them. Then she would give small tokens as rewards to those children who were trying to work. These tokens were just like money, since they could be used to "buy" all sorts of privileges at the school— candy, more recess, attention from the teacher. It didn't take long for Susan and Sam to get the message. Disruptive behaviors disappeared. All of the students were eager for more new projects. The teachers felt better about their work. Performance of the students on intelligence tests at the end of the year was significantly better than at the year's beginning.

Even where students are not paid to learn, a natural process of positive reinforcement by a teacher can have a powerful shaping influence. Think back, for a moment, to the words of encouragement and praise you received from a particular teacher. Did you do better in that class? Did that teacher seem to like you? Were you more involved in the course? How much does your teacher's

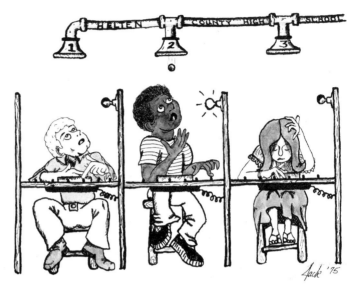

When our behavior is rewarded, we are more likely to repeat it in the future. Some schools use "tokens" as rewards for desired behavior. Teaching machines are based on the same principle: if we learn at our own pace and receive immediate reinforcement by knowing our answers are correct, we will progress all the faster.

attitude toward you influence your progress in learning?

Two researchers experimented in an elementary school to test the influence of the "self-fulfilling prophecy"—that is, the idea that people often live up to what others expect of them. They gave an intelligence test to all the children, but did not report the true results to the classroom teachers. Instead, they randomly picked the names of 20 percent of the students, arbitrarily labeled these students "intellectual bloomers," and told the teachers that these children could be expected to show important gains in their test scores by the end of the year. Eight months later, when the same test was repeated, it was found that those students who had been labeled "intellectual bloomers" showed a substantially greater increase in their scores when compared to other students who were not given this label, even though the *only* consistent differences between the two groups were the teachers' expectations. This experiment provoked much controversy, but the researchers maintain that of 242 similar studies using a variety of subjects and situations (in offices, factories, swimming classes, and the like), 84 studies have demonstrated that teachers' expectations of their students' progress made a significant difference in how those students performed.

Four reasons are suggested for this effect, all of which are forms of positive reinforcement:

> *People who have been led to expect good things from their students, children, clients, or what-have- you appear to:*
>
> • *create a warmer social-emotional mood around their "special" students (climate);*
>
> • *give more feedback to those students about their performance (feedback);*
>
> • *teach more material and more difficult material to their special students (input); and*
>
> • *give their special students more opportunities to respond and question (output).*[7]

Once an environment is restructured using some artificial reward as a reinforcer, must these special conditions be maintained forever to prevent the person from returning to his old "bad" habits? Will the impact of a specific reinforcer, like a token or a pat on the back, gradually decrease with time, so that new rewards must continually be created to keep the person responding appropriately? Skinner rejects these arguments by pointing out that under the influence of the restructured environment, the individual learns new ways of perceiving and behaving which have their own natural rewards:

> *You don't need to maintain a system of contrived reinforcers indefinitely. People get the impression that I believe that we should all get gumdrops whenever we do anything of value. There are many ways of [phasing out] a system of reinforcement Certain schedules of reinforcement permit you to reduce the frequency of reinforcement steadily.* But the main thing is to let noncontrived reinforcers take over. The students who get prizes for doing their homework eventually discover the natural reinforcers of getting work done. *They discover that they are learning something, possibly in contrast with their brothers and sisters in other classrooms, but in any case something which makes them more successful. [Emphasis added.]* [8]

Behavioral Conditioning as Therapy

Can you remember a situation where you were so anxious that you were "clutched," "frozen," "uptight," "paralyzed with fear," or "panicked"? Was it because of an accident? An impending test or athletic contest? Because you were returning home to face your parents after violating their

WHO REWARDS YOU?

1. *Compare these two cases to identify who is reinforcing what behaviors.*

MARGARET is very shy and almost never speaks in class, but the teacher in home economics really got her to open up. Margaret asked a question last week, and Mrs. Shore looked at her for a minute, paused, and then said it was a very good question, that if more questions of that quality were asked, it would be helpful to the whole class. You should see Margaret raise her hand now, at least in that class.

MARLEEN hangs around with a pretty tough crowd that's always pushing through the corridors and doing something they shouldn't be doing during the noon break. Marleen is the leader of the girls in that group, probably because she is the loudest, the most foul-mouthed, and the first to take a dare. She almost prides herself on being a bad student, asking dumb questions in class even when she already knows the answer. When Marleen asked a question in class last week, the teacher commented that it was a good question, that if more questions of that quality were asked, it would help the whole class. Marleen was really embarrassed because some other girls from her group were in the class and they kept making teasing faces across the room. Someone passed a note calling Marleen "the star student." Needless to say, that was the last question Marleen has asked.

Why is the teacher able to successfully reinforce Margaret's class participation but not Marleen's?

What is the new factor that appears in Marleen's case?

Can you think of ways that your behavior is conditioned by reinforcement at school?

2. *Do you think that it is good educational practice to reward children for what they "should" be doing anyway? Or do you think that the children in the class who were paid to learn were simply being bribed?*

Will these children maintain their interest and progress once the rewards are removed?

Would you expect any harmful effects from this type of training?

3. *Would a behaviorist contract work in your family to lessen unpleasant arguments and misunderstandings? Pick out five of your behaviors that you think your family would like to have you change. Next, pick five unpleasant chores that you will agree to do without any prompting if you resort to one of the behaviors on your "to be modified" list. If, for example, you want to stop your habit of tossing clothes around your room, you might agree to do the dishes for two nights if any clothing is found lying around in your room. If the rest of your family agrees, include them in a family-wide contract. To complete the experiment, put your contract into operation for one week.*

Was your behavior modified during the week?

How do you explain what happened?

Did the undesirable behavior return after you stopped the contract?

Are you in favor of extending the contract for a longer time or to other habits?

In what ways is this contract based on reward?

Is punishment being used in this contract?

4. *Can friendship be explained as a type of mutual reinforcement between two friends? Consider the following:*

JOE AND MIKE were inseparable until Joe started working out with the school gymnastic team. Mike wasn't interested in gymnastics at all. For a while they continued to double-date on weekends, but Joe began spending most of his time hanging around with some of the other fellows on the gymnastic team. He had more in common with them than with Mike, who was spending most of his time tinkering with his car or studying.

Skinner says that a behavior will be maintained as long as it is rewarded by the environment. If there is no reward (or punishment), then the behavior will gradually disappear. Do Skinner's thoughts explain why Joe and Mike drifted apart? In what ways do friends reward each other? Can you give an example

> of a friendship where there is no mutual reinforcement?
>
> If you agree that friendship can be explained as a form of mutual reinforcement, would you also agree that love and marriage are based on the same mutually rewarding "exchange"?

clear instructions? Whatever your memory, try to imagine how it felt to be so tense. Keep that image in mind as you read the case study below.

Overcoming Fear (Desensitization)

FRANK was absolutely panic-stricken whenever he found himself in a social situation with a girl.[9] In fact, his anxiety was so extreme that it made him feel nauseous. This reaction was strongest when he arrived at his date's house, and would continue at a high level of intensity as they went out to the event of the evening. Frank's anxiety would diminish and sometimes disappear altogether once things got underway, particularly if the event of the evening was so absorbing that "small talk'" could be kept to a minimum. Needless to say, the pain and embarrassment of this strange fear kept Frank from having many dates and prevented him from living a full and satisfying life.

Frank explained his problem to a private counselor who practiced behavioral therapy. After several interviews with Frank, the counselor decided that the best way to remove this strong and irrational fear might be by a form of conditioning or retraining called *systematic desensitization*. This technique is based on a simple and natural skill that many of us overlook in our daily lives: the ability to relax.

The first order of business was to teach Frank how to put his entire body into a deep state of relaxation, quickly and effectively, whenever he wished to do so. There is nothing mysterious about this process. If you want to try it, find a comfortable place to lie down, and focus all of your attention on first tensing, then relaxing, each group of muscles in your body. Begin with your feet, then slowly work up your legs to your trunk, your fists, your arms, your neck, your face. With each muscle group in turn, tense it as tightly as you can and hold it for a slow count of five. Then relax the muscles, while whispering to yourself, "Relaaaax." Allow twenty minutes for practice, or until you become efficient at this systematic relaxation. Frank, under the direction of the trained counselor, learned to relax rapidly and thoroughly.

Some counseling sessions were spent assembling a list of situations that made Frank anxious, including some that were likely to upset him a lot, some that did not bother him at all, and situations falling between these two extremes. The final list, arranged numerically from the least disturbing to the most disturbing, is called an *anxiety hierarchy*. At the time he sought the help of the counselor, Frank was dating a girl name Alice. Here is his anxiety hierarchy about relating to Alice:[10]

1. Sitting at home in a comfortable chair, thinking only of relaxing.

2. Talking with friends at school; someone mentions "Alice."

3. Relaxing in a comfortable chair at home, thinking of Alice.

4. Writing a letter to Alice in a room at home.

5. Eating dinner with parents, discussing his going to pick up Alice.

6. Driving the car to Alice's house.

7. Reading a letter from Alice at his own home.

8. Talking with Alice on the telephone.

9. Driving past Alice's house, seeing her standing in the distance.

10. Driving up to Alice's house, seeing her coming out and walking toward him.

11. Driving with Alice in the car on the way to go sailing.

12. Walking around the schoolyard with Alice.

13. Talking to Alice inside her room; no one is around.

By now you may recognize that the counselor plans to use a behaviorist principle we studied earlier in this chapter. Frank's behavior will be shaped by overcoming his fears on a step-by-step basis, with each step being a "successive approximation" of the target behavior, which is being comfortable while alone with a girl.

Now that the relaxation training is successful and an anxiety hierarchy has been prepared, the counselor begins desensitizing Frank to the feared situations. Another name for this process is *counter-conditioning*, which means a conditioning designed to reverse a maladaptive or unhealthy conditioning that was instilled earlier. Frank places himself in a state of deep relaxation, and the counselor asks him to imagine as vividly as possible that he is actually experiencing whatever situation is selected from the list. If Frank reacts to this imagery with anxiety, he is to give a prearranged nonverbal signal, like raising a finger.

Since the therapist starts with the neutral situations near the top of the list, Frank does not signal for the first several situations. However, when Item 3 is suggested, he raises his finger. The counselor says "Okay, stop imagining that. Now to help you relax even more I am going to count from 1 to 10, and with each count you'll feel yourself sinking into a deeper and deeper relaxation . . ." As Frank's anxiety drops, he stops the signal, and the therapist then returns to the item ranked one step lower in anxiety and resumes the process.

Gradually, over a number of sessions, Frank learns to dispel the anxiety in all the listed situations by using his new tool, the ability to relax at will. Next, with the assistance of his counselor, Frank begins to transfer this new self-control to actual situations corresponding with items in his anxiety hierarchy. For instance, if he can dine at Alice's house with her parents present, an item causing comparatively mild anxiety, and feel no stomach upset, his confidence grows in his ability to master fears that have proven highly intense in the past. Furthermore, the behaviorist counselor will argue, the impact of this new learning will not be limited to the original circumstances. Frank's training in systematic desensitization has given him a specific skill that he can apply to other problems he may face in the future.

The Token Economy—A Motivating Environment

Imagine that you have just been appointed director of a ward in the state mental hospital. The behavior of the hundred patients in your ward is severely disorganized. They loll about on the beds and on the floors, never talk to anyone, and often refuse to eat. No one who has entered your ward as a patient has ever recovered sufficiently to be released from the hospital. When you took over, your instructions were clear: "Take all the money you need, but we want results!"

As a Skinnerian, you believe that behavior is always a response to conditions in the environment. Therefore, your first task is to analyze the structure of this hospital environment to see what impact it is having on the patients. Some unfortunate patterns of reinforcement are immediately apparent:

1. If a patient refuses to eat, a nurse spends extra time coaxing him, which is clearly a reward for the patient's disruptive behavior.

2. A patient who doesn't talk loses human contact but gains some measure of privacy.

3. All the pleasurable activities in the ward are open to everyone, even those patients who refuse to clean their rooms, who smash things, who cause fights, and are otherwise difficult to deal with.

4. Finally, since the hospital takes care of food, bed, medicine, cleanliness, and literally everything else, there is little *motivation* for patients to work at recovering their lost behavioral patterns that were suitable for independent life outside the hospital. In other

words, the hospital environment systematically
reinforces the very behaviors that it purports to
be curing.

Your next question might be: if you want to change the
environment so that it reinforces only desirable behaviors,
what can you use for rewards? In a real mental hospital,
two young behavioral researchers applied this strategy.[11]
They carefully observed how patients preferred to spend
their time under the existing hospital structure, and they
decided to restrict the patients' access to those desirable
activities. In the new system, to have the things they
wanted, patients would have to work at improving their
behavior—that is, to work at recovering a measure of the
independence and self-control that would eventually
permit a return to the outside world.

Every patient had individual preferences for rewards.
Since his or her reward might not be immediately
available, it was necessary to devise some sort of
temporary reward. The researchers decided to use
tokens, small plastic coins worthless outside the hospital
but very valuable on the inside! Whenever patients acted
appropriately, they were immediately given a specific
number of tokens which could be spent however they
preferred. Many pleasurable events that were formerly
open to everyone were now restricted to patients who
could pay for admission with tokens, including use of the
commissary, outdoor walks, religious services, music,
movies, and admission to the dining hall. The hospital
ward was turned into a small token-exchange system
modeled directly on the money-exchange system of the
outside world. The name of this technique is, naturally

285

enough, the *token economy*. Here is a series of short illustrations of how this process might work:

MR. WEST, a patient for one year, hated the lack of privacy in the ward. He stuffed his few personal possessions and some food items under his mattress, and he usually refused to leave the bedside for fear that another patient would raid his supply. The ward nurses confirmed that several other patients did the same thing. They also commented that almost all the patients went to great lengths to achieve some small measure of privacy in the open, barracks-like ward. As a result, the ward manager established two new reinforcers: (1) a row of locked cabinets with individual keys, and (2) portable canvas screens that could be placed around a bed. Both items were available for a set number of tokens. Soon thereafter, Mr. West, who had formerly avoided most social interaction with the staff or other patients, became more alert and eager to earn tokens whenever an opportunity arose. In a short time, he was able to purchase both a locker and a screen. As a beneficial side effect, his behavior improved markedly with his increased participation in social activities.

SEVERAL FIGHTS broke out in the dining hall over who was to sit at which table. One group of women who were usually in each other's company would try to reserve the table next to the window at each meal. This irritated other patients. Some patients would even get angry if they weren't able to sit in the same chair for each meal. The ward manager decided to adapt these preferences into reinforcers. Accordingly, a master schedule was set up whereby all patients were assigned to eat in different

286

groups on a regularly changing basis. To be exempt from this constantly rotating assignment, that is, to reserve a single chair or to eat with the same group of friends at each meal, it was necessary to spend a set number of tokens. For a group to eat together regularly, it was necessary to cooperate since everyone in the group had to choose to spend some of his or her tokens for this privilege.

Mrs. Smith seldom spoke to anyone; her favorite pastime was walking outdoors. Under the new token system, the nurses were instructed to immediately reinforce any appropriate verbal behavior, both by giving tokens and by taking prompt action to follow up on a request or complaint. For two months, Mrs. Smith would present herself for a walk outdoors, but since she had earned no tokens, she was not permitted to go. Still she did not complain, but simply wandered away dejectedly. On one particularly nice day, when the nurse refused her permission to go out, she muttered "not fair," her first words for many, many months. The nurse promptly handed Mrs. Smith a token, which happened to be the price of admission to the outdoor walk.

This scene was repeated for a week or so. Then, during a weekly staff meeting, a nurse from another area of the ward reported that Mrs. Smith had made her bed and cleaned up her clothes for the first time ever, and that afterwards, she had asked the nurse clearly and distinctly for a token as a reward. The staff was encouraged that Mrs. Smith was starting to recover her desire to communicate verbally.

The basic principle underlying token economies—controlling the structure of an environment in order to motivate a certain set of behaviors—has been applied in many settings. The school where children were paid to learn was a structured environment. Other examples include military training camps, prisons, and some family-style foster homes for delinquent adolescents.

The token economy example gives us some idea about how a behaviorist psychologist might approach social reform. Skinner and his followers believe that we ought to analyze our whole society to determine which types of present behavior we want to reinforce and which we want to discourage, and then design a social environment that fosters the desired behaviors. In a novel called *Walden II*, Skinner described a fictional community that carried out his ideas by organizing their environment to produce people who were happy and fulfilled.[12] Some people have tried to establish real communities based on these ideas.[13]

Many groups—including politicians, religious leaders, minority groups, and other psychologists—have strong opinions for or against Skinner's behaviorist views. Next, we will examine this debate about the issues of "freedom" and "dignity."

Are "Freedom" and "Dignity" Old-Fashioned Concepts?

The intentional design of a culture and the control of human behavior it implies are essential if the human species is to continue to develop. Neither biological nor cultural evolution is any guarantee that we are inevitably moving toward a better world ... extinct species and extinct cultures testify to the possibility of miscarriage.

B. F. SKINNER, *Beyond Freedom and Dignity*[14]

288

The word "freedom" has been used to inspire men and women for many, many years, but during that long life it has accumulated many different shades of meaning. Today, most people who are asked to say what they mean by freedom would probably say something like: "To be free is to do whatever you want or choose to do." The opposite of "freedom," in this popular view, is "control," whether from external sources or from processes inside the person. We also attach certain moral values to these concepts. We say that it is "good" to be free and "bad" to be controlled. We praise someone who performs a socially desirable act only if he "chose freely" to do it. We withhold our praise for someone performing the same act who was "forced to do it," who did it "because he or she *had* to," or who was merely "responding to social control" when he did it.

The implication of this traditional view is that people are "worth" more, are more "praiseworthy," or have more "dignity" if they have the ability to freely choose their actions. As an opponent of this traditional view, Skinner believes that it is a serious mistake to think that the terms "freedom" and "dignity" are *accurate descriptions* of human behavior or *adequate guides* for human values.

Three Cases: Who Should be Blamed? Who Should Be Praised?

Although Mr. Jones came from a very poor family, he worked his way into an important position in his company. He and Mrs. Jones started their own family knowing that they could give their children economic advantages that neither of them had known. Edward was the first child, and he was showered with attention. Each new achievement was noticed and praised. Three years later, Mary was born. Ted followed in two more years. All three children were personable, bright, and enthusiastic.

EDWARD was a dedicated student from the very start. He worked late at night on his homework and consistently brought home outstanding report cards. His mother and father noticed that Edward didn't bring friends home and didn't get involved in extracurricular activities, but they assumed that this situation would change eventually.

MARY followed Edward's lead, working enthusiastically in her classes. She received fewer outstanding report cards, but her personality was more easygoing and friendly. She liked working on committees and always was immersed in the problems of a friend or in group activities. During high school, she participated in every dramatic production by her class, and she hoped to be able to pursue this interest professionally after graduation.

TED, the youngest child, also worked hard in school, but his grades never reflected his effort. He often felt that his parents were disappointed that he didn't succeed in school as had Edward and Mary. Certainly there was never the same celebration when he brought his report card home. However, Ted had a gift for working with people, and from his earliest days always had a group of friends and younger children that wanted to be around him. They were often a boisterous, active group, and when Ted and his friends became teenagers, it was difficult for the high school to adjust to their mischievousness. Ted would never turn down a dare, and he collected a band of loyal followers equally rash and bored with school. It wasn't long before Ted's activities were noted by the local police. Still, his parents hoped that he would "outgrow" this stage. Then there were a series of incidents: shoplifting, driving under the influence of alcohol, and defacing public property. Feeling his parents' strong disapproval, Ted spent more and more time away from home with his friends.

Today, many years later, Edward is the manager of a large city bank and lives in a manner similar to his parents. Mary didn't become an actress, but her performance as a newspaperwoman was so successful that she has been promoted to a supervisory position with a television news staff. Ted, unfortunately, continued to drift aimlessly with a group of similarly alienated friends. He enlisted in the military service to break out of his rut, but two years later he returned with a less than honorable discharge for bad conduct. Only recently has he shown any signs of settling down. He is now working at a gas station and learning something about auto repair.

To understand the force of Skinner's argument, consider the three lives described above. Do you feel that Mary and Ed should be *praised* for making good choices and that Ted should be *blamed* for wasting his opportunities? If your initial response is to say "yes," think about the same question in another way. If you wanted to use the stories of Ed, Mary, and Ted to teach other young people how they should behave, would you be giving them any useful information by saying that Ed and Mary were "good" and that Ted was "bad"? What quality did Mary and Ed possess that Ted lacked? How can your audience *acquire* that quality that you find so praiseworthy? If you are finding these questions difficult to answer, let's look again at a behaviorist explanation.

The lives of Edward, Mary, and Ted diverged, the behaviorist will say, not because Ed and Mary had some inner moral or mental quality that Ted lacked, but because there were many small differences in how each of them was reinforced by the environment. Thus, to praise Mary and Ed while blaming Ted gives others no useful information about those three persons; it only provides information about the speaker himself. The primary function of praising and blaming is to tell the listener what the *speaker* will reinforce in the future: "Behave like Mary and Ed and I'll reward you; behave like Ted and there'll be no rewards!" If you are really interested in discovering what caused Mary, Ed, and Ted to behave as they did, the behaviorist continues, you must carefully examine the interaction between each individual and the circumstances of his or her environment. What each of us chooses to do is not an expression of free will. Behavior is always a response to conditions in the environment, as they now exist or as they existed at some important time in your earlier life. A response that is consistently reinforced will continue, while a response that is consistently ignored either will disappear or, in the case of such physiological needs as hunger, which don't disappear, will be distorted by the deprivation. Because the science of behaviorist psychology is still young and growing, it might not be possible to explain in detail how the lives of Ed, Mary, and Ted were controlled by conditions in their environment. Nonetheless, Skinner believes that eventually such an explanation will be possible.

292

If you accept this behaviorist view, the important issue is not whether actions are "controlled" or "free," for all human actions are controlled by environmental conditioning. Instead, the important issues are: *how* did the environment produce this specific behavior and *how* should the environment be changed to produce new and different behavior? What kind of control was used to condition Edward, Mary, and Ted? What patterns of positive reinforcement or punishment were administered by their parents, schools, church, and peers? What kinds of control might have worked better? Who was in a position to have exercised this new kind of control over the individual concerned?

Designing the New Society: Who Controls the Controllers?

What sort of person would you like to be? Because the prospects for achieving your goal depend basically on your environmental conditioning, another way of asking the same question is: what kind of environment would you like to live in? The behaviorist theories will *not* help you to decide what is desirable behavior, because that is a question of values rather than a question of learning technology. However, once you choose a target behavior, the Skinnerian psychologist will offer to teach you the principles you need to design a new environment, one that is especially adapted to reinforce behavior in the direction of your goals. Unfortunately, *anyone* can learn to use this behaviorist technology. There is no guarantee that it will fall only into the hands of persons who will use it for good purposes.

Dictators have relied, and continue to rely, on punishment as their basic principle of social control.

Indeed, one meaning of "freedom" in its traditional usage is to be rid of someone who can force you to do what you don't want to do, or who can punish you if you disobey his orders. Historically, freedom movements have been directed against this type of control, namely, punishment. Skinner believes that this struggle for freedom was very important and valuable, *but,* he warns, dictators in the future will not have to rely on such crude and ineffective methods of conditioning behavior. They too can read Skinner's books and see that reward is a more effective motivator than fear of punishment. A dictatorship in the future could be built by an effective use of reinforcement.

The critical issue for all humans, then, is: who will be in charge of designing and directing the new environmental structure? Who will control the controllers to insure that they work for the common welfare?

There are no easy answers. Skinner worries that some people do not even see the problem. They don't recognize that we cannot avoid responsibility for constructing our own future.

BEHAVIOR MODIFICATION IN ACTION

1. *Set aside twenty minutes during an evening at home to practice the systematic relaxation exercise described on page 281. Don't force yourself into a rigid pattern or worry that maybe you're not doing something right; just relaaaax. If the room is unavoidably noise-ridden, don't get upset. Let the sounds enter peacefully in one ear and go out the other. Do you feel different after this exercise?*

2. *In organizations like "Alcoholics Anonymous" and "Weight-Watchers," the members help each other to cope with their common problem. How is positive reinforcement used in such situations?*

3. *Do you think it is morally acceptable to set up token economies to control the lives of people who, for one reason or another, are unable to decide whether they want to participate? For instance, should we use token economies in mental hospitals? In nursing homes? In prisons or juvenile correction facilities? In schools?*

   Does the token economy method seem effective to you—that is, does it make people less dependent on the institution that is "preparing" them for outside life?

4. *You have just been notified that you will be a delegate representing young adults at the First National*

295

Assembly to Design Our Future. You will be expected (1) to give a short speech outlining what you believe are the three most important virtues that the nation should foster in young people, and (2) to describe how you want to restructure the present environment to achieve those goals. Jot down your ideas and be prepared to convince your classmates to support you as a delegate.

Will your reconstruction plans be applied to those delegates—and their constituencies—who voted against you, as well as to those who voted with you? If so, is it fair to decide the issue by a simple majority vote of the delegates?

5. *Suppose that you are a congressman or woman when two bills about behavioral conditioning are brought to the floor. The issues are controversial, but you cannot avoid voting. The television cameras are on you as you are called on for your voice vote. Which bill will you support? What reasons will you give to your constituents back home? Here are the bills in question:*

HOUSE BILL NUMBER 1

A bill to authorize $200 million to subsidize the costs incurred by those states that implement a thorough and scientifically valid program of behavioral modification in all levels of their state correction systems. Physical deprivation or torture is strictly forbidden as "cruel and unusual punishment," but in other respects states may permit a wide latitude of experimental modification programs.

The goal of this new program is to provide more effective rehabilitation to all prisoners, for their own good and for the protection of the citizenry, and to save public funds over the long run.

House Bill Number 2

A bill to prohibit the application of any and all theories or practices known as "behavioral modification" to shape behavior of children under the age of 18 in any public school, day care facility, rehabilitation ward, or other publicly supported institution in this nation, including correction facilities.

6. *A psychiatrist with a Freudian approach to personality read this chapter on Skinner's behaviorism. Afterward, he made this comment:*

"Some qualifying statements should be added to this chapter about the *uncertainties* of life, the *unpredictables,* the "grays" between the blacks and whites, about the difficulties of determining what is "good" and what is "bad." I think that it is important to counteract some of the simplicities of behaviorism with a reminder that life isn't all a matter of "right" and "wrong," of simple answers and easy solutions. This is an especially important message for adolescents who are undergoing the emotional turmoil of becoming adult."

How do you think Skinner would answer this psychiatrist? Which view do you find more convincing as a view of human behavior, the Freudian or the Skinnerian?

Suggested Readings

Bry, Adelaide, *A Primer of Behavioral Psychology* (New York: New American Library, 1974).

Carpenter, Finley, *The Skinner Primer: Behind Freedom and Dignity* (New York: The Free Press, 1974).

Goodall, Kenneth, "Field Report: Shapers at Work," *Psychology Today,* November, 1972.

Skinner, B. F., *About Behaviorism* (New York: Knopf, 1974).

Skinner, B. F., *Beyond Freedom and Dignity* (New York: Knopf, 1971).

Skinner, B. F., *Walden Two* (New York: Macmillan, 1948).

FOOTNOTES

1. Adapted from "Systematic Exclusion: Eliminating Chronic Classroom Disruptions," by David W. Keirsey in *Behavioral Counseling: Cases and Techniques* by John D. Krumboltz and Carl E. Thoresen (New York: Holt, Rinehart, & Winston, 1969), pp. 89-113.
2. *Ibid.*, pp. 89-90.
3. Adapted from William W. Cumming, "A Bird's Eye Glimpse of Men and Machines," in R. Ulrich, T. Stachnik, and J. Mabry, eds., *Control of Human Behavior* (Glenview, Ill.: Scott, Foresman, & Company, 1966), pp. 246-256.
4. Adapted from Findley Carpenter, *The Skinner Primer: Behind Freedom & Dignity* (New York: The Free Press, 1974), pp. 5-6.
5. B. F. Skinner, *Beyond Freedom and Dignity* (New York: Alfred A. Knopf, 1971), p. 63. Copyright © 1971.
6. Lois Wille, "Paying Children to Learn? St. Louis Gives It a Try," *The Boston Globe,* November 7, 1971.
7. Robert Rosenthal and Lenore Jacobson, "The Pygmalion Effect Lives." Reprinted from *Psychology Today,* September 1973. Copyright © 1973, Ziff-Davis Publishing Company. All rights reserved.

8. Elizabeth Hall, "Will Success Spoil B. F. Skinner?" Reprinted from *Psychology Today,* Magazine November 1972, pp. 65-72, 130. Copyright © 1972, Ziff-Davis Publishing Company. All rights reserved.

9. Adapted from Thomas J. D'Zurrilla, "Reducing Heterosexual Anxiety," in J. D. Krumboltz & C. E. Thoresen, eds., *Behavioral Counseling* (New York: Holt, Rinehart, & Winston, 1969), pp. 442-454.

10 *Ibid.,* p. 445.

11. Teodoro Ayllon & Nathan Azrin, *The Token Economy* (New York: Meredith Corporation, 1968).

12. B. F. Skinner, *Walden Two* (New York: Alfred A. Knopf, 1948).

13. Kathleen Kinkade, "Commune: A Walden-Two Experiment." Reprinted from *Psychology Today,* January & February 1973. Copyright © 1973, Ziff-Davis Publishing Company. All rights reserved.

14. Skinner, *Beyond Freedom and Dignity, op. cit.,* p. 175.

7.
The Electrical-
Chemical You

You are sitting in a bullring in Spain. A large fighting bull, bred to be so aggressive that it will attack a human, is pacing angrily, staring at a man who, unarmed and without a cape, has just stepped into the ring. This man, José Delgado, is a psychologist about to perform an experiment. His only protection is a small, black radio transmitter. The bull snorts, then charges at full gallop. Just as the horns come within striking range, Delgado raises the transmitter and pushes a button. Abruptly the bull wheels to the side, grinding to a halt within just a few feet of the scientist. The experiment is a success. How did he do it?[1]

You are now watching Delgado perform another experiment. A baby Rhesus monkey clings to its mother, who hugs and nurses it. First, to demonstrate the strength of the mothering instinct in these monkeys, Delgado temporarily removes the baby from the cage. The mother becomes very upset: she paces about, calls to her baby, and threatens other monkeys in the cage as well as the observers standing beside the cage. When the baby is returned, the mother resumes her earlier nurturing behavior.

Now Delgado begins the experiment by pressing his

radio transmitter. The mother monkey immediately drops the baby, moves away, bites her own hand and leg, and begins running around the cage belligerently. She ignores the baby's cries and rejects its attempts to approach her.

After about ten minutes of this strange display, she returns to her earlier, natural behavior just as suddenly as she departed from it. The mother and baby are reunited. Why did this happen?[2]

Delgado's final experiment involves more complex behavior. In the large cage in front of you is a colony of monkeys. You can observe their firm social hierarchy. The "boss" eats first, occupies the biggest share of space, and gets first pick of female companions. To maintain his position, he stares, paws, and growls at lower-ranking male monkeys who get out of line.

Delgado now introduces to the group a specially trained female monkey named Elsa. With Elsa present, the power structure in the colony begins to change. Elsa begins to stare directly at the head monkey—a highly aggressive gesture which provokes an immediate attack. The boss starts to move toward Elsa, but she runs to a part of the cage where a small lever protrudes. As she has been trained to do, Elsa presses the lever. This lever activates Delgado's radio transmitter. Suddenly the chief monkey stops, his fierce grimace disappears, and his other customary displays of power diminish. The lower-ranking male monkeys begin to walk freely around the cage, ignoring the boss's territory with no fear of punishment.

After ten minutes pass, the old power structure begins to reappear. Once again, the chief monkey begins to grimace and stare menacingly around the cage. All the monkeys drop back submissively—except Elsa. She reaches again for the lever, but Delgado takes her out of the cage and ends the experiment. Can you guess what was happening?[3]

Electrical Stimulation of the Brain

In these experiments, one animal—the bull, the mother Rhesus monkey, and the chief monkey—has small metal wires called *electrodes* implanted surgically in its brain. Attached on the outside of the animal's head is a small instrument called a *stimulator-receiver*. When Delgado presses a button on his radio transmitter, the stimulator-receiver picks up the signal and converts it into an electrical impulse. That impulse flows along the electrodes to a specific section of the animal's brain.

In each of these experiments, an electrical stimulus from outside the body sets in motion a complicated set of behavioral reactions: a bull diverts its attack, a mother monkey temporarily abandons her maternal instinct, and the dominance of a monkey chief is temporarily demolished. The type of reaction produced depends on the location of the electrode in the brain. By trial and error, researchers test the effect of stimulation at different locations and "map" which regions of the brain will, if stimulated, produce a certain type of behavior.

These experiments suggest that some sort of "electrical" system is important in starting, stopping, and maintaining a wide range of animal behaviors. Control of various behaviors is localized in specific regions of the brain. The brain also coordinates the specialized regions to produce the organized, purposeful behavior we usually observe in animals.

José Delgado described these experiments in his book, *Physical Control of the Mind.* He is a *physiological psychologist,* one of a group of scientists who believe that behavior can best be explained—and changed—by understanding the physical and chemical processes that occur inside the body. In each of the experiments, Delgado dramatically changed an animal's natural behavior by *intervening directly* in the electrical activity of the animal's brain. In this chapter, we explore this physiological perspective on behavior and contrast it with the perspectives of Freud (who analyzed *inner mental and emotional states*) and Skinner (who studied how the *environment shapes behavior*).

Electrical Stimulation in Humans

The human brain also responds to electrical stimulation. Doctors have applied electrodes to human brains for many years as an aid to brain surgery. By stimulating an area, they determine what function it performs, identify regions that must be protected during the operation, and diagnose disease or abnormalities in the brain. Electrical stimulation of the brain under these circumstances can produce many different types of behaviors such as:

A. Forcing the hand to clasp into a fist involuntarily.

B. Producing a direct sensation of intense pleasure, as indicated by the person's own statements, his outward appearance, and by his desire to continue or repeat the experience.

C. Changing the emotional tone of someone's behavior from one style to another—for instance, changing a person's customary withdrawn silence to a talkative style marked by friendly statements and gestures as long as the stimulation continues.

D. Altering mental and emotional states in otherwise normal persons to produce the following types of reactions:

1. *Illusions (visual, auditory, . . . memory or déja vu, sensation of remoteness or unreality);*

2. *emotions (loneliness, fear, sadness);*

3. *physical hallucinations (vivid memory or a dream as complex as life experience itself);*

4. *forced thinking (stereotyped thoughts crowding into the mind).*[4]

Because artificial stimulation of the human brain with electrical impulses produces such a clear impact on behavior, it is reasonable to expect that some sort of electrical process is closely related to our thoughts, emotions, and actions.

More evidence of our inner electrical activity is provided by the EEG (electroencephalograph) machine that "tunes in" to the short bursts of electricity that constantly fire in our brain. Eight electrodes attached outside the skull monitor the electrical impulses in eight different regions of the brain. These impulses are amplified to swing a thin wire with an inked tip between two magnets. As each wire swings back and forth, it traces a "wave-like" pattern on a paper rolling beneath it. The stronger the electrical impulse, the wider and more spiked the wave tracing.

The term "brain waves" refers to EEG recordings. In

effect, these "waves" are a visual "feedback" of the invisible electrical activity occurring inside the person.

EEG machines are used to study the brain's electrical activity while people sleep, dream, hear, feel, see, or engage in other activities. EEG readings are usually made while the person is lying down. Even the slightest movement of an eyelid produces a marked wave-motion in at least some of the eight tracings as the area of the brain that specializes in eye movement sends out strong electrical impulses. By observing the EEG patterns of many different types of people who are in a resting state, researchers have identified "normal" patterns of brain activity. Doctors can diagnose some brain diseases or disorders by comparing an individual's EEG reading with these "normal" standards. The EEG and similar machines are also important tools in psychological research.

A New Way of Seeing Yourself

You may wonder "What does all this have to do with *me?* What is important in my everyday life are my feelings, my needs, my thoughts—*not* the electrical currents inside me. Of what use is it to me to know that when I get angry, one type of electrical pattern occurs, while when I sleep, another type does?" This example might help answer your question.

Suppose that there were a "link" or "tie-up" between thoughts, feelings, or actions and a specific combination of chemical and physical processes that occurs inside your body. Accordingly, if you were observed to behave in a certain way—for example, to be severely depressed— then we could predict that the specific set of physical and chemical processes that accompany depression is also present. To help relieve your depression, we might

EXPLORING YOUR DREAMS
A SECOND LOOK

What happens to your body while you sleep? Puzzled by this question, William Dement and other physiological psychologists used the EEG and similar machines to measure electrical activity in the brain, in muscles around the eye, and in other muscle groups. They were startled to find that, instead of resting quietly throughout the night, we have periodic bursts of *active sleep*. Breathing becomes irregular, more blood flows to the brain, and small twitches occur in the face and fingers. Although the main muscles of the body are largely immobile, there is a series of rapid eye movement (REM) during active sleep. If the eyelids are pulled back, the dreamer appears to be following something with his or her eyes. If aroused at any point during a REM period, the subjects report dreams in progress that are much more elaborate and colorful than those reported during non-REM periods.

How often do REM periods (which we experience as dreams) occur? Dement writes:

An adult who sleeps seven and one-half hours each night generaly spends one and one-half to two hours in REM sleep . . . we dream roughly every ninety minutes all night long. After offering us several short episodes early in the night, the brain may produce an hour-long "feature film."[5]

Can REM periods (or dreams) be started by some internal stimulus, such as a full stomach or an urge to urinate, or by an external one, such as a sound or spray of water? Dement and his researchers found no relationship between the onset of REM periods, and either external or internal stimuli. For example, subjects who drank large quantities of water before retiring showed no variation from their regular REM cycle. Moreover, other findings indicated that for a short time at the end of all REM periods, no further REM activity will occur—just as a person who has eaten heavily will not feel the sensation of hunger for a while. Dement concludes:

> *The point is that the* occurrence of the REM period is determined by a physiological-biochemical process which is cyclic in nature. *Thus,* REM *periods and their associated dreams cannot be responses to randomly occurring internal or external disturbances.*[6]

Will internal or external stimuli influence the *content* of dreams, even if they do not initiate them? If they do not, then how can Freud's wish-fulfillment theory be true?

To influence the content of dreams, researchers have flashed lights, played the sound of train whistles or of the dreamers' voices, and sprayed water on dreamers' faces. In a sizable proportion of dreams, these external stimuli were incorporated in some related form in dream content, although the degree of incorporation varied depending on the type of stimulus.

The impact of internal stimuli is less clear. Volunteers undergoing prolonged starvation tests during World War II did not report an increase in dreams about food. Dement reports that subjects who were so thirsty that their lips were dry and their saliva gone still did not dream about being thirsty or drinking, although one third of these dreams did refer in passing to liquids.[7]

Citing these studies, Dement questions the Freudian wish-fulfillment theory. There seems to be little need for any dreamer to repress and distort a wish to eat or drink, he argues. Yet even under extreme deprivation, dream content did not incorporate references to hunger or thirst.

However, Dement describes another experiment where the results are less clear-cut. Soon after a REM period began, the subject was awakened, asked about his dream, and fed some banana cream pie. After three repetitions of this, the subject experienced his first dream-reference to food: he reported having coffee and a cigarette in the fourth dream. He ate another piece of pie. In the fifth dream, he was given spaghetti which he scraped into a garbage can. As he was awakened for the sixth time (after a *fifth* piece of pie), the subject reported: "Dr. Dement, I dreamed I was feeding *you* banana cream pie!"[8] A Freudian psychologist might argue that this experiment shows a dream incorporating external events (the pie and the experimenter), internal events (full stomach), and an emotional attitude or wish of the subject (to force the experimenter to eat the pie).

directly intervene to change the physical-chemical combination underlying the depression: a physician might prescribe an anti-depressant drug, or apply some electrical stimulation to your brain to remove the depression. If this were possible, then we would possess an important tool for understanding and curing some types of mental disorders.

In this chapter, we explore some of the present applications of the physiological approach to psychology.

These techniques are not as powerful as the above example suggests. However, the field is rapidly expanding. Therapies that treat the "electrical-chemical you" are usually combined with some of the methods of psychotherapy we have examined in previous chapters.

Some people are disturbed to learn that there are connections between their inner "felt" experience and a combination of physical and chemical processes in the body. "Where will this investigation lead?" they ask. "Using electrical stimulation or a new chemical, could someone turn other persons into 'robots'?" Before answering this question, we need more information about the brain and how it controls our body.

The Human Brain

Your brain is a central processing computer. Into the brain flow messages from your eyes, ears, nose, mouth, skin, muscles, and internal organs. Messages are sent from the brain back out to these parts of the body. The brain itself is composed of a large mass of billions upon billions of *nerve cells*. It is through these nerve cells, strung in long chains throughout the body, that the brain communicates with other parts of the body.

The main track for messages entering or leaving the brain is the *spinal cord*, a bundle of many nerve chains that runs down the center of the spine. At key locations, individual nerve chains split off to head toward other areas of the body. The Figure on page 310 is a simplified illustration of the human brain and nervous system.

The outside of the brain is folded in on itself, as indicated by the curved lines in the drawings. These folds

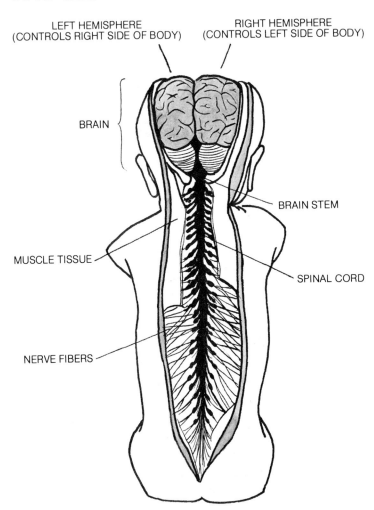

LEFT HEMISPHERE
(CONTROLS RIGHT SIDE OF BODY)

RIGHT HEMISPHERE
(CONTROLS LEFT SIDE OF BODY)

BRAIN

BRAIN STEM

MUSCLE TISSUE

SPINAL CORD

NERVE FIBERS

Information flows to and from your brain through long chains of nerve cells. This simplified drawing shows the relative location of the brain, the central bundle of nerve fibers called the spinal cord, and some of the nerves that branch out to the muscles and organs of the body.

permit many specialized sections to be cramped into the small area inside the skull. Notice that the brain has two halves. The right half controls the left side of the body and the left half controls the right side. Some nerve cells run between the two halves of the brain; these permit the brain to coordinate our behavior in an organized, integrated manner.

Earlier in this chapter, we learned that different regions in the brain specialize in controlling different aspects of our behavior. In fact, there are several "brains" that make up what we generally refer to as a single unit. The Figure on page 312 shows a general division between:

1. the *brain stem,* at the top of the spinal cord, that controls basic functions like breathing, heartbeat, sleeping, and temperature;

2. a centrally located region at the top of the brain stem which we refer to as the *old brain,* which controls, among other things, our emotions, general level of arousal, neuromuscular coordination; and,

3. the *new brain* (neocortex), a large mass with many folds that surrounds the old brain on three sides. The new brain controls a wide range of perceptions and behaviors, including speech, thought, and learning mechanisms.

The old brain and brain stem appeared much earlier in the evolution of life than the new brain. Dinosaurs, living approximately 150 million years ago, had primarily old brain and brain stem components. The modern crocodile,

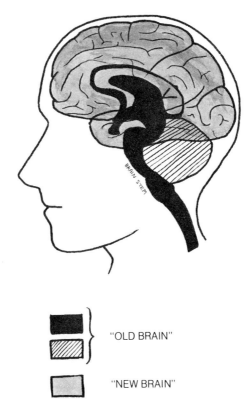

"OLD BRAIN"

"NEW BRAIN"

Several "brains" make up what we generally refer to as a single unit. The "old brain" segments control many bodily functions that seem as if they were automatic, while the "new brain" controls conscious and voluntary behavior.

a survivor of that ancient past, still has only a very thin cover of new brain over the predominantly old brain and brain stem, as illustrated in the Figure on page 316. The behavior of creatures like crocodiles and birds is governed largely by emotion and instinct.

THE RIGHT AND LEFT BRAIN

*If one is a wordsmith, a scientist, or a mathematician,
damage to the left hemisphere may prove disastrous.
If one is a musician, a craftsman, or an artist, damage
to the right hemisphere may obliterate a career.*[9]

Robert Ornstein's statement above about "right and left
thinking" dramatizes recent findings about the
specialization between the two halves of the neocortex,
or new brain. The left half primarily controls logical
thought and verbal expression, while the right half deals
with artistic creation, spatial perceptions (recognizing
faces or other geometrical patterns), general body
awareness and orientation, and the perception of
experience in integrated wholes or *gestalts*.

Evidence of the specialization between hemispheres
of the new brain comes from experiments with "split-
brain" patients. In these patients, the nerve cells
connecting the two halves of the new brain were
severed for medical reasons.

*Despite the radical surgery, these "split-brain"
people showed almost no abnormalities in their
everyday lives. However, Sperry and his associates
discovered, through many subtle tests, that the
operation clearly separated the specialized functions
of the two hemispheres.*

*If, for instance, the patient held a pencil (hidden
from his sight) in his right hand, he could describe it
verbally as usual. But if he held the pencil in his left
hand, he could not describe it at all. Recall that the
left side of the body is connected with the right*

313

hemisphere, which does not possess much capability for speech. With the corpus callosum [connecting nerves] severed, the hemispheres cannot communicate. So the verbal mechanism of the patient literally does not know what is in his left hand. If, however, the experimenters offered the patient a selection of small objects—a key, a book, a pencil, etc.—and asked him to choose the one he had previously held in his left hand, he could select the correct item. The patient could recognize a pencil; he just couldn't talk about one.[10]

Ornstein suggests that the functional difference between the right and left halves of the new brain may provide a physiological basis for Freud's distinction between conscious and unconscious mental processes:

Freud's famous dichotomy holds that the conscious mind largely controls language and rational discourse, while the unconscious is much less accessible to reason or to verbal analysis. The unconscious may communicate through gestures, face and body movements, or tone of voice. In split-brain patients, the verbal, rational system, disconnected from the source of information, may be countermanded by body language. A person may insist "I am not angry," yet his tone and facial expression indicate that he is furious.

Sperry demonstrated the "Freudian conflict" that occurs when the right hemisphere gets emotional input that the verbal hemisphere does not. He showed a photograph of a nude woman, among a series of otherwise dull pictures, to the right hemisphere of a [female] patient. At first the woman said that she saw nothing; but she immediately flushed, squirmed, and looked uncomfortable. Her "conscious" or verbal half was unaware of what had caused her emotional turmoil. All she knew was that something unusual was occurring in her body. Her words showed that the emotional reaction had been "unconscious," unavailable to her language apparatus.[11]

Ornstein's suggestion of a connection between Freud's psychological concepts and the specialization of the physical brain is only speculative. However, this comparison highlights how scientists can investigate a problem from different perspectives: as the product of "inner needs," as Freud did, or as electrical-chemical processes, as Ornstein and Sperry have.

As the new brain area increases, an animal's behavior becomes more complex and less instinctual. Mammals, and especially humans have a large area of new brain folded over the more primitive parts. This accounts for their more complex behavior. Nonetheless, even in the more complex animals, the old brain continues to play an important role through its control of emotional life.[12]

The new brain contains many highly specialized regions. If you apply an electrical impulse along different surface folds, you stimulate different responses. The Figure on page 317 illustrates the variety of reactions to stimulating one side of one fold, running from the top and middle of the new brain down both sides (fissure Rolandi). Because the right hemisphere is pictured, the electrical stimulation produces effects on the left side of the body. The forward side of this fold controls muscle

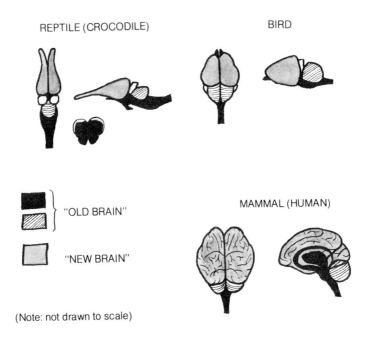

REPTILE (CROCODILE)

BIRD

"OLD BRAIN"

"NEW BRAIN"

MAMMAL (HUMAN)

(Note: not drawn to scale)

Mammals, and especially humans, have larger "new brains" than creatures such as birds and reptiles. As the surface area of the new brain increases by folding in on itself, behavior becomes more complex and less instinctual.

movement in the body. Starting from the top, an electrode touching the surface of the brain would produce movement first in the toes, then the ankles, the knees, the hip, and finally the face.

The distorted human figure stretched along the curvature of the brain illustrates how much of the brain area is allotted to the control of muscle movement in each part of the body.[13] We can see that control of the motor movement of individual fingers requires as much brain area as control of the remainder of the body below the

316

neck. Similarly, control of the motor movements in the mouth region alone occupies a large number of brain cells. A similar "homunculus" or human figure could be drawn to illustrate the sequence and proportional allotment of brain tissue concerned with body sensations which runs along the *rear* side of that same fold (fissure Rolandi). If artificially stimulated, this region would produce illusions of various sensations.

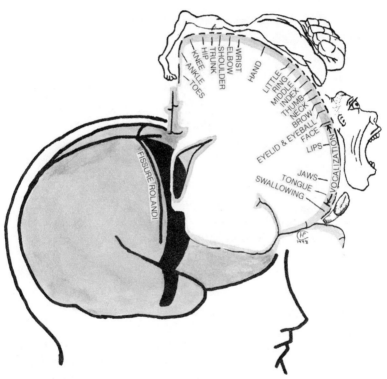

Electrical stimulation of the brain along the front side of the Fissure Rolandi will cause movement in the parts of the body illustrated in this drawing. The distorted features show the relative differences in the amount of brain tissue dedicated to the control of different muscle groups.

The Body's Messenger System

How are we able to produce movements or sensations in the body simply by applying an electric impulse along a fold of the brain? How does the message that a certain part of the body is to be moved get from the region of the brain that is electrically stimulated to the muscles controlling the desired movement? What types of behavior can be produced by this sort of electric stimulation? To answer these questions, we must look at the body's nerve cells that specialize in transmitting electric impulses.

Millions of microscopic nerve cells are strung together in long chains throughout the body. Messages to or from the brain are passed from cell to cell along these nerve chains or pathways. A similar message-transmission service takes place *inside* the brain, which we experience as perception, sensation, or thought. The nerve cells pass messages by means of electrical impulses, not unlike the way a telephone line passes electrical impulses which can be translated into human sounds at either end by the telephone apparatus. The electrical stimulation of the brain is similar to the tapping of a telephone line.

To understand how electrical impulses are passed from cell to cell, look at the Figure on page 319. Part A is a drawing of an actual nerve cell, consisting of a cell body, *inbound* fibers, and *outbound* fibers. Not that the outbound fibers from one cell do not actually touch the inbound fibers of nearby cells. The minute gap between the end tips of two cells is called a *synapse* (pronounced *sin*-aps). Understanding what takes place at this synaptic gap is the key to understanding how electrical stimulation of the brain can produce the results we described earlier.

Imagine for the moment that nerve cells, like people, have problems and make decisions. The basic "problem"

318

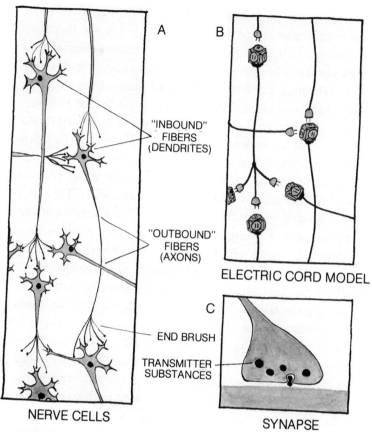

A

B

"INBOUND" FIBERS (DENDRITES)

"OUTBOUND" FIBERS (AXONS)

ELECTRIC CORD MODEL

C

END BRUSH

TRANSMITTER SUBSTANCES

NERVE CELLS

SYNAPSE

This enlarged and simplified drawing of microscopic nerve cells illustrates how electrical-chemical messages are sent to and from the brain. Current flows along the out-bound fiber(s) until the gap (synapse) separating cells is reached. The current then stimulates the release of a transmitter substance which "plugs" the gap, passing the current to the inbound fiber of an adjoining nerve cell (Parts A & C). The electrical extension cords in Part B provide a mechanical analogy of this process.

for a nerve cell is illustrated in Part B of the Figure on page 319. In this drawing, instead of actual nerve cells, there are several specially designed electric extension cords which work similarly to nerve cells. Each has a socket end which accepts inbound current and a set of plugs at the opposite end which carries outbound current. Note that the outbound plugs from these extension cord cells do not touch the inbound sockets of nearby cells. Therefore, this gap must be crossed (just as in actual nerve cells).

Assume for the moment that there *is* some way of stretching the plug end to reach a nearby socket. This does not necessarily solve the problem of how electric current is to be passed along the chain, for the problem then becomes choosing *which* plug is to be united with *which* socket! Many different combinations are possible. What method can be used to select among the alternatives? A switching decision must be made at each link in the chain of tiny extension cord cells.

The real nerve cell pictured in *Part A* has the same problem. To which of its neighbors should the nerve cell pass its message? How can it transmit the message across the synaptic gap? How can a continuous pathway be built so that the electrical impulse from the brain can travel along a chain of nerve cells to reach the target muscle or organ?

Nature has devised an ingenious and complicated switching system for the nerve cells. Nerve cells manufacture a group of specific chemical substances called *transmitters* which are stored in tiny sacs near the tips of outbound fibers. Electrical impulses cause the cells to release some of the transmitter chemical, which then flows across the synaptic gap, setting off an electrical reaction in the inbound fiber of the nearby cell.[14] In effect, the chemical transmitter "carries" the electrical impulse across the gap. (See Part C of the Figure on page 319.)

The chemical transmitters also help *switch* the impulse along the *specific* nerve pathway that it should follow. Although this switching mechanism is still not clearly understood, it appears to depend on the presence of *different kinds* of chemical transmitters which respond differently to various kinds or amounts of stimulation.

Some nerve pathways are already hooked up by the time you are born, including those that govern breathing, sucking, crying, and grasping. But there are many other types of behavior that we must *learn*. This suggests that some of the nerve switching patterns are developed through practice. Do you remember the last sport or handicraft you started to learn? In the beginning, you were probably very clumsy, but careful attempts to repeat the actions in a more controlled fashion eventually resulted in a smooth, sure skill. Scientists suggest that as you continued to use and reuse the same nerve chains during the practice sessions, the chemical transmitters at the tips of the individual nerve cells were affected so that electric pulses flowed more easily along that chain than along other possible routes.

Electrical Stimulation Revisited: Humans and Robots

Now we can return to the question that initiated our investigation. Can electrical stimulation of the brain provide a method for enslaving human beings? Science fiction writing is filled with stories of men and women forced to work for some evil power because electrodes are implanted in their brains. Could electrical stimulation force people to behave contrary to their usual patterns?

Given our present knowledge, the answer is a comforting "No!" *The stimulation of the brain merely sets in motion responses that people already have programmed inside them. It sets off an electrical impulse that runs along the pre-existing nerve pathways.* In Delgado's words, "The final result depends more on the structure and organization of components than on the trigger."[15]

Thus, although an emotional mood can be set, the way a person actually *translates* that mood into behavior will depend on all the complex factors that usually determine a person's behavior: personal history, social context, and the limitations of the physical environment. A skilled behavior can be *activated* if it has already been learned, but electrical stimulation of the brain will not direct the *acquiring* of a new skill. Although lost memories can be revived, strong emotions awakened, or hallucinations provoked by electrical stimulation of the brain, the actual content of these responses will depend on what the person has experienced during his or her life and on how that person learned to express his or her emotions. Simple motor movements or sensations can be stimulated, but it is not possible with our current knowledge to produce a set of coordinated behaviors that would together constitute a meaningful or purposeful action. Imagine how many different muscles and how many subtle judgments about distance, weight, and wind factors have to be coordinated just to throw a ball accurately!

In short, a person cannot impose his "will" on someone else using electrical stimulation of the brain, except perhaps to stop or interfere with some ongoing activity.

While the danger of humans becoming robots seems remote, there are important social issues raised by the use on human patients of electrical stimulation or powerful new drugs. In the following pages, we examine how some people with mental or emotional disorders are treated through techniques based on physiological psychology.

The Anticonvulsant Drugs and Epilepsy

In some historical periods, persons with epilepsy were believed to be "seized" by the gods. (The term *epilepsy* comes from the Greek word meaning "seized.") Alexander the Great and a number of other famous people are believed to have had this "sacred disease." In other eras, persons with epilepsy were regarded as bewitched. Today, with our greater understanding of physiological processes, we know that an episode of epilepsy—that is, a seizure—consists of a temporary change in behavior that occurs when there is a brief electrical disturbance in some part of the brain. The seizure may manifest itself in convulsions or merely a form of unconsciousness (e.g., see the quotation below). It may last from thirty seconds to five minutes. Afterwards, the person may be confused, tired, and sleepy for a short while. Epilepsy is not contagious and not dangerous to other persons. About one person in fifty has this problem. It usually appears before the age of twenty-one.[16]

The Epilepsy Foundation of America gives this generalized description of epilepsy in a pamphlet:

> *Tiny parts of our brain, called cells, give off a kind of electricity. When I have a seizure, it means that, all of*

a sudden, my brain is giving off too much electricity. It's like a lightning storm . . . striking all at once, then going away.

Some seizures are called "grand mal," which means "big sickness." But there are other kinds of seizures, too. Some people have "little" seizures which can look just like daydreaming. Other people make funny movements without knowing it, like pulling at their clothes or smacking their lips.

I don't have seizures very often any more, because I take medicine to keep them from happening . . . it is very important to take my pills every day. About half the people with epilepsy can stop their seizures by taking . . . medicines. Others still have a seizure once in a while, even though they take their pills. . . .

If I ever have a seizure when you're around . . . there's not much you can do. You might make sure I don't fall on anything that'll hurt me. Or if you have a handkerchief, you could put it between my teeth to keep me from biting my tongue. When I wake up, I probably won't remember what happened. . . . [17]

The discovery of anticonvulsant drugs illustrates a physiological approach to understanding and changing behavior. Using EEG machines, scientists observed that seizures were accompanied by unusual brain wave patterns in some parts of the brain. Some nerve cells were apparently discharging electricity prematurely and in a disorganized manner. Is there a drug, researchers wondered, which would reduce the excitability of the misfiring nerve cells? They conducted many experiments with animals, artificially producing seizures and then administering different chemicals. When they found a

YOUR BODY AND YOUR MIND

1. *Why do some people fear research in the physiological roots of human behavior? Do you think that these fears are justified? Is there a limit beyond which psychologists should not go in trying to influence human behavior?*

2. *People who have had bad experiences with drugs often cannot understand why they did not feel "high." Can you find an explanation for this in the discussion of "humans and robots"?*

3. *Imagine that a drug is discovered that produces a feeling of complete satisfaction, no matter what problem a person has. What would be the social implications of such a discovery? In what ways should use of the drug be controlled, if at all? For a fictional account of such a drug, see Aldous Huxley's description of "soma" in* Brave New World.

chemical that effectively counteracted the seizures without harmful side effects, they experimented with human volunteers. As a result, we now have several types of anticonvulsant drugs which are effective for many different (but not all) types of epilepsy. People with epilepsy can lead full and active lives, marrying, working, and playing like anyone else, if they take their medications regularly and take common sense precautions.

The most important problem for epileptics is that

uninformed people may overreact when they learn of the condition. These reactions are unfortunate because the problem can be successfully treated and minimized under medical supervision.

Anticonvulsant drugs are a significant factor in improving the lives of many persons with epilepsy. Chemical treatments have also been developed for certain types of mental illness.

The Psychotherapeutic Drugs[18]

Many people recover from their occasional bouts of sadness and depression either spontaneously or with the help of a friend or psychotherapist. However, sometimes a depression becomes so severe that it cripples the person's ability to perform even the simplest tasks of everyday life. This kind of depression may not respond readily to psychotherapy. However, a new tool for fighting severe depression and other mental disorders has been developed in recent years through biochemical research.

Almost by accident, researchers found a chemical with a structure similar to that of the chemical transmitters that pass electrical messages between nerve cells. Other researchers gave the new drug to severely disturbed mental patients, whose behavior improved significantly. This success set off a world-wide search for other drugs that would produce similarly impressive effects with other types of mental disorders. As a result of this research, psychiatrists today have a variety of drugs that can be used to treat mental disorders. The anti-depressant drugs can relieve the crippling sadness of some patients.

Anti-psychotic drugs can stop hallucinations that occur in some types of schizophrenia or acute drug poisonings, and they can calm the frenetic activity of a person who is manic.

The success of these chemical treatments suggests that some forms of severe depression or psychotic experience are related to a biochemical imbalance or disorder in the brain. How chemicals produce these improvements is still not fully understood. It is likely, however, that the drugs affect the activity of the chemical transmitters in the body's nerve cells, facilitating the passage of electrical impulses along certain nerve pathways and inhibiting passage along other routes.

Not all persons with mental disorders respond to chemical therapies. Therefore, research into the physiological processes underlying mental and emotional disorders continues. The focus of physiological psychologists on understanding the electrical-chemical you will continue to have tremendous importance as knowledge about our bodies expands.

Brain Surgery: The Case of Julia S.[19]

JULIA, an attractive and pleasant blonde who looked younger than her 21 years, developed a rare form of epilepsy after a childhood accident. Occasionally, her behavior became unpredictably violent, which made her a danger to other persons. Once, in the ladies' room of a movie theater, as she was experiencing some frightening thoughts and feelings, a stranger brushed past her arm. In a sudden panic, Julia grabbed a knife from her purse and stabbed the other woman. Another serious attack occurred in a mental hospital. Julia asked the nurse for help, saying that she felt the same strange feelings as before. When the nurse delayed a moment to finish some other task, Julia suddenly grabbed the nurse's scissors and stabbed her.

By the time Julia and her parents came to see Dr. Vernon Mark, a leading brain surgeon, they had tried—without success—all the types of medical treatment that could be prescribed for Julia's problem, including psychotherapy, many different drugs for emotional disturbance and for counteracting seizures, and a long series of electric shock treatments. They came to the hospital as the last alternative to placing Julia in a custodial institution for the rest of her life.

To help Julia, Dr. Mark applied a variety of techniques that we are familiar with from our study of electrical stimulation of the brain. After his initial investigations confirmed the presence of some abnormal electrical discharge patterns in Julia's brain, Dr. Mark worked to pinpoint the exact location of the abnormal waves and to see how the brain waves related to Julia's behavior. He drilled tiny holes in Julia's skull and implanted electrodes in the *amygdala*, a part of the old brain that influences emotion. A "combined stimulator-receiver" (like that used by Delgado) was attached to her head in order to radio reports to an EEG machine. This permitted observation of the electrical activity in those areas of Julia's brain where abnormalities were suspected. Also, at some time during each day, doctors would radio a burst of electrical stimulation to her brain through the "stimulator-receiver" to test its effect on her behavior.

On several occasions during their observations of

Julia, the doctors saw wildly swinging waves appear on the EEG, followed by Julia's characteristic rage behavior. She "narrowed her eyes, bared her teeth, and clenched her fists—that is, she exhibited all the signs of being on the verge of making a physical attack."[20] Some times this seizure was caused naturally. At other times, the same behavior was elicited by the electrical stimulation. In one dramatic instance, Julia was peacefully singing and playing her guitar (with no abnormal wave activity on the EEG). Then an electric signal was sent by the doctors:

> *After five seconds of stimulation, Julia stopped singing and stared blankly ahead. During the next sequence she slipped out of communication and was unable to answer the questions posed by the psychiatrist who was examining her. A cascade of abnormal spike-like epileptic brain waves from her amygdala was then recorded. . . . This was followed by a sudden and powerful swing of her guitar. She narrowly missed the head of the psychiatrist, and instead the guitar smashed against the wall.*[21]

Using these observations, Dr. Mark identified the amygdala as the source of the violent seizures. A small number of these abnormally firing cells were then destroyed, using the electrode. The destruction was very precise in location and very controlled in amount. The risks to Julia were lower than in an open-skull operation where infection or other accidental injury might occur.

What was the effect of this surgery on Julia? Dr. Mark reports that in the five years since the operation, she has had fewer seizures and no attacks of uncontrollable rage. She is able to live at home rather than in an institution and she recently passed her high school equivalency exam. An underlying psychosis (that is, a problem in perceiving and interpreting reality) that Julia already had when she came to Dr. Mark is still present, but the operation was intended to remove only the abnormal electrical discharge and the violent behavior associated with it, not to affect this other problem. The results as reported by Dr. Mark appear to have benefited Julia and her parents, given the unpleasant alternatives that would have been likely if her rage attacks had not been treated. Not everyone agrees with this conclusion, however. There is an intense debate between supporters and opponents of brain surgery.

Brain Surgery—Pro and Con

The basic arguments of each side are presented in the fictionalized account below. Which arguments do you think are most convincing? Why do you think brain surgery causes such marked differences of opinion?

BRAIN SURGEON:

While it *is* true that we don't know everything about the brain, we are not performing these operations without professional justification. There are thirty years of clinical evidence about brain function, many animal experiments with psychosurgical techniques, and even human cases. These have shown that if this type of surgery is properly practiced, it can help alleviate painful behavioral problems that are associated with the abnormalities in the physical functioning of the brain. This type of surgery is restricted to persons who have tried every other form of treatment without success. The fact that our knowledge about the brain is not complete should not stop our use of this type of surgery. After all, many medical treatments that are used routinely today are without any extensive theoretical justification. They just work, so we continue to use them.

OPPONENT A:

The brain is a sacred part of the human being, since consciousness—the unique aspect of mankind that gives us a spiritual existence—resides in that physical material. To allow a part of that matter to be destroyed is irresponsible and immoral. Scientists should not tamper with the core of a person's being.

OPPONENT B:

While there is nothing wrong with this type of brain surgery *in principle*, its present use is premature. We simply don't know all the effects of this surgery on the patient because the whole process is so new. A patient's personality might be irreversibly altered in subtle, unexpected ways that are difficult to detect. The doctors who are performing the operations are the ones who are reporting the follow-up information. They are apt to be biased in their interpretations because they *believe* that they are right. Often these doctors are very specialized, and are neither interested in or trained for analyzing the results in terms of the whole person (as opposed to analyzing the absence or presence of a particular disease).

ANOTHER INTERESTED ONLOOKER:

This field of medicine may have a lot of potential, and it would be foolish to prohibit it outright by enacting state or federal laws. However, there is a critical need to develop standards for how brain surgery is to be used. There is a particular danger that such a powerful and irreversible technique might be used to control persons who cause trouble in large custodial institutions like mental hospitals and prisons. Even in the individual cases that are presented for brain surgery, there is a need to determine that this method is in fact the only alternative treatment left since others have failed. Until legislation is passed to regulate these matters, hospitals should at minimum require an independent and impartial panel to interview the patient and his or her family. The panel should ensure that the patient's and/or family's consent to this operation is given only after full disclosure of information about the benefits and consequences that might result.

Biofeedback Training: Revealing the Body to Itself

You feel tense and on edge. Your body responds with tightened muscles, clammy palms, faint traces of a churning stomach and perhaps even an ache in your neck or forehead. You feel "tight," "anxious," "irritated," "uneasy," "worried," "upset." You probably recognize that these physical symptoms are typical reactions to emotional stress. However, stress has been an unavoidable part of your life for so many years that you no longer concern yourself with it. You can only think of your important responsibilities, of other people's expectations, of an endless list of small duties that must be discharged immediately.

There are many situations in modern life that make it difficult to get away from emotional stress. Getting away from it all is doubly difficult if you don't feel in touch with yourself, if you carry a residue of anxiety and tension learned early in your life. If you can't avoid the stressful modern environment or your own anxious inner feelings, you may feel normal and relaxed even when your body is still mobilizing your muscles, heart, stomach, and other organs for "fight or flight."

Many of these physiological reactions to stress seem to occur automatically, outside your voluntary control. The reason is that these processes are controlled by the old brain and brain stem rather than the new brain. When electric messages pass up the nerve pathways toward the brain, they reach these more primitive areas first. The messages that control heart rate, breathing, temperature, muscle tension, stomach acid secretion, and alertness are screened out and managed in this part of the brain. Because they are not amplified and boosted into the new brain, these messages usually don't come to your attention. This division of labor among brain parts allows you, for example, to sleep without worrying that your breathing will stop, and to run without thinking about each individual muscle movement.

While it works well enough under normal conditions, the old brain may not respond adequately to the rapidly changing circumstances of modern life. For example, it may continue to signal your muscles to tense, your blood pressure to rise, and your heart to pump faster, even though you are supposedly resting at home in your easy chair after a hard day's work. This constant overstimulation of the body, if prolonged over many years, can damage body tissues.

Researchers who study *psychosomatic medicine,* that is, how the mind and body interact to produce or maintain illness, believe that tension and anxiety contribute to many physical ailments, including heart attacks, migraine, low back pain, asthma, obesity, skin rashes, extreme fatigue, and ulcers. Doctors must always be alert to discover and treat psychological factors that are interacting with the physical symptoms of an illness. Unfortunately, there is often no easy way to decrease the strain on the body by relieving tension and anxiety.

Biofeedback training is a new approach to the old problem of how to control our physiological reactions. The basic method is the design of an artificial channel for electrical impulses that bypasses the screen imposed by the brain stem and old brain. Like other body functions, the physiological processes that control the heart, stomach, muscles, and other organs are controlled by the millions of electric messages passing to and from the brain along the nerve pathways. Using special instruments, we can tune in a specific set of electrical impulses, amplify them, and then convert these amplified impulses into signals that can be heard or seen.

One example of a biofeedback instrument is the EEG machine that converts the electrical impulses of the brain into wave-like tracings on a roll of paper. Another example is the famous "lie-detector," or polygraph, which is a collection of several biofeedback instruments. The operator questions a subject while the polygraph records changes in breathing, in blood pressure and pulse, and in the electrical tension of the skin. Because mental and physiological processes are so closely intertwined, questions that provoke anxiety also produce unusual physiological responses. These are picked up by the machine and converted to tracings on a roll of paper. By measuring the anxiety level around a particular issue, the polygraph alerts the operator to probe that issue more thoroughly. An unusual physiological response to a question is not a reliable indicator of guilt or innocence because people might be anxious for many different reasons.

In recent years, biofeedback machines have been used to teach people to control their own bodies more effectively. Once biofeedback reveals the pattern of electrical activity in some part of the body, a person can often learn to change it. At first, this is by trial and error. Later, there is a growing ability to distinguish directly among physiological states. The biofeedback experiments that follow illustrate the dramatic results produced by this new method of training.

ELECTRODES ATTACHED to the scalp and neck muscles of some headache patients fed reports of the electrical activity in those muscle groups into an instrument that produced a series of tones. The tones increased in pitch as the amount of electrical activity (tension) in the muscles increased. After a training period lasting from four to eight weeks, these persons learned to *recognize* rising tension in the head and neck areas even without hearing tones and to *avoid* headaches by relaxing those muscles.[22]

PERSONS WHO HAD LOST an arm or leg were taught to direct the movement of a specially designed artificial limb by tensing specific muscles at the amputation site. To use such a device, the patient was taught to activate individual muscles using biofeedback techniques. A flashing light signaled that the correct nerves were being fired. After some practice, the subjects could separately control the contractions of individual muscles. Once this occurred, these muscles were connected by electrodes with the controls that directed the movement of the artificial limb. By tensing the appropriate muscle, the person produced a corresponding movement in the artificial limb.[23]

WHENEVER SOMEONE FEELS a strong burst of emotion, the skin produces an electrical response. Some experimenters are trying to determine if this reaction can be used by a psychotherapist and patient to identify emotionally troubling areas more efficiently than by unaided discussion. The skin response is also under study as a clue to the presence of certain mental disorders, like schizophrenia.[24]

BIOFEEDBACK RESEARCHERS hope to find the connection between the different wavelike patterns produced by the swinging wire of the EEG machine and specific emotional states as they are felt by the person. While the connection between electrical activity in the brain and inner emotional experience is still speculative, it has been demonstrated that people can learn to control which type of wave they produce. In one dramatic illustration of this control, electrical impulses of the brain were converted into power to run a toy electric train. Whenever *alpha* waves were present, the train began to run along the track, and its speed was proportional to the strength of the alpha electrical activity![25] The finding that people can control which brain waves they produce may become important if researchers can show that certain brain-waves have beneficial effects on emotions and behavior.

Biofeedback instruments help us to identify what is happening inside our bodies and train us to control our own physiological processes. This psychological research may lead to discovery of an early warning system that can predict the potential for future illness by locating the effects of stress on our body tissues. Research may also result in a method for training large numbers of people to live healthier and more productive lives through systematic tension control.

Biofeedback Is Not a Game

One problem with biofeedback, as with any scientific tool, is that it can be used by careless or misguided people as well as by those who are intelligent and well-trained. It is not wise to allow just anyone to monitor your hidden physiological responses and to interpret their meaning to you. Before participating in any experiment with biofeedback instruments, you should make sure that the supervisor is well trained, has a good reputation among scientists or therapists, and that the information will not be used to harm you.

Persons who have unusual or abnormal electrical patterns in the brain should avoid an attempt to artificially influence their brain waves. This is particularly true of persons who habitually use drugs or who have epilepsy.

A final consideration is that the biofeedback instruments must be working properly to provide meaningful results. Thus, if a machine is not well adjusted or is reacting to electricity from sources other than the subject, the readings will be worthless.[26] It is best to treat biofeedback training as you would any strong medicine until we understand more about it and how it affects your personality.

THE NEW TECHNOLOGY:
WHAT ARE THE LIMITS?

1. *A biofeedback instrument has been used in each of the situations described below. As you read each case, decide whether or not you think that the use was good for the person involved, or good for society, and whether or not there are any dangers:*

WILLIAM always feels worried and tense, even though he can't identify exactly what it is that bothers him. When he should be having the most fun—on a date or while playing sports—he clams up, makes mistakes, and generally ruins the activity for himself and the others too. Now he is going to a psychological clinic connected with his school. The counselor there is using some instrument attached to William's skin that registers whenever he feels a strong emotion. William was astounded to see how quickly the counselor could pick out the types of situations that produced especially painful reactions. Their discussions of these items are beginning to help William to identify what types of things bother him and why. He is hopeful that he will eventually be able to remove some of the causes of his anxiety.

LEW is enthused about a new cult he just joined. To join, it is necessary to go through a special process called "coming clear" that Lew found to be very positive for him. Another member of this cult operated a polygraph (lie detector) that was attached to Lew while Lew confessed what it was about his life up to that point that made him feel unworthy. Several times, when Lew tried to downplay certain events in his past that he was ashamed of, the operator noted Lew's emotional reaction on the polygraph and pushed him to tell more about those experiences, to hold nothing back. It was refreshing to get all of that out and to have other people accept you even though they knew so much about you. Now that Lew is a member of this cult, he is learning to be the guide for other newcomers. When you see him at school, he keeps pestering you to come see for yourself what the cult is really like. Should you give in?

You have just graduated from high school and are applying for a job as a bank clerk. After looking thoroughly at the very long questionnaire you filled out, the interviewer asks you if you would mind answering a few questions. "It's just a formality," he says. "Since it's clear from the questionnaire that you have nothing to hide, I'm sure that you won't mind. It'll just take a few minutes." He leads you into the next room, where you see a chair next to a complicated-looking machine with several graphs. You suddenly remember what you learned about lie detectors, and you also recall that you got involved with juvenile court when you were eleven years old for shoplifting. It was your first offense, so the judge dismissed it and ordered the record destroyed. You never got involved in such things again. Still, you are certain that they will ask you now, "Have you ever been involved with the law?" You're going to react to that, they'll find out, and you'll lose the job. What should you do? How do you feel about being put in this bind? Although you're afraid and angry, you believe that a bank needs people it can trust, so maybe it should have the right to subject people to this. What do you think?

2. *Suppose that there is a very effective chemical or surgical treatment that will control persons who commit violent acts. Should society have the right to force persons convicted of violent crimes to undergo this treatment, or should the criminal have the right to refuse the treatment?*

3. *Do you believe that direct manipulation of the chemical and electrical system of the body is a form of treatment as morally acceptable as the psychoanalytic or behaviorist therapies? Why or why not?*

The Complexities of Human Behavior:
Some Concluding Questions

In this section, we have explored three perspectives used by psychologists to explain why we think, act, and feel as we do. What do you think is the most important ingredient in an explanation of behavior? Is it the person's self-awareness and the "push and pull of inner needs"? Is it the pattern of rewards in the environment that really controls behavior? Or is it the intricate interplay of electrical and chemical processes that best explains how we think, act, and feel?

The science of psychology is expanding rapidly and simultaneously along these three paths. Some believe that one approach will eventually dominate the study of behavior, while others believe that the different perspectives will gradually be integrated into a single, coherent theory of human behavior. In the competition among the different scientific theories, the crucial test is whether or not an explanation can *predict* what behavior will result if a certain action is taken. The more effectively a theory can predict the connection between *stimulus* and *response,* the more effective it will be as a tool to change behavior in ways that an individual or society considers desirable.

Personal preference also influences the choice among alternative approaches. A psychologist may begin working within one theoretical perspective because he or she finds it appealing. Usually, this subjective choice will be justified in objective terms: the more *appealing* perspective is seen as most *effective* for predicting behavior.

CHOOSING YOUR PERSPECTIVE

1. *Which of the three approaches do you think gives the most effective predictions of how people think, feel, and act? Do you think that the three perspectives are so different that they can never be integrated into an overall theory of human nature, or do you think that a combination of the three would provide the best explanation of behavior?*

2. *Which of the three perspectives do you find most appealing? Which least appealing? How do you explain your preferences?*

   Suppose that the approach you find *least* appealing began to outdistance the other theories as a predictor of behavior. What implications do you anticipate—both for yourself as an individual and for society—from the widespread acceptance and increasing dominance of that "unappealing" view of human nature?

3. *We studied the three approaches to psychology in separate chapters, each designed to present one view in its most favorable light. Because of this design, some important questions were not addressed. Can each theory explain all kinds of behavior? When is one approach appropriate and another not? Look at the following situations taken from each chapter. Do all three psychological approaches offer a reasonable explanation for that behavior? Which theoretical perspective do you think applies best in each case?*

a. *The case of Stephen B. was discussed in the chapter on B. F. Skinner. How might a Freudian psychologist explain Steve's behavior, using the concepts of id, ego, superego, anxiety, and defense mechanisms? How would he suggest that Steve's behavior could be changed? How would Maslow, Rogers, or Glasser approach Steve's problem? Can you think of any explanation of Steve's behavior based primarily on physiological processes? What methods would psychologists who take this approach use to investigate his problem? If they found some physiological problem, what types of therapies would they be likely to suggest?*

b. *Julia S., the girl who underwent brain surgery, took this dramatic step only after she and her parents had tried every other method of treatment without success. What sort of therapies do you think might have been used with Julia before the brain surgery? (You should be able to suggest one possibility from each of the three chapters, including an electrical-chemical approach other than brain surgery.)*

c. *Select one story that illustrates a defense mechanism in the Freud chapter. How does Freud explain the behavior described? Can you explain how a defense mechanism might be learned and maintained using Skinnerian concepts of reinforcement? Do physiological theories offer any alternative explanations of the "defensive" behavior?*

Suggested Reading

Brown, Barbara, *New Mind, New Body* (New York: Harper and Row, 1974).

Chorover, Stephan, "Big Brother and Psychotechnology II: The Pacification of the Brain," *Psychology Today*, May 1974.

Delgado, Jose, *Physical Control of the Mind* (New York: Harper and Row, 1969).

Hart, Leslie, *How the Brain Works* (New York: Basic Books, 1975).

Huxley, Aldous, *Brave New World and Brave New World Revisited* (New York: Harper and Row, 1932, 1958).

Lykken, David, "The Right Way to Use a Lie Detector," *Psychology Today*, March 1975.

Mazur, Allan, and Leon Robertson, *Biology and Social Behavior* (New York: The Free Press, 1972).

Pines, Maya, *The Brain Changers: Scientists and the New Mind Control* (New York: Harcourt, Brace and Jovanovich, 1973).

Snyder, Solomon, *Madness and the Brain* (New York: McGraw-Hill, 1974).

FOOTNOTES

1. José Delgado, *Physical Control of the Mind* (New York: Harper & Row, 1969), p. 168.
2. *Ibid.*, pp. 166-168.
3. *Ibid.*, pp. 164-166.
4. *Ibid.*, pp. 114, 143, 149, 153.
5. William C. Dement, *Some Must Watch While Some Must Sleep* (Stanford: Stanford Alumni Association, 1972. Subsequent edition, San Francisco: W.H. Freman and Company/ Charles Scribner's Sons, 1974. Copyright © William C. Dement, 1972, 1974, pp. 29, 37, 65, 69.

6. *Ibid.*, p. 37.
7. *Ibid.*, p. 69.
8. *Ibid.*, p. 65.
9. Robert E. Ornstein, "Right & Left Thinking." Reprinted from *Psychology Today*, May 1973, p. 88. Copyright © 1973, Ziff-Davis Publishing Company. All rights reserved.
10. *Ibid.*
11. *Ibid.*, p. 90.
12. Vernon H. Mark and Frank R. Ervin, *Violence and the Brain* (New York: Harper & Row, 1970), pp. 14-24.
13. Mrs. H. P. Cantlie, (c) 1948, in Wilder Penfield & Theodore Rasmussen, *The Cerebral Cortex of Man* (New York: Macmillan, 1950), Figure 22, p. 57.
14. Julius Axelrod, "Neurotransmitters," *Scientific American*, June 1964, Vol. 230, No. 6, p. 58.
15. Delgado, *op. cit.*, p. 182.
16 Epilepsy Foundation of America, *Epilepsy School Alert*, 1973.
17. Epilepsy Foundation of America, *Because You Are My Friend*, 1973.
18. Leon Eisenberg, "Psychiatric Intervention," *Scientific American*, September 1973, Vol. 229, No. 3 p. 117.
19. Mark and Ervin, *op. cit.*, pp. 97-108.
20. Mark and Ervin, *op. cit.*, p. 99.
21 Mark and Ervin, *op. cit.*, pp. 105-106.
22. Thomas Budzynski et al., "Feedback-Induced Muscle Relaxation: Application to Tension Headache," in Theodore X. Barber et al., eds., *Biofeedback and Self-Control*, 1970 (Chicago: Aldine, Atherton, 1971), pp. 447-453.
23. Barbara Brown, "New Mind, New Body." Reprinted from *Psychology Today*, August 1974, p. 84. Copyright © 1974, Ziff-Davis Publishing Company.
24. *Ibid.*, pp. 56, 74.
25. *Ibid.*, p. 51
26. *Ibid.*, pp. 74, 106.

III.

People in Groups

8.

Women and Men in a Changing World

Before you begin reading this chapter, create a short story around each of the following situations. Describe the characters in each story and tell what happens.

Paul and Susan are twins. Both are bright, but their parents can only afford to send one of them to college.

* * * *

Gayle is one of three girls in a physics class of twenty. The professor tells the class he will rank them academically from one to twenty at the end of the semester. Gayle's boyfriend is also in the class.

* * * *

Brenda is interested in government and politics. She decides to go to law school.

Now put your stories aside; we will discuss them later in the chapter.

EIGHT-YEAR-OLD LISA RYAN fell from her bicycle and scraped her knee. She ran to her mother with tears in her eyes. Mrs. Ryan picked Lisa up, gave her a warm, comforting hug, and stroked the tears off her cheeks.

Later that week, Lisa's six-year-old brother, Jim, got into a fight with a classmate on the school playground. Jim came home bruised and tousled. When he saw his parents, he began to cry. All the misery of defeat and humiliation welled up in him. Mrs. Ryan put her arm around Jim, while her husband tried to reason with him. "Come on now, Jim. Stop crying. Try to act like a man."

Why was Lisa allowed to cry, while her *younger* brother was not? What does "act like a man" mean? How *should* a man act?

We have all grown up with certain basic assumptions about what it means to be a woman or a man. As young children, we probably played the "feminine" or "masculine" roles expected of us by our family, our community, and our culture. If you are a girl, did you play "house" and "nurse," decorate your room in pink, and take ballet lessons to become more graceful? If you are a boy, did you play hockey and baseball, prefer blues and greens, and plan to be a doctor or policeman?

Perhaps you assume you did these things "naturally." But what makes dolls and jacks and the color pink feminine? Why are chemistry sets, baseball averages, and the color blue masculine? Why not reverse them? Is it "unfeminine" to want to be an engineer? Or "unmasculine" to cry? Why is it acceptable to be called a tomboy but devastating to be labeled a sissy?

Imagine for a moment that you are of the opposite sex. How different would your life be? Would your temperament and personality be different? Would your abilities differ? Would your parents assign you different responsibilities at home? Would your career goals change? How much of your identity—who you are and what you will become—is defined by your sex?

"COME ON NOW, STOP CRYING; BIG BOYS DON'T CRY."

In our society, boys are expected to "control" their emotions. The young boy faces a difficult task: to be tough, courageous, strong in crises, and generally self-sufficient. This can be a burden and an unnecessary restraint: shouldn't men learn to express the full range of emotions, including crying from joy or sorrow?

351

In this chapter, we explore the psychological differences between the sexes and how biology and social conditioning interact to produce and shape these differences. The person you marry, the job you choose, the way in which you raise your children—in fact, your whole life style—reflects your concepts of femininity and masculinity!

Sometimes both men and women feel pressured to live up to what they *think* is the "ideal" image for members of their sex. To some extent, this is a burden created by advertising and the media. Do you have an image of the "ideal" man or woman?

FEMININE AND MASCULINE: YOUR VIEW

GIRLS:

What is your image of the "ideal" woman?

How do you think that most men would describe the "ideal" woman?

If the descriptions differ, why do you think they do?

How would you describe the "ideal" man?

BOYS:

What is your image of the "ideal" man?

How do you think that most women would describe the "ideal" man?

If the descriptions differ, why do you think they do?

How would you describe the "ideal" woman?

Construct a composite of each ideal from class responses.

Is the girls' composite of the ideal woman different from the boys' composite of the ideal woman?

Is the boys' composite of the ideal man different from the girls' composite of the ideal man?

How do you explain the differences?

"Anatomy Is Destiny"—Or Is It?

Many psychologists have studied newborn humans and animals to try to isolate early psychological differences between the sexes *before learning takes place*. They have found that infant girls and boys differ in behavior at least as early as three months of age.

Boys generally appear more active and aggressive than girls. They also seem more independent and adventuresome. For example, Harvard psychologist Jerome Kagan's experiments have shown that at four months of age, "twice as many girls as boys cry when frightened in a strange laboratory."[1] At twelve months, the girls who become frightened drift toward their mothers; the boys "look for something interesting to do." Kagan has found similar differences in monkeys and baboons, leading him to believe there may be a biological predisposition to such behavior.

Psychologist Michael Lewis has noted similar findings:

> By the time they reach thirteen months, boys venture significantly farther from their mothers, stay away from their mothers for longer periods of time, and look at and talk to their mothers less often than do girls of the same age. Boys play more vigorously with toys, often banging them together, and play significantly more with non-toys (doorknobs, light switches, and other room equipment). A boy also responds with more overt aggression to the frustration barrier; he attempts to get around it, instead of standing in the middle of the room and crying.[2]

Infant girls, on the other hand, are more sensitive and responsive to touch, voice, and facial gestures directed toward them. Girls pick up *social* cues—they seem more attuned to all that is going on around them. They have a longer attention span than boys and they can concentrate better on the complex and subtle activities they see and hear. Perhaps this is why parents usually talk more to infant girls, and why girls learn to speak earlier than boys!

These early basic differences may be partially "built in" to your brain and central nervous system. How these differences affect your behavior later in life depends on many factors: your experiences, your personality, your intelligence, your environment, and your culture. But there is another "biological component" in your behavior as well, one that influences you throughout your life. Your endocrine system produces hormones—chemical substances affecting your sexual development and temperament.

Hormones and Temperament

The male hormones are called *androgens;* the female hormones are *estrogens. Each sex produces both types of hormone, but in different proportions.* The presence of these hormones influences the direction of and the timetable for your sexual development.

These hormones also influence your personality. For example, testosterone, the principal male hormone, stimulates aggressive behavior. It partially affects your sexual "arousability." Women also produce testosterone, but in smaller amounts than men do.

Experiments by Harry Harlow and Stephen Suomi at the University of Wisconsin have shown that the natural play of male rhesus monkeys was "rough and tumble" even when they were isolated from birth so they could not learn or imitate such behavior. Female monkeys were much more passive and "maternal."[3] When Robert Goy of the Oregon Regional Primate Research Center injected male hormones into pregnant monkeys, he found that their female offspring were "masculinized"—they were more aggressive, rough, and active than normal female monkeys! Similarly, female hormones make male monkeys and other male animals more gentle and passive.[4]

The female hormones seem to affect temperament more obviously. Some women become depressed, anxious, and irritable when they experience a tremendous drop in estrogen production. This occurs regularly before menstruation, just after childbirth, and during menopause. In other words, the emotional cycle of women is related to their reproductive system. Before their menstrual periods, they may feel sensitive, tired, and insecure. As estrogen production picks up again with the start of the menstrual cycle, they may feel more alert, outgoing, active, and content. As M. D. Kerr of Cornell Medical School explains, "Estrogen is one of the body's own tranquilizers and anti-depressants."[5] Despite these somewhat predictable emotional shifts in women, specific reactions depend upon individual personality differences.

Studies by Katherina Dalton at the University of London over a fifteen year period illustrate the importance of the female hormonal cycle. She found that:

> 45 percent of female industrial employees who reported sick did so during this time [before and during menstruation].

52 percent of female emergency-accident admissions occurred at this time.

49 percent of females who committed a crime did so during this time.

Students writing exams before and during their periods earned roughly 15 percent lower grades than they did at other times during the month.[6]

These figures do not mean that all or most women become depressed or disabled by their menstrual cycle. Rather, the figures show the delicate interplay between women's physical and emotional selves.

Menopause, the time when the menstrual cycle stops, may also trigger an emotional reaction. Most women reach menopause between the ages of 44 and 53. As their estrogen level drops, an estimated 50 to 85 percent of women experience a variety of such symptoms as depression, tension, anxiety, irritability, fatigue, and headaches.

Menopause may also coincide with other stress-producing situations in a woman's life: her children may be going through adolescence or leaving home for college or marriage. She may be taking stock of her life or becoming anxious about widowhood. She may also be concerned about changes in her sexual life or her inability to have children. It is therefore hard to separate all the factors which may lead to depression. Difficult as all these physical and emotional changes are, most women are able to adjust and lead healthy lives.

Many people believe that men, as the level of their male hormones decreases, go through a stage similar to women's menopause called the *male climacteric syn-*

drome. Little research has been done on this syndrome and some doctors question whether "male menopause" really exists. Male hormones decrease much more gradually than female hormones do.

It is important to remember that *hormones may influence the direction of your general mood, but your specific behavior is the product of everything else that you are: your personality, your attitudes and your self-confidence.*

A Question of Anatomy

Sigmund Freud based his theory of the psychological differences between the sexes on biology. Stated briefly, Freud believed that the obvious anatomical differences between the sexes caused important differences in personality development. He felt that children become curious about their genitals around the age of five. Girls notice that they have no penis and feel cheated and inferior to boys. Girls, therefore, turn their affections toward their fathers, blaming their mothers for their "incompleteness." This creates the so-called *Electra complex:* a young girl's desire to possess her father. Freud believed that "penis envy" has an important, far-reaching effect on the female personality. He felt that it led to the self-contempt, shame, and envy he attributed to all women. He also believed women were more passive, secretive, insincere, dependent, and lacking in a sense of justice—all because of their anatomy.

A boy, on the other hand, prizes his penis. He fears that if he angers his father, he may be punished or castrated. A young boy must therefore control his sexual desire for his mother (which Freud called the *Oedipus complex*), so that he will not anger his father. (A more complete discussion of the Oedipus complex can be found in Chapters 1 and 5.) The boy therefore learns to copy his father's behavior, hoping that he, too, someday will possess a woman like his mother. It was Sigmund Freud who said, "Anatomy is destiny."

Many people have challenged Freud's conclusions. Freud lived in a moralistic era and worked with a small group of disturbed middle-class women. His clinical experiences were limited. Many of his followers believe Freud overemphasized sex as the major determinant of behavior.

Erik Erikson, for example, believes Freud was wrong to dwell only on what a woman is "missing." Instead, he thinks the focus should be on *what a woman does have: a creative "inner space."* A woman has potentials, such as the ability to have a baby, which a man does not. Erikson believes that a person's sex may *predispose* one to certain characteristics and traits, but he notes that many of these "inclinations" can be "unlearned or relearned."[7]

Freud and Erikson present two masculine interpretations of sex differences. What does a female researcher think? Psychoanalyst Karen Horney (1885-1952) sharply disputed Freud's view. In 1926, she wrote, "I, as a woman, ask in amazement, and what about motherhood?" Horney noted that ". . . when one begins, as I did, to analyze men . . . one receives a most surprising impression of the intensity of this envy of pregnancy, childbirth and motherhood, as well as of the breasts and the act of sucking."[8] She said "I know just as many men with womb envy as women with penis envy."[9] Horney did not believe that people are *born* with psychological differences because of their sex.

While anatomy may not be "destiny," certainly the way you feel about your body is important to your self-esteem and personality. Your central nervous system and your hormones do affect your behavior. Your "biological self" is, therefore, one important factor in defining your identity. Perhaps it can best be described as the foundation upon which you build your personality, abilities, and attitudes. *Far more important, however, are the social factors in your environment—for it is as you grow up that you truly learn what is "feminine" and what is "masculine" in your society and culture. Moreover, in a changing world there is opportunity for you to participate in the redefinition of the terms "feminine" and "masculine," and to help others understand the breadth of these terms.*

Socialization—The Early Years

From the moment of birth, when an infant is taken home in either pink or blue, most parents react to their child in terms of sex differences. Little girls are handled more delicately than boys and are surrounded by dolls. Young boys wrestle playfully with their fathers, crawl around in overalls, and receive building sets, trucks, and trains for toys.

Studies have shown that by the age of three, most children cannot only tell you their sex, but also what jobs are typically chosen by each sex. They know that in this country men are bus drivers, policemen, and doctors; that women are nurses, teachers, and housewives. Perhaps this perception will change now that both women and men in our society are beginning to hold a greater diversity of jobs.

YOUR BIOLOGICAL SELF

1. *Do you think biological differences between the sexes (in strength, aggressive inclination, hormonal cycle) should influence job or career choices? Explain your response.*

2. *Women tend to live longer than men. Find out why. To what extent does this fact relate to their biological make-up and/or their social roles?*

Independence and Aggression

At first, age is more important than sex to a young child. Age determines the skills he or she can master, such as walking and talking, and the privileges that can be earned. But as a young boy approaches the age of five, he begins to learn that it is not "proper" for him to hover around his mother. He is expected to become more independent. And if, with all his energy and playfulness, he gets into a fight or falls down, he is encouraged to be brave and hold back his tears. The message to a young boy is clear: you are ready to "act like a man"!

This early training boys receive in *not* expressing their feelings can be a burden to them all their lives. Shouldn't men express the full range of emotions, including crying from joy or sorrow? The young boy faces a difficult task: to be tough and courageous; to be strong in crises; to be reserved in touching others unless genuine affection is involved; to be self-sufficient.

Young girls are allowed to be both affectionate and tearful much longer than boys. They learn to play quiet games such as "school" and "house," acting out the interpersonal relationships they see in their small worlds. When girls prefer to climb trees and play baseball, parents usually smile and say "she'll outgrow it," even though they may secretly view such skills as an achievement. Tomboys may please a father who really wanted a son. Young girls are thus permitted a much wider range of behavior than boys. They are also allowed to remain dependent on their parents for a longer time.

Psychologist Judith Bardwick believes this pressure on a boy to become independent has one very positive effect: it helps him to build his self-esteem based on *his own tangible achievements*. He gains confidence as he masters each new skill or situation without the help of his parents. He learns to trust himself.[10]

Photo courtesy of Kenneth M. Bernstein

Our society encourages boys to be rough and aggressive on the playing field, strong and assertive in their relations with others.

Being more dependent, girls try to please their parents and other adults so they can keep their love and affection. Bardwick thinks that girls create an image of themselves based much more on *how other people react to them* than on what they can accomplish on their own. This may make a girl more sensitive in relating to others, but it also makes her more vulnerable. She does not learn to rely on her own appraisal of her merits. Her confidence is more easily shaken and her feelings hurt by how other people judge her.

Society also teaches boys and girls to express aggression differently. Boys are encouraged to be rough and aggressive on the playing field. An occasional black eye in a neighborhood fight is treated like a "coming of age." After all, "boys will be boys," and no one likes a sissy. Boys are also physically punished more than girls, and usually it is the father who carries the strap. Thus, boys learn to identify with a more direct, open form of aggression.

Girls tend to learn more subtle forms of expressing anger. They are not permitted to physically fight their way out of an argument. They therefore may use sarcasm, stubbornness, or rejection to get even. They may threaten, "You'll be sorry," or "If you do that, I won't like you anymore!" Young girls are verbally and socially more sophisticated than boys—and words can hurt as much as a black eye!

Learning and Achievement

At the age of six, girls are better prepared to begin school: they are more mature, more verbal, more interested in pleasing adults, and more accustomed to controlling their impulses. Girls seem to value success in school as a way to achieve self-esteem and they are better able to adjust to the required school behavior.

Boys find it harder to sit still, concentrate, and "be good." They have higher energy levels and they are absorbed in their struggle to become independent. Competition with their friends is important. Recess may be their favorite period. Boys are apt to have discipline problems. School may not be as positive an experience for them as for girls. Although there is no measured difference in overall intelligence between the sexes, young girls are more likely to achieve good grades—a pattern that continues throughout elementary and high school.

Aptitudes and interests also seem to differ. Girls are usually better with language skills and concepts. Boys often excel in mathematical and mechanical reasoning. They are more analytical. *Early learning experiences probably contribute to this difference.* Boys are encouraged to take initiative, to explore, to play with a variety of objects to see how things work. Girls are more involved in people-related games and activities. Also, they are, as noted previously, more responsive to verbal stimuli early in life.

Psychiatrist David Levy has found that often boys who are particularly good with words, yet weak with figures, have been overprotected by their mothers.[11] Their early learning experiences were similar to those of girls! Research has also shown that girls who do well with mathematical and spatial learning problems were often left to work alone by their mothers, as most boys are.[12]

There is, however, a *wide* overlap: many girls are

mathematically inclined and many boys are highly verbal. Since aptitude and interest differences seem to be learned rather than inborn, the differences described above may begin to fade with the changing times.

Sex-Role Models and Stereotypes

Parents are the most important role models in a child's life. They teach the child what it is like to be feminine and masculine. They influence the child's attitude about his or her sexual identity.

Paul Mussen and Eldred Rutherford of the University of California studied what factors are important for a parent to be a positive role model.[13] They found that:

> "The most crucial determinant of the development of masculinity in young boys is the nature of the father-son relationship." A father must have a warm, loving relationship with his son to encourage masculinity. It helps if his son also considers him "a powerful person in his life—instrumental in both rewarding and punishing him." In other words, a boy will identify with his father as a whole person— loving, powerful and competent.

> Highly feminine girls had mothers who were satisfied with their own identity—*self-accepting and self-confident*. Their mothers also provided warm mother-daughter relationships. The mothers were not necessarily more "feminine" in their own activities, nor did they encourage their daughters to be. But the fathers were more "masculine," and they did encourage their daughters to be "feminine."

> The parental role was more important for a daughter's sex role identification.

LEARNING SEX ROLES

1. *In what ways did your parents encourage you to become more feminine or masculine? To become more independent? List the cues about your sexual identity that you received as you grew up.*

2. *When you were angry or upset as a child, how did you express this to your parents? to your friends? in school? Did you use verbal or physical aggression? Did you cry?*

3. *What games did you play when you were young? Were these played only with children of your own sex? If so, why?*

   Observe elementary school children on the playground. What sex-based patterns can you identify?

   Is there any value in sex segregation at this age? Explain your response.

4. *Describe your two most memorable experiences from your first years of elementary school. Are they action-oriented or people-oriented?*

   Do they involve success or defeat?

   Are there sex differences present in the "themes" of your stories?

5. *List the subjects you enjoy most in school. Compare the boys' list to the girls' list in class. Are there sex differences? If so, what reasons can you give for them?*

Society clearly defines appropriate masculine behavior and values masculine achievement. Thus, a boy receives support and encouragement from all of society's socializing agents. His family's role fits in with a larger, consistent picture.

Our culture is not so clear about what are desirable traits in a woman, nor does it value the feminine role as highly. Girls, therefore, need positive role models even more than boys. Many women have mixed feelings about their femininity. They may wonder how to balance their desire for achievement with their desire to raise a family. A mother who is "experiencing conflicts about her own femininity . . . cannot support her daughter's self-esteem or serve as a successful role model."[14]

Young children are constantly presented with a simplistic version of "typical" feminine and masculine behavior through toys, books, movies, and television. While role models are necessary and helpful, stereotypes can be harmful.

Men have been portrayed in exciting, stimulating activities. They are the heroes, explorers, scientists, and lawyers. They control power and make important decisions. Their women have awaited them in supportive roles: as wife, nurse, or secretary. We are beginning to see signs of change in the media as female police detectives,

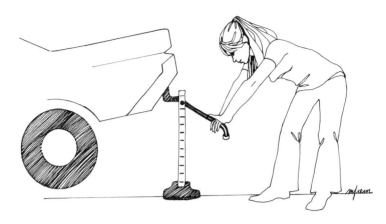

The kinds of activities that women and men do *not* perform have little—or nothing—to do with their potential. Women have the strength and skill to function as carpenters and auto mechanics. Men are perfectly capable of sewing a button on a shirt and cooking a soufflé for supper—if they are willing to try. As stereotyped notions of people's "proper" roles break down, both women and men will experience success in ever-broadening areas.

doctors, lawyers, and construction workers are spotlighted, but at present women are still generally portrayed in less important and less exciting roles. Perhaps this is why studies have shown that four out of five girls at some point in their lives wished they were boys!

Recently, a study was completed of 2,760 stories in 134 school books by 14 different publishers.[15] Here are the results:

More than two-thirds of all stories are about boys and men.

Boys are presented in active, creative situations, like

368

building walkie-talkies, or using their wits in capturing hijackers, dealing with a genie, or solving problems for girls or even mother.

Girls are pictured quietly watching boys play, or in domestic activities like cooking, cleaning the house, or sewing. Often girls are teased by boys for their stupidity when they make mistakes.

Men are illustrated in a variety of occupations, 147 in all. Women are shown in only 26 occupations, most of them mere extensions of household labor.

Fathers solve problems for everyone and frequently participate in joint activities with their kids.

Mothers, however, rarely have a life apart from housework, seldom leave the kitchen, and are more likely to scold than play with their children.

The effects of these stereotypes can be seen on the playground. Girls do not usually play boys' games—they cheer boys from the sidelines. The sexes segregate and each plays in an "appropriate" way.

From these stereotypes, children learn what will be expected of them by their culture at an early age. Radcliffe president Matina Horner describes an incident with her daughter, who was five at the time:

> One day she came into my room and said to me: "Mommy, Daddy must love you very much." "Why do you say that?" I asked her, pleased that she had made such an assumption. "Because he doesn't want you to be tired," she said. "He does the dishes so that you won't be tired."[16]

This was her way of explaining the fact that her father was doing a "feminine" job!

Adolescence: Consolidating Your Image

From the age of five, a boy learns to accept his masculine identity; he becomes more independent, he learns to compete and to assert himself, and to limit his show of emotions. He gains satisfaction from and confidence in his own achievements. He begins to define his career goals from the many opportunities society offers him. Adolescence presents new challenges and responsibilities, perhaps a rethinking of values, but the foundation of his male identity has already been developed. It just awaits testing.

A girl begins adolescence without this clear image of her sex role. Pressures on a girl to become feminine have been gradual, and perhaps as a tomboy she has "achieved" in the male world. When she physically matures and her friends begin to date, a former tomboy must suddenly confront her feminine identity and change her means of gaining self-esteem. Likewise, the school achiever must now decide if her popularity will be affected by her ambition and good grades. Will she still seem feminine if she wants to be a lawyer or a sports reporter? Can she afford to be aggressive and independent? How will boys react to her? This may be less of a problem for girls in the future, as our society begins to accept women in leadership roles and challenging careers. But girls have learned to be more concerned than boys about *how others see them*. They must therefore define for themselves what is "appropriate" feminine behavior—and they do this in adolescence.

Girls may also view sexual relationships quite differently than boys do. Boys have learned to think of sex primarily as a way to achieve pleasure, but many young girls have received a "double message"[17] at home: sex is pleasurable, but only at the proper time; menstruation is the entry into womanhood, but it is messy and brings cramps; childbirth is fulfilling and creative, but awkward, painful, and requires medical help. Young girls may not be as eager as boys to grow up!

Adolescents today have a much more relaxed view about sexual relationships than did previous generations. Yet the feminine and masculine attitudes may still differ. Having a sexual relationship may bring a boy status in his peer group and reaffirm his sense of masculinity. Girls feel less pressure to "prove themselves" in this way. Boys are also more easily aroused sexually, and initially they may not invest the same kind of *emotional commitment* in a sexual relationship as girls generally do. Most adolescent girls need reassurance not only that they are attractive, but also that they are liked as people. They tend to worry more about being used and being rejected. Girls associate sex with love and parenthood much more than do boys.

Adolescence, then, is a time to consolidate your self-image. As you become more independent, you must make important decisions about your career goals, your view of love and sex, your life style. While boys must decide *how* to achieve, girls must decide *whether* to achieve. Girls must define what it means to be "feminine" in our changing times.

SOCIAL CONDITIONING:
LEARNING YOUR IDENTITY

1. a. *Ask a group of third graders what they want to be when they grow up. Compare the girls' answers with the boys' answers.*

   What are the differences?

   Does one list reflect higher aspirations than the other?

   Which list is larger and more diverse?

   Which list has more achievement-oriented jobs?

   Which list has more people-oriented jobs?

   You might also ask, "If you were of the opposite sex, what would you want to be?" Do the children give different answers than they did for their own sex?

   b. *Now have the members of your own class list their goals and career objectives—are there similar differences?*

2. *Young girls often role-play with their dolls; they play the mother and their dolls are their children. Girls also babysit more than boys.*

   Does this kind of social conditioning for a maternal role help a girl to adjust to having younger siblings?

372

Is there less sibling rivalry and jealousy among girls than among boys toward younger children in the family?

Should boys also be encouraged to play with dolls and babysit more?

Will this affect their sibling relationships or prepare them better for fatherhood?

3. *Observe the tasks of each member of your family at home. How are family responsibilities divided? Are the assignments interchangeable? Are they related to sex? For example, who babysits? Who wipes the dishes? Who pays the bills?*

How will you want household duties divided when you get married?

4. *Clip out of a magazine any five advertisements with people in them, or cite them from T.V. What roles do women and men play in them?*

What societal values is the advertiser capitalizing on?

How would you describe the people in the ads?

5. *What signs of change have you noticed in the media about sex-role stereotyping? Cite some examples.*

6. *Name two people in your life who were important*

role models for you. What traits do they have which you admire?

7. *If you were a member of the opposite sex, describe how different you imagine your life would be.*

Photo courtesy of Kenneth M. Bernstein

As we begin to re-examine what is "feminine" and what is "masculine," we find many new roles and career possibilities opening up to both women and men.

374

8. *Is there a greater value placed on physical appearance in either sex?*

    What are the advantages and disadvantages of physical attractiveness?

9. *If you have children, how do you think they will view masculine and feminine roles? How would you like them to?*

10. *How do you feel the Women's Liberation Movement has changed society's notion of feminine and masculine?*

    How do you feel this change, if any, will affect you?

    Are men reassessing *their* roles because of it?

11. *Is there a Women's Liberation Movement in other countries? Check the role of women in China, Japan, the Middle East, and India. What political factors are involved in defining the role of women?*

Adulthood: Different Paths to "Success"

> *He saw her lift her eyes: he felt*
> *The soft hand's light caressing,*
> *And heard the tremble of her voice,*
> *As if a fault confessing.*

"I'm sorry that I spelt the word:
I hate to go above you,
Because,"—the brown eyes lower fell,—
Because, you see, I love you!"

JOHN GREENLEAF WHITTIER,
from *"In School-Days"*

Should a girl lose to a boy in a spelling bee? In 1870, when Whittier wrote this poem, the answer was yes, if she likes him! Have things changed in the past hundred years? Let us look at this special dilemma for girls: the *fear* of success.

Early in life, school is a major source of self-esteem for girls. Yet by the time they reach high school, girls begin to tone down their ambitions. Despite their better grades, they show less confidence in their abilities than boys do. Girls are also more nervous and shy in class and are more likely to avoid competition. They are usually less willing to borrow money or work to further their education. When they reach college, often their aspiration level drops, their goals become less challenging. They are more likely to accept routine jobs with little hope of advancement. Why?

In 1964, Matina Horner began a study of the motivation of college women to achieve. Ninety women and eighty-eight men, all undergraduates at the University of Michigan, participated in her first experiment. She asked the students to complete a story based on a brief "cue." The men created stories around the following line:

After first-term finals, John finds himself at the top of his medical school class.

Here is a response typical of those made by the men:

John is a conscientious young man who worked hard.

He is pleased with himself. John has always wanted
to go into medicine and is very dedicated . . . John
continues working hard and eventually graduates at
the top of his class.

In response to this cue, more than 90 percent of the
men "showed strong positive feelings, indicated increased
striving, confidence in the future and a belief that this
success would be instrumental to fulfilling other goals
such as providing a secure and happy home for some
girl."[18]

Women were asked to respond to a similar cue:

*After first-term finals, Anne finds herself at the top of her
medical school class.*

The typical women's responses were much different:

Anne will deliberately lower her academic standing
the next term, while she does all she subtly can to
help Carl. . . . His grades come up and Anne soon
drops out of med school. They marry and he goes on
in school while she raises their family.[19]

Anne is an acne-faced bookworm. She runs to the
bulletin board and find she's at the top. "As usual,"
she smarts off. A chorus of groans is the rest of the
class's reply. Anne was always praised for her
initiative and study habits—mainly because these
were the only things one could praise her for. She
studies twelve hours a day, and lives at home to save
money. She rents her books. 'Well it certainly paid
off. All the Friday and Saturday nights with my
books, who needs dates, fun—I'll be the best woman
doctor alive!' And yet, a twinge of sadness comes
through—she wonders what she really has. But, as is

> her habit, she promptly erases the thought, and goes off reciting aloud the 231 bones in her wrist.[20]

> Anne is really happy she's on top, though Tom is higher than she— though that's as it should be. Anne doesn't mind Tom winning.[21]

Horner found that 65 percent of the women were "disconcerted, troubled, or confused" by their cue. The women either denied the story was possible, changed the story content, made success seem almost accidental, or doomed Anne to the life of a social outcast. The study showed that these women were not afraid to fail—*they were afraid to succeed!* Their self-esteem depended upon being accepted. They worried that if they were too smart, too independent, too aggressive, too competitive, and too career-oriented, they would not find husbands!

Moreover, Horner found that their fear increased with their ability level and increased as they progressed farther in school. Female college juniors would often switch from pre-law to teaching. Studies at other colleges produced similar results. Male law students described a successful woman as overaggressive, unpopular, and unattractive. Horner feels that these negative attitudes toward career women persist, despite the efforts of the Women's Liberation Movement. It will be interesting to test this out in *your* generation.

When T. Neal Garland and Margaret M. Paloma interviewed fifty-three women who were either physicians, attorneys, or professors, they found that almost all of the women placed motherhood above job aspirations.[22] They made sure their work would fit in with their family responsibilities. Increasing numbers of women, however, do want to have *both* a career and a family. Diane Hatch surveyed women completing their freshman years at the University of Michigan in 1968 and 1969. She asked them what they wished to be doing in fifteen years, and found that "86 percent wanted to be married and 63 percent wanted a career too."[23]

Our society reverses priorities, then, for women and

"When I grow up I am going to be a judge." More women than ever before are eager to have both a family *and* a career.

379

men. A "successful man" must achieve in the business world. A "successful woman" must have a husband and children. Of course, most men also want families, and most women will work before or after they raise their children. The important point is that women are now beginning to look at a wider variety of options and roles in order to achieve self-fulfillment. As Bardwick notes:

> ... neither men nor women want to be constricted to only one set of roles. ... A person is most likely to feel fulfilled if he or she participates in several roles and is able to gratify several major motives and abilities. Then retirement does not mean despair; divorce does not mean disaster; the natural termination of one role does not mean that meaningful life has ended.[25]

The Women Who Work

According to the United States Department of Labor, nine out of ten girls will work at some time in their lives. Women constitute nearly 40 percent of the labor market (as of 1972), but they tend to be clustered in the lower paid, less influential, and less prestigious jobs. For example, the median income for full time working women in 1971 was only three-fifths that of men.[25] While earnings will vary according to education, skill, seniority, and supply and demand, some women have been paid less than men doing the same job at the same level. Legal action has been chipping away at this kind of inequality, and women are just beginning to move up the corporate ladder. Yet they still face distrust and suspicion in competing for higher-level jobs.

Women are now trying a variety of jobs once reserved for men only.

Many people do not realize how significant this situation is to those women who work. U.S. Labor Department statistics show that "of the nearly 34 million women in the labor force in March, 1973, nearly half were working because of pressing economic need. They were either single, widowed, divorced, or separated, or had husbands whose incomes were less than $3,000 a year."[26]

What problems do women face in competing for high-level jobs? Many women are out of the labor market for ten to fifteen years while raising a family. Those fifteen years are the crucial ones during which ambitious young men begin to create their career reputations. Also, when a woman is ready to return to a job, she may be fearful of competing with younger, more recently trained applicants. She may lose confidence in herself.

Another reason for the low status of women in the business world may be the attitude and temperament they bring to the job. Precisely those assets which society seems to value as feminine—gentleness, dependency, consideration, and sensitivity—may be disadvantages in a highly competitive business. A woman is more likely to take a "helping" job such as teaching, nursing or social work—jobs which pay less and consequently, in our society, have less status.

Women who grow up with stereotyped notions of "male" and "female" careers may have trouble seeing themselves in challenging and demanding work positions. As previously noted, they may lower their career aspirations in the fear that they would otherwise be considered aggressive or "unfeminine." Many women have never considered the wide range of jobs for which they would qualify; this is now changing as sex-role stereotyping is beginning to break down. In fact, engineering schools are recruiting women, and law, business, and medical schools are also receiving applications from and accepting larger numbers of women.

Even when women have the ability and desire to get ahead, they may face serious roadblocks. Bardwick explains, "Managers do not give women real responsibilities, acknowledge their capabilities or ambitions, or promote them to positions of authority. In turn they get predictable results: women who are afraid to compete, to assume responsibility; women who remain emotionally dependent on others' evaluation of them; women with low self-esteem, cautious of direct confrontation with management. Organizational resistance to placing women in power makes predictions of women's inadequacies self-fulfilling."[27]

It is therefore not surprising that even in families where the mother works, most children perceive the father as the breadwinner. They assume their mother's income will provide the "extras."

Another factor we tend to overlook is the low status of household work. How much is housework worth? Two Cornell researchers found that its financial value is as much as $10,000 in large families (according to 1971 New York State pay rates) and $8,600 in a family of four with two young children.[28] Yet if a man cleaned the house while his wife held a job, would it be considered strange?

The world of work has been an uncertain arena for women. They must resolve the conflicting demands of career and family. It may be difficult to straddle both worlds, but frustrating not to. While men may also face difficulties and pressures, they suffer no such ambivalence—they are expected to work all their lives.

Conclusion

Are there psychological differences between the sexes? In our culture, women tend to be more dependent, noncompetitive, sensitive, nurturing, and interpersonally oriented. Men tend to be more aggressive, task-oriented, and independent. Are these differences inevitable?

ANALYZING YOUR STORIES

Let's review the stories which you wrote at the outset of this chapter.

Who went to college, Paul or Susan? Why?

What did the other do? How did he/she feel about it?

Who did better in physics, Gayle or her boyfriend?

What happens to each? What are they like?

Is Brenda successful in law school? What type of person is she?

What conclusions can you draw about your image of the proper role for women and men?

Compare the boys' stories to those of the girls. Are there major differences?

Try similar experiments on people out of class. See if you get similar results.

Do you think these attitudes are changing?

❖ ❖ ❖ ❖

Name some famous women who are (or have been) in the following fields:

Art	Law
Music	Medicine
Business	Education

Sports   Politics

If you find this difficult to do, how would you explain the reason for it?

Anthropologists have found that in almost every society men control the government, business, religion, fighting, and marriage arrangements. Is this evidence that they are following "biological predispositions"—that men have a more aggressive, energetic nature, and women a more gentle, maternal temperament?

Actually, it appears that social conditioning plays a much more decisive role than biology in shaping sex differences. In her study of primitive cultures, Margaret Mead found that sex differences in temperament were the reverse of ours in a few small tribes: "the Arapesh ideal is the mild, responsive man married to the mild, responsive woman; the Mundugumor ideal is the violent aggressive man married to the violent, aggressive woman. In the third tribe, the Tchambuli, we found a genuine reversal of the sex-attitudes of our own culture, with the woman the dominant, impersonal, managing partner, the man the less responsible and the emotionally dependent person." Mead states, "The biological bases of development as human beings, although providing limitations which must be honestly reckoned with, can be seen as potentialities by no means fully tapped by our human imagination."[29]

We all originate in the womb with both male and female characteristics. Therefore, it is possible to influence the direction of later development. For example, Dr. John Money, a researcher at Johns Hopkins, cites cases in which children had to be raised as the opposite sex due to accidents before or after birth—and they learned to act, feel, and look like a member of that sex."[30]

Your identity, then, is the result of a "complex interweaving" of biological, social, and individual forces. Members of each sex have the potential to develop traits more commonly associated with the other sex. There is a wide overlapping between the sexes in personality characteristics and behavior. Men who are confident in their masculinity can also be gentle and sensitive. Women who are sure of their femininity can afford to be assertive and ambitious. It is clear that in today's world, people have much greater freedom to define for themselves what it means to be "feminine" and "masculine."

It is important for people to choose the roles and lifestyles—traditional or non-traditional—that are most satisfying and comfortable for them. This may mean different roles at different times in life (student, accountant, mother, businessperson, etc.), or it may mean carrying out several roles simultaneously (mother, druggist, musician, etc.). These options are available to both sexes.

No one can deny that sex differences exist. We do not have to be the same to be equal. Yet neither should we be locked into stereotypes. The more we can embrace the positive characteristics attributed to both sexes, the more *complete* and *total* human beings we will be.

YOUR FEELINGS ABOUT
WOMEN'S LIBERATION

1. *List the jobs of all the people with whom you come into contact during one week. Compare the lists of women's jobs to men's. What patterns are there?*

2. *How do you feel about:*

   - Men opening doors and walking behind women?

   - Women retaining their maiden names when they marry?

   - *Boys:* marrying a woman more successful than you?

   - *Girls:* marrying a man less successful than you?

   - Working for a female executive vs. a male executive?

   - Girls calling boys for dates, deciding where to go, initiating sexual relations?

   - A woman leaving her job because her husband must relocate for his?

   - A man leaving his job because his wife must relocate for hers?

   - Athletic teams being open to women?

   - Job competition between a single woman and a man with a family—should that matter in deciding who is hired?

Between a single man and a woman who must support her family?

- A woman as a minister or rabbi? a woman as President? Are there any occupations inappropriate for either women or men?

3. *How do you feel about the responsibilities of marriage versus the demands of a career? Would you give one or the other priority? Explain your response.*

4. *How do your parents view the role of women in work and marriage? Do their views differ from yours?*

5. *What work arrangements could be made to accommodate those women or men who have family responsibilities? For example, could two people split one job? Would this be unfair to an employer?*

   Will child-care centers ease the situation? What alternative life styles would help to accommodate women's work aspirations?

6. *Many single-sex colleges have recently become coed. Which atmosphere (a coed or single-sex college) do you think encourages women to achieve more?*

   To raise their career aspirations?

   To gain greater self-esteem?

   Which seems healthier socially?

In which setting do women and men develop their potentials more fully?

7. *How does your* economic *level influence your view of femininity and masculinity?*

How does *ethnic* or *social* background influence your view? For example, discuss sex roles in minority cultures in America—among Chinese, Blacks, Italians, Jews, Hispanics.

Suggested Reading

Bardwick, Judith, *Psychology of Women* (New York: Harper and Row, 1971).

Boslooper, Thomas, and Marcia Hayes, *The Femininity Game* (New York: Stein and Day, 1973).

Boston Women's Health Collective, *Our Bodies, Ourselves* (New York: Simon and Schuster, 1972).

Brenton, Myron, *The American Male* (New York: Coward-McCann, 1966).

Bullough, Vern and Bonnie Bullough, *The Subordinate Sex: A History of Attitudes Toward Women* (Urbana: U. of Illinois Press, 1973).

Fasteau, Marc, *The Male Machine* (New York: McGraw-Hill, 1974).

Friedan, Betty, *The Feminine Mystique* (New York: W. W. Norton, 1963).

Gornick, Vivian *Woman in Sexist Society* (New York: Basic Books, 1971).

Horney, Karen, *Feminine Psychology* (New York: W.W. Norton, 1967).

Janeway, Elizabeth, *Between Myth and Morning: Women Awakening* (New York: William Morrow, 1974).

Komisar, Lucy, *The New Feminism* (New York: Watts, 1971).

Mead, Margaret, *Male and Female* (New York: William Morrow, 1949).

Mead, Margaret, *Sex and Temperament in Three Primitive Societies* (New York: William Morrow, 1935, 1950).

Money, John, and Anke Ehrhardt, *Man and Woman, Boy and Girl* (Baltimore: Johns Hopkins, 1972).

Roszak, Betty, and Theodore Roszak, *Masculine/Feminine* (New York: Harper and Row, 1970).

Schulman, L.M., *A Woman's Place* (New York: Macmillan, 1974).

Tripp, Maggie, *Woman in the Year 2000* (New York: Arbor House, 1974).

FOOTNOTES

1. *Time,* March 20, 1972, p. 44.
2. Michael Lewis, "Culture and Gender Roles: There's No Unisex in the Nursery." Reprinted from *Psychology Today* May 1972. Copyright © 1972 Ziff-Davis Publishing Company. All rights reserved.
3. M. Scarf, "He and She: The Sex Hormones," *The New York Times Magazine,* May 7, 1972, pp. 106-7.
4. *Ibid.*
5. Dr. M. D. Kerr, *Psychiatry,* 1972.
6. Lionel Tiger, "Male Dominance? Yes, Alas. A Sexist Plot? No," *The New York Times Magazine,* October 25, 1970.
7. Erik Erikson, *Identity, Youth and Crisis* (New York: W. W. Norton and Company, 1968), pp. 267, 291.
8. Karen Horney, "The Flight From Womanhood," *Feminine Psychology* (New York: W.W. Norton, 1967), pp. 54-70
9. Rona and Laurence Cherry, "The Horney Heresy," *The New York Times Magazine,* August 26, 1973, p. 75.
10. Judith Bardwick, *Psychology of Women* (New York: Harper and Row, 1971). Copyright © 1971 by Judith Bardwick. By permission of Harper and Row, Publishers, Inc.
11. *Time,* March 20, 1972, p. 44.
12. *Ibid.*
13. C. Himber, "So He Hates Baseball," *The New York Times Magazine,* August 29, 1965. © 1965 by The New York Times Company. Reprinted by permission.
14. *Ibid.*
15. Ilene Barth, "Do Kids' Schoolbooks Distort Sex Roles?" *Parade,* July 1, 1973, p. 6.
16. Vivian Gornick, "Why Women Fear Success," *New York,* December 20, 1971, p. 53.
17. Bardwick, *op. cit.,* p. 48.
18. Gornick, *op. cit.,* p. 50-52.
19. *Ibid.*
20. Bardwick, *op. cit.,* p. 182.
21. *Ibid.*
22. Judith Bardwick, "Women's Liberation: Nice Idea, But It Won't Be Easy." Reprinted from *Psychology Today,* May 1973. Copyright © 1973, Ziff-Davis Publishing Company. All rights reserved.
23. *Ibid.*

24. *Ibid.*
25. "Women Workers Today," U.S. Department of Labor; Employment Standards Administration, Women's Bureau, Washington, D.C., 1973.
26. "The Myth and the Reality," U.S. Department of Labor Employment Standards Administration, Women's Bureau, Washington, D. C., May 1974.
27. Bardwick, "Women's Liberation," *op. cit.*
28. "Household Work—a $10,000-a-Year-Job?" *The Boston Globe,* March 29, 1973.
29. Margaret Mead, *Sex and Temperament* (New York: William Morrow and Company, 1950) pp. 205-6.
30. *Time,* January 8, 1973.

9.

Group Dynamics

JAMES CROSSED HIS ARMS and chuckled to himself. It was clearly a standoff and he was glad to be an observer. Richard and Bess wanted to use the class money for the graduation dance, as seniors had done in past years. Bob and Rita represented a small group of students who wanted to send the money to victims of a flood in North Rivertown.

James hadn't taken either side. In fact, he hadn't spoken at all. He didn't like these committee meetings anyway. They wasted so much time without accomplishing anything. Still, he was irritated that no one had asked for his opinion.

He watched Richard hogging the floor, as usual. "Why should I support him," he thought sourly, "if he doesn't even care what I think about it?" Richard was tall, self-confident, and a star athlete. Richard had stopped him in the hall before the meeting to emphasize how important it was to have a good band this year for the dance. James was inclined to agree, but he didn't like to be ordered around. Richard seemed to have convinced Bess, the girl who was always combing her hair in class and who turned in the best term papers.

James didn't know Bob very well, although they passed frequently in the halls. Bob had a friendly face that peered out from behind his heavy eyeglass frames. Rita was probably the mastermind behind this new proposal. She was a "fireball," as James would put it. This scheme to save the flood victims was only the last in a string of socially significant causes that Rita had championed in the school. She was popular, at least with a substantial minority of the students. She lost the class presidency to Richard by only a few votes. Rita sat beside the new girl, Pat, who was even quieter than James!

Richard was still talking, trying to bully the group into agreement: " . . . and, besides, even if we do give the class money to the flood victims, it won't help them enough to matter. What can three hundred dollars do for a thousand people who need everything? There are all sorts of government agencies to help people in disasters, so I don't see what right we have to take dues that were paid with the idea of having a graduation dance and to give them away in a hopeless gesture. It's important, I think, for the class to have something to remember Rivertown High . . ."

"I agree," Bess chimed in, "and both Richard and I have talked to a lot of other students who want to spend the money on the dance."

"May I say something?" Pat asked timidly.

"It's a free country," James thought to himself, "Why does she need Richard's permission to speak?" Pat had a prim stiffness about her. She seemed to be waiting for either Richard or Bob to respond. She didn't even look in his direction.

"Sure, Pat," Bob replied. "In this group everyone just says what's on his or her mind."

394

"Well, then, I think that Mr. Jones, our class adviser, should be asked how we can settle this argument, since there seems to be a split in this group."

A short silence was broken by Bess. "If we keep at it, we can work this out by ourselves, don't you think?" The question was directed to no one in particular. The discussion resumed by general assent without a consideration of Pat's proposal. "I think," Bess continued, "that if Bob and Rita and their friends want to give money for charity, they should do it themselves. They shouldn't try to make the rest of us feel guilty to get us to do something

Photo courtesy of Kenneth M. Bernstein

People function differently in groups than they do as individuals. "Leaders" and "followers" will emerge in a group.

we don't want to do. Why can't they take up a special collection from those students who want to contribute to the flood victims and leave the class funds for their originally planned use?"

"Well put," James thought to himself. "Another point

for Bess." Secretly, of course, he agreed with Bess and Richard. There should be a dance . . .

"James, you're not saying much. What do you think we should do?" Bob's question was unexpected, but James recovered quickly and smiled. Bob's friendly face peered at James through the thick glasses. At least Bob wasn't trying to railroad the group like some other people, James thought. However, James wasn't too excited about spending his money on someone other than himself.

"Well," he said, wrinkling his face under the strain of having to tip the balance. "I think that there are . . . ah . . . arguments on both sides, and . . . "

"That's why I suggested that we call Mr. Jones," Pat interrupted.

"Pat, we're not babies! Students must think for themselves," Rita's response was curt and conclusive. It was clear that Pat just didn't understand about these things.

"Hey, let's not fight about it. At least Pat suggested a solution. Remember that this is her first meeting with us." Bob was trying to make peace, but his comment was not quick enough to save Pat's feelings. She pressed her lips tightly together and began fiddling with a pencil in her lap. James was surprised that she would be so dense as to miss the signals everyone gave when she brought up the Mr. Jones issue the first time. At any rate, Pat was clearly not going to contribute anything else during this meeting.

Working in Groups

Let's temporarily suspend this committee meeting to make a few preliminary observations about groups in action. What are the common characteristics of personal interaction in groups, whatever their size, composition, or purpose?

"Task" vs. "Process"

A useful way to begin our study of groups is to distinguish "task-oriented" behavior, which is focused directly on achieving the group's goal, from "process-oriented" behavior, which is designed to maintain smooth functioning among group members. There are at least three examples of "process-oriented" statements in the case study above. The first is Bob's giving Pat "permission" to talk. Identify other examples. How many persons make comments designed to help everyone work as a group?

In this chapter, we adopt a *process* orientation. We will be concerned with patterns of interpersonal behavior that occur in groups with very different tasks. Once you can recognize these processes in operation, you have taken the first step toward using them productively.

You can identify yourself as a member of many groups: your family, your special friends or gang, your sports companions, your school classes, your committees and clubs, your co-workers on the job. The skill in interpersonal relations that you acquire in these and other groups may in large part determine whether or not you achieve your career goals, establish meaningful relationships with other people, and earn the economic resources to live life as you choose.

Norms: The Unspoken Rules

Once the members of a group begin working together,

they develop shared expectations about what is and what is not appropriate behavior in the group. These standards are called *norms* because they define what the members of that social system, be it as large as a nation or as small as a couple, accept as "normal" behavior. Someone who violates a norm runs the risk of punishment (*sanctions*) from other members of the group. In the case study, Pat, the new member of the committee, violated a norm by proposing that the students call on a teacher to help make the decision. At first her suggestion was politely rebuffed, but when Pat didn't take that hint, Rita applied more forceful sanctions against her.

Norms may differ drastically from the "official" rules governing the group. For example, a boss of a roofing gang officially expected each worker to apply ten squares of shingles in one eight-hour day. Among the workers, the norm was no more than seven squares per day. When a worker consistently met the boss's standard and violated the workers' norm, then:

> ... strange things tended to happen. For example, he would come to get more shingles from his pile and find a fellow worker sitting on the pile having a cigarette and offering him one. This would slow him down by ten to fifteen minutes. If he persisted in breaking the norm, he might go down to get more shingles and come back to find his roofing hatchet missing or in severe cases his nail bag nailed to the roof. In fact, there were dozens of tricks that the roofing gang could employ to insure that all members of the crew [cooperated]. . . . [1]

Can you think of a similar conflict in your school

between the official code of behavior and the unspoken rules? Although officially each student is supposed to study hard, listen attentively in class, and volunteer to participate in discussions, there is often a norm among students that is more influential in determining what "should" and "shouldn't" be done. In your classes, when (and for how long) is it proper to talk? Do students admit to each other how much they studied for a test? What disruptions will students tolerate from one of their number? Which will they discourage? What sanctions are used?

A person who consistently violates the norms of his or her group, even after sanctions have been applied, is usually excluded from the group. Where circumstances or authorities will not permit a physical exclusion (for example, in a classroom) the disapproving students may isolate the violator psychologically. This can be accomplished by ignoring the "deviate" person, avoiding contact with him or her, and discriminating against the person whenever an opportunity presents itself.

Even when group norms are incorrect or morally wrong, it is still difficult for a member to act against them. In the next chapter, "Perception and Persuasion," we explore this issue in some detail.

Let's return to our case study.

"WE CAN'T KEEP THIS bickering up forever," Bob continued. "Isn't some compromise possible?"

Rita took the hint. "Bess, you reported in our last meeting about the several different cost estimates for the dance. What was the least expensive alternative you suggested?"

"It all depends on the quality of the band. There is a group of students here at Rivertown High who have a band that is at least passable, and they're much less expensive than an import. If we used them, we could probably get by with 200 dollars total cost."

"But the students want and deserve a better band," Richard objected, "and the extra 100 dollars would make the difference. On the other hand, it wouldn't even begin to help the flood victims."

"Richard, hold up a minute. Clearly, there are some students who do not agree with you. Now if we can discuss the possibility of mutual concessions instead of repeating past arguments, we might be able to finish this meeting with a decision." James had to respect Bob for guiding the group toward a solution, even though he agreed with Richard about the issues. He smiled at Bob just to let him know that there was support among group members for his leadership. Bob returned the smile.

"Not a bad fellow," James thought, "Not bad at all." James appreciated someone who cared what others in the group were thinking. Just because he didn't talk all the time didn't mean he had no opinions.

Richard crossed his arms and tipped his chair back with disgust, but Bess, who was formerly his chief ally in the group, refused to follow his lead and instead joined the new movement toward compromise: "Listen, Bob and Rita, suppose we work it out this way. We give 50 dollars of class dues to the flood victims. I know that won't help much, but it establishes your general point that the class should be concerned with socially significant purposes. Then—and here's the key point—we will support your friends if they want to take a voluntary contribution on behalf of the flood victims during the lunch hour. I suggested that before, if you recall. Now, this will leave 250 dollars for the graduation dance, which will permit us to get a suitable band, if not the best. What do you say to that?" Bess ran her fingers through her hair and looked proud of herself.

Heads nodded around the circle. "Hmmm. That might work," Bob said, "Why don't we get everyone's opinion on that proposal."

One by one, each member agreed, except Richard. James was the last in line to vote. He felt Richard watching him. Even though he had already lost the vote, Richard expected James to join his dissent based on their talk before the meeting. But it was Bob, not Richard, who had really been concerned with what James felt about the issues.

"I vote yes," James said. It was four votes to one. The meeting was over.

✿ ✿ ✿ ✿ ✿

Why do you think James voted as he did? Are personal relationships among members in this group an important influence in the decision-making? Who is the leader of this committee? Or is there more than one leader? What makes someone a "leader"?

Leaders and Leadership

Business and military organizations have sponsored much of the research about leadership. They have very practical reasons for wanting to make their groups as effective as possible. Specifically, they want to know how a person can be *trained* to be a better leader or a more effective group member.

At first, psychologists searched for a unique personality trait such as "charisma," "personal magnetism," or "authoritarianism" as the key to understanding leadership. They soon abandoned that approach. The trait theory was oversimplified. Groups differed in styles of leadership, tasks, characteristics of the individual members, and amounts of authority officially delegated to the leader. All of these factors seemed to contribute to the success or failure of the leader in a specific situation.

One researcher divided a study group of recognized leaders into two categories based on their leadership style.[2] A leader was called *person-oriented* if he was generally permissive, democratic, preferred general instead of detailed supervision, and tried to involve all members of the group in decision-making. A leader was called *task-oriented* if he was controlling, authoritarian, took personal responsibility for decision-making, and tried to direct the individual actions of group members. Which of these two styles do you think would be more effective?

The study showed that the relationship between the orientation of the leader and the effectiveness of his or her actions in the group was complicated. The formal authority given the leader because of rank or job status was only a contributing factor in the leader's influence. First in importance was the leader's personal relationship with the group members, which reflected his skill in interpersonal transactions. Second in importance was the nature of the task itself. If the goal required a detailed, step-by-step approach using a well-established procedure, then a task-oriented leader who exercised

402

tight control over the group often produced the best results. On the other hand, if the task was novel or uncertain, if it required creative invention to discover a means for accomplishing the task, then the person-oriented leader who encouraged the participation of all group members in decision-making seemed to produce better results.

Leadership thus has three main components. In decreasing order of importance, they are: the interpersonal skill of the leader, the structure of the task itself, and the amount of formal authority vested in the leader from outside the group.

Perhaps the most useful way to explain leadership is by reference to group needs. An effective group must have certain functions performed by its members. Goals must be set, methods devised, resources located, and—to maintain a stable and productive membership—the personal needs of individual members must be at least partly satisfied. The *functional* theory of leadership says that when any member of the group performs an act that helps achieve one of the group functions, then he or she is "leading" the group at that moment. The term *leader*, as we normally use it, refers to those persons who perform acts of leadership for the benefit of the group more often than other members.

This theory is useful because it emphasizes that leadership is a *skill* which can be *learned*. A person can be taught to recognize what group functions need to be performed if progress is to occur, and he can also be taught to make the type of intervention that is likely to help.

In the dance committee meeting, the leadership role

passed back and forth. Initially, Richard appeared to be a strong leader in the group. However, because he limited himself to repeating a single viewpoint, he soon lost pace with others who were more flexible. Bess took the lead in proposing task-oriented solutions. Bob emerged as a process-oriented leader because he tried to minimize bickering, to ask everyone's opinion, to shame members who were unwilling to compromise, and to state openly his intuition of the prevailing mood of the group (for example, "Isn't some compromise possible?"). Note how Bob responds to the personal needs of the two withdrawn members of the group, Pat and James. He tries to protect Pat from attack and gives James the friendship he seems to crave. In fact, the story implies that James voted in favor of the proposal mainly because of Bob's kindness toward him.

The "Role" of a Leader

As the members of a group interact, they begin to develop shared expectations about how each individual will behave. Thus, in addition to evolving group norms, they also start to view each other as having *roles* to perform in the group. For example, a person who performs group functions more often than other members soon assumes the role of leader, that is, he or she is *expected* to continue helping the group with the same approximate frequency.

Often, however, roles are not left to evolve naturally. Instead, some authority establishes *positions* which have implicit role expectations for whoever assumes that slot. Government, business, and military positions often have role expectations that exist independently from the person

404

who happens to occupy the position at a particular time.

When the expectations attached to a role are very different from those you, as the occupant, want to play or are accustomed to playing, the resulting discomfort is called *role strain*. If it is not adequately recognized and managed, role strain can produce emotional disturbance or even physical illness.

There are some situations where we can predict that role strain will occur. A person who is promoted from a field worker to a foreman, or from a foreman to a desk-bound supervisor, is likely to experience some emotional discomfort if he or she is not prepared for the change in roles or is not supported during the transition into the new set of expectations. Suppose, for example, that you have a good friend with whom you spend much time and to whom you customarily defer in important decisions. One day, both of you are appointed to the same committee and the supervising teacher asks you to be the leader. Your committee must work hard if it is to clean up the gym in time for an important party. Everyone grabs a broom and dustpan and begins working, except your friend, who wanders around the gym talking to the workers.

Your friend is a deviate from the group norm: he is the only one not preparing for the dance. If his challenge to the group's task and its unspoken rules is allowed to persist, it might undermine the morale of those students who are working. It might also indicate that you cannot perform one key function of a leader, that of enforcing group norms. You are now in a bind. On the one hand, because of your leadership role, you are expected to punish this student's behavior. On the other hand, because of your friendship role, you are expected (at least by the friend) to defer to his wishes as you have in the past. What strain would you feel facing this conflict in roles? How would you handle the situation?

The Pattern of Personal Preferences

Another important aspect of group process is the pattern of personal attractions or dislikes among group members. If you know this pattern, you can anticipate how information (or rumors) will flow through the group. You will know who the natural leaders are, who the isolated members are, what alliances are likely to develop in a group conflict, and how tightly knit or *cohesive* the group is.

Social scientists analyzing small groups sometimes administer *sociometric* tests to get the information necessary to diagram the pattern of attractions and dislikes. The test contains several questions with this general form:

"With whom do you like to work in this group?"
"With whom do you not like to work in this group?"

or

"Whom would you most like to have as the leader in this group?"
"Whom would you least like to have as the leader of this group?"

The answers of all members are combined and plotted in a *sociogram*. Each individual in the group is represented by a circle, attractions are represented by arrows running from chooser to chosen, dislikes by dotted arrows, and isolation by the absence of any arrow at all. The figure below is a sociogram based on our brief observation of the school dance committee described at the beginning of this chapter.

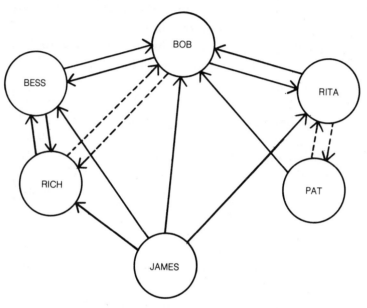

The Sociogram: A Diagram of Interpersonal Relationships

Why do these patterns of preference develop within a group? Can we predict which persons in a group will be chosen most often by others in the group? What accounts for their popularity? Social psychologists who have studied these questions suggest that there are several factors that contribute to status or popularity within the group.[3]

First, we are more likely to choose to associate with or

be led by someone who appreciates us in return.

Second, we are more likely to choose someone who reflects our own attitudes, social background, or other characteristics we find important. By so doing, we strengthen our confidence in our own interpretation of the world. Since it is possible to view the same events in many different ways depending on our culture or our level of personal defensiveness, it is always reassuring to find someone else who seconds our interpretation. This is called *consensual validation.*

Third, we are more likely to choose someone with whom we have already had several exchanges. Someone who is conveniently located may meet other members more frequently and may become popular partly because of this greater exposure. For example, persons living near doors or elevators in apartment houses are more likely to run into their neighbors, find that they have things in common, and develop a pattern of mutual preference. Similarly, if a boy and girl sit next to each other in several classes, the chance of an attraction between them may increase.

Fourth, we are more likely to choose someone who represents the values and standards prized by the group. Thus, if the group values skill at talking, the talkers are more likely than the non-talkers to be ranked highly in a sociometric test. Similarly, if the group values defiant rejection of authority, the most daring rebel will be the most highly ranked.

Fifth, and finally, there is the member's interpersonal skill. Some people are just more pleasant to be around than others. Another way of saying the same thing is that some people are rewarding to interact with while others impose costs in time and frustration on those who interact with them. We are more likely to choose someone who rewards other members by helping them, defending them, solving conflicts, suggesting new ideas, and giving fresh hope and courage when it is most needed. Such a person is less likely to impose his or her own personal problems on others in the course of a casual exchange, thereby relieving the other people of the need to spend time and energy in issues they would prefer to avoid. By contrast, people who are inconsiderate, aggressive, or cannot control their own emotions make it costly to interact with them. This will lessen their ranking in the preference poll.[4]

One reason that a sociometric test succeeds in identifying the "natural leaders" of a group is because their contributions in achieving group goals and in maintaining the satisfaction of other members are reflected in the ratings they receive. Using the characteristics listed above of a frequently chosen person, we can say that a natural leader is more likely (1) to appreciate more of the other members, (2) to offer consensual validation of the group's view of the world, (3) to exemplify the values held by the group, (4) to have frequent interactions with the other members, and (5) to reward fellow members rather than impose costs on them during those interactions.

We have explored some of the general processes that occur in all groups, as if we were studying a road map of unfamiliar territory to find landmarks to guide our driving. Many people absorb this general information quickly and then ask a more urgent personal question: "How can I *improve* my interpersonal skills? How can I learn to be more effective in groups?" We will consider this question next.

PERCEIVING GROUP PROCESSES

1. *Select a television series with a regularly recurring group and analyze the interactions of the group members in one episode, using the concepts studied in this chapter.*

    Does the group have norms? If so, how are they enforced?

    Who is the leader? What functions does he or she perform for the group?

    What patterns of personal preference exist among the members? How do these patterns influence the course of the episode?

    What roles do various members play?

2. *Bring a collection of blocks of various shapes and sizes to class for use in a "building" experiment. Select six or seven persons to "build something" with the blocks in a five-minute period, without any verbal communication among them. Those who are not in the group should observe what happens. After the five minutes are up, let the group members discuss how they felt during the exercise. What goals were each of them pursuing? Who cooperated with whom? What frustrations did they feel? Now add the observations of the students who were not in the building group. After some discussion, six more persons can begin "building" while the first group acts as observers.*

    Discuss your experiences in these nonverbal

groups using the concepts you studied in this chapter. Use the questions in the first part of this exercise (above) to analyze the process in your group.

Training Groups: Learning Through "Feedback"

What does it mean to say that someone is or is not effective in interpersonal relationships? Chris Argyris, a social psychologist, suggests that there are three signs that someone possesses "effective interpersonal competence."[5] First, the person perceives and interprets situations accurately. This is fundamental because a person who distorts information as it is sent or received multiplies the chances for misunderstanding and conflict. Second, he is able to solve problems in such a way that they remain solved rather than reappear in a different form. Third, the person finds solutions that permit parties to continue working with each other at least as effectively as when they began to solve the problem. Of these three criteria, the first—the ability to send and receive information with a minimum of personal distortion caused by one's own needs and emotional defenses—is the basic skill underlying the other two.

Self-Awareness: The Key

A first step to improve your skill in groups, then, is to become aware of those processes inside yourself that may distort your view of your own behavior or that of other members. Although conflicts still may exist even when both parties assess the situation accurately, many battles occur because one or both of the persons involved mistakes the true nature of the situation.

To illustrate the relationship between your own self-knowledge and other people's attitudes and beliefs about you, two researchers named Joe Luft and Harry Ingham designed the "Johari window:"[6]

To be effective in interpersonal relationships, we must perceive and interpret situations accurately. Sometimes it is helpful when friends tell us their reactions to our behavior; we become more aware of how others see us, and we may change our behavior accordingly.

	KNOWN TO SELF	NOT KNOWN TO SELF
KNOWN TO OTHERS	*Free Area*	*Blind Area*
NOT KNOWN TO OTHERS	*Hidden Area*	*Unknown area*

Two squares do not pose problems of communication. The free area refers to information about you that is already known to both you and others. The unknown area refers to information about you that cannot be communicated because neither you nor others are aware of it. The remaining squares do raise communication problems, however, because one party to the transaction has more information than the other. The blind area refers to information about you which, although it is easily observable by others, remains unknown to you. The hidden area refers to information which you are aware of but hide from other people. An example is the "hidden agenda," where you have secret needs and purposes that you hope to fulfill without revealing them to others.

The more information about you (and about other members of the group) that falls within the free area, the clearer communications will be among the group members. This free area of information shared by all participants can be increased if each member discloses any "hidden agendas" he has, and if members help each other to understand individual "blind spots." A method for doing this was discovered by Kurt Lewin, a social psychologist.

Discovery of the T-Groups[7]

In 1949, a government commission hired Kurt Lewin and his associates to train community leaders to cope more effectively with interracial problems. Their workshop began like many: the participants brought up problems they had faced at home, and the group considered methods to deal with them. Sometimes participants assumed the roles of opposing parties to act out how they would behave if placed in a difficult situation. As the groups worked, Lewin had observers record what happened in each session. These observers met in the evening to compare groups and to discuss the events of the day. When some of the participants in the workshop heard about these nightly meetings, they asked to attend. After initial hesitation, this was permitted. The results were astounding. A participant would object to an observer's comment about him. The observer would tell why he felt as he did, and the other participants would support or criticize from their points of view. Soon everyone at the workshop came to the evening meetings for the exciting interpersonal exchanges.

> The staff immediately realized that they had, somewhat inadvertently, discovered a powerful technique of human relations education: group members may profit enormously by being confronted, in an objective manner, with observations about their behavior and its effects on others; they may learn about their interpersonal styles, the responses of others to them and about group behavior and development in general.[8]

Thereafter, the focus of the Training-group activity

shifted from discussion of events in the participant's home towns—the "there-and-then" approach—to a discussion of the interpersonal processes among the persons present at the time—the "here-and-now" approach. People continued to be emotionally involved in the original task of studying interracial problems, but, at the same time, tried to maintain a detachment that would permit them to analyze their own behavior and that of the group. Lewin called this dual task of a T-group member *observant participation.*

Lewin also coined the term *feedback* to describe the fresh information that people acquired when they heard the other members' responses to their behavior in the group. Feedback often "thaws" a person's habitual patterns of interacting with others. The result of this thawing is a new sense of uncertainty about one's own behavior. The T-group permits the person to cope with this emotional discomfort by experimenting with new ways of relating to other people. In turn, these experiments provoke more feedback. Through this continuing process, the members of the group become more aware of what is happening both inside themselves and in the group as a whole.

> *In the first session of a group of nonpatients (business executives) meeting for a five-day, intensive (fifty-hour) human relations laboratory, one member, a twenty-five-year-old, boastful, aggressive, swaggering individual who had obviously been drinking heavily that day, proceeded to dominate the meeting and to make a fool of himself. He boasted of his accomplishments, belittled the group, monopolized the meeting, interrupted, out-shouted, and insulted*

every other member. All attempts to deal with the situation failed. Feedback from members about how angry or hurt he made them feel, interpretations about the meaning and cause of his behavior—all were ineffective. Then my co-leader commented quite sincerely, "You know what I like about you? Your fear and lack of confidence. You're scared here, just like me; we're all scared about what will happen to us' this week." At that point the [person] instantaneously discarded his facade, eventually becoming a most valuable group member; further- more, a softer, accepting style of relating became an important part of the group culture.[9]

After a T-group experience, people are often more skilled at recognizing unfulfilled needs of the group and in effectively performing the functions necessary to meet those needs. Hopefully, they will become leaders in the old groups they return to and introduce the benefits of more open communication to members of these groups, making this openness the new group norm.

Psychotherapy in Groups

The power of feedback has also been harnessed for the benefit of people who lack basic skills of interpersonal competence. Those who have a regular pattern of misinterpreting the behavior of others and of getting involved in self-defeating transactions with others often experience intense inner suffering. To control this inner pressure, they are likely to sacrifice their ability to perceive themselves and other people accurately in exchange for some form of "protective armor." The mental and emotional difficulties give them a *survival orientation* toward life instead of the *competence orientation* of the well-functioning member of society:

> *The important point is that the individual with neurotic defenses is frozen into a closed position; he is not open for learning, he is generally searching not for growth but for safety. . . . Through the use of defense mechanisms he withdraws, distorts, or attacks the environment.*

✿ ✿ ✿ ✿ ✿

> *The survival-oriented individual does not give or accept accurate feedback; if left to his own devices he will generate those kinds of experiences which will strengthen his defensive position. He may, for example, be particularly attentive to feedback that confirms the rationality of his having to be closed. Similarly, the feedback he gives to others may be highly colored by his survival orientation: he may be far more concerned with engendering in others certain attitudes toward himself than with giving accurate feedback.*[10]

A group experience where all the members are strongly committed to helping themselves and fellow patients can sometimes break this closed and self-defeating cycle. Each patient in a therapy group can be expected to import into the group environment the same inappropriate tactics that he uses in daily life. As the patients begin to interact with each other, a *social microcosm,* a small version of the outside world, develops in the group. This process permits the therapist to observe the patient's "problem" directly instead of only hearing about it through the biased report of the patient. The therapist can call attention to a behavior when it occurs, and the interpretations and reactions of other group members can be marshalled to reinforce points for the patient. Occasionally, the therapist will offer interpretations of some patient's behavior. For example, he might point out that the patient is displacing anger unconsciously from one member who provoked it onto another, weaker member who is an easier target to attack. The therapist might expose how a patient's reactions to parental figures in the past are being "transferred" into the

Often, people join therapy groups in order to gain a better understanding of their feelings and behavior. As the people begin to interact with each other, the group becomes a "social microcosm": a small version of the outside world. This process permits the therapist to observe a patient's problem directly, instead of only hearing about it. Other group members can also provide helpful feedback on how they view a person's behavior.

group context. Or he might show why a patient who has repressed some quality in his or her personality feels a strong negative response to another member who has that same quality.

As in T-groups, feedback from other group-therapy patients clarifies for the individual just how self-defeating some of his behavior can be. When the individual finally builds up the confidence to experiment with new ways of relating to other people, the group feedback provides consensual validation for this improved interpersonal style. Franz Alexander, describing the purpose of individual psychoanalysis, suggested that therapy "exposes the patient, under more favorable circumstances, to emotional situations which he could not handle in the past. The patient, in order to be helped, must undergo a *corrective emotional experience* suitable to repair the traumatic influence of a previous experience."[11] The same dynamics are at work in group therapy. (Remember, however, that a behavioral psychologist might explain this *same process* as a "re-learning" that takes place in a specially structured environment—the group.)

Finding a Therapy Group

Sometimes people who *think* they would like to be in a therapy group because of something they have read or heard from their friends are not good candidates for group treatment. An important first step for any person who wants help is to get advice about which of the many different styles of therapy is most likely to be suitable in his or her individual case. This type of "screening" function is often performed by counselors or mental health workers attached to community mental health centers, local schools, university health clinics, hospitals, or similar institutions. Also, some big cities have group psychotherapy associations that will advise whether or not group therapy is appropriate, and, if so, what group best matches the applicant's needs.

If you find that your behavior consistently makes you unhappy or gets you into trouble with other people, you may want a screening interview with a mental health professional. The purpose of a screening interview is not to *treat* you but rather to gather some information from you about the problem as you see it, to determine if you would benefit from psychological counseling, and, if so, to decide what type of treatment would be best. The purpose of the interview(s) is exploratory, with no commitment on your part of follow up on the advice given.

Unfortunately, some groups are not so careful in determining who should and should not participate. Therapy groups usually have a clear commitment to healing and to relief of emotional suffering, and they are usually associated with a recognized professional mental health program. They should be distinguished from unsupervised groups which are often unpredictable in goals. If you are thinking about entering an unsupervised group, you should pay close attention to the "consumer's guide" that follows.

Encounter: A New Use of Groups

Some people believe that everyone can benefit by participating in a group where open and honest expression of emotions is encouraged. These groups are formed under many different names: encounter groups, awareness groups, personal growth groups, gestalt therapy, sensitivity training, and an ever changing kaleidoscope of labels, leaders, and techniques is used. For simplicity, we refer to all these groups with the single name, "encounter." If you look in the newspaper or on the bulletin boards in many public locations, you will often find advertisements like those below:

NEW PATHS

Primal groups for emotional identity. Call 888-8888

W.I.N.

Personal growth groups. Individual, couples, and family counseling. Fees negotiable. Call 555-5555, 555-5556.

SLEEP AND DREAM WORKSHOP

A few openings in August. Call Bill at 333-3333.

B.E.S.T.

At B.E.S.T. Institute, we have your integral intensive group: Gestalt, sensitivity, bioenergetic, primal, and emotional training. R. Yoga. 111-1111, 111-1122, 111-1133.

NOTICE

Rolfer—V.I. employing psychic visualization. Sponsored by the Collective Group Movement for Therapy. Private sessions Dec.-Jan. Call 999-8888.

Like T-groups and therapy groups, these encounter groups rely on the social microcosm concept: that each individual will import the emotional restrictions, defenses, and strengths he exhibits in the outside world into the group environment. Encounter groups also rely on the basic mechanism of feedback, and often use special exercises that speed up this process. For example, a "trust walk" exercise might be introduced. In this event, the group members form pairs; one person in each pair is blindfolded; and the remaining person then leads the blinded one in a nonverbal exploration of the immediate area. After a short while, the pair switches roles. Then everyone returns to one circle, where the participants are encouraged to tell how they felt trusting someone so completely or to tell what they could silently sense about the person who guided them. A different type of exercise might involve a "hot seat," where one member becomes the sole focus of the group's attention. Feedback about that member's behavior is then administered in a heavy dose.

Despite some similarities with T-groups and therapy groups, encounter groups have one important difference: they do not have an easily definable purpose or goal. T-groups are designed to improve communication skills in normally functioning people. Therapy groups are designed to provide a "corrective emotional experience" for

422

persons who are not relating well to other people. By contrast, the aims of encounter groups and their leaders are as diffuse and varied as the motives of persons who attend them. The authors of an extensive research project on encounter groups suggested that the major purpose of such groups may be ". . . not for people-changing, but for people-providing."[12] Those who participate agree to suspend many customary rules of social interaction in order to facilitate and intensify their interpersonal experiences.

> The techniques encounter leaders use to create excitement, to create closeness, to create openness become more understandable viewed in this perspective. The psychological meaning to participants of the well-known "trust walk," the exercise which perhaps most epitomizes the encounter movement, may be clearer when viewed as functioning not to change people but to provide them with a replica of an experience felt to be too rare or too costly to acquire from the interactions of everyday life.[13]

A Dangerous Underside

One important fact to remember about the different types of encounter groups you might contact is that some may be harmful. Observing groups and leaders under carefully supervised conditions, a Stanford University research project found that 8 percent (or about one in twelve) of those who started in these groups became "casualties": their experience was so negative that they had to seek professional psychological help to recover.[14] Also, 30 percent (almost one in three) had a lasting negative reaction of lowered self-esteem or lowered confidence in interpersonal relations.

The theories or philosophies of the group leaders (which ranged among psychodrama, Gestalt, transactional analysis, Synanon, marathon, Esalen, and others) did *not* appear to have any relation to the number of casualties produced. What was important was the *actual behavior* of the leader as opposed to his or her theoretical beliefs. Some leaders appeared less able to understand and utilize group processes skillfully, less able to judge when someone had been pushed enough, and less caring toward the members of their group. These deficiencies were an important contributing cause of negative outcomes for participants.

In the Stanford study, the leaders were handpicked and highly regarded in their field. However, in the world-at-large there are *no restrictions on who can be a group leader*. Anyone can be an encounter group leader, without any professional training and even without any intuitive skill. Although most leaders have had some personal experience in groups, that is not necessarily a qualification to manage complicated group processes. There is no screening procedure to ensure that the leader does not have personal problems which will distort his supervision of the group. What was "high-risk" in the Stanford study becomes even riskier in the open market.

Casualties and negative outcomes may also occur in professionally supervised therapy groups, but these groups usually take more responsibility in identifying such persons at an early stage and helping them to find other kinds of psychological help.

The "High-Risk" Group: A Consumer's Guide

The authors of the Stanford study recommend that you take the following precautions before entering any type of encounter group:

First, do some preliminary self-assessment on your own.

> *What are one's hopes for the experience, and one's own view of self? Persons who feel essentially cut off from other people, dislike their own behavior, and see it as less than adequate, and, in addition, believe that encounter group experience will somehow beautifully, magically, and safely liberate them from themselves, should take care. Such inflated expectations—and they are perhaps too easy to caricature—can lead not only to frustration, but to negative outcomes. It is simply suggested that potential group entrants examine realistically where they are, and what they might hope, practically speaking, to obtain from the experience. It should be kept in mind that one's chances for clear positive benefit are only about one in three. A person who feels, essentially, that he or she is in psychological distress should ordinarily be considering counseling or psychotherapy rather than an encounter group experience.[15]*

Second, talk to persons who have been in the groups led by the leader you are evaluating. It is better to ask after several months have elapsed, because the Stanford study found that some persons who initially had positive outcomes later changed to negative, whereas there were few cases that went the other way with time.

The most productive question to ask is: "Would you like to be in a group again, led by this leader?" Negative answers should be taken rather seriously. Positive answers should be taken skeptically; one should talk to another group member, or preferably several. Past group members can also be asked about the general group climate, especially the degree to which, in the latter part of the group, anger and attack took place. Such groups should be entered with caution, if one's hoping for learning and for avoiding negative effects are high.

Questioning past group members as to whether anyone got hurt in the group, and getting details of this, is also especially productive in locating groups which might be damaging.[16]

Third, if you do enter a group, remain aware of your position in the group and be a "comfortably active" group member.

Persons who, by the middle of the group, find that they have been largely passive, "out of it," do not like the group particularly, do not sense that they are respected and liked by the other members, never have a feeling of "communion" with them, and do not feel able to disclose their inner thoughts and feelings, will probably get little out of the group experience.[17]

Fourth, you should avoid (a) being overoptimistic about what the group can do for you, or (b) being too naively trusting in the goodness of the group or the leader, or (c) being "out on the edge of the group."

> *Mild skepticism, the attitude that the group can be used for one's purposes, but [that it] may not automatically be the best or safest of environments, appears to be the most productive stance.*[18]

Fifth, there is a better chance of having a positive learning experience if you *think* about what is happening in the group as well as reacting emotionally.[19]

Sixth, never forget that you can always leave the group if it is "proving steadily unproductive, stressful, or damaging. . . . Not all persons and all learning environments can be perfectly matched."[20]

Seventh, and finally, remember that local mental health professionals can often advise you about the desirability of entering a particular group.

Games People Play—A Transactional Analysis of Group Process[21]

One aim of people who enter therapy groups (or psychotherapy in general) is to gain insight into self-defeating patterns of behavior that they tend to slip into. The proverb, "Forewarned is forearmed," applies. If the person can be taught to anticipate what will happen if events continue on the same track, then he can decide to move out of the way of an onrushing problem.

A useful way to teach people to anticipate problems is to describe interpersonal transactions as if they were games. One player makes the opening move, the opposing player chooses a response from several available alternatives, the first player makes another

FOCUSING ON FEEDBACK

1. *Bring blindfolds to class and experiment with the "trust walk" described in the discussion of encounter and sensitivity groups. After everyone has had a chance to lead and to be led, discuss your feelings about being dependent on someone and your nonverbal perceptions about the person who was leading you.*

2. *Invite a local mental health professional who leads therapy groups to class to discuss: what happens in these groups; when group therapy is preferable to individual counseling; and how the therapist can tell when a person no longer needs to continue the group therapy.*

3. *In a social microcosm, people bring their characteristic styles of dealing with others into the small groups they participate in. How would Freud explain this type of transference of behavior from one context to another?*

   How would Skinner explain the persistence of a behavioral style in different contexts?

   In Freud's view, how could feedback change behavior?

   In Skinner's view?

4. *Suppose that a friend has just disclosed to you that he*

or she is planning to enter a personal growth group. What questions would you want to ask to help him or her reach a good decision? Role-play a conversation between you and your friend in class using the ideas in the "consumer's guide" discussion.

move, and this alternation continues until someone wins the game. Eric Berne, a psychiatrist, often observed such predictable alternation of move and countermove when two or more persons interacted. There seemed to be a purpose to the transactions, even though the purpose was not always to "win" something. Some transactions followed such regular patterns that it seemed as if the interacting persons were following imaginary rules. Berne decided to record the different *scripts* that people seemed to be following as he observed them.

Because of his psychoanalytic training, Berne believed that behavior reflects the influence of id forces (basic drives and wishes), ego forces (realism), and superego forces (moral standards). However, he decided that these Freudian concepts were too complicated to be useful to most people. He wanted to transform them into practical terms that could be easily applied in everyday life.

If a person's superego strongly influences his behavior, Berne reasoned, then he tends to act like a parent would act. With reference to such a set of acts or statements, an observer could say: "That is your 'Parent' behaving now." By this, the observer *means* that the person has assessed the situation to be one calling for behavior that is judgmental, moralistic, authoritarian, and evaluative.

Having made this assessment, the person is now imitating whatever behavior he learned from his parents.

"That is your Parent" MEANS:

> *"You are now in the same state of mind as one of your parents (or a parental substitute) used to be, and you are responding as he would, with the same posture, gestures, vocabulary, feelings, etc."*[22]

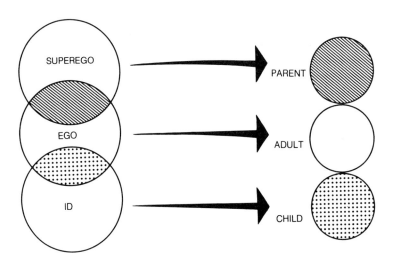

When you communicate with someone, are you being judgmental and moralistic (as a parent might be)? Impulsive or playful (like a child)? Or rational and mature (like an adult)? Eric Berne has proposed a system for understanding interpersonal communications. It is called transactional analysis, and it is based on the Freudian heritage of the id, ego, and superego.

The advantage of using this kind of statement is that people do not need extensive training to understand what the terms mean. Everyone has had a parent (or parental substitute) and can recognize how a parent tends to behave.

If the id impulses strongly influence a person's behavior, Berne continued, then he tends to act like a child. The situation is assessed as calling for behavior that is submissive, impulsive, self-centered, pleasure-seeking, playful, pleading or begging, or something similar. Of this set of acts or statements, the observer could say:

> *"That is your Child"* MEANS:
>
> > *"The manner and intent of your reaction is the same as it would have been when you were a very little boy or girl."*[23]

Since everyone has experienced what it is like to be a child or to be around children, this observation can also be applied intuitively.

Finally, if the rational ego is clearly in control, then the person tends to act like a mature adult: he assesses the situation as requiring rational analysis and calculation. Thus, the observer could say:

> *"That is your Adult"* MEANS:
>
> > *"You have just made an autonomous, objective appraisal of the situation and are stating . . . the conclusions you have come to, in a non-prejudicial manner."*[24]

If we use Berne's system of Transactional Analysis,

then whenever someone communicates with another person, we can describe what happens using one of three possible statements:

(1) "That is your Child speaking."

DIAGRAMMED AS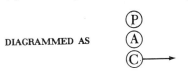

(2) "That is your Adult speaking."

DIAGRAMMED AS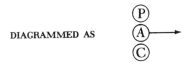

(3) "That is your Parent speaking."

DIAGRAMMED AS

In the maps or diagrams illustrated above, Berne represents each person by a series of three circles (P stands for Parent, A for Adult, C for Child). When a communication is "sent" from one person to another, that transaction is mapped by an arrow drawn *from* the appropriate level of the sender's personality *to* the level of the receiver's personality at which it was directed. A similar arrow is drawn in the opposite direction to map how the receiver responds.

Here are some examples of transactions between two people, X and Y, mapped using Berne's diagrams:

TRANSACTION #1

X   Y

Ⓟ   Ⓟ
Ⓐ⇄Ⓐ
Ⓒ   Ⓒ

X: *"Where is my book?"*

Y: *"On the table."*

TRANSACTION #2

X   Y

X: *You should do the dishes now."*

Y: *"Why are you always criticizing me?"*

TRANSACTION #3

X   Y

X: *"Where are my keys?"*

Y: *"Don't act like a child; if you'd pick up, you wouldn't lose things."*

The first transaction is Adult-Adult. Because both persons are using a matching level of communication, Berne calls this a *complementary transaction.* The second exchange is

Parent-Child, but it is also complementary because the response returns along the same route as the initial communication. By contrast, the third example is a *crossed transaction*. While the sender is attempting to communicate at the Adult-Adult level, the response comes at a different level, that of Parent-Child. Needless to say, crossed transactions cause much misunderstanding and trouble between people.

Another source of misunderstanding occurs when there is a *double message* in the communications between two persons. When a hidden or unconscious communication passes at the same time as the observable "social" communication, it is called an *ulterior transaction*. An example is the salesman (S) whose aim is to sell an appliance by appealing to the buyer's (B) unconscious needs.[25]

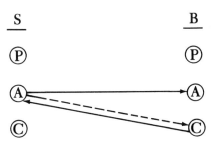

S: *"This one is better,* B: *"That's the one*
   but you can't afford it."   *I'll take."*

The statement by the salesman is apparently factual, directed from his "Adult" to the buyer's "Adult." But the salesman is also sending a hidden message (indicated by the dotted arrow) which, loosely translated, might be: "This product is too good for you," or "You'll have to prove yourself if you want to buy *this* product." If the buyer's "Adult" were in control, he or she might see the salesman's ulterior motive and simply ignore it. For example, the buyer might reply "Yes, you're right, that seems to be the best product, but you're also right that I can't afford to buy it now." However, this buyer falls for the salesman's trap. The buyer's "Child" wants to beat the salesman at his own game by proving that he or she *can* afford "the best," even when that is not true. The buyer chooses to protect his self-esteem instead of his money.

People who communicate with each other using ulterior transactions usually have secret goals. They are looking for a "payoff" that will satisfy whatever need motivated them to send a hidden psychological message. Instead of communicating honestly and openly with each other, they are hoping to "win" something from the other participants in the transaction. If one person sends both an overt and a hidden message, then the receiver has two choices: either to play along by the sender's rules, in which case the hidden psychological needs of the sender are gratified, or to ignore or deflect the hidden part of the message, in which case the sender must either give up his ulterior motive or look elsewhere for someone who will fall for the trick.

When people interact using hidden communications which "fit together" or "complement" each other and progress by steps to a predictable ending, they are taking part in what Berne calls a *game*. The two important ingredients for a game are, first, a hidden communication, and, second, the existence of a payoff. People who play games cannot have the honest and open interpersonal relationships that many people seek. For a specific example of a game, see the box on pages 437-440.

Berne believed that people could be happier and more productive if they were able to avoid playing such games. His method of transactional analysis is designed to give people the ability to recognize these games as self-defeating behavior and to avoid being trapped into playing them. In a group therapy situation, the members help each other to see which "games they are playing" by giving honest feedback to one another.

Conclusion

Why do some groups achieve their goals more effectively than others? Why do some groups provide more satisfaction to their members than others? Why does a person choose to join one group rather than another? Why does he or she assume a particular role in the group? Psychologists who study these issues often focus their attention on the processes of personal interaction that are common to most groups. They chart how norms, individual roles, and alliances among members evolve in groups. Once it has evolved, a group's structure has an important impact on the thoughts, feelings, and actions of each member as well as on the group's overall effectiveness. There is a constant and complex interplay between the individual's influence on the group and the group's influence on the individual.

A group's processes may be applied in a conscious attempt to change the behavior of its members. A person who receives frank responses to his statements and actions

"WHY DON'T YOU—YES, BUT"

In his popular book Games People Play, *Berne analyzed the scripts of many typical games, including "Kick me," "Alcoholic," "See what you made me do," "Blemish," and "Let's you and him fight." The game described here is one that Berne observed to be "most often played at parties and groups of all kinds, including psychotherapy groups." This game is called "Why Don't You—Yes, But," which is abbreviated in this passage as* YDYB.

White: "My husband always insists on doing our own repairs, and he never builds anything right."

Black: "Why doesn't he take a course in carpentry?"

White: "Yes, but he doesn't have the time."

Blue: "Why don't you buy him some good tools?"

White: "Yes, but he doesn't know how to use them."

Red: "Why don't you have your building done by a carpenter?"

White: "Yes, but that would cost too much."

Brown: "Why don't you just accept what he does the way he does it?"

White: "Yes, but the whole thing might fall down."

Such an exchange is typically followed by silence. It is eventually broken by Green, who may say something like, "That's men for you, always trying to show how efficient they are."

YDYB can be played by any number. The agent [in the above situation, White] presents a problem. The others start to present solutions, each beginning with "Why don't you . . .?" To each of these White objects with a "Yes, but. . . ." A good player can stand off the others indefinitely until they all give up, whereupon

White wins. In many situations she might have to handle a dozen or more solutions to engineer the crestfallen silence which signifies her victory. . . .

Since the solutions are, with rare exceptions, rejected, it is apparent that this game must serve some ulterior purpose. YDYB is not played for its ostensible purpose (an Adult quest for information or solutions), but to reassure and gratify the Child. A bare transcript may sound Adult, but in the living tissue it can be observed that White presents herself as a Child inadequate to meet the situation; whereupon the others become transformed into sage Parents anxious to dispense their wisdom for her benefit.

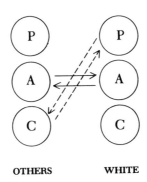

OTHERS   **WHITE**

S: *Why don't you . . ."*   R: *"Yes, but . . ."*

Why Don't You — Yes But

This is illustrated in [the Figure above]. The game can proceed because at the social level both stimulus and response are Adult to Adult, and at the psychological level they are also complementary, with Parent to Child stimulus ("Why don't you . . .") eliciting Child to Parent response ("Yes, but . . ."). The psychological level is usually unconscious on both sides, but the shifts in ego state (Adult to "inadequate" Child on White's part, Adult to "wise" Parent by the others) can often be detected by an alert observer from changes in posture, muscular tone, voice and vocabulary.

In order to illustrate the implications, it is instructive to follow through on the example given above.

Therapist: "Did anyone suggest anything you hadn't thought of yourself?"

White: "No, they didn't. As a matter of fact, I've actually tried almost everything they suggested. I did buy my husband some tools, and he did take a course in carpentry."

Here White demonstrates two of the reasons why the proceedings should not be taken at face value. First, in the majority of cases White is as intelligent as anyone else in the company, and it is very unlikely that others will suggest any solution that she has not thought of herself. If someone does happen to come up with an original suggestion, White will accept it gratefully if she is playing fair; that is, her "inadequate" Child will give way if anyone present has an idea ingenious enough to stimulate her Adult. But habitual YDYB players, such as White above, seldom play fair. . . .

The example given is particularly dramatic, because it clearly illustrates the second point. Even if White has actually tried some of the solutions presented, she will still object to them. *The purpose of the game is not to get suggestions, but to reject them.*

While almost anyone will play this game under proper circumstances because of its time-structuring value, careful study of individuals who particularly favor it reveals several interesting features. First, they characteristically can and will play either side of the game with equal facility. This switchability of roles is true of all games. Players may habitually prefer one role to another, but they are capable of trading, and they are willing to play any other role in the same game if for some reason that is indicated. . . .

In summary, then: while each move is amusing, so to speak, to White, and brings its own little pleasure in rejecting the suggestions, *the real payoff is the silence or masked silence which ensues when all the others have racked their brains and grown tired of trying to think of acceptable solutions. This signifies to White and to them that she has won by demonstrating it is they who are inadequate.* If the silence is not masked, it may persist for several minutes. In the paradigm, Green cut White's triumph short because of her eagerness to start a game of her own, and that was what kept her from participating in White's game.[26]

(feedback) from fellow members of the group can learn important lessons about himself. For someone who already has an acceptable level of interpersonal competence, feedback from a group may improve his communication skills. T-groups apply group process in this way. In carefully supervised therapy groups, feedback may help those who lack basic interpersonal skills to achieve a more adequate level of functioning. Finally, feedback may be used to intensify emotional exchanges among individuals, as in personal growth, encounter, or sensitivity groups.

Because so much of our lives is lived in groups, the exploration of group dynamics will continue to be an important focus of psychological investigation.

ANALYZING SOME TRANSACTIONS

1. *Role-play the situations described below. Using Berne's transactional analysis, describe the short conversations in terms of the parent-like, child-like, and adult-like levels of communication.*

    A mother and father are reluctant to let their son take the family car.

    Two couples on a double date are trying to decide what to do.

    A salesperson is helping someone to look for new clothing.

    The boss has called a meeting of three employees. He wishes to describe a task that must be finished immediately and to assign jobs.

    Four students meet each other outside school and begin to talk.

    Two roommates argue about who should do which chores and who is not carrying his (or her) share of the general upkeep.

2. *Why might it be an advantage for someone to recognize games or ulterior transactions in operation?*

    How could this new knowledge be used to help the person?

In Berne's view, what part of the personality makes use of the knowledge?   In Freud's view?

How would Skinner explain a change in behavior that occurred after someone learned that he or she was "playing a game"?

Suggested Reading

Berne, Eric, *Games People Play* (New York: Grove Press, 1964).

Harris, Thomas, *I'm OK-You're OK* (New York: Harper and Row, 1969).

James, Muriel, and Dorothy Jongeward, *Born to Win: Transactional Analysis with Gestalt Experiments* (Reading, Mass.: Addison-Wesley, 1971).

Klein, Alan, *Role-Playing in Leadership Training and Group Problem-Solving* (New York: Association Press, 1956).

Lawless, David, *Effective Management* (Englewood Cliffs, N.J.: Prentice-Hall, 1972).

Rogers, Carl, *On Encounter Groups* (New York: Harper and Row, 1970).

Verny, Thomas, *Inside Groups: A Practical Guide to Encounter Groups and Group Therapy* (New York: McGraw-Hill, 1974).

FOOTNOTES

1. David Lawless, *Effective Management* (Englewood Cliffs, N.J.: Prentice-Hall, 1972), p. 265.
2. F. E. Fiedler, *A Theory of Leadership Effectiveness* (New York: McGraw-Hill, 1967).
3. Lawless, *op. cit.*, pp. 208-213.
4. Lawless, *op. cit.*, pp. 214-215.
5. Chris Argyris, *Interpersonal Competence and Organizational Effectiveness* (Homewood, Ill.: Dorsey Press, 1962).
6. Reprinted from *Group Processes: An Introduction to Group Dynamics*, by Joseph Luft, by permission of Mayfield Publishing Company, formerly National Press Books, Palo Alto, 1970, p. 11.
7. Excerpts from *The Theory and Practice of Group Psychotherapy*, by Irvin D. Yalom. © 1970 by Basic Books, Inc., Publishers, New York, pp. 343-352.
8. *Ibid.*, p. 344.
9. *Ibid.*, p. 92.

10. *Ibid.*, pp. 367-368.
11. Franz Alexander, "Unexplored Areas in Psychoanalytic Theory and Treatment," in G. Daniels, ed., *New Perspectives in Psychoanalysis: Sandor Rado Lectures 1957-1963* (New York: Grune and Stratton, 1965), p. 75.
12. Excerpted from Chapters 16 and 17 of *Encounter Groups: First Facts,* by Morton A. Lieberman, Irvin D. Yalom, and Matthew B. Miles. © 1973 by Morton A. Lieberman, Irvin D. Yalom, and Matthew B. Miles, Basic Books, Inc., Publishers, New York, p. 453.
13. *Ibid.*
14. *Ibid.*, adapted from Chapters 16 and 17.
15. *Ibid.*, pp. 440-442.
16. *Ibid.*, pp. 440-442.
17. *Ibid.*, pp. 440-442.
18. *Ibid.*, pp. 440-442.
19. *Ibid.*, pp. 440-442.
20. *Ibid.*, pp. 440-442.
21. Eric Berne, *Games People Play* (New York: Grove Press, 1964). Reprinted by permission of Grove Press, Inc. Copyright © 1964 by Eric Berne.
22. *Ibid.*, p. 24.
23. *Ibid.*, p. 24.
24. *Ibid.*, p. 24.
25. *Ibid.*, p. 33.
26. *Ibid.*, pp. 111-120.

10.

Perception and Persuasion

Psychologists have long recognized that how a person perceives or "takes in" the world determines how he or she reacts to it. Two people may react very differently to the same situation. For example, one student may see a teacher as frightening and difficult. Another student in the same class may view the same teacher as challenging and stimulating. The first student may react by avoiding the teacher or giving up on the work; the second may try to get to know the teacher and do well in the course. Each student's actions are determined by his own view of "reality."

Despite such individual differences, psychologists have found that it is still possible to predict how most people will react to certain situations or environments. In this chapter we examine how the environment influences us on three different levels. First, we discuss *psychological settings*: how the "atmosphere" of our everyday surroundings shapes our moods and feelings. Next, we focus on obvious and direct forms of *social influence*, the media: how do advertisers and journalists affect our behavior by their methods of presentations? Finally, we explore how strong *social pressures* in our environment actually change or distort our expected behavior.

Psychological Settings

Can a person's environment influence his thinking, mood, and behavior? Each time you enter a room or any confined space, you are consciously or subconsciously aware of its tone or atmosphere. The atmosphere may make you relaxed or tense, cheerful or depressed, alert or bored. Look around the room you are in right now. How does it make you *feel*? What factors contribute to your reaction?

Psychologists are now studying the influence of environment on human behavior, asking such questions as: Does a room suit the purpose for which it was created? Does its decor support the feelings and mood desired in that room? To analyze its atmosphere, they look at a variety of factors: spaciousness, arrangement and type of furniture, lighting, colors, textures, and noise level.

Space and Comfort

Anthropologists have found that a person perceives and uses space as *territory*, in that he assigns meaning and value to the space which surrounds him. If someone comes too close to him, he may perceive that person as threatening or inappropriately intimate. You may remember an incident when you felt uncomfortable and backed away from a person who moved too close to you.

Edward Hall is a pioneer in the field of *proxemics*, the study of man's use of space. Hall has suggested four basic spatial zones for Americans:

1. *Intimate distance* (0-18 inches): man's closest and most private spatial zone, where the greatest sensory stimulation occurs and the undesired

446

presence of others causes alarm or defensive alertness.

2. *Personal distance* (1½-4 feet): the zone in which people most commonly communicate with others.

3. *Social distance* (4-12 feet): the zone used to conduct business and matters of less personal involvement.

4. *Public distance* (12 feet plus): the most impersonal zone requiring the least involvement, which is used for the most formal events.[1]

Hall then breaks these spatial zones down into "close" and "far" phases, cautioning that they vary in use and extent according to cultural and personal differences.

These zones may be visualized as concentric cylinders surrounding a person. Each cylinder defines a zone in which certain kinds of behavior are considered appropriate. The occurrence of inappropriate behavior in a zone may alter normal or expected reactions. Someone you know well and trust, such as a boyfriend or girlfriend, may comfortably stand next to you in the close personal zone. But if a stranger invades this zone, you may become flustered, tense, or angry. People seem to need inviolate personal space as well as more public, interactive spaces. The absence of either kind of space in the environment can influence behavior and alter responses.

Overcrowding reduces, distorts, or eliminates normal spatial zones. People may respond to overcrowding by withdrawal, avoidance, aggression, mental or physical illness, or some form of atypical behavior.

How can proxemics be used to create the proper

Photo courtesy of Kenneth M. Bernstein

Space, distance, and seating arrangements all affect the way in which we interact with each other. People interact most when facing each other in small groups.

atmosphere for a room? In designing classrooms, for instance, one might want to provide both personal spaces where people can be alone and public spaces where people can interact. When personal spaces are not provided, students tend to be less productive and to lose their sense of identity.[2] Students also may withdraw and become less active and involved. Spatial factors thus can affect learning.

Osmond distinguishes between spaces that bring people together and support social relationships and spaces which keep people apart and frustrate social relationships.[3] For example, a traditional classroom arrangement with all the desks in rows may protect one's personal space and territory. Yet such a rigid arrangement makes it difficult for students to interact. A math teacher may want such an arrangement so that students will concentrate better. A social studies teacher who wishes to promote discussions in the classroom would have to change the seating pattern.

A space that is too open and unstructured may make people feel just as uncomfortable as a space that is too closed and structured. If you were alone in the gym, how would you feel?

Patterns of Interaction

The pattern of communication is an environmental factor closely related to space; where people sit in a room affects how they communicate or interact. There is usually greater interaction among people in small groups than in larger ones. As group size increases, two-way communication or interaction decreases. P. E. Slater suggests that five is the best size for a small group.[4]

Using that same number, H. J. Leavitt found that the seating arrangment of a small group affected group feelings and behavior.[5] He observed that a highly centralized group, with its leader clearly indicated by his or her centrally located seat in an X or Y pattern, tends to be more productive than a group with a noncentralized seating pattern such as a circle. Centralized groups solve more problems with greater accuracy and efficiency. While noncentralized groups with circular seating may not be as productive, they have higher morale and more positive feelings of satisfaction and involvement in their work.

In the classroom or office the seating arrangement of a group can be altered to reinforce the behavior desired.

One pattern would be used if the *product* (the solution of the problem) is most important. Another pattern may be selected if the *process* (responsiveness to the members' personal feelings) is of greater concern. The best seating pattern to solve a chemistry problem is different from the best pattern for a group therapy session.

Researchers have also found that people who sit *opposite* each other in small, circular groups tend to interact much more than people sitting side by side.[6] Yet as the group increases in size, and the circle gets larger, communication begins to occur *around* the circle.

Psychologist Robert Sommer has found that pairs of students prefer to sit side-by-side at a table when engaged in cooperative activities, but prefer to be further apart and face-to-face across a table when engaged in competitive activity.[7] These studies support the idea that types of space and communication patterns influence perception, mood, and behavior. The environmental designer must take this into account in selecting and arranging furnishings if he is to reinforce the behavior desired in a given setting, be it classroom, office, hospital, or prison.

Appealing to Our Senses

Hall has also discussed the effects of *visual* space, *auditory* space, *tactile* space and *olfactory* (smelling) space. Any source originating outside man himself and affecting any of his senses can be considered an environmental factor.

Visually, for instance, people respond to colors in various ways. Warm colors such as yellow and red are generally perceived as *activating* colors and therefore are used in classrooms to encourage activity and excitement.

Cool colors such as blue and green are generally perceived as more restful and calming.[8] Accordingly, cool colors are used in quieter areas. While dark shades of red, violet, and black often intensify and arouse emotions, pastel shades of these colors are soothing and restful.

Color, sound, smell, climate, and space all affect our perceptions of our environment. They subtly appeal to our emotional rather than our rational sides. We may intuitively "sense" an atmosphere when we walk into a room, or we may not be consciously aware of it. Nonetheless, these environmental factors influence your behavior. Psychologists are now learning how to structure spaces better suited to their purposes by choosing colors, fabrics, lighting, and furniture to promote desired behavior and feelings.

The Media: Powers of Persuasion

We have seen how environment and atmosphere influence our mood and behavior. A more direct and immediately recognizable form of persuasion occurs in advertising.

Advertising

> The woman said, "The serpent beguiled me, and I ate."
>
> Genesis 3:13

Suppose that you are the director of a small public relations firm. A client asks you to plan the advertising for his new toothpaste company. Your job is to:

1. Pick a name for the company.

CREATING MOODS

1. *Divide your class into six groups. Each group should meet separately to decide on the interior design and atmosphere of one of the following:*

Psychology classroom	Elegant restaurant
Dentist's office	Factory assembly-line
Church sanctuary	Den of a home
Discotheque	Police interrogation cell

Consider the following factors in creating your ideal room:

a. *Purpose of the room*

Characteristics of the group which will use the room

Types of activities which will go on there

b. *Shape and size of the room*

c. *Spatial Factors* and *Communication Patterns*

d. *Furnishings*

Kinds of furniture, rugs, decorations

Quantity and arrangement

e. *Visual Space*

Kinds of light (artificial, natural; bright, dim)

Choice of colors

Shapes and forms in the room

f. *Tactile Space*

Two- or three-dimensional objects

Textures

g. *Kinesthetic Space*

Movement and flow patterns, freedom, direction

h. *Auditory Space*

What sounds should and should not be heard

Noise level

i. *Climate*

Heat and air circulation

Temperature and humidity

j. *Olfactory Space*

Odors, natural or artificial

When all the groups are finished, a spokesperson for each should tell the whole class:

What the room they designed looks like.

Why they chose that decor and what mood they expect it to create.

2. *Try out different seating arrangements in your class. One day, have a class discussion with your seats*

*arranged in rows; the next day, try a circle arrange-
ment; the third day, place seats about at random.
What is the effect of each pattern?*

*Try solving a problem in the X or Y pattern; then
try another problem in the circle arrangement. Which
works better? How does each make you feel?*

3. *Select a cafeteria, library, or other public gathering
place and observe how people respect, invade, or
maintain personal space. Record your observations.
Consider:*

How far apart do people sit who are not together?

How does interaction change in relation to the
number of people around a table, or their seating
arrangement?

Do people leave when their personal territory is
invaded?

2. Totally design a container for the product—size,
   shape, color, wording.

3. Decide how to advertise the toothpaste: radio,
   television, magazines, newspapers, handbills,
   posters, etc.

4. Choose an "image"—format, idea, concept—for
   the advertising.

Think about each task for a few minutes. How would you

"Wow, the toothpaste that will make your dream come true!" Advertisers often imply that their products will bring you love, adventure, and success. They create an image for their products to appeal to your needs and desires.

persuade people to buy your client's brand of toothpaste? How would you differentiate it from all the others on the market?

Advertisers ponder such problems every day. It is not

easy to sell such common items as milk, soaps, deodorants, tissues, light bulbs, and razor blades, because the products are very much the same whatever the brand. When appeals to reason and logic are not sufficient, advertisers have to think of other ways to convince you that their product is better than their competitors'. Advertisers have to become experts in psychology, learning what motivates people to buy and how to make their brand more appealing. Marketing specialists play a vital role in the manufacturing industry.

In an age of self-service supermarkets and department stores, products must sell themselves. The personal touch of olden days, when the farmer or craftsman talked directly with a customer, is practically gone. The modern consumer makes a choice based on commercials, slick packaging, an image of the product, and occasionally the advice of a friend.

In the late 1940's and early 1950's, *motivational research* became important in the advertising industry. Psychologists were asked to explain why people often behaved illogically or unpredictably in buying various items. Why would someone buy a more expensive stereo when a cheaper model was just as good? Why did most people reach for the blue and white box rather than the yellow one? Why would people eat plums but not prunes?

Psychologists used a variety of techniques to find the answers. They interviewed potential consumers of these products to check their likes and dislikes. Some used personality tests to match types of people to their products, and then created consumer profiles describing the age, personality, and social class of their target population.

456

Word association tests were given to check the image of products. For example, test experts would say the word "car" and see what it made people think of. Did they associate it with power, status, convenience, efficiency, or adventure? Advertisers then could market their products with the needs of specific people in mind. Even the eye-blink rate of subjects was measured as they looked at various items, because blinking reflects tension!

To understand human motivation, they probed all three levels of consciousness: the conscious, rational level, "where people know what is going on, and are able to tell why;" the subconscious level, "where a person may know in a vague way what is going on within his own feelings, sensations, and attitudes but would not be willing to tell why. This is the level of prejudices, assumptions, fears, emotional promptings and so on;" and the unconscious, "where we not only are not aware of our true attitudes and feelings but would not discuss them if we could."[9] Could repressed desires, perhaps tied to sex or aggression, influence which brand was selected?

The researchers studied not only *motivation*, but *perception* and *learning* as well. Why do people see certain colors more clearly than others? How long do they remember a name or a fact about the product? What attracts the eye and the ear? What texture should the product have? In effect, advertising firms became psychology laboratories, learning how to interpret and then influence human behavior. Many of these research methods pioneered in the decade or so after World War II are still being used to prepare products for marketing.

Consumer research techniques are now applied to a variety of situations. For example, lawyers find such techniques helpful to screen who should be chosen for the jury in a client's trial: lawyers may veto potential jurors who would be unfriendly to their client's cause because of bias toward such matters as the client's race or occupation. Television networks use sample audiences to preview programs before they decide to put them on the air.

Most people base their decisions to buy a product on a variety of complex reasons: need, timing, product appeal, image, efficiency, price, and so forth. Yet psychologists have been able to define some *general needs* we all have:

To be liked and loved.	To be fulfilled.
To be secure.	To maintain health.
To be considered attractive.	To feel vital and active.
To be respected.	To have adventure.
To have a sense of identity.	To be comfortable.
To be remembered after death.	

Advertisers keep these needs in mind as they appeal to the many facets of our personalities. Let us examine some of their psychological techniques.

Associations: The Problem with Prunes

What do you think of when someone mentions a prune? Say the first words that come to mind.

Several years ago advertisers realized that the prune had a bad image. When the word association game was tried, people thought of "dried up," "dark and wrinkled," "an old maid," or "good for constipation." Obviously, people had hidden resistances to prunes—they were just not in a class with apples and oranges! So advertisers decided to create a new look for the prune. Vance Packard describes the "prune campaign" in his book *The Hidden Persuaders.*

First, the advertisers livened up the prune, surrounding it with bright colors in their advertisements. The drab prune looks better on a checkered tablecloth. Then they put young, vital people into the advertisements, perhaps a swimmer or someone on the way to play tennis. Suddenly the prune became a "wonder fruit" for the physically fit. And sure enough, sales went up. What happened? People began to associate prunes with youth, health, and cheerfulness, all of which they desired. Subconsciously, they must have decided to see if prunes could bring such benefits to them. After all, it seemed to work for the people in the advertisements, didn't it?

There are many products that have similar emotional overtones. Instant coffee and quick cake mixes may taste just as good as the "real thing" but somehow they seem inferior to us. Why? It was too easy to make them! We assume that quality must take time and effort. And we may even be hurt that someone did not spend that extra time trying to please us and pamper us. A cake made from scratch is considered a sign of love!

Many advertisers try to implant a definite image of their products in our minds. Think of Salem cigarettes. What do you see? A handsome young man and a beautiful woman walking hand in hand through the countryside. It's sunny, it's spring, and everything is blossoming, including love. Subconsciously you are left with the question, "Will Salem cigarettes bring me romance?"

In another cigarette advertisement, you are supposed

to *identify* with a rugged, masculine outdoorsman: the Marlboro Man. He may be on his horse riding through a snowstorm or corralling cattle—the height of adventure and excitement. Because male smokers outnumber female smokers, many cigarette advertisers deliberately focus their appeals on men. The message seems to be, "You, too, can feel masculine and strong, be exciting and intriguing, *with Marlboros.*"

Why must advertisers tie cigarettes to love and adventure? Cigarettes, like toothpaste, do not differ much. Therefore, each must create an "image" apart from its quality. Why do people smoke? To relax? To be sociable? To seem sophisticated and suave? To look strong and mature? Understanding these motivations, advertisers deliberately tie their cigarettes to our emotional needs for love, for relaxation, for self-esteem, or for adventure. A smoker may not be able to recognize his or her cigarette in a taste test, but will nonetheless be very loyal in buying it.

How successful have the advertisers been? Think of Hathaway shirts, Ivory Snow, Crest toothpaste, Ultrabrite toothpaste, Cadillacs, Volkswagens. What images does each conjure up? Some brand names now even stand for the product itself: Kleenex, Band-Aids, Xerox, Jello. Other brands represent status: KLH stereos, the Mercedes-Benz, Saks Fifth Avenue clothing. Here again we may be paying not only for quality but for an image, and may worry that if a similar brand is cheaper, it cannot be as good. We may feel "secure" if we pay more.

Another advertising technique is to have someone famous or authoritative sell a product. Can Joe Namath sell shaving cream better because he is a symbol of rugged masculinity, or because people trust or idolize him? Prince Spaghetti takes you to Boston's North End, right into a "real" Italian home. If the mother uses Prince, is it the best? Do people react more positively to a celebrity selling them a product, or do people prefer to identify with the common man or woman in an advertisement? A debatable question. Consider the Alka-Seltzer advertisements. Do you see yourself in the man who ate too much?

Perhaps because we hear commercials day and night, we are often able to tune them out. It is possible to watch a commercial and not be able to repeat it thirty minutes later. Psychologists have found that "people can forget as much as 60 percent of what they have learned within an hour after learning and as much as 75 percent within 24 hours. Usually pleasant or congenial things are remembered better than unpleasant ones, and things perceived in isolation are remembered better than things preceded or followed by similar ones."[11] A remedy? Repetition! Count how many times the product's name is mentioned in a thirty second commercial. Often a melodic tune is created so that you will sing or whistle about the product as you do your day's work.

Eye-Catchers

Do colors have their own personalities? Do reds and oranges make you feel warm and cheerful? Are blues and greens cool and fresh? Is pink feminine? Black sophisticated? Deep brown rich? Researchers have found that the color and shape of a package, its visual appeal, make a big difference in whether it sells. Packard tells of a study done by The Color Research Institute which proves this point. Women were given three boxes of the same detergent, one box predominantly yellow, one mainly blue, the third, blue with some yellow splashes. While the detergent in each was the same, the women thought that there were three different detergents.

After using the detergent in each of the three boxes, the housewives reported that the one in the bright "yellow box was too strong; it even allegedly ruined their clothes in some cases. As for the detergent in the predominantly blue box, the wives complained in many cases that it left their clothes dirty looking. The third box, which contained what the Institute felt was an ideal balance of colors in the package design, overwhelmingly received favorable responses. The women used such words as "fine" and "wonderful" in describing the effect the detergent in that box had on their clothes."[12]

Advertisers not only worry about color, but also about shape and wording. Too much small print may turn us away.

Additionally, the location of their product on the supermarket shelf makes a big difference. Is it at eye level and visible, low down on a shelf and easily missed, or too high to reach? Is the product close to the check-out counter so that you might buy it on an impulse? Or is it in the rear of the store where you must seek it out, and therefore may forget it?

Subliminal Perception: The Sneak Attack

Can you be influenced without realizing it? A few advertisers have tried to reach into your unconscious to implant their messages. The advantage to this technique is that if you are unaware of the sales pitch, you cannot critically evaluate its worth. Yet, you might respond to its message as though it were your own idea. How is this done?

In 1957, James Vicary demonstrated the *tachistoscope*, a film projector which flashes messages on a screen lasting just a fraction of a second. While the conscious mind did not pick up these messages, the unconscious mind often did. This is because although our visual and hearing perception is limited to a definite range of light, speed, and sound, our unconscious mind responds to a broader range. Information we miss at one level of consciousness actually registers at another: the unconscious. This is called *subliminal perception*. How does it influence our behavior? Wilson Key explains:

> *During one six-week test of the machine in a theater, involving 45,699 patrons, messages were flashed on alternate days: "Hungry? Eat Popcorn," and "Drink Coca-Cola." During the six weeks, popcorn sales increased 57.7 percent and Coca-Cola sales 18.1 percent. Though all people cannot be influenced so simply, a statistically significant number of people in any audience will obey the commands given subliminally, apparently, as long as there is no deep conflict about the command within their mind.*[13]

People were outraged when they found out that they were being manipulated.

Because the public questioned the morality of such advertising, most companies decided not to use it. Yet occasionally there are still some hints of this subliminal technique. For example, emotionally loaded words may be embedded or hidden in advertisements. The word "love" may be etched onto the ice cubes in a glass or be planted in the scenery. Perhaps you will not consciously pick up such a cue. Yet these advertisers hope that your unconscious will absorb the message and associate love with the product being advertised.

The theory behind all this is that if we are caught off guard, with our defenses down, we are more open to suggestion and manipulation. Yet no one has proven that this technique really works. Most advertisers do not wish to risk their reputations on a gimmick that may be both ineffective and highly unethical.

The Whole Story

Is one brand of aspirin really the best and the fastest? We are asked to accept the advertiser's word as fact. Yet who has the time or interest to prove differently? Of course, the manufacturer can be held legally responsible to prove any claims or promises. Messages are therefore carefully worded: general, yet *suggestive*. The facts given may be true but perhaps they do not tell the *whole* story. For example, Brand X aspirin may have been proven most effective in "a test." But what test? Where? How many competitors was it matched against? Were they respected brands? The advertiser may say that more doctors recommend Brand X, but how many were asked? What brands were they asked to choose from? How was the question phrased? Did the researcher ask, "Would you recommend Brand X as an aspirin?" Or, "Of all the different brands of aspirin, which would you recommend to your patients?" The first version is *slanted* to gain a positive reply. The second question is neutral and fair.

The consumer is being subtly manipulated if such "facts" are not evaluated critically.

The News of the Day

When we think of the media, we are more likely to think of Walter Cronkite, *The New York Times,* and *Newsweek* than advertisements for aspirins and Volkswagens. We have focused on advertisements because their *whole purpose* is to try to influence us, and

Perhaps because we hear commercials day and night, we have become used to tuning them out. It is possible to watch a commercial and not be able to remember it thirty minutes later.

so they clearly illustrate different methods of psychological manipulation. Can we assume, however, that news programs and articles are totally objective? Or are they, too, subtly influencing us? While most reporters try hard to be *neutral* and *factual,* hidden bias can creep in. Look at these two descriptions of the same event:

POLICE CALLED TO QUELL VIOLENCE: ABSENTEEISM HITS NEW HIGH

Serious incidents were reported in several of the city's schools yesterday during the fourth week of court-ordered integration. Police had to be called in to restore order. Meanwhile the absenteeism rate continued to soar, hitting a new high of 35 percent. Angry parents gathered outside the superintendent's office to demand greater protection for their children.

SCHOOL ATTENDANCE AT 65 PERCENT: MINOR SCUFFLES REPORTED

Attendance in the city's schools was recorded at 65 percent yesterday during the fourth week of court-ordered integration. A few scuffles were reported at three schools, but teachers were able to handle the problems before the arrival of extra police officers. A group of concerned parents asked the superintendent to ensure greater protection for their children from now on.

React to these two news briefs separately. How did each make you feel? Which article alarmed you? Which version calmed your fears? Examine each for: (a) emotionally loaded words; (b) point of view; (c) content emphasis.

Inescapably, a news event is described from the viewpoint of the person who witnessed it. Two people may view the same event very differently.

The extent to which a story is covered, if at all, and where it will be placed in the newspaper or broadcast are also decisions which shape our view of the news. When we rely on the media to present the news to us, we are accepting other people's judgments about what we should know. We are rarely aware of what we are *not* being told. If a story is buried on a back page with a bland headline, we may either miss it or pay little attention to it.

Robert Cirino cites one example. Information about the harmful effects of smoking was available as early as 1938. In 1953, a summary of thirteen separate medical studies was reported, showing that "the prolonged and heavy use of cigarettes increased up to 20 times the risk of developing cancer of the lung."[14] Yet on the day the summary was made public, this important finding could only be found on page 16 of *The New York Times*. From 1938 to 1955 there were no major network (radio or television) documentaries on smoking.

The impact of the media is enormous. Robert Cirino notes ". . . modern man can hate a person he has never talked to or seen face-to-face. . . . He can become sad because of a tragedy which happened to someone he has never met in a place he has never seen. He can approve of a person he has never talked to or seen. He can be persuaded by leaders he's never talked to, to kill someone he has never seen, or to give up his life for reasons he's never really considered."[15]

Newspapers and networks reflect the bias of the people who control them; whether they are well-intentioned or practice distortion does not alter this fact. While editorials present their opinions directly, these people also influence the general tone of the paper or program more subtly. They decide which feature stories to run, whom to interview, what polls to take, what photographs (flattering or not so flattering) to use, what advertisements will be accepted. Will the political candidate of their choice be smiling on page one while his opponent is frowning on page ten? We cannot avoid such media manipulation in a complex society, yet we need to be aware of it. Professional standards and free competition among papers and networks help to safeguard us from serious distortion of the news.

Friendly Persuasion

The art of friendly persuasion is practiced by all of us, not just by the media. It is an essential skill for parents, teachers, lawyers, politicians, clergymen, and salespeople.

It is important to know how to present your views clearly and effectively. Whether you are making a point in class, bargaining for extra allowance, or being interviewed for a job, you are, in effect, selling yourself and your ideas. It can be very frustrating to have a good idea and not be able to convince others of its value. So the art of friendly persuasion is not necessarily negative or devious. It is a useful skill if you are to accomplish your goals in life.

Even advertising, with all its questionable techniques, can have a positive effect on our lives. Advertisements help us sort out products and tell us what we can expect from the products we buy. We can legally hold a company to its published word. Therefore, advertisers are careful to be technically honest in their claims. Colorful packaging is meant to attract us, and it does. But if the product is poor, we will not buy it again. Consumers are more sophisticated today and expect quality *in* the product, not just colorful wrapping *around* it.

We may *want* to hear persuasive arguments from the media for and against an issue before making a judgment. Most of us do not have the time to research both sides of an issue on our own. We depend on others to do it for us. Most people are exposed to many views during the course of a day, from newspapers, magazines, radio, television, and fellow workers. We therefore have the opportunity to judge which views make the most sense to us.

In any case, we all have *selective perception*. We tend to see and hear what we *want* to see and hear. Irrelevant and competing ideas often do not register in our minds. So it is not likely that our opinions will be radically altered by any *one* source. Attitudes change gradually by persuasion from many sources.

How Social Pressures Influence Our Behavior

Sit back and imagine for a few moments how you would react in the following three situations.

1. The Electric Shock Experiment

You have volunteered to take part in a study of memory and learning directed by psychologists at a local university. You have been paid $4 plus carfare for an hour of your time. Before you begin, you sign a simple release

WHAT IS PERSUASIVE?

1. *Examine a variety of advertisements in magazines, newspapers, on different radio and television stations. Select one for analysis.*

   At whom is the advertisement directed?

   Why did the advertiser choose that medium for his product?

   What technique is the advertiser using? Is it effective?

   What kind of advertisements appeal to you most?

2. *Make up your own advertisement for a product of your choice. Explain to whom you are trying to appeal and why you think your technique will work.*

3. *Try the word association game with the following products:*

Cadillac	National Airlines	Excedrin
Volkswagen	Tareyton Cigarettes	Pepsi
Alka-Seltzer	Charmin toilet paper	Dentyne
Geritol	Levis	Crest toothpaste

4. *Make a list of "emotionally loaded" words which might be used in a news story or advertisement.*

5. *In the course of a day, how often do you use the art of persuasion? Cite some examples.*

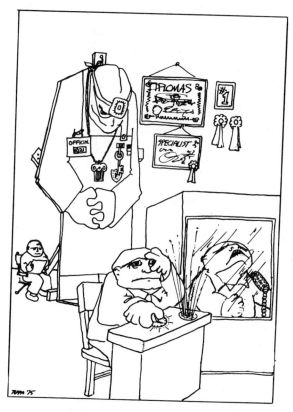

You have agreed to participate in a learning experiment. You have been told to administer an electric shock to the "learner" each time he makes a mistake. As you proceed, the shocks become more intense and the learner pleads with you to stop the experiment. You turn to the director of the experiment. He tells you to continue. What will you do?

agreeing not to hold the university responsible for any legal claims relating to this experiment.

You and another volunteer are led into a laboratory. The experimenter tells you that he wishes to study how punishment affects learning. You will be the "teacher" in this experiment; the other volunteer will be the "learner."

You watch as the learner is seated in an adjoining room. His arms are strapped to his chair and the experimenter attaches an electrode to the learner's wrist. He is told that he must learn a list of word pairs, and every time he makes a mistake, "he will receive electric shocks of increasing intensity."[16]

You are now escorted back into the main room. You are asked to sit down in front of a shock-generating machine with a line of thirty switches ranging from 15 volts to 450 volts. The machine is marked to show what voltage will produce a "Slight Shock," all the way up to "Danger—Severe Shock."

You are now told to give the learning test to the person in the adjoining room. When he gives the right answer, you can move along to the next item. When the learner makes a mistake, you are to give him an electric shock, increasing the intensity by 15 volts each time. Thus, for the first error he would receive a 15-volt shock; for the second, a 30-volt shock.

It all sounds strange, but you decide to proceed. As the learner makes mistakes, you shock him. "At 75 volts, the 'learner' grunts. At 120 volts he complains verbally; at 150 he demands to be released from the experiment."[17] The learner pleads that he has a heart condition. You look to the experimenter. He tells you to go on; that the shock may hurt but it won't cause permanent injury. At 285 volts the learner lets out an "agonized scream,"yet the experimenter nods you on, emphasizing the importance of the study.

• What will *you* do? Should you continue or should you stop? Why?

2. The Mock Prison

YOU HAVE AGREED to participate in a two week study of prison life. You are a college student anxious to earn the $15 per day offered by psychologists at the university. You have been interviewed and judged to be stable, healthy, and mature.

Suddenly one summer morning, a screeching police car comes to a sharp halt before you as you are walking down the street. In this surprise arrest, you are charged with a serious crime, searched, handcuffed, and brought back to the police station for booking and fingerprinting. You are isolated, blindfolded, and carted off to prison. There you are stripped, searched, deloused, and given a uniform. You are told to learn "sixteen basic rules of prisoner conduct"which include periods of silence, addressing other inmates only by ID numbers, and so forth.

The cell is small and stuffy. You must ask permission from the guards (also college student volunteers) for such routine activities as smoking or even going to the bathroom. You cannot tell what time it is. There are no windows. Right after you fall asleep, you are rudely awakened by a harsh whistle for a "count." You are ordered to perform tedious and meaningless tasks for hours on end. You never met the other "prisoners" or "guards" before, but you know they are also students.

• What kind of prisoner would you make? Could you stand the petty rules, the drills, and harassment from guards? Would you continue in the experiment if you were ordered to stand on your feet for several hours? What if you were put in solitary?

• Imagine that you were made a guard. How would you play your role? What would you do if the prisoners talked back to you? If they refused to return to their cells? How would you feel about your power?

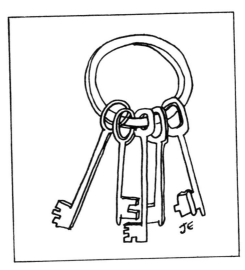

One summer morning, you are walking down the street when suddenly you are stopped by a policeman and arrested. You are carted off to prison, and placed in a small, stuffy cell. You are given a uniform and a set of rules. You are ordered to perform meaningless tasks by a group of hostile guards. What kind of prisoner will you be?

3. Matching Lines

SUPPOSE YOU ARE PART of a group seated around a table for an experiment. You are asked to match a given line of a certain length with one of three other lines. Since the three lines do differ in length, you are fairly sure you know which of the three will match the given line.

One by one, each person makes a choice. You are soon shocked to find that everyone is choosing a different line from the one you had picked. It is now your turn to announce your selection.

Which line will you choose: the one you had originally picked, or the choice of the majority of the group? Why?

Each of these experiments is real, and each has demonstrated the strong influence of social pressures on the individual. Most of us feel sure that we know how we would act in almost all situations. We assume that we have fixed values which will dictate our behavior wherever we are. We think our behavior will be consistent, predictable, and rational in almost all cases.

Let us look more closely at these experiments and then ask ourselves again, how would we act? Are our social selves different from our individual selves? Can group pressures manipulate us? Just how malleable are we?

The Electric Shock Experiment: OBEDIENCE TO AUTHORITY

The electric shock experiment actually took place at Yale University under the direction of a social psychologist, Stanley Milgram. It has since been repeated at several universities all over the world, involving more than 1,000 participants. What did Milgram want to find out?

While each volunteer was told that he was part of a learning experiment, the real focus was on *obedience to authority*, not on learning! The only genuine volunteer was the "teacher." The "learner" and the experimenter were just playing prescribed roles. Although the "teacher" did not know it, the "learner" was never being shocked. The groans and pleas were part of an act. What Milgram wanted to find out was: just how far will an individual go in inflicting pain on an innocent victim before he or she finally refuses to obey the instructions of an authority figure (the experimenter)?

As social beings, we have all learned to accept a society based on rules. We have been taught to respect authority figures in a variety of different situations: parents, teachers, policemen, judges, theater ushers, lifeguards, etc. What happens, then, when there is a conflict between what we are ordered to do by an authority figure and what we feel is right? Milgram's experiment shows the extent to which a social pressure (the desire to obey) can influence an individual's judgment and behavior.

An astonishing 65 percent of all the participants at Yale delivered the *maximum* shock to the learner, despite the victim's strong protests and the fact that this was only supposed to be a "learning" *experiment*. The volunteers ranged in age from 20 to 50 and came from a wide range of socioeconomic and ethnic groups. They were recruited through newspaper advertisements and mail solicitations. They were people like you and me. Yet, when they played their roles in this experiment, they acted much differently than we would expect. Milgram notes:

> *It is the extreme willingness of adults to go to almost*
> *any lengths on the command of an authority that*
> *constitutes the chief finding of the study . . . ordinary*
> *people, simply doing their jobs, and without any*
> *particular hostility on their part, can become agents*
> *in a terrible destructive process. Moreover, even*
> *when the destructive effects of their work become*
> *patently clear, and they are asked to carry out actions*
> *incompatible with fundamental standards of morali-*
> *ty, relatively few people have the resources needed*
> *to resist authority.*[18]

Why? Are people really just aggressive and sadistic? Milgram says no. These people shocked their victims "out of a sense of obligation." Despite their own anguish and turmoil, they felt it was their "duty" to carry out the experiment. They were following their orders.

To do this, the volunteers had to "adjust" their thinking. For example, they got *"absorbed in the narrow technical aspects of the task"*[19] so that they lost sight of its "broader consequences." They concentrated on teaching the word pairs, and tried to block out of their minds the reactions of their victims.

Because the experimenter insisted that they continue, many teachers *rationalized* that they were no longer responsible for what might happen. The experimenter would be to blame if the learner had a heart attack! The teachers felt that they could always tell themselves that they had wanted to stop but were not allowed to. They did not recognize that in fact they could have stopped at any time. This was only an experiment. No one was controlling them! The teachers also seemed to assume that verbal objections were sufficient to release them from their responsibility in this situation. But is a value real if you do not act on it?

A third defense mechanism which helped many teachers handle their own self-conflict was to *depersonalize* the task. Forgetting that this was just a study created by a person to help other people, some teachers allowed the experiment to take on, in Milgram's words, a "life of its own." As one anguished teacher repeated, "It's got to go on. It's got to go on."[20] But he did not ask himself *why* or *who said so*? Some people justified their actions by saying that "science" would benefit.

When the experiment was changed so that the victim was closer and more visible to the teacher, the situation became more human and personal. The teacher was then more likely to rebel.

Another interesting defense mechanism was for the teachers to *devalue* their victims. In order to live with their actions, the teachers wanted to believe that the learners were not cooperating with them. One teacher commented, "He was so stupid and stubborn he deserved to get shocked."[21]

Did people obey because they were awed by the prestige of Yale? Milgram moved his experiment to Bridgeport and advertised for volunteers under the name Research Associates of Bridgeport. In this setting, using a rundown building and without a university connection, 48 percent of the teachers still gave the maximum shock. When the volunteers were asked to sample the shocks themselves, the teachers were usually not willing to receive shocks as harsh as the ones they had delivered. A woman who gave the 450-volt shock three times said she would only be willing to take a 15-volt sample! At the end of each experiment, all participants were reassured that they had not really hurt their victims and the purpose of the study was explained.

What is the significance of an experiment on obedience in a psychologist's laboratory? If people can be so easily manipulated in a simple research experiment where they have little to lose by rebelling, how will they act in a real life situation where they may find it dangerous to disobey?

Think of the German officers at the Nuremberg Trials who claimed that they were just following orders. Consider the incidents in Vietnam where civilians were massacred because soldiers no longer saw them as people, but instead depersonalized them into "the enemy." The defense mechanisms used by Milgram's volunteers—absorption in a task to block out the victim's suffering, rationalization that only the person issuing the orders is responsible, depersonalization and devaluation of the victims—are the same ones which have been used throughout history by soldiers in battle and people who have persecuted others.

Milgram's study helps us to understand how some people resolve the inner conflict between two important and widely held values: obeying orders and doing a job well versus disobeying authority and standing on one's personal beliefs. Obedience is a necessary element in any society, but we must also be aware of its power to control us to the degree that we forfeit our own judgment. "Behavior that is unthinkable in an individual who is acting on his own may be executed without hesitation when carried out under orders."[22]

The Mock Prison: ROLES PEOPLE PLAY

The mock prison was the creation of psychologist Philip Zimbardo and his colleagues at Stanford University. They wished to study the effects of imprisonment on the average person and the process by which "guards" gain social power through their control of prisoners.

Why not study this in a real prison? First, Zimbardo felt that "prison.systems are fortresses of secrecy, closed to impartial observation," and more importantly, ". . .in any real prison, it is impossible to separate what each

Both "prisoners" and "guards" learned to play the roles expected of them in the "mock prison." Guards harassed and mistreated the prisoners with their newly won power. Prisoners suffered such mental and physical stress that some had to be released; the others became resigned to their fate.

individual brings into the prison from what the prison brings out in each person."[23] The researchers felt that they would not be able to tell whether the real prisoners were (a) acting out their own problems or (b) reacting to the conditions of imprisonment. So the experimenters decided to create a mock prison filled with normal, well-adjusted people.

Ten "prisoners" and eleven "guards" were selected for the experiment. All were average, stable, middle-class college males interviewed in advance. The twenty-one volunteers were split into the two groups randomly. Everyone was sure that he could endure the two-week experiment.

The basement of Stanford's psychology building was converted into a prison. Cameras and microphones were hidden to record all events and conversations of both prisoners and guards.

First, both the prisoners and the guards were *de-individualized*. The prisoners had all their personal belongings taken away. They were given smocks and caps to wear and placed in barren cells. They had only I.D. numbers for names. They were no longer unique individuals, but rather dependent and helpless beings who had to get permission for every trivial need. The guards were given "identical khaki uniforms and silver reflector sunglasses that made eye contact with them impossible."[24] They were also given handcuffs, billy clubs, whistles, and keys—symbols of their power.

The guards were not trained, but rather were given considerable freedom in how they maintained "law and order." A "rebellion" broke out on the second day when the prisoners barricaded themselves inside their cells.

From that moment on, when the guards had to use force to regain control, the guards began to harass and mock the prisoners:

> *They made the prisoners obey petty, meaningless and often inconsistent rules, forced them to engage in tedious, useless work, such as moving cartons back and forth between closets and picking thorns out of their blankets for hours on end. (The guards had previously dragged the blankets through thorny bushes to create this disagreeable task.) Not only did the prisoners have to sing songs or laugh or refrain from smiling on command; they were also encouraged to curse and vilify each other publicly during some of the counts. They sounded off their numbers endlessly and were repeatedly made to do push-ups, on occasion with a guard stepping on them or a prisoner sitting on them.*[25]

How did the prisoners react? They became "resigned to their fate." They talked mainly about prison issues, never getting to know each other personally. Since they saw each other constantly being humiliated, and taking it, they could not give each other the respect and support they needed. When the guards ordered them to curse each other, they did. The prisoners learned the "safest strategy to use in an unpredictable, threatening environment from which there is no physical escape—do nothing, except what is required. Act not, want not, feel not and you will not get into trouble in prisonlike situations."[26]

Within the first 36 hours, prisoner "8612" had to be released "because of extreme depression, disorganized thinking, uncontrollable crying and fits of rage."[27] On each of the next three days, another prisoner had to be released due to similar "anxiety symptoms." A fifth prisoner developed a "psychosomatic rash over his entire body (triggered by rejection of his parole appeal by the mock parole board)."[28] Finally, after only six days and nights, the experiment had to be prematurely ended.

What are the implications of such an experiment? Zimbardo and his staff explain, "It was remarkable how readily we all slipped into our roles, temporarily gave up our identities and allowed these assigned roles and the social forces in the situation to guide, shape, and eventually to control our freedom of thought and action."[29] Even though the experiment was just a psychological game, and everyone knew it, it was remarkable how each person became totally involved. People acted in this group situation in ways they would not have been able to act as individuals. At one point or another, all of the guards behaved sadistically. Not one ever came to a prisoner's aid when he was being mistreated, and many actually admitted that they had enjoyed their power over others. In an amazingly short time, the prisoners were dehumanized: they felt helpless, dependent, and uncharitable toward each other. "The potential social value of this study derives precisely from the fact that normal, healthy, educated young men could be so radically transformed under the institutional pressures of a prison environment."[30] What, then, are *real* prisons doing to both prisoners and guards?

On a more abstract level, how do we all become "psychologically imprisoned" by the roles that we play?

To what extent do we allow ourselves to become imprisoned by docilely accepting the roles others assign us or, indeed, choose to remain prisoners because being passive and dependent frees us from the need to act and be responsible for our actions? The prison of fear constructed in the delusions of the paranoid is no less confining or less real than the cell that every shy person erects to limit his own freedom in anxious anticipation of being ridiculed and rejected by his guards—often guards of his own making.[31]

Matching Lines: THE NEED TO CONFORM

In the electric shock and prison experiments, clear lines of authority were set up. The social pressures were obvious. Obedience was demanded. But how important are the more subtle pressures on our daily lives? How often do we find ourselves doing what we think others expect of us? How readily will we conform, or go along with friends and family, rather than exercising our own independent judgment?

In Solomon Asch's experiments, 95 percent of the subjects tested could make the correct judgment about which lines matched when they were not in a group. So Asch had eight accomplices pretend that they were volunteers. The accomplices purposely chose the wrong lines. They were seated around the table in an order that meant the geniune volunteer would announce his choice near the end, after listening to the others.

What happened when it came time for the volunteer to announce his choice? The majority of subjects usually remained independent, choosing the line they perceived to be correct. Yet between 30 and 40 percent of the volunteers did go along with the group's judgment, denying the validity of their own perceptions. Three-fourths of the subjects agreed with the group *at least part of the time.*[32] If asked to explain *why* afterwards, they would usually attribute it to poor vision or misjudgment rather than to group pressure. People did not want to *admit* that group influence was the reason for their altered decision; it did not seem justifiable to them!

Factors which affected whether an individual changed to the group choice were: (a) how clear the differences in the lines were; (b) "the degree to which the opposition was unanimous and the size of the group in opposition";[33] and (c) the character and personality of the individual subject.

Asch's studies show the impact social pressures can have on a person's judgment *even when one has freedom of choice.* When anxious and insecure, we are often more ready to accept the opinions of others than to trust ourselves. We all use our friends as reference points, checking to see if they agree with us on how we view a particular issue. We all depend on reassurance that our decisions are correct. And when we stand alone on an issue, we cannot help but worry that we may be wrong!

People may conform out of insecurity about their own judgment or out of a need to be liked and accepted. Whatever the reason, we are all keenly aware of how our individual behavior will fit into our own social setting.

Social pressures can be positive as well as negative influences on our behavior. Rules and standards help us to live together peacefully. We expect others to be polite, respectful, and fair, and we know that this is also expected of us. We learn to adapt our behavior to get along with others, and to be liked. We may feel pressured to do well, or to be responsible. These are all positive effects of social living. But it is important to be aware of just how much our behavior is constantly influenced by those around us. No one is a totally independent agent, free from these social influences.

FACING SOCIAL PRESSURES

1. How do *you* feel about obedience, loyalty, and individual morality? Consider:

   The Nuremberg Trials (after World War II)

   Lieutenant Calley and Vietnam

   Daniel Ellsberg and the Pentagon Papers

   Under what circumstances should people obey orders? disobey orders?

2. *To obey or not to obey? How would you handle the following situations:*

   - You are stopped for speeding and you know you were under the limit. Will you pay the $25 ticket?

   - Your children are supposed to be bused to a neighboring school district to achieve integration. You had wanted them to go to the school closest to your home.

   - A teacher tells you to rewrite a composition you feel is excellent. He does not like your style.

   - The library claims that you owe $10 for a missing book you think you returned.

   - The supermarket manager tells you, the stockperson, to put the old bottles of milk up front so that he can get rid of them before people take the new ones.

3. *In what ways are the defense mechanisms described by Milgram also used by prejudiced people?*

4. *What could be done to humanize prisons for the sake of both prisoners and guards?*

5. *Try out the Asch experiment on friends. Can you influence their judgments?*

6. *The three experiments described in the chapter all place people in artificial, although extremely dramatic, situations. How would you feel about being part of such experiments? Is it morally acceptable to "set people up" in this way?*

7. *How many different "roles" do you play as you move from one situation or group to another? Describe them.*

   What "social pressures" do you feel from day to day? Are some of them conflicting? (For example: the need to do well in school versus the desire not to be considered a "grind.")

8. *In adolescence, peer group pressure is a strong influence on one's behavior. What kinds of things would you do to please your friends which you might not do on your own?*

Suggested Reading

Allport, Gordon, *The Nature of Prejudice* (Reading, Mass: Addison-Wesley, 1954).

Baker, Samm, *The Permissible Lie: The Inside Truth About Advertising* (Boston: Beacon Press, 1971).

Cirino, Robert, *Don't Blame the People* (New York: Random House, 1972).

Elms, Alan, *Social Psychology and Social Relevance* (Boston: Little, Brown, 1972).

Hoffer, Eric, *The True Believer* (New York: Harper and Row, 1951).

Milgram, Stanley, *Obedience to Authority: An Experimental View* (New York: Harper and Row, 1974).

Mills, Judson, *Experimental Social Psychology* (Toronto: Macmillan, 1969).

Packard, Vance, *The Hidden Persuaders* (New York: D. McKay, 1957).

Schiller, Herbert, *The Mind Managers* (Boston: Beacon Press, 1973).

Toch, Hans, *The Social Psychology of Social Movements* (New York: Bobbs-Merrill, 1965).

FOOTNOTES

1. E. T. Hall, *The Hidden Dimension* (Garden City, New York: Anchor Press/Doubleday and Company, 1966).
2. G.F. McVey, *Sensory Factors in the School Learning Environment* (Washington, D.C. : National Education Association, 1971).
3. H. Osmond, "Some Psychiatric Aspects of Design," in L. B. Holland, *Who Designs America?* (Garden City: Anchor Books/Doubleday and Company, 1965).
4. P. E. Slater, "Contrasting Correlates of Group Size," *Sociometry,* 1958, *21,* 129-139.
5. H. J. Leavitt, "Some Effects of Certain Communication Patterns on Group Performance," *Journal of Abnormal Psychology,* 1951, *46,* 38-50.
6. B. Steinzor, "The Spatial Factor in Face-to-Face Discussion

Groups," *Journal of Abnormal and Social Psychology,* 1950, 45, 552-555.

7. R. Sommer, *Personal Space: the Behavioral Basis of Design* (Englewood Cliffs, New Jersey: Prentice-Hall, 1969).

8. F. Birren, *New Horizons in Color* (New York: Reinhold, 1958); also, McVey, *op. cit..*

9. Copyright © 1957 by Vance Packard, from the book *The Hidden Persuaders,* p. 25, published by the David McKay Company, Inc. Reprinted with permission of the publishers.

10. *Ibid.,* p. 137.

11. John Wright, Daniel Warner, Willis Winter, Jr., *Advertising* (New York: McGraw-Hill, 1971), p. 87.

12. Packard, *op. cit.,* pp. 16-17.

13. Wilson Key, *Subliminal Seduction* (Englewood Cliffs: Prentice-Hall, 1973), p. 23.

14. *The New York Times,* December 9, 1953, p. 16.

15. Robert Cirino, *Don't Blame the People* (New York: Random House, 1971), pp. 27-28.

16. Stanley Milgram, *Obedience to Authority: An Experimental View* (New York: Harper and Row, 1974), p. 3.

17. *Ibid.,* p. 4.

18. *Ibid.,* pp. 5, 6.

19. *Ibid.,* p. 7.

20. *Ibid.,* p. 9.

21. *Ibid.,* p. 10.

22. *Ibid.,* p. xi.

23. Philip Zimbardo, "A Pirandellian Prison," *The New York Times Magazine,* April 8, 1973, p. 38. © 1973 by The New York Times Company. Reprinted by permission.

24. *Ibid.,* p. 39.

25. *Ibid.,* p. 44.

26. *Ibid.,* p. 49.

27. *Ibid.,* p. 48.

28. *Ibid.,* p. 48.

29. *Ibid.,* p. 46.

30. *Ibid.,* p. 56.

31. *Ibid.,* p. 60.

32. Alan Elms, *Social Psychology and Social Relevance* (Boston: Little, Brown, 1972), p. 138.

33. Arthur Cohen, *Attitude Change and Social Influence* (New York: Basic Books, 1964), p. 110.

II.

The Psychology of Moral Development*

Here are two stories, each followed by a number of questions. Get together with four or five other students in class and discuss these stories, answering each of the questions. Then report as a group to the class on your discussion and the conclusions you reached.

Jan's Dilemma

JAN EDWARDS discovers one day that her friend Susan is into the drug scene at the high school which they both attend. Not only is Susan using speed, "downers," and L.S.D., but she is also selling them to other students. Jan decides to talk to Susan. Susan tells her that she knows what she is doing and that nothing bad is going to happen. But she pleads with Jan not to tell anyone. Now Jan has to decide if she should tell anyone or just keep quiet about it.

1. What should Jan do? *Why?*

2. How many different alternatives does Jan have?

---

* By Dr. Paul Sullivan with Dr. Ralph Mosher.

What are the reasons for doing or not doing each of these?

3. If *you* were in Jan's place, what would you do?

4. Susan is selling drugs which might hurt other people. Does that influence what you think Jan should do? What if Susan were selling only marijuana? Or heroin? What if she were also selling to younger children? Are there any circumstances under which Jan should report Susan to the police?

5. What if Susan were not Jan's friend but just someone Jan knew around school: What should Jan do in that case? Why? What if Susan had just started dating a boy Jan really liked?

6. Suppose that a good friend of Jan's had almost died of an overdose of drugs last year. Should that influence her decision? Why?

7. What are the best reasons for Jan telling someone? What are the best reasons for her not telling?

The Fire Chief

IN EUROPE DURING WORLD WAR II, a city was often bombed by the enemy. Each man in the city was given a post he was to go to right after the bombing to help put out the fires and to rescue people in the burning buildings. A man named Diesing was put in charge of one fire engine post. Because the post was near where he worked, he could get there quickly during the day; however, it was a long way from where he lived. One day there was a heavy bombing and Diesing left the shelter where he worked and went toward his fire station. But when he saw how much of the city was burning he got worried about his family. He had to decide whether or not to go home first to see if his family was safe, even though his home was a long way off. The station was nearby, and somebody had been assigned to protect his family's area.[1]

1. Should Diesing go to his post or go home first to check on his family? Why?

2. What *reasons* are there for Diesing to go to the fire station? What reasons are there for him going home? Which reasons are the best? Why?

3. Imagine *you* are Diesing. Would you go to your post or home first? Why?

4. Does Diesing have a responsibility to the other people in the city whom he is supposed to protect from the fires? Why? Does he have a responsibility to his family? Which is more important?

5. Suppose Diesing were an unpaid volunteer fire fighter, rather than an appointee. Would that make a difference as to what he should do?

6. Suppose other firemen were going to check on their families. What should Diesing do? Does what other people were doing make a difference in your view of the situation?

7. Suppose it were against the law not to go to your post and Diesing and a few other men broke this law. Should Diesing be punished? What should his punishment be? Why do we punish someone who breaks the law?

In this chapter, we examine the psychology of moral or ethical development. Each person has a specific way of looking at moral questions. We shall look at whether there are any *patterns* to how people think about moral issues. Do people change in their way of thinking about moral questions over a period of time? Understanding an individual's development in regard to moral questions helps us to understand human development in general.

What Are Moral Issues?

What is a moral question or issue? At first glance, the answer may seem easy; but the more you think about it, the harder it becomes. What makes moral and non-moral questions different? Think about what the word "moral" means to you.

One possible definition of a moral issue or question is one which in some way affects people's happiness, welfare, or rights. For example, whether you should break your promise to help a friend study for an important exam so you can go to the movies may be a moral question. We may have a moral responsibility not to break our promises to other people without a very good reason. Which of the topics below would you say involve moral concerns? Why?

1. Smoking three packages of cigarettes a day.

2. Cheating on an exam.

3. Keeping your car in safe running condition.

4. Whether to go on vacation to the seashore or the mountains.

494

5. Marrying someone because he or she is rich.

6. Deciding what to have for lunch.

7. Whether to read *Time* or *Newsweek*.

8. Whether or not to assassinate Adolph Hitler.

9. Jaywalking.

10. Abortion.

11. Smoking pot.

12. Whether to walk to school or take your car.

13. Ignoring parking tickets.

14. Taking care of your parents when they get old.

As you can see, there are moral aspects to many types of questions and issues. The following activities will help you understand more fully what a moral issue is.

Two Theories of Moral Development

Two of the most prominent psychologists who have studied moral development are Jean Piaget and Lawrence Kohlberg. There are many ways of looking at moral development. Because time and space do not allow us to go into depth with all approaches, we have chosen to limit ourselves to careful consideration of the *cognitive-developmental* approach of these two psychologists.

Jean Piaget and the Child's Moral Development

To understand how younger children think about moral issues, we would like you to interview some children using three brief stories.

WHAT IS A MORAL ISSUE ?

1. *Write a definition of what you think a moral issue is. In class, get together with five other students and come up with a group definition of "moral issue" and of the term* moral. *Decide what these mean to you. Discuss them in class.*

   Check your definition against those in two dictionaries. What does your definition include which the dictionary definitions do not? What, if anything, do the dictionary definitions add?

2. *Make your own list of moral concerns and a separate list of non-moral concerns. Discuss them in class.*

3. *Discuss in class the list of topics on pages 494 and 495. Does everyone agree on which are moral concerns and which are not? Look carefully at the concerns which you have decided are non-moral. Are there any circumstances in which these non-moral concerns might be seen as moral?*

4. *For each of the next three days, make a list of moral issues which you or people you know come across. Describe the situations in which you or your friends encountered the moral issue. Hand in your list and descriptions each day* without *putting your name to your work. The teacher will select a list of some of these for discussion. Are they all moral issues? Why?*

Discuss how you would resolve some of these moral issues.

First, find three different children, one in each of the age ranges three to four, five to seven, and nine to ten. You can interview younger brothers and sisters, children from your neighborhood, any child who meets the age restriction.

Photo courtesy of Kenneth M. Bernstein

Children do not think like adults about what is right and wrong. They have their own characteristic moral reasoning. This may seem funny or exasperating to parents and adults, but the reasoning is very real and persuasive for the child.

Second, read each of the three brief stories to them.

Third, after each story, have them retell it to you before asking any questions. Write down the way they tell the story to you.

Fourth, ask the questions which follow the particular story and write down the child's answers. Be sure to write down exactly what the child says and *not* what you think he *meant* to say.

I. SUZIE AND CAROL

Suzie was helping her mother set the table. Accidentally, she dropped five plates and broke them.

On that same day, Suzie's friend Carol was not allowed to go out and play. She got very angry and grabbed a plate and broke it on the floor.

Have each child retell the story. Write down his or her words and then ask: Which girl was naughtier? *Why?*

II. BILLY AND JOE

Billy would not eat his dinner. When his mother left the room for a minute, he threw the dish on the floor and broke it to pieces. When Billy's daddy came home, he gave Billy a lollipop.

In the house next door, Joe was trying to help his mother put the dishes away. He tripped on the rug, dropped three dishes and broke them. When his father came home, he spanked Joe.

Have each child retell the story. Write it down and then ask: Which boy was naughtier? *Why?*

498

III. TWO BROTHERS

A boy broke a toy belonging to his little brother.

Ask the child: Should the boy give his little brother one of his own toys? Or should he pay for having the toy fixed? Or should the boy not be allowed to play with any of his own toys for a week? *Why?*

In class, make a list on the blackboard of the responses you got to each story from each age group.

What similarities are there in the answers of each age group?

Were you surprised by any answers you got? Which ones? Why?

Are the answers younger children gave different from those of older children? How are they different?

Jean Piaget, the Swiss psychologist whose ideas you have already read about in Chapter 1, did some of the earliest research on moral development. The stories which you read to younger children are similar to ones used by Piaget in his research. He observed how children's thinking about moral issues changes and develops as they grow up. He described changes in the moral judgment of children aged four to fourteen. Below is a brief summary of his findings.

Moral realism is an important part of the thinking of younger children. Moral realism means that a child decides the goodness or badness of an action based on the

The young child relies on rules made by adults to decide what is right or wrong. The child decides what is bad by what is punished.

physical consequences of the action in the real world. The child does not consider what the person wanted to do (his intention). In the case of Suzie and Carol, younger children will generally say Suzie was naughtier because she broke five plates while Carol only broke one, even though that Carol broke the plate on purpose while Suzie did it accidentally. How naughty is decided in the child's mind by *how many* plates each one broke, the physical consequences of what she did. As the child grows older, he or she pays more attention to what a person *intended* to do. By age nine or ten, the child no longer uses such moral realism in his thinking.

Another aspect of moral realism is shown in the second story. Younger children usually decide that Joe was naughtier not only because he broke more dishes but also because Joe got punished (a spanking) while Billy was rewarded (a lollipop). Once again, the child does not take account of the *intentions* of the two boys. Billy broke the dish deliberately while Joe did it accidentally. For the young child, the fact that Joe was punished makes him the naughtier one. The child relies on rules made by adults to decide what is morally right or wrong: what is bad is what is punished. The young child even believes that the forces of nature help adults to punish wrongdoers. If he hears a story in which a bridge collapses under a boy who has just stolen an apple, the very young child believes the bridge is punishing the boy for stealing. Once again, as the child gets older, this type of thinking disappears. The older child decides if an action is right by whether it is fair or unfair to the people involved.

The third story illustrates what Piaget discovered about children's ideas of justice or fairness. For the young child, wrongdoing such as breaking a toy must be punished. Usually, he believes that the more severe the punishment, the better. For the older child, justice is not punishment for the sake of punishment but a process which may educate and reform the person who has done something wrong. In other words, the punishment should be made to fit the crime. The wrongdoer should correct what he did and in the process he will learn not to do it again. Justice is being fair to people, treating them equally.

In summary, Piaget found that the young child makes moral decisions on the basis of fear of punishment and moral realism. Morality is defined by adults who create unchangeable rules. But as the child grows older, he gains more experience cooperating with other children. The child begins to respect others as equals. This experience of equal cooperation with other children changes the individual's moral ideas. He realizes that moral rules are not unchangeable orders handed down by adults, that rules are made by equal individuals who cooperate for their own benefit. If a rule does not promote the good of people, it can be changed. The child begins to decide moral questions on the basis of his own moral values, not those of adults. The fairness or unfairness of an action determines whether it is good or bad.

Piaget showed that there are at least two different ways of looking at moral questions. People move from an earlier to a later stage as they mature. Social scientists and educators no longer view the child as a miniature adult, having the same moral ideas as adults but fewer of them. Indeed, it is now recognized that children do not think like adults about what is right or wrong. They have their own characteristic moral logic. This logic may seem funny or exasperating to parents or adults. But it is very real and persuasive to the child. Children can only "become adult" over time.

Piaget, however, did not follow up on his studies of moral judgment once he began studying intellectual development. The man who has produced the most complete theory of moral development based on Piaget's work is Lawrence Kohlberg.

Kohlberg's Theory of Moral Development

Kohlberg developed a questionnaire to measure a person's level of moral reasoning. Here are two stories from this questionnaire. This time, we would like you to interview adolescents and adults.

First, select any two or three adults or adolescents.

Second, read them each of the stories below and write down their answers to the questions. You may want to save yourself time and energy by writing out the stories and questions on separate sheets of paper. Give the sheets to the person to read and to write out his answers to the questions.

Third, be sure the person writes *why* he answers the questions the way he does, that he gives reasons for his thinking.

Fourth, compare with other students the answers you got. Are there any similarities or differences? How many different kinds of thinking can you see?

I. SHOULD HEINZ STEAL?

In Europe, a woman was near death from a special kind of cancer. There was one drug that the doctors thought might save her. It was a form of radium that a druggist in the same town had recently discovered. The drug was expensive to make, but the druggist was charging *ten times* what the drug actually cost him. He paid $200 for the radium and charged $2,000 for a small dose of the drug. The sick woman's husband, Heinz, went to everyone he knew to borrow the money, but he could get together only about $1,000. He told the druggist that his wife was dying and asked him to sell it cheaper or let him pay later. But the druggist said, "No, I discovered the drug and I'm going to make money from it." So Heinz got desperate and broke into the man's store to steal the drug for his wife.[3]

1. Should Heinz steal the drug? *Why* or *why not?*

2. Which is worse, letting someone die or stealing? Why?

3. What does "the value of life" mean to you?

4. Is there a good reason for a husband to steal if he doesn't love his wife?

5. Would it be as right (or wrong) to steal the drug for a stranger as for his wife? Why?

6. Heinz steals the drug and is caught. Should the judge sentence him or should he let him go free? Why?

II. MERCY KILLING

A woman had terminal cancer. There was no treatment known that could save her. Her doctor knew that she had only about six months to live. She was in terrible pain, but she was so weak that an effective dose of a pain-killer like ether or morphine would make her die sooner. She was delirious with pain; in her calm periods she would plead with the doctor to give her enough ether to kill her. She said she couldn't stand the pain and she was going to die in a few months anyway.[4]

1. Should the doctor give her the drug that would make her die? Why?

2. What does her husband have to do with the decision?

3. Do you think the woman should have the right to

make the decision to die? Or should the right to decide be the doctor's? The court's? Why?

4. What should the doctor do if he wants to respect the woman's rights? Why?

5. Does a person have a duty or an obligation to live when she does not want to?

6. Should there be general guidelines for doctors about mercy killing? If so, who should set them? Why? What should they be?

7. The doctor kills the woman and is brought to court. He is found guilty of murder. The usual sentence is life imprisonment but it is up to the judge to decide. What should he do? Why?

Lawrence Kohlberg is a psychologist who has studied how people think and reason about moral issues. He has created a theory about how moral development occurs. Kohlberg claims that a person's thinking may be at any of six stages of development. There are four general characteristics of these stages:

1. Each stage involves a basically different way of thinking about or solving moral questions.

2. Individuals must go through these stages *in order* without skipping any. You cannot go from stage 1 to stage 4 without also going through stages 2 and 3.

3. The way a person thinks at a given stage is applied to most moral situations he encounters.

505

It is a general point of view or way to solve moral dilemmas.

4. Later stages of moral development reflect earlier ways of thinking, but in a new and more complex form. Moral development proceeds from the simple to the more complex. Moral judgment at the *later* stages takes into account more aspects of a situation.

Kohlberg says that there are three levels of moral reasoning, each of which is divided into two stages.

LEVEL I: Preconventional Level
Stage 1: Punishment-Obedience Orientation
Stage 2: Instrumental Relativist Orientation

LEVEL II: Conventional Level
Stage 3: Interpersonal Concordance Orientation
Stage 4: Law and Order Orientation

LEVEL III: Postconventional Level
Stage 5: Social Contract-Legalistic Orientation
Stage 6: Universal Ethical Principle Orientation

I. PRECONVENTIONAL LEVEL

The Preconventional Level of moral reasoning is common in children until the ages of 10 to 13. *Stage 1* is called the *Punishment-Obedience Orientation*. At this stage, what physically happens to a person as a result of a specific action decides for the child if the action is good or bad. The child tries to avoid punishment. He obeys those who have more power than he does. Moral rules are set by other people; the child only obeys. He is also very

506

In Stage One the child decides whether his actions are good or bad based on the *consequences* he will face. The child obeys others to avoid punishment.

concerned about his own welfare. You can see the parallel to Piaget's earliest stage of development.

In describing each of the six stages, we shall provide a statement about Heinz's dilemma (whether or not Heinz should steal the drug to save his wife). Each statement will be typical of the sort of thinking a person might use at that stage.

Typical Stage 1 thinking: No, Heinz shouldn't steal the drug. After all, he might get into trouble and be put in jail for doing it.

Stage 2 is called the *Instrumental Relativist Orientation,* or "You scratch my back and I'll scratch yours." The person at this stage is primarily concerned with getting good things for himself. Sometimes he is concerned with

The person at Stage Two is primarily concerned with getting good things for himself. Sometimes he will be concerned with helping others, but usually this is in order that the other people will do things for him. This is the "You scratch my back and I'll scratch yours" stage!

helping others, but usually this is so that the other people will do things for him. The child at this stage may interpret the Golden Rule in an interesting way. If he is asked what the Golden Rule says you should do if someone comes up to you and hits you, he often responds, "Hit him back! Do unto others as they do unto you." This of course is not the ideal version of the Golden Rule which says, "Do unto others as you would have them do unto you." The individual who reasons in *Stage 2* terms thinks that a person in a situation which calls for a moral decision should do whatever is best for himself or whatever he *feels* like doing.

> *Typical Stage 2 reasoning:* Heinz should steal the drug if he wants to. He doesn't have to, but someday he might need his wife to steal a drug for him. Besides, it would be hard for him to get another wife to take care of him.

II. CONVENTIONAL LEVEL

In the age period ten to thirteen, most children start to move to the Conventional Level. Stage 3 is called the *Interpersonal Concordance* or *"Good Boy-Nice Girl" Orientation*. Here the person decides what is good or right behavior by what he thinks pleases or helps other people and what is approved by other people. This person is concerned about what other people think of him, especially those who are close to him such as his family and friends. He wants others to approve of him. He can now put himself in the place of others in a moral dilemma (see things the way they do) and make decisions on that basis. But he often finds it hard to decide which person's

The individual whose thinking is at Stage Four looks at moral questions according to the existing rules of important social groups like the government or church. "What does the law say?" "What is the church's position on this question?" He supports these social authorities because he believes that order is what makes possible all the good things society can provide, including justice.

510

place to put himself into. He may decide to take the side of relatives and close friends because these are the people he most wants to please.

> *Typical Stage 3 thinking:* Yes, of course, Heinz should steal the drug if he wants to be a good husband. He must love his wife and saving her means more than anything to him.

At Stage 4, the Law and Order Orientation, what is morally right is to do your duty and show respect for the rules of the society in which you live. For there to be justice or moral right, the basic laws and structure of society must be maintained. The individual whose thinking is at Stage 4 looks at moral questions according to the existing rules of such important social groups as the government or church. "What does the law say?" "What is the church's position on this question?" He supports the government, the law, and other social authorities because he believes that order is what makes possible all the good things society can provide, including justice.

Stage 4 may seem like Stage 1 because it emphasizes obeying the law. In Stage 4, however, one has respect for authority because he believes that order must be kept in society for the benefit of everyone. By contrast, at Stage 1 a person obeys out of fear of punishment.

> *Typical Stage 4 thinking:* No, to steal the drug would be wrong because Heinz was breaking the law no matter how you look at it. Although I can see why he would have done it, I don't think he was justified. If he had thought long enough he probably would have come up with some legal way of getting

the drug. You just can't have people breaking the law whenever they feel like it. It would mean chaos.

III. POSTCONVENTIONAL LEVEL

The individual begins to move from the Conventional to the Postconventional Level in the age period 15 to 19. However, these stages are usually not thoroughly developed until the person is in his twenties or later. *Stage 5* is the *Social Contract-Legalistic Orientation.* As an individual moves from Stage 4 to Stage 5, he may begin to see that different societies, for example the United States and Nazi Germany, can have very different moral or legal codes. Should a person always obey the rules of his or her society, as a person at Stage 4 would tell us? What if they are the laws of Nazi Germany? How does a person decide which moral rules should be used in a society and what a person's moral duty is?

In Stage 5 reasoning, the individual recognizes individuals "join together" to form an agreement or "social contract" among themselves to solve this problem. People in the society do not have to sign a written agreement; an individual becomes part of the contract by living in society and accepting the benefits, rights, and responsibilities of that society. The contract tells how fair rules for the society can be made and how they can be changed to take account of new situations. The purpose of the agreement is to provide the greatest amount of good for the greatest number of people in society.

The agreement also includes certain *basic rights* such as life, liberty, and property which the society guarantees to every person. These rights are even more important than the rules of society. The purpose of the rules is to

512

protect these rights. If the rules of society do not protect people's rights or promote the good of the people, a person at Stage 5 would reason, then the rules should be changed. This is a basic difference between Stage 4 and Stage 5. At Stage 4, one seeks to preserve the laws and rules of society as they are. At Stage 5, one sees laws and rules as a means for protecting individual rights and promoting the welfare of all the people. When this is not being done, the laws must be changed. It is a law-creating way of seeing society.

> *Typical Stage 5 thinking:* Yes, I feel Heinz should steal despite the fact that he is breaking the law. The law should be written to take care of this sort of situation but it isn't and there isn't time to get it changed. Heinz is doing more good in saving a life than he is causing harm by stealing.

Kohlberg's final stage is the *Universal Ethical Principle Orientation, Stage 6.* The morally right thing to do is determined by abstract moral principles which the person has carefully examined and accepted. The principles are justice, considering every person and his point of view equally in every situation, and respect for the dignity and value of human life. An individual at Stage 6 applies these principles to all situations (they are universal), and he is willing to have these same principles applied to him and any moral situations in which he finds himself. The person at Stage 6 believes that the principles of justice, equality, and respect for people are fundamental. Therefore these principles are higher than the social contract or the laws established under the social contract, and a person always has an obligation to do what these principles tell him to do.

Typical Stage 6 thinking: Heinz should steal the drug. It is wrong legally but right morally. A person always has a duty to save a life and so his moral duty outweighs his legal duty not to steal. The only just thing to do is to steal. Even if I knew I would be the druggist in this situation I would still think stealing was right.

Everyone's reasoning starts at Stage 1 but not everyone develops to the same final stage. An individual's thinking may stop developing at any of the stages from 1 to 6. Most adults in every country which Kohlberg has studied are at 3 or 4. Only a small percentage of adults remain at Stages 1 or 2. Kohlberg suggests that fewer than 20 percent of adults in the United States reason primarily at Stages 5 or 6.

Why Is Moral Development Important?

As we have already seen, Kohlberg says that most people do not develop beyond Stages 3 or 4, the Conventional Level of moral reasoning. In the United States, he suggests 80 percent of the people never use Stage 5 or 6 reasoning consistently. This is especially ironic because our Constitution is based on Stage 5 reasoning! The majority of citizens may be unable to fully understand the moral ideas which are the basis of the Constitution.

Studies have also shown that only those at Postconventional stages of moral reasoning are consistently able to resist the pressure put on them by other people to act in immoral ways. William Calley, an Army lieutenant in Vietnam, searched a Vietnamese village for Vietcong. In the process, he ordered his men to line up over 100 Vietnamese women, children, and old men in a ditch and

514

WHAT STAGE?

This is an exercise to help you become familiar with the various stages of moral reasoning. There are two moral dilemmas followed by several people's statements about the dilemmas. Try to decide what stage of moral reasoning each of the people is using. Remember that at each stage an individual can say that the person in a dilemma either should or should not do something. Whether a person says Heinz should steal the drug or not steal the drug tells us little about that person's stage of moral reasoning. It is the reasons why he says Heinz should or should not steal which determine his stage of moral development.

STORY 1:

Reread the "Fire Chief" story, the second in this chapter. The following statements are about that case.

A. I guess he should have gone to see about his family. After all, he loves them very much and as a good husband and father he has to take care of them. I mean, the reason he wants to go home first is because of his love for his family. That's certainly a good reason.

B. He really shouldn't go home. His wife and family may be important to him, but it would be dangerous for him to travel from the city and he has to look out for himself. But I guess it depends on how much he likes his family and if they're important to him.

C. No, he shouldn't go home. He has the responsibility

for many lives. Certainly he should care about his family, but by becoming fire chief he made sort of a "contract" with the other people in the city. By breaking this "contract" he'd be endangering many people and going back on his word in a way. He has to take account of social responsibility and his moral duty to help save lives.

D. Legally, he probably shouldn't go. There must be rules saying men must report right away. But the husband does have an obligation to his wife and family as well as to the government. He has the God-given responsibility to look after them. So I guess going home would be justified in that way.

E. Sure Diesing should go and take care of his family if that's what he wants to do. After all, he has to look out for himself and his family. They do things for him, so he may want to help them. Other people are probably looking out for themselves.

F No, he shouldn't go home to his family. It must be against the law and he"ll get put in jail or something. Of course, it would be OK if he wasn't going to get punished.

G. No, he definitely shouldn't do that. I'm sure there are rules or a law which says he should report to his post. What if all the fire chiefs and other people with duties went to look after their families? There'd be chaos and many people would be hurt. For a society to operate, people have to obey the laws even if they don't always like them.

H. Well, I know he loves his family and everything, but

everybody else is probably going to their places and they wouldn't think much of Diesing as a fire chief if he left to take care of his family. There are lots of people who are depending on him as fire chief and he shouldn't let them down. Other people will take care of his family. And I'm sure his family would want him to stay at his post.

STORY 2: THE RUNAWAY SLAVES

Before the Civil War, we had laws which recognized some rights of men who owned slaves. According to one law, if a slave escaped he had to be returned to his owner or turned in to the legal authorities. It was felt there would be chaos in the Southern states if slaves were able to run away and not be returned. A person who didn't turn in a runaway slave could be jailed himself. Some people who believed slavery was wrong disobeyed the law, hid runaway slaves and helped them to escape even though it was against the law.[5]

A. No, they shouldn't help those slaves to escape. If they were caught, they'd be put in jail and their families and people who love them would suffer. They have to think first about those people who love them. If they put themselves in the place of their families, they would see they shouldn't do it. People would think they weren't very good husbands and wives or mothers and fathers if they risked going to jail like that.

B. This is really a difficult problem because it's not really right to break the law, but slavery goes against a higher law, the law of God or something like that, I guess. I suppose from that point of view you ought to obey the higher law and help the slaves to escape but it's hard because you should obey the rules of society too. After all, without rules and laws society would just break down.

C. I really don't think that they should have helped the slaves. After all, they were risking being put in jail and what would they get out of it? The slaves should be able to look out for themselves. The slave owners weren't hurting them, so why should they hurt the slave owners by helping the slaves to escape?

D. No, I don't think that those people should have helped the slaves. Those people had agreed with the other members of their society to obey the laws which their representatives made. Those representatives had made the laws, and now the people have to live up to their part of the agreement and follow the law even though they might not agree with it. What they should do is protest and work to have their representatives change the law if they disagree with it.

E. If they put themselves in the place of the slaves, I'm sure they'd want to help them. The slave owners were being mean anyway. All good people would see that the slaves ought to be helped. They'd certainly want someone to help them if they were the slaves.

F. Yes, I think they should have helped the slaves even though it was against the law. In most cases people should obey the law because they've sort of entered into an agreement with other members of their society to obey the rules which they together agree on. But in this case, the majority which made the rule is wrong. This is an unjust law which violates basic human rights of the slaves. Laws are supposed to protect those rights. The rights of the slaves to freedom take precedence over the property rights of the owners. In order to protest the laws and maybe to help change them, these people should break the law if there's no other way to change things. Of course, they have to be ready to accept the penalties of the law too.

G. Sure they should help the runaway slaves if they want to. Everyone should be treated the same as everyone else and the slaves certainly weren't. Besides, later on the slaves might be able to help them with their farms or something to pay them back.

H. No, they shouldn't have broken the law and helped those slaves. The law is the law and you can't have people breaking every law they don't like. There'd be chaos if everyone broke the law whenever he disagreed with it. Who are they to decide what's right and what's wrong? The good of society has to be considered here even though you feel bad for the slaves too and may not like the law much.

I. They shouldn't help the slaves to escape because if they get caught they'll get put in jail or something.

On separate pieces of paper write "Stage 1," "Stage 2," etc., through "Stage 6." Have six people each draw one of these pieces of paper out of a hat and not tell anyone which stage they have drawn. These six people then discuss a moral dilemma, possibly one of the two dilemmas from the previous activity, using reasoning of the stage they drew. (The person who draws the slip of paper saying "Stage 4" uses Stage 4 reasoning, and so forth.) The rest of the class observes closely. After the discussion is over, the rest of the class tries to decide which stage each person was using.

Or, the entire class can divide into six groups, with one representative of each group drawing a stage. The members of each group decide what arguments the group will use in the whole-class discussion. After the discussion, groups try to decide which stage of moral reasoning other groups were using.

Another possibility is to assign each stage to two individuals or two groups. One individual of the pair or one of the two groups uses that stage of moral reasoning to argue that the person in the dilemma *should* do something. The other person or group—using the same stage of reasoning—argues he *should not* do it. For example, in the Diesing dilemma, one person or group uses Stage 3 reasoning to argue that he should check on his family, while the other person or group uses Stage 3 reasoning to argue that he should not.

kill them. The only man in Calley's platoon who would not do as Calley ordered was Postconventional in his moral reasoning.

In the Milgram experiments which you have already read about, the only subjects who consistently refused to give supposed electric shocks to another person were also Postconventional. Kohlberg's studies in prisons seem to show that a high proportion of adults in prisons are at Stages 1 or 2 in moral reasoning. These findings underscore the importance of having people develop to the highest level of moral thinking which is possible for them.

How Does Moral Development Take Place?

Kohlberg believes that there are two basic ways through which moral development is stimulated. The first is called *role-taking*. When the individual role-takes, he becomes aware that there are other people in the world who are like himself but who have different specific feelings, desires, and ways of seeing the world. The individual also begins to look at his own actions and behavior from the point of view of these other people. When the person puts himself in the place of others, sees things from other people's points of view, he is recognizing that others are equal to himself and that he and other people have to depend on each other. Being able to put yourself in another person's place is being *empathic*. Both empathy and justice are important aspects of moral development.

A person usually develops the ability to role-take through taking part in a variety of social groups: family, peer groups, government, colleagues at work. The individual has to be able to communicate and interact with the other people in these groups. To do this well, a person must be able to put himself in the place of others and understand how they see various situations. He also must understand how these other people see him. Then, when there is a moral conflict, a person will consider other people's viewpoints in arriving at a solution.

The other way in which development of moral reasoning can be stimulated is by facing moral dilemmas indirectly through discussion. Here the person can role-

521

play by putting himself in the place of all the people in the dilemma. While discussing the dilemma with other people, he may hear arguments which are more complex, which seem to provide a fairer solution to the dilemma. Research has shown that when this happens the person sees that the new type of reasoning is more adequate and tries to change his own way of thinking accordingly.

People are most effectively attracted by reasoning which is one stage above their own stage of thinking. They are not attracted to thinking at stages below their own because it is not as satisfactory for dealing with the moral dilemma. Thus, people tend to change their way of thinking about moral issues as they hear more adequate arguments and see the limitations of their own reasoning. But it takes time for a person to have enough diverse experience to change his thinking significantly.

Ways to Discuss Moral Dilemmas

There are a number of ways to discuss dilemmas in class:

1. Discuss what should be done in the moral dilemma situation. It is important for as many people as possible to give their opinion. Be sure to ask *why* each person says what he does.

2. Have people who disagree on what should be done discuss their reasons with each other.

3. List each of the possible solutions to the dilemma on the blackboard and examine each one to see what good or bad effects it might have.

522

WRITING YOUR OWN DILEMMAS

To understand the various aspects of moral situations more fully, write for class discussion some moral dilemmas similar to those at the beginning of this chapter. Write the dilemmas by yourself or in small groups. These are the steps in developing a dilemma:

1. Decide what sort of moral situation to write about. You can write about a situation of which you have personal knowledge or simply a moral situation you make up.

2. Next, develop the dilemma story. Write the dilemma so that it leaves the moral problem to be decided by the people who read and discuss the dilemma. There should not be a final answer to the dilemma when you write it. The dilemma should not be too long or involved.

3. Write some questions about the dilemma which can be used to guide discussion. Look at the questions following each of the dilemmas in this chaper for models.

4. Use the other questions about the dilemma to discuss different aspects of the problem.

5. You do not need to get agreement among everyone about what should be done. But it is important to have everyone give his reasons and think carefully about all the reasons presented.

Another way of approaching a moral dilemma is to put yourself in the place of each person in the dilemma situation. See the situation as you think each person would see it, and then make the fairest possible decision for all the people involved. We can see how this is done by looking at a specific example. Reread the Heinz case (stealing the drug) which you used in interviewing adolescents and adults. Then try to put yourself in the place of Heinz, his wife, and the druggist, using the following questions:

First look at HEINZ. Try to put yourself in his place and understand his feelings and actions. Make a list of the things you imagine he might be thinking about or feelin as he tries to decide whether or not to steal the drug. Wha things might make him think he should steal the drug? What reasons might he have for not stealing the drug? How would he feel if he stole it or did not steal it? Why? What might happen to him if he did or did not steal it? Should he think first of himself or his wife? Why? Does he have any obligation to society? You can think of other questions which might be looked at.

Then look at HEINZ's WIFE. How would she feel about his stealing the drug? Would she want him to steal it? Why? Why not? What reasons might she have for not wanting him to steal it? What are the results for her if Heinz steals or does not steal the drug? Would she feel he owed it to her to steal it?

If you were THE DRUGGIST, how would you feel about Heinz stealing the drug? What would be the consequences for the druggist of Heinz stealing the drug? Why wouldn't the druggist give Heinz the drug at a reduced price? How would you feel if you were the druggist and did not give Heinz the drug and his wife died?

524

After looking at the dilemma from the point of view of each of the people involved, do you think Heinz should steal the drug or not? Make lists of the reasons you think Heinz should or should not steal it.

Now suppose that you knew you were going to be one of the people in the situation but you did not know which one you were going to be: Heinz, Heinz's wife, or the druggist. You have an equal chance to be any one of them. Knowing this, now what do you think Heinz should do? For what reasons should he do it? Remember that you could as easily be Heinz's wife, or the druggist, or Heinz. Has your decision about what Heinz should do changed from what you thought before? *This procedure is known as deciding from behind the "veil of ignorance."*[6]

Of course, there are many other ways of approaching moral dilemmas. You could have people act out the roles of the various people in a dilemma, sort of a moral play. Design some of your own ways of dealing with dilemmas. Use some of these ways to discuss dilemmas you wrote. Also, look through parts of this book which you have already read and see if there are moral issues which you did not notice originally. For example, in the previous chapter, "Perception and Persuasion," there is a detailed description of the Milgram experiment. What are the moral issues there? Are there moral dilemmas in Chapter 2, "Adolescence"?

Suggested Reading

Beck, Clyde, *Ethics* (Montreal: McGraw-Hill Ryerson, 1972).

Blatt, Moshe, Ann Colby, and Betsy Speicher, *Hypothetical Dilemmas for Use in Moral Discussions* (Cambridge: Moral Education and Research Foundation, 1974).

Frankena, William, *Ethics* (Englewood Cliffs, N.J.: Prentice-Hall, 1973).

Gardner, Howard, *The Quest for Mind* (New York: Vintage, 1972).

Kohlberg, Lawrence and Carol Gilligan, "The Adolescent as Philosopher: The Discovery of Self in a Post-Conventional World," *Daedalus*, Fall, 1971.

Kohlberg, Lawrence, *Collected Papers on Moral Reasoning* (Cambridge: Center for Moral Education).

Lockwood, Alan, *Moral Reasoning: The Value of Life* (Columbus, Ohio: Xerox Education Center, 1972).

Piaget, Jean, *The Moral Judgment of the Child* (New York: The Free Press, 1965).

Rawls, John, *A Theory of Justice* (Cambridge: Harvard U. Press, 1971).

Wright, Derek, *The Psychology of Moral Behavior* (New York: Penguin Books, n.d.).

FOOTNOTES

1. From the "Kohlberg Moral Judgment Interview, Long Form." Used with permission of the Center for Moral Education, Harvard University, Cambridge, Mass.
2. Jean Piaget, *The Moral Judgment of the Child* (New York: Free Press, 1965).
3. From the "Kohlberg Moral Judgment Interview," *op. cit.*
4. *Ibid.*
5. *Ibid.*
6. John Rawls, *A Theory of Justice* (Cambridge, Mass.: Belknap Press of Harvard University Press, 1971).

526

IV.

Emotions
and Their Expression

12.
The Ambivalence of Emotions: An Introduction

Life without emotions would be bleak indeed. Imagine, if you can, what it would be like never to laugh or cry, never to know the joy of winning a race, or the sorrow of missing a very close friend. Sometimes you may even cherish the physical sensation of a thumping heart, sweaty palms, and a giddy head as you wait suspensefully to hear if you have won a prize. So important to life are emotional feelings that some people even take risks like racing automobiles or riding a roller coaster to experience thrills and heighten excitement.

In Albert Camus' novel *The Stranger*, the protagonist, Meursault, regards his life as so humdrum and empty that he is driven to kill a man in order to experience feelings. It is Meursault's absence of feelings, his inhumanity, his indifference, that makes him appear odd—a stranger.

Emotions are also known to drive people to commit "crimes of passion." We speak of emotions as "good" when they seem to enrich life, as "bad" when they bring sorrow, harm, or pain. How can similar feelings be, at the same or at different times, both acceptable and unacceptable? How can we tell which is the "healthy" expression of anger and which is the "sick"? If you recall how many times you have laughed or cried at the same thing, or how "you always hate the one you love" you will realize that all emotions, in a sense, have two heads. It is this duality, this ambivalence, that causes the problem of distinguishing between normal and abnormal, healthy and sick, good and bad. Usually we end up frustrated at trying to make clear-cut distinctions and begin to realize that most things in life are not just black or white but rather are different shades of gray. It is important to keep this in mind as we talk about emotions, especially when we try to understand what is meant by mental illness as the term is commonly used.

Reality of Emotions

Even though it is difficult to define feelings or emotions, everyone knows they exist, that they are as real and essential to life as eating and breathing. It may not be clear what a person actually *feels*, unless he lets us know through words, facial expressions, behavior, thoughts, or emotional reactions. Sometimes we *assume* from what we observe that people are feeling a certain emotion because we tend to think that others will react the way we would in the same situation. This may not always be true. Still, we do not need to be told that someone is sad when we see him cry, just as we do not need to be told that the wind is blowing when we see the leaves rustle.

Sometimes feelings are confusing, and take a while to sort out and to understand. Reading a sensitive poem, identifying with a certain character in a novel, seeing a sad or a happy movie or television show often helps us to get a better grasp on what we feel. Some people have a special talent for translating their feelings into writing, drawing, and composing or playing music. Some may develop an unusual ability to understand and empathize with others because they are "good judges of people." Still others may seem incapable of feeling very much, or appear not to be bothered by things that seem to bother almost everyone else.

Why do we find such variety in how people deal with and express their emotions? What does it mean when we say that some people are "easily hurt" and others are "as tough as nails"?

Varieties of Emotional Expression

Do you remember the first time you felt like running away from home? If you can recall it, you might remember that you were angry at your parents or someone else and that you had fantasies about how sorry they would be when they couldn't find you, especially if you got hurt. You may even have started out on your escape from home, only to sit on a street corner, have a good cry, and then come back home, to discover, alas, that nobody even realized you were gone. On the one hand, you were disappointed, but on the other, you were relieved that no one knew what you were thinking.

Another child might have yelled at his mother, "I hate you!" and been done with it, unless he happened to be yelled back at, slapped, or punished in some other way. Yet another child might not even have recognized that he was angry at a parent, and might have hit his baby sister instead.

What determines which way a person reacts to his feelings? This question should not imply that there is any totally satisfactory answer. The question has puzzled scientists and others for centuries, and despite the tremendous increase in our knowledge about the physiological, endocrinological, neurological, and psychological aspects of emotion, there is still much that we do not know.

There are, however, some fairly well established facts. We are all born with a certain constitutional make-up which lays the groundwork for how we experience feelings. Superimposed upon that basic foundation is the kind of learning that occurs during growth and development. For example, a child punished for his sexual curiosity may repress the feelings associated with sexual development. The kinds of attitudes one is taught by others about what is "masculine" and what is "feminine" may teach us that some feelings are "acceptable" and others are not. In our society, fear, sadness, and crying are often ridiculed and regarded as weaknesses, especially in males, while happiness, courage, and inhibition of certain feelings are usually praised. One can hear it in the parent's simple remark to the baby boy who cries after falling: "Big boys don't cry." One can hear it in the doctor's office with the promise of a lollipop if the child holds back his tears when painfully stuck with a needle. One can hear it in school when teachers too quickly dismiss a discussion of feelings in class in order to "get on with the work." How can anyone reassure a child that "there is nothing to be afraid of" until some time is spent in trying to learn more about just what it is the child fears?

The child grows to adulthood carrying the ingrained messages from his early experiences. Certain feelings are admired, others are disparaged. It is difficult to decide for oneself what is okay to feel and okay to express. It is difficult even to make judgments from observing public figures. Do we envy and admire a woman who holds back her tears and maintains her composure when her husband is assassinated? Are we moved by and sympathetic to a man who can tremble and cry as he speaks of his dead brother?

Some people are said to be "sensitive," with feelings that are "easily hurt." If a person feels ashamed or embarrassed about this, he or she may try "not to show it." There is often a fear of ridicule, a sense of being thought "sissyish" or "peculiar," and a belief that it is not only bad to *have* feelings but it may be even worse to *show* them. So we may laugh in order not to be seen as sad, be extra friendly to disguise anger and resentment, try to "look cool" to avoid betraying frightening insecurity. It is always easier, therefore, to know what a person is *doing* than to know what he is feeling. Feelings are more subjective and actions are more objective, but both can express emotion.

The style of expression which any individual develops depends upon many factors: self-image, sense of "what is right," peer values and pressures, and previous experience and memories of being "hurt." If one grows up with the idea that being sad, feeling lonely, or crying is bad or abnormal, then his defense mechanisms may go to work to disguise his true feelings, "to put on a happy face," "to put the best foot forward," "to whistle in the dark." While the person may actually *know* how he feels, his mask may help to fool others. (Clowns are often very sad people beneath the paint and comedy.) And if the defenses are working extra diligently, the person may even hide his

Without the expression of emotions, life would be a bore. Often we do not have to say a word: our body language communicates our happiness and joy, our sadness, our fear or anger.

feelings from himself. To use the language of Freudian psychology, the feelings may be repressed so that they remain unconscious, and only reveal themselves (a) through distorted actions and speech, (b) in symbolic expression (through fantasy or creativity in art or music), or (c) when the censor is relaxed, through dreams, jokes, or "slips."

Strangely enough, while some people consider "sensitivity" abnormal, others see it as enviable and admire a person who is compassionate, in touch with others' feelings, imaginative, and creative because of ease in understanding and coping with feelings.

Clearly, there is nothing wrong with having feelings.

534

Without them, life would be a bore. True, feelings may hurt, but coped with constructively, they can broaden and enrich your life. Feelings have so many dimensions. There is joy, excitement, elation, and delight, as well as fear, rage, anger, and shame. How you "get it all together" depends partly upon what you are born with, partly upon developed skills, and partly upon the people who have inhabited your enlarging world since childhood.

There are other ways to tell indirectly that we are experiencing an emotion, even though we don't "feel" its presence. Having feelings is only one way of experiencing emotions. Thoughts will sometimes reveal what a person feels. Words of self-criticism, failure, and negativism may tell us that one is depressed. Or the difficulty a person has in presenting his ideas clearly before a group may tell us he is anxious and inhibited. On the other hand, a thought may in itself provoke a feeling state. The memory of a happy time can evoke warm, pleasant feelings. Thoughts about the death of a loved one on the anniversary of that death may revive all the pain and grief felt long ago.

Sometimes behavior itself tells us a lot about what a person feels. In 1872, Charles Darwin wrote a book called *The Expression of the Emotions in Man and Animals*. He was a meticulous observer of the physical signs which revealed the likely existence of feelings. Careful observations of the smallest of facial muscles and the gesturing of the body taught Darwin much about emotions and their muscular accompaniment. Centuries ago, actors learned how to mimic an emotion by reproducing bodily movements, facial contours, and postural gestures that have come to be assigned to specific feelings. The more effective they are in their art, the more successful they are in producing audience reaction (feelings) through identification with artificial characters. And as testimony to the old saying "there is nothing new under the sun," what Darwin noted years ago is now more popularly described as *body language* in a number of recently published books. We are told in these writings how every slouch, every gesture, every posturing or muscle twitch can *nonverbally* communicate our mood, our disgust, our resentment, our sexual arousal, or our disappointment to others.

The body speaks a language not only through physical movement, but also through aches and pains and deformities which can be caused by emotional distress. We speak at times of hypochondriacal worries which occur when a person is depressed or anxious. Conversion reactions of blindness, loss of speech, paralysis, and inexplicable physical symptoms are sometimes caused by deep-seated, unconscious emotional conflicts. These unhealthy ways of handling emotion will be discussed more fully in Chapter 15, "Darker Shades of Gray: Mental Illness."

13.

Normal-Abnormal:
A Spectrum of Grays

Trying to define normality is like bobbing for apples. First
you think you've got it and then it's gone. When the poet
Ezra Pound was allowed to go into the city from the
psychiatric hospital in which he was being kept, he was so
appalled by the behavior of those outside the hospital that
he said he felt much safer with his fellow patients, and
promptly returned. Some interpreted this as further proof
of Pound's "abnormality," but others conceded that
perhaps he had a point.

What is considered normal today may be considered
abnormal tomorrow and vice versa. Times change and so
do attitudes, habits, dress, customs, values, and behavior.
When the anthropologist Margaret Mead studied the
island of Samoa and its people, it was quite "normal" for
the natives to go naked and feel no shame, in contrast to
our own customs in this country at the time. Now it seems
that circumstances have been reversed, with primitive
tribes learning about clothes and civilized countries
becoming more accepting of nudity.

If the dividing line between normal and abnormal is so
fuzzy, how does anyone determine what is healthy and
what is sick? This question is important not just
philosophically, but also because it has a lot to do with

how we think and feel about ourselves and others. It is risky to attach labels to certain kinds of behavior, certain kinds of thinking, even certain kinds of people. Calling someone sick because he is a nonconformist may cause him to lose his job or may alienate him from others. Labeling a person as "crazy" may cause him to be hospitalized or even jailed. Notions about normality are affected by individual attitudes and public pressures. For example, a law may be changed to make alcoholism an illness rather than a misdemeanor, or homosexuality a "normal variant" rather than a "perversion." People may be treated very differently, depending on which label is used.

Scientists, physicians, psychiatrists, lawyers, judges, politicians, and teachers have a great influence on establishing guidelines for what is considered normal or abnormal at any time in a given society. It is partly their position of authority and esteem which places them in this crucial role. A biological researcher may inform us that males and females in this country reach sexual maturity about four years earlier than they did a century ago and thereby influence our ideas about the "normal" age for onset of puberty. Many studies have shown how readily we accept what people in authority say about art, music, plays, books, and so on; few individuals have the knowledge or time to challenge these authoritative opinions.

Certain individuals who have been considered important authorities on the subject of child-rearing have enormously influenced changes in attitude about what is normal and what is abnormal development, growth, thinking, and behavior. For example, Freud influenced our ideas about normality. He endured ridicule, humiliation, and ostracism for his monumental discoveries about the unconscious mechanisms of the mind, about personality development, and about the normality of sexuality in human behavior. His discoveries illustrate how concepts of "normality" change from one era to the next. It took years to convince the medical and lay public that "infantile sexuality" was a "normal" part of development.

Freud did try to develop an individualized, humanistic approach to the notion of normality. He believed that normality should be considered in terms of the ability of the ego to maintain a comfortable balance between reality (as it existed in each individual's experience) and the buried, unconscious wishes, drives, and urges which he called the id. The extent to which a person's ego could maintain this balance indicated the degree of psychological or emotional normality. This idea is contained in the expression "a well-balanced person."

For some psychologists, the individualized approach to an understanding of normality, focusing on what is right for a particular person, has not been specific enough. They have used other definitions of normality. One approach employs a kind of statistical timetable of development. To discover the "right" time for a child to be walking or talking, for example, large numbers of children were studied to discover the ages at which these behaviors occurred. A simple statistical average was then obtained and considered the *norm* against which interested and concerned parents and doctors could measure the growth of a child. A similar concept is often used on your Scholastic Aptitude Tests or on grades in your classes which are based on your deviation from the average grade of the class. Tests which claim to measure

I.Q. also work in this way. Your score is compared against the average of other people of your age, sex, and cultural background. Note that if you have *higher* than the average I.Q., this is considered to be statistically "abnormal" because it falls outside the range of the average or "normal" score. Of course, no one feels especially upset about *this* kind of abnormality.

The statistical approach to normality is fairly rigid and is applied to such things as blood pressure, pulse rate, visual acuity, height, weight, and other physical characteristics. Usually such measurements consider something "normal" if it falls within certain boundaries which permit *some* individual variation. But even this degree of flexibility usually does not take into account the broad spectrum of differences in people. *It also does not acknowledge that people may not be "normal" all the time, especially in the areas of emotional reactions or health.* For example, getting an occasional cold or having an outburst of anger does not make one "abnormal" or "sick." Furthermore, having an "abnormal" temperature (a fever) is a "normal" response to getting an infection.

We see, then, that any concept of normality must take into account the full range of a person's behaviors, circumstances, values, unique responses, and adaptability—in other words, his or her totality! "Normal" people may act "abnormally" in certain situations. (Remember the Milgram obedience experiment described in Chapter 10.)

While some people mistakenly equate "normal" with "perfect" or "ideal," we need only recall Sir Francis Bacon's remark that "There is no exquisite beauty without some strangeness in the proportion." Very few of us would want to be either the "ideal" or "average" person.

540

We cherish our imperfections which make us different and distinct. It is usually our differences which create our character. Even if it *were* possible to achieve perfection, the person who strives for it may find himself being too intense, too "uptight" and excessively concerned about what others think about him. While some people regard conformity as a sign of normality, it is not hard to see that excessive conformity can rob a person of his spontaneity, make him compliant and dependent to an extraordinary degree, and totally submerge his individuality. On the other hand, anyone who completely ignores the acceptable standards of his social environment and gives in to his basic urges all the time will certainly be regarded as "abnormal" by others.

To adapt to our inner and outer requirements, we must steer some kind of middle course between our individual needs and the acceptable limits of behavior imposed upon us by our surroundings.

As you can see, establishing a clear-cut definition of normal and abnormal is extremely difficult. For this reason, many psychology textbooks do not make the effort. There are almost as many definitions of abnormality as there are schools of psychology. The existentialists and humanists, on one hand, argue that each individual has his own baseline of normality. The behaviorists, on the other hand, are inclined to consider this a "Humpty Dumpty" approach. (In Lewis Carroll's *Through the Looking Glass*, Humpty Dumpty said, "When I use a word . . . it means just what I choose it to mean—neither more nor less.") To avoid this "loose" definition of normality, the behaviorists have developed techniques for "objectively" measuring all aspects of human behavior. Because they omit anything which cannot be measured—including feelings, fantasies, unconscious symbolism, perception, or will—they have been criticized for being too rigid, dehumanized, and mechanistic.

Even members of a particular school do not all agree. Thomas Szasz, a humanistic psychiatrist and psychoanalyst, for example, believes that society (and the psychiatrist as a representative of society) imposes on individuals labels ("diagnoses") which are meant to keep certain people in power and others oppressed. He believes that labeling a person's problems as mental "illness" is wrong, that "what gets diagnosed as 'mental illness' is usually just behavior that other people don't want to tolerate."[1]

Yet, despite the difficulties in distinguishing the normal from the abnormal (or pathological) in personal and emotional matters, one cannot dismiss altogether the usefulness of making an attempt. For, as Seymour Halleck states, "it is hard to imagine how anyone could practice psychiatry without some idea of what behavior is good for people and what is not. There must be some standard of normality in order to decide whether a given person needs treatment, how he should be treated, and what should be the treatment goals."[2]

We must think carefully about what we mean by commonly used terms like "adequacy of performance," "conformity to established standards," and "cultural expectations." We must think about *whose* standards are being applied and what the *effects of labeling* a person "sick" or "abnormal" could be. A broad definition of the normal person in our society is offered by Norman Cameron:

> *First of all [he] gains a basic confidence or trust*
> *through his interactions with a mother figure early in*

> *life. This leaves him free to take a great deal for granted in his relationship to the world around him, to feel reasonably secure about himself and others. adulthood, has managed to weather the succession of weanings and emotional crises which all maturing normally entails. He has been able to resolve his major conflicts without the serious personality distortions which leave a person vulnerable to adult psychopathology. He has learned to give and to get love and loyalty, at each phase of his development, in ways that are appropriate for each level. He has learned to control his aggressions without becoming passive, without losing enterprise and initiative, and without missing the enjoyment of competition and cooperation. He takes pleasure in mutual interdependence, in needing others and in being needed by them. He is a person who experiences a reasonable degree of self-fulfillment in his major social roles, feels warmth toward other human beings, and is able to communicate his feelings acceptably in such a way that they are reciprocated by other persons in his daily life.*[3]

To fulfill oneself in ways that are compatible with one's own potential, satisfaction, and concern for others is a "normal" objective in life.

How Do I Know I'm Healthy?

Even though it's difficult to clearly distinguish between what is normal and what is abnormal, most people, as they grow up, spend a lot of time and energy wondering whether or not they're healthy and sane. We all seem to want to be normal even if we don't know exactly what it is. This dilemma partly reflects the confusing messages we

WHAT IS NORMAL?

1. *Think about movies, books, and the use of language today and try to compare them to their counterparts of ten or fifteen years ago. What do they tell us about the changing concept of normality? Ask your parents to tell you how they talked, behaved, danced, . . . as youngsters.*

2. *Imagine being forced today to enter a mental hospital as a patient. You protest to the doctor that you are normal and a mistake has been made. He asks you to tell him why you think your behavior is normal. Write your reply.*

3. *Have you ever noticed yourself or someone else using labels like "sick" or "paranoid" or "crazy" to describe someone you are angry at? How do you explain this commonplace practice? What are the dangers of this behavior?*

4. *Can you think of any circumstances in which it might be considered normal for a person to:*

   Commit suicide?

   Misinterpret reality?

   Kill another person?

   Lie or cheat?

   Steal?

Have the class write a definition of normal behavior. *Then think of several situations with which to* test *your definition. Refine your definition as you go along.*

receive from our parents, our teachers, our peers, and our social institutions. As children, we are urged by our parents not to let kids beat us up, but to fight back. In church, we're taught to love all human beings. But if we're drafted into the army, we're taught the necessity of killing our enemies. No wonder people get confused!

As children, we may have invented imaginary friends and even had conversations with them when no one was around. Later on we hear people speak of others who talk to themselves as "crazy" or "looney." We may worry that there is something wrong with us.

We read about emotional reactions, about defense mechanisms, about physical symptoms, and we wonder whether what we read applies to us. Even in reading about definite indications of mental illness, we think we recognize ourselves in the descriptions.

This always happens when someone first begins to learn about emotional or physical illness. The reason is simple: while we each have individual characteristics that make us different from every other person, we share much in common. Basically, we all have the same physical equipment and experience the same emotions; we simply develop our own styles of expression. Who does not know what it is to feel happy, to feel sad, to feel blue, to feel nervous? Who has never felt jealous, angry, competitive, "mixed up," excited, guilty, inadequate? How is it possible to cry and laugh at the same thing? To love and hate the same person? To desire and fear a specific objective? To be "psyched up" for a basketball game one time and to be disinterested the next? Who has not daydreamed, had nightmares, flights of fantasy, and grandiose plans? Perhaps there have been times when you were glad you got sick and thereby avoided an unpleasant situation.

None of these situations necessarily makes you a candidate for mental illness. The reason we recognize ourselves in those who are described as mentally disturbed is that they have all the same feelings, thoughts, and behaviors that we have had at one time or another. But there are major differences—in the *intensity* of the reactions; in the time *when* they occur; in the *degree* to which they persist; in the *extent* to which they *interfere* with ability to function; in how they *prevent* the development of *relationships* with others; and in the degree to which they *ignore current realities*.

We might say that mental health and mental illness are matters of degree. As with normality and abnormality, there are many shades of gray rather than just black and white. Before you can comfortably read about mental illness, it is important to realize that we all have emotional feelings and sometimes we even express them in ways

Who does not know what it is to feel happy, to feel sad, to feel blue, to feel nervous?

that make others and ourselves unhappy. *Defense mechanisms do not cause mental illness* any more than white blood cells cause infection. Defense mechanisms protect us from the strains and stresses of everyday experience. They help us to rationalize, repress, deny, project, avoid, displace and sublimate in ways that smooth out the rocky road of life. Without such protections, we would be at the mercy of every scary situation that came our way. We would be like one big raw nerve ending, hurting at every unpleasantness we encountered. *We experience trouble only when our defenses do not work effectively or when they work too intensely.*

During adolescence—or any other time for that matter—a person encounters many difficulties that cause conflicting emotions, frustrations, disappointments. It is not unreasonable to be upset, especially when you are "experimenting" with ways of getting along with your peers. You are growing physically as well as emotionally, and there are many obstacles along this path. It is not uncommon to "fly off the handle" once in a while.

Despite all the reassurance you get from others, you probably still worry about whether or not you are a normal adolescent. Maybe you find yourself worrying too much for a while about your body or your "image," maybe you get discouraged about school and even oversleep occasionally to avoid an exam. You may even get "ticked off" at your best friend. But as long as this does not remain a constant pattern, there is little cause for concern. You are probably quite healthy if:

You know what you get disappointed or angry about.

Despite disappointments, you generally find your life interesting and satisfying.

You are able to exercise a fair degree of control over expressions of feelings when it is appropriate to do so.

You can get along fairly well with your classmates and teachers and parents.

You do not shirk your responsibilities even when they don't appeal to you.

You sleep and eat well and exercise reasonable concern about bodily functions and hygiene.

You have a sense of humor, an interest in new things, and motivation for new challenges.

It is also a sign of health to be able to discuss your concerns with another person and to ask for assistance from parents, teachers, or counselors if at any time you have worries about yourself, your feelings or your behavior.

So Who Isn't Anxious and Depressed?

There is no such thing as pure pleasure;
some anxiety always goes with it.

OVID *Metamorphoses VII*

There's post-operative depression, post-partum depression, post-graduate depression and post-marital depression (sometimes called "the honey-moon").

ERIC HODGINS, *Episode*

How many ways do you use the word "anxious"? When you say "I'm anxious to find out my grade," you mean you're eager to know. When you say "I'm anxious about my part in the play," you mean you worry about learning your lines and hope you won't embarrass yourself on opening night. When you say "I'm anxious about flying to California next Sunday," you probably mean that you feel nervous and tense about flying, have fantasies about the plane crashing, and worry about getting physically ill. Sometimes you say you're anxious and you're not even sure why.

We have all known the discomfort of anxiety—the dry mouth, the dripping palms, the fidgety feet, the swirling thoughts, the pounding heart, the tense muscles, the knotted stomach, and the quivering bladder or bowel. A little of this feeling may prepare us to be on guard, motivated, concerned enough to want to do a good job at whatever makes us anxious. A *lot* of the same feeling may make it impossible to work: we are easily distracted, keep getting up to sharpen our pencils and straighten our desks, go to the refrigerator, or "just take a little nap before studying."

If we become anxious enough, we may reach the level of panic and decide to "chuck the whole thing"—go for a walk, take in a movie, or play a vigorous game of handball until the feeling passes. Our lives are punctuated here and there with varying degrees of anxiety, but fortunately, these interruptions are usually temporary and we function—work and play—adequately. Only when the distressing times begin to outweigh the comfortable ones do we begin to have a serious problem. We may begin to look for excuses to describe our plight—not enough sleep, too much hard work, excessive physical distress, and so on. But, these situations seldom account for anxiety. Rarely, for example, is hard work in and of itself responsible for a nervous breakdown or emotional exhaustion.

In "The Push and Pull of Inner Needs," we spoke of Freud's efforts to distinguish different kinds of anxiety. We mentioned that everyday fears or anxieties are usually related to definite events, people, or things. But the anxiety that has no obvious cause, that seems built into the personality and internal workings of the body, is called *free-floating anxiety*. It is this kind of anxiety that causes the greater distress because it seems so purposeless, so unpredictable, so persistent, and so frustrating.

Freud identified another kind of anxiety—*signal anxiety*—which was a milder warning that something threatening to the individual might be just around the corner. This type of anxiety allows the individual to "gear up" to protect himself from danger. It is much like the instinctual reaction of animals to a life-threatening situation.

The more the anxiety becomes a continuous reaction, the closer it comes to being pathological (unhealthy). At this end of the spectrum, we refer to *anxiety states* or *anxiety neurosis*. (These conditions are discussed in Chapter 15, "Darker Shades of Gray: Mental Illness.")

It is probably impossible to speak of one emotional state without considering others. George's experience illustrates this "connectedness" of emotions.

GEORGE had seen Gloria in several of his classes. He liked the way she walked, the way she wore her hair, the sexy way she dressed. She had become quite a distraction for him. Practically all he could think about was how he would like to ask her for a date. The more he thought about it, the more absurd he thought it was—"She would never be interested in me," he thought. "She's practically the most popular kid in the school, and she seems to go for the brainier guys."

One day, George found himself sitting next to Gloria in assembly and struck up a little conversation with her. He felt encouraged. After fretting over it for about three days, he finally called her and asked if she'd go to a party with him. He wanted desperately for her to say yes, but underneath he didn't have very high hopes. He was surprised and elated when she accepted. He could hardly concentrate on his studies—or anything else—for the next two days.

On the evening that he was to call for Gloria, he was a "nervous wreck." George decided that the clothes he had been perfectly satisfied with before just didn't look right. He had more than the usual difficulty combing his hair. As he rushed to get ready, his mother called him for supper, but he said he wasn't hungry. He paced around the house, kept looking at his watch, and finally left in time to meet Gloria. He wasn't outside two minutes when he realized he had forgotten his wallet. Returning to his house, he also discovered he had forgotten his keys; his heart raced wildly as he rang the doorbell—it seemed like an eternity before his mother answered. He rushed up and down the stairs again, out the door and managed to get to Gloria's just a couple of minutes late.

The party turned out to be a bore. George felt self-conscious because most of the other kids knew each other and were dressed much more casually than George. Not only that, Gloria seemed to spend more time talking to other guys than she did to him. They seemed to "hang looser" and to have a better sense of humor than he did. He felt himself becoming tense and angry, but he didn't want to show it. He tried to join in, but he was not really interested in these other kids, just in Gloria. His heart began to pound, the room seemed stuffy, and he felt a little sick to his stomach. He wanted to ask Gloria to go outside with him, but he felt she'd see how upset he was and would consider him weak. So he told her he was going out for a walk in the fresh air. As he walked, he realized how frustrated and disappointed he was. He felt a little sad and wiped a tear from the corner of his eye. He and Gloria got a ride home later with a group of kids; they left Gloria off at her house. He rode the rest of the way home in relative silence, slouched off to his room and spent a restless and sleepless night thinking, "I guess I blew it."

In a matter of a few days, George went from one experience of elation, through a very anxious period, to the opposite feeling of dejection and disappointment. It was not the first time he would feel such mixed emotions.

Many of us have experienced just such swings in our moods. We have all had times when we just haven't felt very happy, or when we have been sad or morose. Hardly anything seemed to capture our interest, and our friends told us we were "pains" or "party-poopers." We were fed up, discouraged, disappointed. The easiest thing to do seemed to be to stay in bed. Strange and frightening thoughts may have entered our minds, like not caring what happened to us, or worrying that we had some incurable illness. Surprisingly enough, we awake to another day full of new energy—like a recharged battery—looking at the previous day's experience as something already deep in the past.

Normal development is riddled with disappointments. It is disappointing to be told to go to bed, that you can't watch another television program, that you can't go out until you put out the garbage, that you have to stay home and babysit while your parents go out for the evening. Every disappointment is like a small loss—a loss of freedom, a lost hope, a lost fantasy or daydream.

This is only the beginning of a series of losses, but in a way they prepare us to know how to handle bigger and more important losses: the loss of the pleasures of childhood when we finally reach adolescence with all its new responsibilities; the loss of a girlfriend or boyfriend; the loss through death of a close relative. In later life, we experience the loss of our youth, our looks, our capacity for sexual enjoyment, our children who go off to school, our physical prowess, our enthusiasm; and later yet, the loss of our mental sharpness and interest in new challenges. All are shades of gray along the spectrum of emotions. Disappointment blends into sadness, into grief, into bereavement, into depression. But all of this is within the realm of normality. Only when the grays shade off into darkness, when the feelings of depression lead to a sense of worthlessness, failure, helplessness, and hopelessness do we begin to consider sadness or depression an illness.

A Look at Some Basic Emotions

There is great variation in our capacity to express the basic, everyday emotions which we all share. Each of us

WHAT ARE HEALTHY EMOTIONS ?

1. *In what kinds of situations is it considered "permissible" to express one's emotions freely? In what situations is one expected to "control" oneself?*

    To what extent is it helpful or harmful to control emotions?

    How do *you* decide when to express your feelings?

2. *How many different kinds of anxiety can you describe?*

    What useful purpose does anxiety serve?

    How can anxiety be disruptive?

    Can you recall what experience caused you the greatest anxiety?

3. *What is the difference between sadness and depression?*

4. *In the story about George and Gloria, how do you think George's expectations influenced the kinds of feelings he had at different times in his pursuit of Gloria?*

5. *Why do we so readily consider ourselves "sick" when we read stories of illness in others? Can you think of*

any novel you've read in which you were upset about identifying with a specific character?

handles emotions in his or her own way. While we all have some idea of what we mean by emotions, there is still no scientific agreement about how emotions develop or what part the "mind" plays in its interaction with the body.

In the early 1890s, the prevailing scientific notion was that we first perceive or sense something, which then

We all share the same basic emotions, although we may express them differently. A smile, a tear, a frown may speak for us more clearly than our words. Our body has a language all its own.

Photo courtesy of Kenneth M. Bernstein

555

causes bodily changes that produce an emotional reaction; for example, we see a tragic event, we cry, and *then* feel sorry. This was called the *James-Lange theory of emotions*, named after the two men who devised it. In the 1920s this concept was replaced with the *Cannon-Bard emergency theory* which held that emotions prepare the body for "fight" or "flight." According to Cannon and Bard, we *first* experience the emotion; then activity in the brain, especially in that part called the hypothalamus, results in bodily changes.

Through the ages, there has been considerable controversy over the extent to which emotions are an inborn phenomenon and the extent to which they are determined by the learning which occurs in our particular environments. Early psychologists believed that all infants were born with a physical capacity to react with fear and rage and that these later became modified by *conditioning* into other emotional responses.

Scientists are still attempting to clarify these puzzles. They are studying the nature of the brain and central nervous system, the hormones, and the adrenal and pituitary glands. All of these factors have much to do with bodily changes, resistance to disease, growth rate, and emotional states. But until we have better answers, we will continue to puzzle over the nature of emotional expression.

Love and Sex: Sweet Mysteries of Life!

*I never could explain why
I love anybody or anything*

WALT WHITMAN

556

How difficult it is to say what love is, yet how much has been written about it—volumes of poetry, philosophy, psychology, even biology! Still, we find it virtually impossible to offer more than simple-minded clichés like "Love is blind," "All is fair in love and war," "Love makes the world go round," and the like. For years people have memorized Elizabeth Barrett Browning's poem "How Do I Love Thee" and have sung all the popular songs about love that always seem to say it better than we can. We are constantly groping for some way to explain what we think we feel—some intense but vague and complicated sensation we call love.

Whatever love is, we know that it can have profound effects on every aspect of our existence. It can make us speechless, forgetful, foolish, helpless, pained, ecstatic, sad, sick, possessed, jealous, deaf, blind, humble, proud, timid, bold, romantic, sentimental, thoughtful, reminiscent, nostalgic, scorned, mad . . . Our dreams about "true love" are shaped by movies, TV, songs, advertising, and what others tell us. Some go through life asking forever what it is, while others settle early for a quick but narrow answer. Voltaire's notion that "Love is a canvas furnished by nature and embroidered by imagination" is as useful a starting point as any.

Nature's Canvas

Probably our ideas about love are formed for us in earliest infancy, when close attachments to parents and other caretakers create the backdrop upon which we will "embroider" our own special meanings of closeness, affection, devotion, and love. As babies, we are totally dependent upon others for comfort, support—for life

557

How difficult it is to say what love is, yet how much has been written about it! We are always groping for some way to explain what we think we feel—some intense but vague and complicated sensation we call love.

itself. How our needs are met, the people who meet them, and the environment in which this all takes place create a setting for feelings to develop. If the circumstances of early life make affection a rare commodity, a child may grow up not knowing what love is, yet still miss and long for it. Illness in a family, absence of one or both parents, hard times and lack of nourishment, the sharing of cramped quarters with many other family members may all interfere with the necessary development of healthy attachments to other people later on. The canvas upon

558

which one embroiders may be full of holes. Later, good experiences help patch the holes. But if the cloth sometimes wears thin, help can be obtained from the "tailors" of human behavior, professionals who know about the processes of early development.

The First Love

Naturally, the first and most intense attachment for everyone is the mother. Life flows with the blood through the umbilical cord before the doctor ties it off and slaps the newborn to start it breathing on its own. The transition is abrupt and the new world is strange. It will take time for the new baby to begin to feel comfortable and to learn how to do more for itself. In the meantime, the child's dependence upon the biological (real) mother is great, although "mothering" (warmth, holding, caressing, rocking) may come from mother substitutes (surrogates).Fathers can do the "mothering." Whatever its source, this is the time of *first love* for the baby. Without fairly constant exposure to this love, a more "mature" love may never develop.

This early love, says psychologist Harry Harlow, is a child's best insurance against becoming an emotionally disturbed adult. This may sound strange coming from someone who spent a lifetime studying the behavior of monkeys, but Harlow believed that humans go through stages of affectionate relationships in much the same way as monkeys do. He designed a "wire mother" and a "cloth mother" and showed that the bond was created more by the "feel" of the "person" doing the holding than by the feeding itself. He also showed that the absence of love early in a monkey's life led to an inability to love and to

YOUR SELF

take care of one's own children. It led to social and sexual problems, and even to violence. Monkeys, he said, went through stages of love just as humans did: from self, to mother, to father, to peer, to mature sexual attachments.

Self-love: Necessity or Selfishness?

It is probably very confusing to be told by friends or parents that you are too much in love with yourself, and then at the same time to be told by teachers, clergy, and counselors that if you don't have love for yourself, you will be unable to love another. How can we reconcile these two ideas? Is it possible to be self-loving yet unselfish?

Part of growing up involves the development of a healthy self-reliance. But trust and confidence in one's own ability can only grow from trust in others. If we are well cared for as infants, if all our needs are satisfied, if we are consistently made to feel comfortable and safe, then we learn to trust others. The baby develops a sense of self as he gradually realizes that he is a separate person. He develops a sense of self-awareness and begins to feel secure enough to explore his own small world—to try things out for himself. Soon he does not need to be held and fed, but can sit in a chair and feed himself. However, he still needs intermittent encouragement in order to be successful in his attempts. While he can satisfy himself to a greater degree, he still looks for the comfort of love and is occasionally fearful that he may lose it.

If successes outnumber failures in his efforts at self-fulfillment, the child begins to develop self-confidence, a capacity and willingness to be away from his "caretakers" for longer periods of time, a desire to "go it alone" for a while. Confidence leads to competence. The child is encouraged, praised, and loved for his self-achievements. He becomes proud, content, secure, and he experiences a sense of his own *worth*.

The feeling that "I am worth loving" is the basis of *self-love*. This is not the same as greediness or selfishness or a haughty feeling of great importance. It is comfort with what one is and an ability to be sufficiently satisfied with oneself to be able to pay more attention to *others*. The idea that reasonable self-love prepares a person to respect and love others is pointed out by psychoanalyst Erich Fromm:

> *The idea expressed in the Biblical "Love thy neighbor as thyself!" implies that respect for one's own integrity and uniqueness, love for and understanding of one's own self, cannot be separated from respect and love and understanding for another individual.*[4]

With a secure sense of self-love, the child can afford to be less selfish, to make fewer demands upon others.

By developing a sense of individuality and separateness, the child has greater freedom to make new attachments. A comfortable balance between self-love and interest in others is part of maturity. Too much self-love can result in isolation, false confidence, and a lack of experience. It also may lead to a turning inward of feelings, which causes problems in adjusting to others. Finding this balance between love of oneself and love of others does not come about abruptly, or without discouragement, disappointment, sadness, and emotional pain.

Making the Transition

For the first few years of life, the child gloats in the joy of *receiving* love. He is grateful for the care he gets, basking in the warmth and comfort of those who fulfill his needs—those who love him. But through a very gradual transition—not fully understood—he finds new satisfaction in giving as well as receiving, sharing instead of taking. Somehow his self-love branches out to involve others. Not only is he loved *by* the parents, he can now reciprocate by loving them back.

He may go on a search for others to love—to siblings, playmates, schoolmates, pets—because the need for extending and fulfilling oneself is so strong. During the early stages of this search, he may take his comforters along, to avoid feeling too lonely. Linus, of the cartoon "Peanuts," comes to mind. With his thumb in his mouth and his blanket to his face, he seeks out Lucy or some other appealing person, yet he does not feel secure enough to leave these attachments aside. Do you remember loving a teddy bear or a favorite doll, or even a ratty old blanket when you were little? These early experiences were not mature love, but they seemed very important at the time. These loves were not sexual, nor a quest for permanent relationships—merely a need to reach out beyond ourselves to become something more than we can be alone.

Maslow spoke of the need for the ego to transcend itself in order to achieve self-actualization. Others who followed Freud believe that the emotional pain and anxiety of separation from one's parents causes a strong biological pull back to the original state of attachment. Erikson speaks of the need for mutual trust, for intimacy and mutual recognition.

Whichever psychological theory one subscribes to, the capacity for love as an emotion is thought to pass through stages. Some of the earliest "romances" of nursery

Photo courtesy of Beth Nicholson

For the first few years of life, the child basks in the joy of *receiving* love. He is grateful for the care he gets, for the warmth and comfort of those who fulfill his needs—those who love him. But through a very gradual transition—not fully understood—he finds new satisfaction in giving as well as receiving, sharing instead of taking. Somehow his self-love branches out to involve others. Not only is he loved *by* the parents, he can now reciprocate by loving them back.

school and kindergarten are called "puppy love," perhaps because the affection shown is similar to that showered upon one's pet. Learning to *give* love outside the home is a big step on the road to maturity. *Reciprocal giving and getting* are important aspects of the ability to love. It is usually at this time that we discover that we can develop no further alone, that we have a need for relationships with others who appeal to us, who have values we admire, characteristics that attract us, qualities that enrich us. We find that another's pleasure is our own pleasure.

During adolescence, there may be a series of platonic attachments where communicating thoughts and ideas in a kind of spiritual or idealistic way is more important than a sensual relationship. "Falling in love" in adolescence is considered by Erikson to be part of developing one's identity, a way to get feedback from others about who we are, about what others like or dislike about us. This process is often seen as somewhat *narcissistic* (egotistical) because we tend to like others who like us, or who look like us and share our views. Platonic loves are not sexual, but they give people practice with some of the issues they will face as biological changes contribute a more frankly sexual aspect to a love relationship.

In healthy individuals, love and sex are usually intertwined, although each can exist separately. Maslow says that self-actualizing individuals do not seek sex for its own sake. Genuine love can even tolerate the absence of sexual fulfillment. A love relationship in which neither partner seeks to exploit the other, or to dominate or disparage the other, can develop a spontaneity, a naturalness, and a sense of comfort and satisfaction which encompass a variety of mutual satisfactions, including sexual ones. Usually there will be an occasional infatua-

LOVE: A PERSONAL DEFINITION

1. *Think up your own definition of love. See if you can describe all the different kinds of feelings that make up love.*

2. *Is there any special poem or song that you feel captures, for you, the feeling of love? Explain why it does.*

3. *What is the difference between self-love and selfishness? Can you think of circumstances in a person's life that would interfere with the development of a healthy self-respect?*

4. *How many different kinds of love can you name (for example, parental love, love of work, love of beauty, etc.)? What are the distinguishing qualities of each?*

tion or experimental relationship before an individual settles into a more or less permanent love relationship.

Out of all these experiences emerges a sense of one's own needs and capacities, an appreciation of what one seeks in a deep personal relationship, a sense of respect and responsibility for self and others, an ability to care and to give and to interact in fulfilling ways with another individual. A good relationship permits closeness without discomfort or over-possessiveness. There is a mutual strengthening rather than a loss of individuality. This is the real embroidery which is woven onto the canvas of one's earliest experience.

Anger and Aggression

Imagine for a moment that you find yourself in the following situation. It is the end of a long week and you've finally finished your tests. All week you have counted on relaxing Friday night, on having a good time at a party with some friends. At five o'clock that evening, your mother comes into your room to say the babysitter just called in sick. You will have to stay home with your younger brother because your parents are going out to dinner with another couple. How do you feel?

Here is how five different people responded to this situation:

> Fran looked at her mother blandly and said, "All right. I'll stay home. I didn't want to go to the party anyway."

> Bob began to argue. He told his mother that his plans were just as important as theirs. He slammed his desk drawer closed and began to pace back and forth.

> Carol dissolved in tears. She said she was terribly disappointed.

> Ted said nothing. He just walked out of the room. Saturday evening, his mother reminded him that he had forgotten to pick up his father's shirts at the cleaners during the day.

> Mark kept reading his book. He began to feel depressed. This was not the first time he had been called to the rescue.

Which of the five would you consider angry?

If you answered all five, you are probably right. Each person handled the anger differently. Fran tried to deny that she was angry. Do you believe her? Bob was forthright in his anger. Carol called her anger "disappointment," but doesn't all disappointment carry with it some resentment? Ted used the "silent treatment." Did he just "forget" to go to the cleaners, or was he getting even with his parents? Mark turned his anger inward; depression is a sign of bottled-up anger.

Anger is a normal reaction when you feel frustrated, helpless, pressured, or disappointed. Yet sometimes you may not even recognize that you are angry. Often anger is expressed indirectly. You may get into your car and speed recklessly down the highway, even have an accident. You may flunk an exam your parents expected you to do well on. You may go out on the tennis court and slam the ball at your opponent with a vengeance. You may get careless and break a dish. You may tell a sarcastic joke. Or you may get a headache, or feel nauseated, or depressed. Your blood pressure may soar.

We all invest a lot of energy in anger. It can wear us down, especially if we do not learn to recognize it and express it constructively. How do our bodies react to anger? How do we block anger or distort it? How can we express it safely and feel relieved? Anger is a *powerful* emotion. Without proper restraints, it can lead to rage or violence.

Ready for Battle

When you get angry, your body chemistry begins to change. Your blood pressure rises, your body sugar

567

increases, and your heart beats faster, providing you with extra energy. You start to breathe more quickly. Your muscles tense up, ready for action. You become less tired and more alert. The pupils in your eyes widen, allowing you to see better. Your senses are dulled so that you can withstand injury better. In fact, your whole body is preparing you to fight! Although the mind can distinguish anxiety from fear or anger, the chemistry of the body responds in a similar way to all.

What happens, then, if you do not discharge some of this energy? Your body remains in a "*chronic* [continuous] state of preparedness,"⁵ which is physically and emotionally unhealthy. Your anger may trigger one of a variety of symptoms such as a headache—often brought on by tension—or an ulcer. Asthma, skin disorders, stuttering, high blood pressure, and arthritis are sometimes linked to repressed anger. The businessman who remarks, "I am so angry that I could burst a blood vessel" is not really joking. Anger can make existing illnesses worse or prevent a speedy recovery.

Hold That Line!

We are all born with the capacity to get angry. It is only *how* we express our anger that is learned. Some people grow up with the warning, "Your friends won't like you if you get angry," or "Nice people don't argue." Often these people learn to hold their anger in and smile so that everyone will like them. Theodore Rubin calls this "the be-a-nice-guy-don't-make-waves" syndrome. He explains that ". . . don't-make-wavers are generally people who predicate their whole lives and personalities on being 'nice guys' and on being universally liked. Of course they feel

Anger is a normal reaction when you feel frustrated, help-less, pressured, or disappointed. Yet sometimes you may not even recognize that you are angry. Often, anger is expressed indirectly. You may flunk an exam, break a dish, tell a sarcastic joke, get a headache, or feel depressed.

that anger, especially if it shows, will destroy the image they live by. . . . Since being universally loved is seen as the only way to be safe in this world, anger—especially anger that causes retaliation by the other fellow—is of course felt as a terrible threat. The 'nice guy' is therefore forced into constantly playing a role."[6] Think about it. Do you know anyone with a frozen smile?

Some people block their emotions with "the mind-your-own-business"[7] syndrome. They reason that if they do not get involved with anyone, they cannot get hurt. After all, anger means that they *care*, that they are vulnerable. To avoid being hurt, they retreat. If they keep far enough away, no one can touch them.

You have probably met the "I-couldn't-care-less" person who denies his anger; the "I'm-angry-but-I'll-get-over-it" person who refuses to deal with his anger; and the "I'd-like-another-chance-to-tell-him-what-I-really-think" person who puts off his anger.

Some people *displace* their anger. Instead of arguing with the boss, they lash out at their spouse or children, who are "safer" targets. And how about the person who explodes over a trifle; he has been saving up all his anger from other sources and, wham, it's all yours! There are those who try to "dilute" their anger with rationalizations. They may say, "Well, she's moody because she isn't feeling well," or "He's had a tough life—how can I upset him?" As Rubin notes, these are all ways in which we pervert our emotions, denying them a healthy outlet. Our anger becomes distorted and returns to haunt us in a variety of disguises. In *The Angry Book*, Rubin portrays these many masks of anger. Here are some of them:

> *Guilt and Depression*[8]—often the result of anger turned inward. Some people berate themselves rather than focusing their anger on the proper targets.

> *"No Sleep and Sleep Sleep"*[9]—It is very difficult to fall asleep when you are really furious at someone. A more passive person, however, may seek to escape his anger and depression by sleeping too much. You

feel no pain when you are asleep. Both symptoms reveal anger.

"Tomorrow and Tomorrow: Chronic Anticipation, Obsessive Ruminating . . ."—"There are people who spend half a lifetime and nearly all their energy in self-destructive preoccupation with pasts that cannot be undone and futures that will never arrive."[10]

"Self-Sabotage"—"Its most important function is to keep its victim striving for impossible and "ideal" goals in quest of neurotic glory. Each failure to be gloriously ideal is met with self-hate, which in effect provides the whip to push the victim up the impossible trail again and again."[11]

"Sweet, Sweet, Sweet, and the Blood Pressure Goes Up, Up, Up"[12]—Bottled-up anger that turns into a physical symptom: a migraine headache, colitis, or a stiff neck, perhaps.

"No Talk"[13]—the icy treatment. You feel like shaking the person and shouting, "Say something. Anything!" This person cuts you off and won't let you reach him. He is expressing anger.

"Let's Pretend"[14]—Some people talk *about* their anger but don't *feel* it: they intellectualize. In a calm, cool voice they may say, "I am furious with you," but their anger stays tightly controlled and plastic. Others "act angry" because they think they ought to in a certain situation: the teacher who first blasts you for being late and then feels guilty and laughs it off with, "Well, don't worry!"

"Supersweet Talk"[15]—the apple-polisher who plays up to his potential enemies so that he is "safe but

utterly lacking in happiness or honesty."

"Don't Worry about Me"[16]—This is the person who manipulates someone close by challenging his love and making him feel guilty. A popular example: the lonely mother who tells her son, "I didn't feel well this afternoon, but it's all right for you to go out and have a good time tonight."

"Subtle Sabotage"[17]—the ill-timed laugh, the forgotten task, a late arrival, a bit of misinformation. All of these may be safe ways to get even.

How many of these people do you recognize? We all have probably used one or another of these disguises to hide our anger. That is why we must remind ourselves that it is *normal* to become angry when provoked. The unruffled person is unreal.

Letting Go

How can we express our anger in a healthy, constructive way? First, we must recognize *when* we are really angry, without apologies, rationalizations, guilt, or embarrassment. Emotions are real, whether they are justified or not, and therefore we must be willing to accept them.

Next, we must decide *why* and *at whom* we are angry. Are we upset over a single incident or an accumulation of woes? Are we venting our anger on a "safe" target, but the *wrong* one?

Some people worry that they will endanger a relationship with someone they love if they get angry. Actually, a relationship can remain vital only when two people are honest with each other. Love is not always harmony. Rubin explains:

> . . . *we generally get angry at people who have some meaning for us. . . . an expression of anger. . . means that one cares enough to want to see remedial action take place so that a relationship can continue and grow. An expression of anger also demonstrates respect for the individual in question. This is so because in expressing anger one is investing emotion—showing how one feels and saying in effect, "I respect you enough to want to share this part of myself with you." This kind of expression also shows considerable confidence in the strength of the relationship. The feeling here is that the relationship is important and strong enough to withstand bumps in the road. It will not come irreparably apart at the first gust of strong feelings. If anything, it will be strengthened as a result of increased understanding between the people involved as well as the increased feelings of reality that always follow clearing of the air.*[18]

A relationship which dissolves over the first show of emotions was not solid to begin with!

A third factor is *timing*—when we sit and simmer, the issues become distorted and the message loses its impact. A grudge poisons the holder more than the target.

A warm, healthy expression of anger is direct and honest, but also sensitive to the other person's feelings. It is important to attack the central issue, not the *total* person. After all, you are not out to demolish someone—just to share your feelings in the hope of correcting a bad situation. There is quite a difference in saying, "It makes me angry when you are late," instead of "You are such a selfish, egotistical person—you only care about your own time." No one rebounds well from sarcasm or the digging up of old grudges and irrelevant side issues.

It is also not fair to explode and then walk away. If you respect the other person enough to get angry, you owe him the courtesy of listening to his response, allowing him to maintain some self-respect as well.

The word "mad" can mean both angry and crazy. Are they the same? Not at all! When you express your anger, you are actually protecting your sanity! Repressed anger impairs your judgment and may make you anxious, depressed, or physically ill. When you release the energy you have invested in anger, you feel relieved. You no longer have to carry it around as excess baggage. However, just unloading your emotional baggage on someone else is not the way to achieve mental health. The constructive use of anger requires tact, control, timing, respect, and reasonableness.

What's Wrong with Aggression?

The word aggression has appeared in several sections of this book. Usually this word calls to mind unpleasant words—hostility, rage, jealousy, violence. Like other emotions, however, aggression covers a wide range of feelings. The word aggression is used by different people to mean different things. Perhaps you have seen movies showing how animals behave, how they fight and kill not only to survive but also to maintain their own territory. This behavior is considered by many biologists and some psychologists to be innate, an instinct with which the

It is important to learn how to express anger in a healthy, constructive way. We must recognize when we are really angry—without apologies, rationalizations, guilt or embarrassment—and then express this anger in a direct and honest, yet sensitive manner.

animal is born. Others believe that it may be learned. But most agree that the *purpose* of this aggressive activity is first to protect the individual, and then the "family" (or species) to which the individual belongs.

When we speak of aggression in the human species, we usually mean more than fighting and killing. Even if the individual is born with aggressive instincts—and there is great debate over this—learning which occurs in a civilized society can change aggressive tendencies into more constructive behaviors. While aggression can be used tactfully and productively to "get ahead," it can also be abused in a "dog eat dog" way. Raw aggression can be tamed to become reasonable self-assertion, which gives rise to self-confidence, self-esteem, and motivation. Healthy competition which develops from aggressive behavior can bring pleasure and the satisfaction of achievement and sportsmanship. Creative uses of aggression are seen in playful sarcasm, cleverness, satire, wit, and humor.

During adolescence, all feelings are not easily tamed. They may not always find positive and constructive expression. Most. of us have at one time or another experienced pangs of jealousy or envy and had the feeling of "wanting to get back" at another person. We have even experienced something like the sense of "territoriality" seen in animals when we feel that others have "overstepped their bounds" or "imposed on our rights." When we feel furious with a teacher or jealous of a classmate or sibling, the expression of our feelings may be blocked. While we might have fantasies of "tearing someone apart" (again, like the animal fighting for self-preservation), the fear and control that we have over such impulses keep us from acting on these fantasies.

Some people worry about the power of their thoughts and have a tremendous fear of losing control. They may "let off steam" by being bossy, verbally abusive, or even cruel, but rarely do they become violent or destructive. In the language of Freud's psychology, the superego helps to bring these urges under control and the ego finds socially acceptable ways to express them.

Whether you believe that aggression is an instinct with which we are born or a kind of behavior and emotion we learn, the topic is clearly of wide interest. Aggression, like anger, can be put to work for us in creative, healthy ways. We must first acknowledge its existence and then learn how to tame it.

EXPRESSING ANGER

1. *Think back to three times when you felt particularly angry at someone or something. How did you handle your anger? What was the result? How might you have handled it differently?*

2. *What habits of other people irritate you most? Do you tell them so?*

   What kinds of things do you do that sometimes bother your parents? your brothers and sisters? your teachers? Why do you think you do these things?

3. *For what reasons do you get angry at yourself? How do you cope with such feelings?*

4. *When you feel generally angry and tense, how do you "let off steam?" Are there particular activities that help you to relax?*

Humor and Laughter

When did you laugh last? At the *fun* of an off-color joke? In the *joy* and *glory* of an athletic victory? Out of *nervousness* when you were called to the principal's office? In the *triumph* of a sarcastic comment that hit its mark? In *relief* that you were not the one who tripped? Out of *embarrassment* that you made everyone late for the show? In *surprise* when you were caught off guard by a tap on the shoulder? To *teach* someone a lesson who is acting foolishly? As an *accommodation* to the boss who thinks he's funny? Or just to feel *part of a group* that's having a good time?

How can laughter express so many different moods and feelings? Basically, laughter is a *discharge of pent-up energy* that relieves and relaxes us. When we are tense and anxious, angry or serious, and someone cracks a joke, all our defenses suddenly come down: we laugh, and

Laughter can express so many different moods and feelings. Basically, laughter is a discharge of pent-up energy that relieves and relaxes us. It is a uniquely *human* method of communication; we laugh *at* and *with* people.

Photo courtesy of Kenneth M. Bernstein

somehow we feel better. Laughter is a uniquely *human* method of communication. We laugh *at* and *with* people. And when we laugh at ourselves, it is because we have been reminded that we, too, are human and therefore may at times be pompous, foolish, rigid, or too serious, and thus laughable.

What triggers our laughter? How does laughter express our hidden desires? Why do we laugh more when in a group? Why is it a "relief" to laugh? Let us look at the "mystery" of laughter.

Jokes and Laughter: Evading the Censor

Remember the id, that part of the personality which expresses your instincts and desires? And the ego and superego which keep it in check? It was Sigmund Freud who explained how jokes and laughter are tied to your id and unconscious. As you grow up, you learn that you cannot gratify all your desires: you cannot punch the boy next door who rode off on your bicycle; you cannot continue to get into bed with your parents each time you have a nightmare; you cannot disobey the teacher when he asks you to come in from recess. In your childhood, you are *socialized* to speak and behave "properly."

What happens, then, to all your hidden desires and fantasies? You *repress* them, pushing them down into your unconscious. You control your aggressive impulses and "inhibit" your natural responses so that they will be considered socially acceptable. Yet through your dreams you may still fulfill your fantasies symbolically. Occasionally, through a Freudian slip, you may blurt out what you are *really* thinking. And through *the joke*, you may express your instincts—whether lustful or hostile—in a socially acceptable way!

How many times have you heard sexy, biting, or nasty jokes that cause someone in the group to flinch, and heard the others remind him, "It was just a joke!"? Freud believed that jokes reach into your unconscious, allowing you to express those aggressive and sexual thoughts and desires that under other circumstances would be censored. Whether you make the joke or just hear it, you thus feel gratified. Your laughter is a pleasurable release of the psychic energy which you are not using to inhibit or suppress your real desires. Your laughter is a "safe" rebellion against your "civilized" nature! Freud explained:

> . . . the joke will evade restrictions and open sources of pleasure that have become inaccessible. . . . It will further bribe the hearer with its yield of pleasure into taking sides with us without any very close investigation, just as on other occasions we ourselves have often been bribed by an innocent joke into overestimating the substance of a statement expressed jokingly.[19]

Humor helps us deal with a variety of sensitive topics: relatives, ethnic groups, alcohol, religion, sex, race. A joke may be totally innocent and playful, or it may be pointed and hostile. Surprisingly enough, uncontrolled laughter sometimes gives a sense of control over something which is frightening, mysterious, and puzzling. Laughing at others' deformities, peculiarities, and differences makes us feel protected against the fear that we ourselves may become sick or "crazy."

Hostile Humor

> *In laughter we have always an unavowed intention to humiliate and consequently to correct our neighbor, if not in his will, at least in his deed.*

> HENRI BERGSON, *Laughter*

The power of laughter is amazing. While an innocent joke may cause only slight embarrassment, hostile humor can make its victim feel degraded, rejected, and punished. Because no one enjoys being laughed at, the victim will usually take great pains not to be caught in the same situation again! So laughter is a socializing agent, reminding people of their quirks and bad habits. It is a prod to better behavior

Humor often disguises aggression. It enables one to disarm his victim coolly and calmly. Its cleverness and wittiness may delight the onlookers who laugh and thereby diminish the seriousness of the situation. Humor takes the potential danger out of a highly charged emotional atmosphere. It often prevents retaliation, because the victim may be too overwhelmed to be equally clever. And the humorist can always claim it was "just a joke"!

Think of all the satires and cartoons which chide our politicians. They capture the truth, destroy pretensions, point out absurdities, and make us laugh all at once! Wit can also be a weapon against oppressors. Here is a story that circulated in Poland many years ago:

> *Little Ladislaw was called upon to recite for the benefit of a Communist official checking up on education under the Polish People's Republic.*

581

> *"Who is your father?" the teacher asked.*
>
> *"Stalin," said Ladislaw promptly, "the father of all progress."*
>
> *"Very good," said teacher. "And who is your mother?"*
>
> *"The Soviet Union, mother of all peace-loving people."*
>
> *"Excellent!" the official broke in. "And now tell me, my little man, what would you like to be when you grow up?"*
>
> *"An orphan," replied little Ladislaw.*[20]

The element of wit and surprise in its ending makes you laugh, but the message is clear. Here again, humor allows for a safe rebellion.

Laughter as a Relief

Many years ago, political theorist Thomas Hobbes described laughter as a sense of "sudden glory" that arises in us when we feel confidently secure while others stumble. Think of how often you laugh at other people's troubles out of relief that it didn't happen to you! You laugh when your friend is the subject of a practical joke, or comes in from the rain looking wilted, or drops a bundle. Your silent thought is, "It might have been me!"

Laughter may also be a release when other emotional outlets are blocked. It may reflect an effort to cope with anxiety. How about the nervous laugh before a test? The inappropriate smile or chuckle when confronted with a mistake? The shallow laughter of depression? The forced laughter of embarrassment? Laughter may *mask* many emotions. During the grim days of the Civil War,

Abraham Lincoln said, "I laugh because I must not cry. That is all. That is all."[21]

The Fellowship of Laughter

Babies smile and laugh before they learn to speak. Laughter is a form of communication often more expressive than words. Laughter is a *social* act. You tend to feel more comfortable laughing alongside others. It is a way of *sharing* a mood.

Humor reflects the character, personality, intelligence, cultural background and social class of a person. The kinds of jokes you tell and enjoy, and even the tone and fullness of your laugh mirror your personality. A study of humor is a study of people: how they feel about themselves and others, the temper of their times, their outlook on life.

Photo courtesy of Kenneth M. Bernstein

In a group, laughter becomes infectious. It unifies people, allowing them to drop their defenses and forget their inhibitions. You will often laugh at things in a group that you would be embarrassed to laugh at when alone. Think of how a joke you picked up at a party will fall flat when repeated to a single friend. As Bergson explained, "Laughter appears to stand in need of an echo. . . . How often has it been said that the fuller the theater, the more uncontrolled the laughter of the audience!"[22]

Even when you laugh quietly to yourself, laughter is a social act. According to Joyce Hertzler, the individual is:

> . . . communicating with himself . . . . One part of his personality may be joking with another part, or kidding it. Much of his laughter and smiling reflects reminiscence of some relation . . . with other people; . . . the happy recall of a loved one or a happy occasion . . . amusement at some real or imagined social situation. . . . Even when we laugh at ourselves, we take the attitude of others toward us, as these attitudes reflect standard group conceptions of humorous, especially ludicrous situations.[23]

The ability to laugh at ourselves is a sign of mental health and maturity. It is important to be able to step back mentally and review our own behavior. Are we taking ourselves too seriously? Have we been pompous? Or foolish? Too cynical or too idealistic? Laughter reminds us that we are human and helps us bounce back from our mistakes.

The Laughter of the Times

Men show their character in nothing more clearly than by what they laugh at.

GOETHE

Let me hear the jokes of a nation and I will tell you what the people are like, how they are getting on and what is going to happen to them.

STEPHEN LEACOCK

Humor reflects the character, personality, intelligence, cultural background, and social class of a person. The kinds of jokes you tell and enjoy, and even the tone and fullness of your laugh mirror your personality.

Do you enjoy ethnic, racial, practical, sex, or "sick" jokes? Do you like puns, satires, slapstick, or cartoons? Do you laugh easily, loud and long? Or do you smile a lot? Do your jokes usually focus on a particular subject? Is your humor playful or aggressive? Can you laugh at yourself?

Sophisticates may prefer political satire to slapstick. Ethnic groups sometimes create humor around their own habits. Upper-class people often laugh cautiously and smile quietly. Working-class people may laugh more fully and loudly. Part of your identity, then, is your sense of humor and how you use it.

Historians often look at the humor of an era to understand its people better. In the 1930s, there were depression jokes. In the 1940s, there were war jokes. In the 1960s, the focus shifted to hippies and the war. A study of humor is a study of people: how they feel about themselves and others; the temper of their times; their outlook on life. It is a superb psychology lesson!

WHAT'S IN A LAUGH?

1. *What makes you laugh most readily? What kinds of humor appeal to you? In the next few days, note each time you laugh. Then jot down what made you laugh and why. What does it tell you about yourself?*

2. *Examine different kinds of humor: slapstick, "sick" jokes, satires, puns, etc. What makes each type work? Bring some jokes to class. Analyze them: What kinds of humor are expressed? Why are they funny?*

3. *Think of a movie, television show, or book which made you laugh. What form of humor was used?*

4. *What kinds of humor do people at different stages of their life enjoy (children, adolescents, young adults, the middle-aged and old-aged)?*

Fear

The only thing we have to fear is fear itself.

FRANKLIN D. ROOSEVELT,
First Inaugural Address,
March 4, 1933

Franklin Delano Roosevelt is remembered by as many people for this saying as he is for his political accomplishments. In 1933, people may not have known precisely what his words meant, but it seemed very reassuring when spoken by a man with great authority at a time when the country was on the verge of panic.

Roosevelt's expression suggests that fear has a tendency toward self-perpetuation, usually out of all proportion to the event that triggers it. If allowed to continue, it can lead to overwhelming anxiety, panic, and paralysis—in an individual, in a group, or in a whole nation. Perhaps more than anything else, Roosevelt's words reminded a nation of frightened citizens to stop for a moment, to look at reality, and to regain control of their emotions. His admonition is not so very different from the way some people make themselves count up to ten when they're afraid of saying the wrong thing. This gives them time to gain some perspective on the situation and to control their impulses.

In an infant, fear is generally indicated when he screams, kicks, thrashes, stamps, or holds his breath in response to a loud noise or some other abrupt stimulus. This is sometimes called a *startle pattern*. When the child is older, he can usually tell us what he fears. The list is long: the dark, loud noises, being alone, hurting, automobiles, guns, strangers, dogs, elevators, funny costumes, insects, swimming, nightmares, thunderstorms, and so on. With parental guidance, a child begins to sort out certain fears which he may consider reasonable. Being afraid of automobiles whizzing down the street helps him to learn not to step off the curb without looking very carefully. Fear of burns prevents him from touching a hot stove. Other fears are not so protective and may, at times, even immobilize a child—or an adult. He can't take a trip because he is afraid of trains or planes. He can't see the panorama of the city because he is afraid of high buildings. He can't go to a movie because he's afraid of crowds or public places.

It is sometimes difficult to distinguish between the kind of fear that is realistic or appropriate and the kind that is irrational and highly exaggerated. A phobia is an irrational and exaggerated fear. The more overwhelming, persistent, paralyzing, or disabling such a fear becomes, the more likely it will be considered a *phobia*.

Sometimes we fear not only external objects and situations but our own imaginings and fantasies as well. These may be more terrifying than anything we would actually encounter in real life. A fear of experiencin certain feelings, wishes, or impulses may be so intense that we are overcome with anxiety. The discomfort of this anxiety motivates a search (consciously or unconsciously) for ways to alleviate the unpleasant feelings.

The defense mechanisms we spoke of earlier help us to accomplish this. For example, a frightening thought or image may be *denied* and *projected* onto something or someone else. We can then say that we are afraid of something *outside* (instead of inside) ourselves. When this projected fear becomes very intense, it is called a phobia. In a sense, people use phobias to fool themselves into thinking that it is the thunderstorm or the dark or certain people or things that provoke their fear instead of their *own* feelings, thoughts, or wishes. Isn't it *less* scary, for example, to be afraid of something identifiable and avoidable like elephants, high buildings, or bridges than to constantly feel anxious about our own unconscious wish that something bad would happen to someone we love?

Ben Jonson, a 17th-century English writer, once said: "All fear is painful, and when it conduces not to safety, is

WHAT'S TO BE FEARED?

1. *Fear can be both helpful and destructive. Give examples of both situations from your own experience. What do you do to cope with your fears?*

2. *How many phobias have you heard of? Name them.*

   What phobias do you, your friends, or members of your family have?

   To what extent are they a problem?

3. *How do fire drills reduce the likelihood of panic in schools, hospitals, and other institutions? What turns fear into panic?*

painful without use. Every consideration, therefore, by which groundless terrors may be removed, adds something to human happiness."

The Mind and the Body: An Inseparable Twosome

Imagine yourself seated in a chair, with wires attaching you to a small electronic device that records blood pressure, respiration, heartbeat, and perspiration. An examiner asks you a number of questions, some more personal than others. Although you find the examiner friendly and you want to cooperate, you have mixed feelings about giving exact answers to some questions you have special feelings about. Despite your decision to hold back certain information, you observe that when you are confronted with sensitive topics, the little automatic pens on the machine begin to jump around wildly, making squiggly lines very different from the otherwise regular tracings. You may not even be aware of the subtle change in heartbeat, the quickening respiration, the ever-so-slight increase in skin moisture, the tightening of the muscles as you sense a twinge of guilt or embarrassment or resentment at some of the questions. If measurements were also made of the lining of your stomach, of the activity of the adrenal and pituitary glands, or the size of blood vessels in various parts of the body, equally impressive changes would be recorded.

Here is a vivid demonstration of the spoken word being transformed into an emotional feeling which is then expressed through physiological changes in the body. What we have just described is a basic technique used by experimental psychologists to study the interactions of mind and body. It is also the mechanism of a lie-detector machine.

This description of the sensitive intertwinings of mind and body probably holds no surprises for you. In your own experience, you have made similar observations. How often, for example, have you had a sickish feeling in the pit of your stomach before an exam? Do you remember feeling sad or crying at the loss of a pet? Have you ever found yourself blushing uncontrollably when hearing an off-color story or being paid a compliment in public? Have you noticed yourself becoming physically tense or developing a headache when angry or frustrated?

Prehistoric man barely made the connection between

his behavior and his inner experiences. When he was frightened, he ran. When he was angry, he attacked. But to explain what happened, he had no such concepts as mind-body relationship, psychophysiological response, or psychosomatic reaction. For the most part, emotions and behavior were attributed to the power of natural events, like the sun and the moon, to the gods, to storms or floods, or to a swarm of insects. Even theories associating the mind ("soul") and body with "devils" or "witches" were far more advanced than these earlier notions. Not until the 17th, 18th and 19th centuries were ideas about mind and body removed from the realm of philosophy to the field of medicine. For example, Beaumont, a 19th-century American physician, made some imaginative, unusual, and important discoveries. Stationed at an isolated frontier post, he was called upon to treat a hunter who had sustained a gunshot wound in the stomach. Though the patient lived and recovered, the belly wall did not completely heal and there remained a kind of "window" into the stomach, through which Beaumont could directly observe reactions of the gastric (stomach) wall. His carefully recorded notes revealed much about how gastric activity was related to emotional disturbance.

This work led the way to more complicated scientific investigation that became the basis of a whole field, *psychosomatic medicine*. Many physicians had observed in their clinical practice relationships between depression and gout, or gall bladder, or thyroid disease. Some doctors observed that moral conflicts seemed to cause skin eruptions, or that hair would occasionally fall out after a frightening experience. Some people had convulsions when they were angry. Menstrual flow was affected by emotional trauma. Anxiety or fright increased the need to urinate or to evacuate the bowel. The term *psychosomatic* gave scientific respectability to these puzzling observations. Still, the "leaps" from a thing of the mind to a thing of the body remained baffling.

Other researchers began to explore the effects of different types of personality on how the body expressed certain feelings or emotional conflicts. Experiments with hypnosis showed how suggestion could affect the motor function of the limbs or raise a blister on the skin. More refined techniques showed the many complex forces which linked mind and body: constitutional factors, interpersonal relationships, early childhood experiences, attitudes and beliefs, social environment, learning and training, emotional and physical resistance to stress, and so on. Adolf Meyer, a physician who considered himself a *psychobiologist*, said in 1951:

> A *sufficiently organized brain is the central link* [*between mind and body*], *but mental activity is really best understood in its full meaning as the adaptation and adjustment of the individual as a whole, in contrast to the simple activity of single organs such as those of circulation, respiration, digestion, elimination or simple reflex activity.*[24]

Despite the trend in medicine to focus on the clearly physical diseases, many investigators were fascinated by the ways in which the mind and body interacted to determine a state of health or disease. New technology has made it possible to study the most intricate changes both within the body and in the environment. It has been recognized that the body, through all of its defense mechanisms (both biological and psychological) tries to maintain a *steady state*, sometimes referred to as *homeostasis* or *constant milieu*. While the requirements for a steady state vary according to age and levels of development, a "vital balance," as Karl Menninger called it, is essential for good health. When emotional upsets, significant losses, fears and stresses affect bodily reactions through changes in body chemistry and altered perceptions, there is a disruption of this healthy balance between body and mind, "psyche" and "soma." Some researchers believe that even cancer may one day be explained this way. This constant interaction, this striving to maintain a balance, exists from birth to the end of life.

While usual and unusual stresses constantly threaten the balance, this does not mean that all stress is bad. In fact, without stress, without frustration, there would be no growth. The struggle to cope with stresses helps the ego to develop new techniques of adapting, to find new and higher levels of development, and to discover greater sources of satisfaction. The child who is overprotected and has everything done for him will become an emotional and physical invalid!

In the following chapters, we will examine what happens when the ego attempts to cope with the stresses of everyday life. We will see how various illnesses reflect a disruption of the vital balance between mind and body. We will examine in more detail what is meant by psychosomatic illness.

Suggested Reading

LOVE

DeRougemont, Denis, *Love in the Western World* (New York: Pantheon, 1956).

Fromm, Erich, *The Art of Loving* (New York: Harper and Row, 1956).

Fromme, Allan *The Ability to Love* (New York: Farrar, Straus and Giroux, 1966).

Maslow, Abraham, *Motivation and Personality* (New York: Viking, 1971).

Moustakas, Clark, *Loneliness and Love* (Englewood Cliffs, N.J.: Prentice-Hall, 1972).

ANGER AND AGGRESSION

Bach, George and Herb Goldberg, *Creative Aggression* (Garden City, N.Y.: Doubleday, 1974).

Fromm, Erich, *The Anatomy of Human Destructiveness* (New York: Holt, Rinehart and Winston, 1973).

Golding, William, *Lord of the Flies* (New York: Coward, 1962).

Lorenz, Konrad, *On Aggression* (New York: Harcourt, Brace and Jovanovich, 1966).

Madow, Leo, *Anger* (New York: Charles Scribner's Sons, 1972).

Rubin, Theodore, *The Angry Book* (New York: Macmillan, 1969).

Storr, Anthony, *Human Aggression* (New York: Atheneum, 1968).

HUMOR

Bergson, Henri, "Laughter," in *Comedy* (Garden City, N.Y.: Doubleday, 1956).

Freud, Sigmund, *Jokes and Their Relation to the Unconscious*

594

(New York: W. W. Norton, 1960).

Hertzler, Joyce, *Laughter* (Jericho, N.Y.: Exposition Press, 1970).

FEAR

Cantril, Hadley, *The Invasion from Mars: A Study in the Psychology of Panic* (Princeton, N.J.: Princeton U. Press, 1947).

Sugarman, Donald and Lucy Freeman, *The Search for Serenity: Understanding and Overcoming Anxiety* (New York: Macmillan, 1970).

FOOTNOTES

1. Maggie Scarf, "Normality is a Square Circle or a Four-Sided Triangle," *The New York Times Magazine,* October 3, 1971.
2. Seymour Halleck, *The Politics of Therapy* (New York: Science House, Inc., 1971).
3. Norman Cameron, *Personality Development and Psychopathology* (Boston: Houghton Mifflin, 1963), p. 13.
4. Erich Fromm, *The Art of Loving,* (New York: Harper and Row, 1956), p. 58.
5. Leo Madow, *Anger* (New York: Charles Scribner's Sons, 1972), p. 73.
6. Theodore Isaac Rubin, *The Angry Book* (New York: Macmillan Publishing Company, Copyright © 1969 by Theodore Rubin), p. 15.
7. *Ibid.,* p. 16.
8. *Ibid.,* p. 38, 40.
9. *Ibid.,* p. 42.
10. *Ibid.,* p. 44.
11. *Ibid.,* p. 52.
12. *Ibid.,* p. 55.
13. *Ibid.,* p. 61.
14. *Ibid.,* p. 66.
15. *Ibid.,* p. 71.

16. *Ibid., p.* 95
17. *Ibid.,* p. 83.
18. *Ibid.,* p. 134-135.
19. Sigmund Freud, *Jokes and Their Relation to the Unconscious* (New York: W. W. Norton and Company, Copyright © 1960 by James Strachey).
20. Richard Hanser, "Wit as a Weapon," *Saturday Review,* November 8, 1952, p. 13.
21. Joyce Hertzler, *Laughter* (Jericho, New York: Exposition Press, 1970), p. 71
22. Henri Bergson, "Laughter," in *Comedy: Two Classic Studies* (Garden City: Doubleday and Company, 1956), p. 64.
23. Hertzler, *op. cit.,* p. 31.
24. Adolf Meyer, "The Role of the Mental Factors in Psychiatry," in *Collected Papers of Adolf Meyer* (Baltimore: Johns Hopkins Press, 1951).

14.
Coping with Crisis:
The Attempt to Adapt

Envy and wrath shorten the life.

Ecclesiastes 30: 24

As long ago as 200 B.C., it was recognized that our feelings have a strong impact on our physical health. Today, this is a fairly well-accepted belief. In the preceding chapter, we mentioned the tendency of the body to maintain a balance, a steady state, a stable adaptation—physically, psychologically, and socially. This was referred to as *homeostasis*. Environmental forces, constant changes of one sort or another, are always affecting this balance, with each stimulus calling forth a counteraction in the body to maintain homeostasis.

Any force or stimulus which threatens to disrupt this important balance is called a *stressor*. The disruption itself is considered the emotional or physical *stress*. To maintain its balance, the body must "figure out" a way to *adapt* to this stress. It does this by using all its *defenses* to *cope* with the disturbing situation. Successful coping means that the balance is maintained.

The Stresses and Strains of Everyday Life

Stresses or tensions may be mild, or moderate, or severe. They can occur under pleasurable kinds of stimuli such as sports, sex, excitement; or under unpleasant circumstances such as fear, threat, or physical harm. We may

* please come by
and simplify
my life for me

be fully aware of being stressed, as when menaced by a barking dog, or we may be totally unaware of stress reactions such as might be caused by the anniversary of a significant event in our lives. We may be stressed not only by an *excess* of stimulation but also by its absence (as in *sensory deprivation*). We may feel the strain of a single sudden experience, or the cumulative effects of a series of small, seemingly insignificant irritations.

Mentally and physically, we react to *failure* and other unhappy conditions, but our endocrine system and our emotions may react just as severely to success. Success brings responsibility and a need to maintain the achievement. This, in turn, can arouse anxiety. The "successful" executive with a stomach ulcer is a stereotyped example of such a stress response.

Internist and psychoanalyst George L. Engel offered a working definition of stress: "Psychological stress refers to all processes, whether originating in the external environment or within the person, which impose a demand or requirement upon the organism, the resolution or handling of which requires work or activity of the mental apparatus. . . ."[1] We have discussed the psychological mechanisms of defense: denial, projection, avoidance, displacement, fixation, repression, and regression. They are always at our disposal to cope with crisis. Almost by reflex, they help us adapt physically and emotionally.

When the psychophysical defenses are overwhelmed, however, there is a *failure to cope*. The otherwise smooth-functioning complex operations of the body become disorganized, causing symptoms of disease. In our attempts to adapt, we sometimes try to assist our *natural* mechanisms by resorting to *artificial* ways of dealing with stress, such as smoking, drinking alcohol, or taking drugs. Often in these efforts to cope with stress, we fail to realize that we may merely be substituting one stress for another. For example, how many adolescents recognize the significance of smoking their first few cigarettes? It means they have dramatically increased their chances of

599

becoming a confirmed smoker for the next twenty years, thereby running the risk of getting diseases like emphysema, lung cancer, stomach cancer, and heart disease. Or how often do we think about the possibility that the use of drugs to cope with stress *decreases* the long-term *natural* ability of the body's mechanisms to cope?

Stresses may be triggered by very personal events like an argument with a friend or an embarrassing situation. They may also follow a national tragedy like a war, a threat to internal security, or uneasiness about economic conditions. Even common events like moving, taking a trip, or visiting the doctor may be experienced as significant stress. The degree of stress may be related to the *intensity* of the frustration or disappointment, or to the *symbolic significance* of a loss. It may be related not so much to the strength of the event as to its *unexpectedness*, its suddenness. We can become just as distressed over the *anticipation* of an event as we might be at the event itself. Just *thinking* about something in the future can stir up stressful fantasies, daydreams, fears, and anxieties.

Symptoms of stress may or may not be visible. We might become depressed or restless, but we might just as readily develop headaches, palpitations, body aches and pains, fatigue, or stomach upset. Some changes may be neither felt nor seen, but can be detected only by special tests of blood that measure hormone levels, changes in blood components, and rearrangements of enzymes in the body. Researchers have begun to accumulate evidence that suggests that cancer may be affected by stress.

The Ravages of Stress

The term stress is sometimes used loosely to refer to extreme environmental conditions, physical threats, or disturbing stimuli that strain the adaptive capacity of the ego. More often it relates to the *internal reaction* to these things—the anxiety, the emotional distress, the threat to security, the arousal or activation of certain psychological experiences. In keeping with our belief that mind and body are inseparably intertwined, it is clear that stress must refer to *both* psychological and physiological changes. It is the interaction of mind and body which makes psychosocial factors so important in fully understanding the development of disease.

While stresses and strains occur from birth to death, each phase of life is characterized by a few specific stresses which challenge the individual's ability to cope. The challenge is not met without frustration and disappointment. Indeed, the absence of frustration and disappointment guarantees a limited growth. The human being develops only by strengthening his coping mechanisms in the face of manageable threats, demands, and frustrations.

Childhood presents the task of learning how to separate from the mother. The prospect of this separation may lead to fear, anxiety, sleeplessness, nightmares, diarrhea, poor eating, and other symptoms. The fears may intensify with each anticipation of separation and may take on the proportions of a phobic reaction. For example, unreasonable fears of animals and darkness may develop. The greatest fear may occur when the BIG separation comes on the first day of school. Mastery of these stresses, with support from parents and teachers, prepares the child to defend himself against the stressful "battles" of adolescence.

At that time, he or she must cope with complex biological, social, and psychological developments:

assuming more adult responsibilities; relating to the opposite sex in new and sometimes frightening ways; struggling with the ambivalent wish to retain the satisfactions of dependency upon parents while wanting to have more freedom. It is a time of conflicting feelings—a feeling that you want to stay, but also a feeling that you want to go. Earlier, we described the major adolescent task of developing one's identity, and its accompanying "crisis."

Mastering this adolescent turmoil prepares a person to cope better with the post-high school years, whether in college or in work. By then he is more familiar with life's disappointments and the uncertainties of the future.

Dating, marriage, and family life introduce the stresses of trying to work out intense meaningful relationships and of assessing oneself as an adequate sexual partner, as a husband or wife, and as a father or mother. The honeymoon itself may not be the storybook experience: it may introduce new anxieties about sexual identity and sexual performance; it may lay the roots of a "bad" marriage, with a prospect for divorce later on. And soon after may come in-law problems, financial concerns, and disagreements about religion, child-rearing, compromise, and sharing.

Pregnancy and childbirth present unusual physiological and psychological stresses—not only for the woman whose womb contains the growing child but also for the concerned husband who may even develop "sympathetic pains."

Occupational stress arises in a variety of ways, some obvious and others quite imperceptible. There are relationships to be worked out with co-workers, bosses and supervisors, questions about job definition, advancement, and wages. There are also noises, pollutants, and potential hazards which one may "take for granted" as part of the job, but which may silently be working away at one's defenses. A steelworker walking high above the city streets constantly copes with stress.

In middle age, there is the frightening and unpleasant prospect of illness, greater responsibility, and uncertain employment. The prospect of the deaths of loved ones compounds the anticipated "mid-life crisis." *Successful coping with earlier experiences prepares one to weather these storms and to adapt in flexible ways.* The normal process of grief and mourning then becomes an adaptive process rather than a maladaptive, prolonged depression.

The aging and the elderly must be prepared to cope with the special physical and emotional crises of this stage. Feelings of uselessness, fear of loneliness, the loss of friends and social position, and retirement impose stresses of great magnitude. Aging persons may look at young people "on their way up" and regard themselves as "on the way down." But, on the other hand, they have had a lifetime to perfect a system of coping techniques which permit a fulfilling adaptation even to this.

Research psychiatrists Thomas Holmes and Richard Rahe have accumulated data that suggest that illness is related not so much to the intensity of stress but rather to the experience of *change*. To study their hypothesis, they devised a Life Change Scale, listing representative life change experiences one can have and assigning numerical values to these events.[2] When the total score of a person reached 300 in one year, that was considered to be a "danger point." By studying patients who reached that level, they discovered that 80 percent of them became seriously depressed, had heart attacks, or were subject to other serious diseases during the following year. Life change units correlated not only with stress and disease, but also with the excretion of the hormone adrenalin. New research in psychiatry has shown correlations between blood levels of this hormone and certain types of mental illness.

On page 606 is a Life Change Scale devised by Holmes and Rahe. They believed that even a joyous occasion could be considered a stress if significant change were involved, so they picked an arbitrary value of 50 and assigned it to marriage. All other events were then given values according to whether the degree of stress involved seemed greater or less than that connected with marriage. While changes like moving or starting school may be considered stressful for some people, Holmes and Rahe found that most persons assigned these lower values than marriage. On the other hand, the death of a spouse, the loss of a job, and divorce were considered much more emotionally stressful. It is therefore clear that it is not just the intensity of one event which is important in influencing disease, but also the number of changes with their cumulative stress. Studies by Holmes and Rahe found that it was the *degree of change over a certain period of time* which influenced the risk of developing disease in the near future.

We have come a long way in understanding the impact of stress on mind and body. But there is still much to learn about the details of these complex processes. How do some people develop such effective coping mechanisms, while others with similar experiences have so much trouble? Why are some people afraid to cross the street while others can fly a rocket to the moon? Some scientists explore the internal workings of the mind and body to explain these differences. Other researchers take a hard look at *social* conditions to try to understand how some people cope with extraordinary adversity.

In our next section, we examine a universal stress with which everyone eventually must cope: death.

Significant changes in life, such as moving, can be experienced as stress. The degree of stress may be related to the *intensity* of the frustration or disappointment, or to the *symbolic significance* of a loss. The degree of stress may also be related to the *unexpectedness* of the event, its suddenness. We can become just as upset over the *anticipation* of an event as we might at the event itself. Just *thinking* about something in the future can stir up fantasies, daydreams, fears, and anxieties.

LIFE CHANGE SCALE*

RANK	LIFE EVENT	MEAN VALUE
1	Death of spouse	100
2	Divorce	73
3	Marital separation	65
4	Jail term	63
5	Death of close family member	63
6	Personal injury or illness	53
7	Marriage	50
8	Fired at work	47
9	Marital reconciliation	45
10	Retirement	45
11	Change in health of family member	44
12	Pregnancy	40
13	Sex difficulties	39
14	Gain of new family member	39
15	Business readjustment	39
16	Change in financial state	38
17	Death of close friend	37
18	Change to different line of work	36
19	Change in number of arguments with spouse	35
20	Mortgage over $10,000	31
21	Foreclosure of mortgage or loan	30
22	Change in responsibilities at work	29
23	Son or daughter leaving home	29
24	Trouble with in-laws	29
25	Outstanding personal achievement	28
26	Wife to begin or stop work	26

*The authors are indebted to Drs. Thomas Holmes and Richard Rahe for permission to reproduce this Life Change Scale.

606

27	Begin or end school	26
28	Change in living conditions	25
29	Revision of personal habits	24
30	Trouble with boss	23
31	Change in work hours or conditions	20
32	Change in residence	20
33	Change in schools	20
34	Change in recreation	19
35	Change in church activities	19
36	Change in social activities	18
37	Mortgage or loan less than $10,000	17
38	Change in sleeping habits	16
39	Change in number of family get-togethers	15
40	Change in eating habits	15
41	Vacation	13
42	Christmas	12
43	Minor violations of the law	11

Life Change Scale ranks life events in descending order; highest values require greatest adaptation and are most likely to trigger disease.

Adjusting to Mortality

He who should teach men to die would at the same time teach them to live.

MONTAIGNE

Facing death is one of the most important experiences in life. Through medical progress and technology we have improved and prolonged our years. Yet despite our "sophistication," we are probably less prepared than our ancestors to cope with the inevitability of death.

It is not easy to think about death. Occasionally we may daydream about the loss of someone we know, or even about who would miss us if *we* suddenly died. But we dismiss our fantasies quickly, unconsciously clinging to the notion that neither we nor the people close to us will die—at least not for a very long time. As Freud wrote, "it is impossible to imagine our own death." Man believes in his own immortality,because his own death is too frightening to think about.

Today, death has been "removed" to hospitals and

It is not easy to think about death. Yet, in understanding our feelings about death, perhaps we will learn more about what we want from life. Confronting the idea of death is one of the most compelling ways to take stock—to see if we are really leading a life which we can look back on with satisfaction.

STRESSES AND STRAINS

1. *Everyone experiences some kind of stress in his or her life. What kind of events do you remember most vividly as being stressful to you? Compare your experiences with others in the class and note whether different people experience the same kinds of situations as stressful.*

2. *If you were to make up a Life Change Scale like that of Holmes and Rahe, would you assign the same relative values to life events? Create your own scale, rating the stressfulness of events in your everyday life. Compare your chart to those of your classmates. How do you react to and cope with these everyday stresses?*

3. *How is it possible for a person to experience success as a stressful experience?*

4. *Think about smoking and drinking in terms of stress. What are the benefits and what are the risks?*

5. *Considering what you have read about the life cycle (Part I), list the stresses one can expect at different phases of a person's life.*

nursing homes. There it has become more business-like, impersonal, sterile. Many years ago, life on the farm, close to nature, gave people intimate experiences with life and death. The aged grandmother used to live with her children and grandchildren and died in the front bedroom surrounded by her family. In small towns, a funeral was a social gathering. Everyone knew everyone else and always paid his final respects. The shorter life span and high infant mortality rate made funerals a more frequent occurrence. Death no longer follows this familiar sequence of events. Death, like anything else with which we are inexperienced, is therefore more terrifying to face.

For those who are not religious, death may be all the more frightening. It is difficult to justify suffering and pain without the thought of heavenly reward.

Religious customs and rituals help to guide the bereaved through the grief process. They provide an organization and structure for the mourning period, and they offer spiritual comfort at a time of despair, pain, and emptiness.

610

What can learning to cope with death teach us about life? In understanding our feelings about death, perhaps we will learn more about what we want from life. What are our values? How can we enhance the quality of our lives? Who is important to us? What are we bringing to life? What are we learning from it? Psychologist Abraham Maslow survived a massive heart attack and afterwards expressed his feelings:

> *My attitude toward life changed. The word I use for it now is the post-mortem life. I could have just as easily died so that my living constitutes a kind of extra, a bonus. It's all gravy. . . . One very important aspect of the post-mortem life is that everything gets doubly precious, gets piercingly important . . . I guess you could say that post-mortem life permits a kind of spontaneity that's greater than anything else could make possible.[3]*

Not only those who personally face death are changed by the experience. Friends and family of the terminally ill often gain a new appreciation of life. The sister of a cancer patient expressed her feelings in this way:

> *My sister knew she was going to die. I knew it too. Yet in her last two years it was she who taught me how to appreciate each new day. Certainly I miss her. Yet when I think of her now, there is no bitterness in me. For I remember how close we became and how much of the joy of life we were able to share.*

> F.H.

611

Some people, even after a long life, feel that they are not ready to die—especially if they think they have not lived a meaningful life. Others can reconcile themselves to a premature death if they are satisfied with the quality of their lives. Confronting the *idea* of death is one of the most compelling ways to take stock—to see if we are really leading a life which we can look back on with satisfaction. Facing the possibility of death puts life in perspective.

Terminal Illness: The Patient and His Family

A family's emotional reactions may vary with the way a member's death occurs. Accidental or sudden death usually overwhelms the family with shock and disbelief. They have not had the time to anticipate and prepare for the loss of a major figure in their lives. The shock, coupled with a lack of experience in dealing with death, leaves one less able to cope with the problems which ensue.

Coping with the stress of terminal illness and *anticipation* of a major loss present different kinds of problems. For example, should the patient be told that he is dying? Most families and many physicians agonize over this decision, for it is as difficult for them to accept the truth themselves as it is to reveal it to the patient.

Concerned about the lack of attention paid to the dying, Elisabeth Kübler-Ross, a physician, has extensively studied the needs of both patients and their anguished families. Ross worked with over 200 patients who became her teachers in helping her to learn about the "final stages of life." She found that many doctors and hospital personnel were more reluctant than the patient himself to face the truth about the patient's condition. Because their

FACING DEATH

1. *Do you ever think or talk about death? How is it handled in your family?*

2. *What bothers you most when you think about death?*

3. *When you die, how would you like to be remembered? Write a paragraph describing personal traits, relationships, deeds.*

   Do you think that people would describe you this way now?

4. *Can you think of situations in life that would be worse than death?*

5. *Are there people or causes you would be willing to die for?*

6. *In what ways does scientific progress affect the way we think about dying? Perhaps you could invite a physician in your community to lead a discussion of this topic.*

goal is to prolong and save lives, some doctors and nurses feel the loss of a patient is a personal defeat.

Ross found that *whether a patient was told or not, he*

usually understood that he was dying and wanted to share his concerns. She suggests that perhaps it is better not to tell the person he is dying, but to *let him tell you!* This enables *the patient* to decide when he is ready to discuss his feelings. She writes, "When a patient is severely ill, he is often treated like a person with no right to an opinion. . . . It would take so little to remember that the sick person too has feelings, has wishes and opinions, and has—most important of all—the right to be heard."[4]

Other "students" of the dying have confirmed Ross's observations. Herman Feifel, a psychiatrist, wrote, "For the terminal patient . . . getting people to listen is perhaps as difficult as getting them to talk. And what the patient may very well want to tell the physician is, simply, that he knows he is dying."[5] He further suggests that many terminally ill patients who are able to discuss their condition adjust as well as or better than those who are shielded from the truth.

Of course, sensitivity is important. A patient will cling to some hope, and that is necessary. It is enough to understand and reflect the patient's feelings, and not to go beyond them to drive the message home.

Often the patient is more worried for his family than for himself. You may have read the story by John Gunther, *Death Be Not Proud*, which describes the terminal illness of his seventeen-year-old son, Johnny. The surgeon had explained the nature of the illness to the boy. His response was, "Do my parents know this? How shall we break it to them?"[6]

Ross and her associates noted the following psychological stages the patient goes through in adjusting to his impending death. These emotional reactions are *defense mechanisms* which help the patient to cope gradually with the reality of his death.

DENIAL AND ISOLATION

... most reacted to the awareness of a terminal illness at first with the statement, "No, not me, it cannot be true."[7]

Denial functions as a buffer after unexpected shocking news, allows the patient to collect himself and, with time, mobilize other, less radical defenses.[8]

ANGER

"Why me?"[9]

There is also a feeling of envy and resentment toward those who are healthy. The person cannot believe that although he has been "good" in his personal life, he is being "punished" by an illness.

BARGAINING

A patient ... had a son who proceeded with his plans to get married as the patient had wished ... she made all sorts of promises if she could only live long enough to attend the marriage. The day preceding the wedding she left the hospital as an elegant lady. Nobody would have believed her real condition ... I wondered what her reaction would be when the time was up for which she had bargained.

I will never forget the moment when she returned to the hospital. She looked tired and somewhat exhausted, and before I could say hello—said, "Now don't forget I have another son!"[10]

Many "bargains" are directed to God for just a little more time.

DEPRESSION

The patient is in the process of losing everything and everybody he loves. If he is allowed to express his sorrow he will find a final acceptance much easier, and he will be grateful to those who can sit with him during this stage of depression without constantly telling him not to be sad ... preparatory grief is much more a feeling that can be mutually expressed and is often done better with a touch of a hand, a stroking of the hair, or just a silent sitting together.[11]

Of a patient: *He was sad that he was forced to struggle for life when he was ready to prepare himself to die.[12]*

It is this discrepancy between the patient's wish and readiness and the expectation of those in his environment which causes the greatest grief and turmoil in our patients.[13]

ACCEPTANCE

Patients die easier if they are allowed and helped to detach themselves slowly from all the meaningful relationships in their life.[14]

The patient does not want to have to make conversation. Nonverbal communication is important. The patient needs reassurance that he will not be left alone even when he does not want to talk. Just sitting quietly in his room provides this kind of support.

These stages are not clear-cut. Emotional reactions vary, fluctuate, and overlap. Hope persists through all of them. While these stages help us to understand the general process of dying, we should also remember that each individual death is as unique as the person himself. To overlook the specialness of one's personality is as much an indignity as to deny the importance of his death.

Ross also interviewed family members. She found that they go through stages similar to those of the patient: shock, denial, anger, guilt, the wish to make up for missed opportunities, preparatory grief. Sometimes relatives and friends are hesitant to visit the dying person. They feel uncomfortable or "don't know what to say." It is likely that the visit arouses fear of the awareness of their own mortality.

The more the patient and his family are able to share their feelings, the more they can relieve their anxieties. If a patient and his family play the game of pretending he will get better, then both have the added burden of isolation and loneliness which comes from inability to communicate honestly. They do not have a chance to resolve past conflicts or to prepare for final separation. Each has the impossible task of trying to bolster the other, without being able to share feelings, doubts, and fears.

The real need is for empathy, support and communication. The empathic person can accept the genuine feelings of another person—he can identify with his fears, concerns, feelings of guilt and anger, and *never judge* him for these. Joan Barthel, a *New York Times* reporter, wrote a touching story about the death of a close friend. It clarifies the meaning of empathy:

*When Eleanor opened her eyes for a moment and
saw me sitting by the bed, she reached toward me.
"I'm afraid," she whispered. I didn't know how to
respond, so as soon as the day nurse came in, I asked
her advice. "You'd better ask the doctor," the day
nurse said. The doctor didn't come, so I went to the
night nurse when she arrived. "What can you say?"
the night nurse murmured, patting my arm. "You
should call the chaplain. Let him reassure her."
Eleanor did not believe in churches or chaplains, so I
asked the resident when he came by on his rounds.
"You have to give her some supportive psychotherapy," he said. "Just tell her there's nothing to
be afraid of." I didn't agree, and when her doctor
appeared, I asked him. He looked troubled and a
little embarrassed. "Tell her she isn't afraid," he said
slowly. "Tell her . . . tell her she's apprehensive." A
little student nurse looked in at the door, a beautiful
blue-eyed child in a starched pinafore, and, cruelly, I
asked her: "What should I say when she tells me she's
afraid?" The little nurse bent her head quickly and
stared at the tips of her shoes. "Aw gee," she said
softly. She raised her head and looked at me, her eyes
gleaming with tears. "Aw gee," she said again. Here,
at last, was an answer I could understand.[15]*

The Grieving Process

*Mourning—the expression of grief—after the death
of someone close, is not only valuable to us but
necessary for our well being.[16]*

HARRIET HARVEY COFFIN

Grieving is hard work, an emotional and physical stress.
When someone close to us dies, it is like losing a part of

WHAT DO YOU THINK?

1. Would you want to know if you were dying? Explain your response.

2. Who would you want to know that you were dying? Family? Close friends? Relatives? Acquaintances? People you work with?

3. What kinds of things would you want to communicate if you were dying? To whom?

4. How could you be helpful to a dying friend?

5. Have you ever visited someone with a serious illness? Can you describe how you felt and how you talked with the person?

ourselves. Yet the more civilized we have become, the more we have tried to control our emotions. Our society praises the courageous mourner, the "man of steel." Actually, it is important to our well-being that we express our grief openly and unashamedly—the way our ancestors did. We should not "be brave." "It is natural and necessary to cry, to be angry, to be disorganized. The seemingly courageous people may eventually suffer more. Months, or perhaps years later, they may become depressed and unhappy, without knowing why."[17] Freud emphasized the power of repressed feelings over our

619

Grieving is hard work, an emotional and physical stress. Yet, "it is natural and necessary to cry, to be angry, to be disorganized. The seemingly courageous people may eventually suffer more. Months, or perhaps years later, they may become depressed and unhappy, without knowing why." HARRIET HARVEY COFFIN

future mental and physical health. Recent studies of bereavement have shown that stress caused by the death of a loved one can increase the risk of physical and mental diseases and even death.

John Bowlby, an English psychoanalyst who studied children's reactions to death, describes three stages in the grieving process.[18] First, there is *numbness, shock, and disbelief*. The mourner may feel angry at the person for dying and deserting him, and at himself for having these feelings. He may feel guilty about unresolved problems with the deceased. "Much grief is selfish. It is the grief . . .

of not giving, of not receiving, of not doing, of not being. Our tears are often shed for what might have been or what we might have done for others."[19] Mourners become preoccupied with the deceased and attempt to work through all their complex feelings about him. Even in the most caring relationships, there is bound to be some hidden anger, guilt, and resentment. It is usual to have a wide range of feelings.

The second psychological stage the mourner experiences, according to Bowlby, is *pain, despair, and disorganization.* The mourner begins to accept the death—it becomes real to him. He will probably feel helpless, lonely, and sad. As Erich Lindemann notes, "The bereaved is surprised to find how large a part of his customary activity was done in some meaningful relationship to the deceased and has now lost its significance."[20] Lindemann lists several "normal" physical symptoms of the grieving process: tightness in the throat, shortness of breath, sighing, an empty feeling in the stomach, lack of muscular power, tension, restlessness, a slight sense of unreality, exhaustion. There is also a loss of warmth in relationships with other people.

In Bowlby's third stage, the mourner begins the *reorganization* of his life. There is *hope,* the *building of new relationships,* a *new style of life.* It will take a long time to adjust to the loss, but most human beings have the resilience to start anew—they realize that their lives must go on. Religious customs support this reaffirmation of life, and ceremonial rituals help to organize and prescribe behavior. For example, some religions require the family to go out of the house and rejoin the community after the seventh day of mourning. Religious beliefs also provide the reassurance that the deceased will live on—whether through an afterlife as in Christianity, or through a "spiritual legacy," as in Judaism.

Sometimes in the case of a terminal illness, mourning takes place *before* the person dies. Just as the patient goes through stages of grief in preparing for his own loss, so too may his family grieve in advance. Often the family members will be physically and emotionally spent by the time the person dies, and they may have few tears left when friends and relatives arrive for the funeral. The immediate family may feel relief that the long ordeal is over.

Grieving is a necessary life experience. It is a crisis which produces stress. The way in which one copes with it will determine the extent to which it is healthy and adaptive. The failure of "grief work" leads to pathological (abnormal) grief reactions and depression. These will be considered in the Chapter "Darker Shades of Gray."

Children and Death

While grieving is a truly painful task for an adult, it is even more difficult for the child. Until children reach the age of about six, they cannot accept the finality of death. They think the deceased has gone on a trip or is temporarily asleep. They can only connect death with their own experiences of leaving and returning, sleeping and waking, losing and finding. When children do begin to realize the *permanence* of their loss, they are often so deeply affected that they pretend that it has not happened. They use denial as a defense against their overwhelming anxiety.

THOUGHTS TO SHARE

1. *How do you feel about the open expression of grief?*

2. *How many different rituals of various religions can you think of that have to do with death? What do you think the psychological reasons are for these customs and ceremonies?*

   Why do people light candles?

   Why do some religions require a specific period of mourning and prayer?

   Why do some religions suggest viewing the embalmed body on the day prior to the funeral?

   Find out the customs of your religion concerning death, and explain them to the class.

3. *In old Ireland, a wake was a time for feasting and drinking. The "keening" of (wailing for) dead persons by family and friends was a feature of the burial. Often, professionals called keeners or banshees were hired to lead or add to the crying. They also joined the feasting. Remnants of these customs can still be observed. How did these customs serve a useful purpose in the work of grief?*

4. *Many Jews stay at home for a week following a family funeral and receive friends and relatives. Why is this a helpful custom?*

5. *If someone in your school dies, how do you think teachers and students should handle this? Should it be openly discussed?*

6. *How can the family physician help during the mourning period?*

7. *Explore the beliefs and rituals of Buddhism, Islam, Hinduism, and the American Indian concerning death.*

How should children be told about death? First, children should be given an accurate description of the cause of death. As Coffin notes, "If the cause of death isn't made clear, children make up their own reasons why people die."[21] Children have vivid imaginations. Usually their fantasies are much harder to deal with than the truth, for children believe that bad thoughts as well as bad acts can kill—and they may hold themselves responsible for a parent's death.

Children may also feel that a parent's death is a punishment: ". . . bad things happen to them because they are naughty. Therefore, they feel desertion, which is the most painful thing in the world, must be a punishment for their wrongdoing."[22]

Adults tend to use euphemisms in describing death to children: "Your father has gone on a long trip," or "your father has gone to sleep." Trying to talk around the subject may backfire. The child may then fear that he, too, will die if he goes to sleep, or he may continue to believe that father will return or wake up.

Children should be allowed to grieve, when they are able, with the rest of the family. Whisking children away to a friend's home to spare them the pain and sorrow only makes death more frightening and mysterious to them. They, too, have feelings to express. They are angry, resentful, profoundly saddened. And they need the support of the rest of the family. As Coffin so eloquently explains:

> *To help a child face and master loss, even smaller losses than death, is to help him master a most important job in life, and all concerned will be strengthened by it. We want him to replace the loss, not with self-love (out of fear that any other love is too dangerous), not with the substitution of objects for people, and not by clinging for too long a time to a longing for the dead person. We want a child to accept his memories and then find other people to love.*[23]

The Condolence Call

We all feel a little bit anxious when we pay a condolence call. "Will I say the right thing?" "What if the family wants to be left alone?" "How will I know how long to stay?"

Visitors are actually very helpful to the mourner. He is reminded that others share his grief and understand his pain. The condolence call also helps provide a bridge between the past and the future. The mourner is reassured that his friends will be there to help fill the gap in his life.

A YOUNG GIRL'S THOUGHTS ABOUT DEATH

Some children have an unusual capacity to understand
and express their thoughts and feelings about death, and
need the permissive setting in which to do so. Not
everyone is able to recapture his feelings later on. The
following story by Ruth Saltzman, a high school
student at the time she wrote this, recollects the
thoughts of a nine-year-old girl with unusual sensitivity
and clarity.

LITTLE KIDS don't think about death that much. I suppose
they don't think about the fact that they are living either.
You can't think about one without arriving eventually at
the other. But when I was nine everyone was dying. . .

I lay awake in bed one night for some ridiculous
reason like a horror movie I had seen earlier . . . I played
a little game with my mind, trying to recall the faces of
the many old friends who had died, and I found that I
couldn't. Part of me wanted to play some more and the
rest of me resisted, sensing, I suppose, the danger in vile
games of that sort. But I was strongly attracted to the
game and curious to find out where it would lead, so I
stopped resisting and allowed my mind to wander. I
picked my parents to be my new challenge, and I tried
and tried and couldn't remember their faces either, and
I stopped playing then and it was dark and I was
suddenly very frightened and screamed for my Momma.

She came and held me until I stopped crying, and
then she asked me what had happened. I was
embarrassed about my thoughts, especially since they

concerned her death and the death of my father. I didn't want her to think that I thought about it because deep down inside it was something I wanted. But she wanted to know, and I wanted to be comforted and reassured, so I told her all the same. She gave me all the reassurance I needed so late at night in the dark, telling me not to worry because she and my father were strong and healthy, and they would live to be one hundred and twenty. I took her word for it. . . .

When ugly thoughts of the loneliness I would feel after my parents' death began creeping up on me. . . . again in the night, I turned to the one thing I knew could prevent their death, if anything could—God. I compiled lists and lists in my mind of all my relatives and friends and every night I prayed that God would grant each one a "long, long life and a happy one, with many blessings." I thought that by not asking for one for myself, He would think I was being generous and kind, and not that my prayers were instigated by a selfish fear of being left behind and alone.

At that time, I wasn't concerned so much with the idea of dying myself, or even with what would happen to me and my family when we died. What bothered me was that I didn't want to have to live without them. I could just as easily have prayed that God would cause each of us to die at the same moment, all together, but prolonging life was a more comfortable and natural alternative.

As long as I thought I could achieve this and defy the life expectancy statistics through prayer, I was relieved for a while of my fears and worries and could live and sleep in comfort. But God must have known that I was taking him on because my grandfather got very ill and died, and I had prayed for him.

I was already a veteran when my grandmother got sick a few months later and I'd stuff my ears with my top

sheet whenever I would hear the phone ring late at night, because I knew it could bring awful news. My parents would sit together in the living room and their quiet talk about lung cancer and heart complications would filter through my partially opened door. I did not know what those words were exactly, but I knew they had something to do with being very sick. I understood that I was losing my grandmother, and I felt very helpless because I wanted to see her once more so that I would be able to remember her, but they didn't let little kids into the hospital. When we came home one day from school, my mother was slowly stirring some macaroni in a double boiler and she turned towards me and hugged me. Her face was strangely twisted and she said that she had some sad news. I didn't want to hear because I remembered that twisted face, and I ran to the window, pressing my hot face against the frosted pane. I wasn't putting an end to the news by running from it. My mother still went to the funeral where they put grandma in the ground, and I stayed behind at home wondering if she had remembered me before she died.
. . .

I didn't understand how my mother was able to live after both her parents had died, because I thought it would be awfully lonely not to have parents to talk to. My momma tried to explain to me that part of maturity is that you grow away from your parents and begin to depend more on a person with whom you choose to spend the rest of your life, and on your children, and they all depend on you. "It's a very sad thing to lose your parents," she said. "But you find other people in life who love you and will listen to you, and you won't be alone."

It seemed to me that if you really loved your parents it wouldn't be possible to learn to depend on someone else. . . .

But my momma thought that that was wrong. Her

mother, she said, had a fantastic sense of humor and love of life and if she knew that my mother was spending the rest of her life grieving, she'd be horrified. "Besides," she'd add, "it doesn't do your parents any good if you prove your love for them *after* they're gone."

It was no wonder that I felt suddenly compelled to affirm my love for my parents over and over. I'd call them into my room late at night and ask them to talk with me, even though I was the one who always did the talking. I'd get worried if they looked unhappy, and I'd ask them if they were "mad at me," because I didn't want to be the one who made them sad. . . .

But I'd forget that when I'd become angry also, and I'd say awful things that I never would have said had I remembered. I'd shout things that I didn't mean; once I even said "I wish you were dead." Then I'd run to my room, slam the door , and cry for hours, not because my mother had raised her voice or hand to me, but because I had let something slip out that could prove that I didn't love my parents at all and couldn't care less what happened to them. I was never sure whether or not God heard every little thing I said, and I'd get frightened that he would fulfill my wish just to punish me, and my parents would get very sick and would have to go to the hospital and they don't let kids into hospitals and my last words to them would have to be "I wish you were dead" when I didn't at all and not "I love you Momma and Daddy" the way it should be. . . .

I thought it was unfair anyway that you could love your parents so much and be so close to them that they know and understand every aspect of your personality and you theirs and then one day it's time for them to die and they just drop out of the picture.

"They never drop out of the picture," Momma said. "As I get older my hands look more and more like

Grandma's hands; I was shocked when I looked down at them one time and saw my mother's knobby knuckles and not my own. If you want to find your parents you only have to look at yourself or at your sisters, because between you, you have inherited every trait that we have. And you inherit much more than that. What do you think your parents' job is? It's to teach their children everything that they themselves know and feel, and if they have succeeded, you won't need their bodies around to help you and guide you because the essence of what they were has been passed on to you, and you will only have to search in yourself to find the answers. . . .

I couldn't be comforted by a one-way communication with memories, and I didn't need my parents around necessarily because I couldn't take care of myself. I wanted to be able just to talk to them, even about silly things like how I hated school today and about that icky kid Debby in English class. Our relationship was much more than essential; I didn't want to lose it, or substitute something for it. . . .

I lay awake in bed one night. . . . I wanted to feel that closeness to my parents which always drove out thoughts of death. So I went to wake them up and as I reached towards my mother's shoulder to shake her awake I noticed her puckered upper lip, and vivid memories of my grandmother as she slept in the bed next to the one Serena and I shared whenever we went to her house, floated through my mind. I also noticed that the pinky of my outstretched hand was crooked, just like my father's, even though he always attributed his to a badly caught baseball.

And I was comforted. . . .

YOUR EXPERIENCES WITH DEATH

1. *Write a story about any experience with death you may have had, or one you imagined.*

2. *How does separation by death compare to other separations, like a divorce of the parents, for a young child?*

3. *Does Ruth Saltzman's story express any of your own early memories and ideas about death? How many themes besides death can you pick out in the story— e.g., guilt, dependency, religious belief, etc.?*

4. *What ideas do you have about how to prepare a young child to deal with death, a memorial service, and a funeral? Draw on your own experiences.*

Perhaps a few suggestions may be helpful. A visitor should be willing to share his memories of the deceased with the mourner. He should not avoid the subject and try to distract the mourner with more pleasant thoughts. The mourner wants to talk of his loss and a visitor should encourage him to do so.

A friend should not "presume to judge another's loss— neither maximize nor minimize the sadness of the situation."[24] Sometimes when an elderly person dies, we may play down the sadness: "Well, she had a good life." Or "She lived to a ripe old age." Yet her child may still feel tremendous grief and find such comments insensitive.

Except for these few cautions, a visitor should not worry too much about what he says—his caring will come through. So long as the visitor is a good listener, can accept the grief of the mourner, and has patience with the grief process, he will be providing a great service to the bereaved. Sometimes the most comforting experience is just the silent presence of another.

There are no set rules for calling on a friend. Howard Thurman eloquently expressed the only necessary ingredient, empathy:

I share with you the agony of your grief,
The anguish of your heart finds echo in my own.
I know I cannot enter all you feel
Nor bear with you the burden of your pain;

I can but offer what my love does give:
The strength of caring,
The warmth of one who seeks to understand
The silent storm-swept barrenness of so great a loss.

This I do in quiet ways.
That on your lonely path
You may not walk alone.[25]

Sir Thomas Browne wrote, "Many have studied to exasperate the ways of Death, but few hours have been spent to soften that necessity." In learning how to cope with loss and grief, we will be learning one of life's most important lessons, for "if we accept being alive, then we must accept the fact of death."[26]

DEALING WITH DEATH: SUGGESTIONS FOR CLASS

1. *Death is a universal theme. People throughout history have reacted to and thought about it. Select one (or more) of the following quotations and develop your own thoughts on the subject in a brief essay.*

Grief is the price we pay for love.

PAUL MCELROY, *Quiet Thoughts*

To die is the great debt and tribute due unto nature.

STERNE, *Tristram Shandy*

Sunset and evening star
And one clear call for me!
And may there be no moaning of the bar
When I put out to sea. . .

TENNYSON, *Crossing the Bar*

The goal of all life is death. FREUD

Live mindful of death; the hour flies.

PERSIUS, *Satires*

We are but tenants, and . . . shortly the great Landlord will give us notice that our lease has expired.

JOSEPH JEFFERSON,
Inscription on his monument

For dust thou art, and unto dust thou shalt return.

Genesis

When death comes, he respects neither age nor merit. He sweeps from this earthly existence the sick and the strong, the rich and the poor, and should teach us to live to be prepared for death.

ANDREW JACKSON

Tis not to die we fear, but to die poorly,
To fall forgotten, in a multitude.

JOHN FLETCHER, *The Humorous Lieutenant*

Death is rather to be chosen than a toilsome life.

AESCHYLUS, *Fragments*

Grief is itself a medicine.

WILLIAM COWPER, *Charity*

Grief makes one hour ten.

SHAKESPEARE, *Richard II*

He mourns the dead who lives as they desire.

YOUNG, *Night Thoughts*

Suppressed grief suffocates. OVID, *Tristia*

2. *Invite the following professionals to lead discussions with the class:*
   A clergyman   *A cancer specialist*
   A social worker or psychiatrist   *A funeral home director*

The Failure to Cope

We have all admired the physical stamina of an athlete who can run or swim great distances. We are often astonished at stories of human endurance: the mountain climber who trudges through snow and wind for days without food; the elderly man who single-handedly sails around the world, always on the brink of catastrophe; those who survive the tortures of war, the unthinkable existence in a concentration camp, the devastation of chronic famine and poverty. But we also know that everyone has his limits, the point at which the individual falls from sheer exhaustion.

Those who have known such endurance experiences insist that physical resistance is not the whole answer. Whether we call it attitude, emotional strength, ego adaptability, faith, determination, or will power—we must acknowledge the contribution of some psychological factors.

The ability to cope with all of life's stresses is not a simple or single skill. We can list a few factors besides physical constitution which probably contribute: early upbringing, interpersonal relations, self-image, confidence, motivation, the "will to live," variety of accumulated experience, religious belief, adaptability, flexibility, and so on.

While we are impressed with unusual demonstrations of coping behavior, we are less surprised by the many failures to cope. Failure to cope with adversity, disappointment, loss, competition, hardship, and obstacles is certainly much more widespread.

The stresses of everyday life are sufficient to cause such occasional failures. Indeed, failures are to be expected and should be considered within the range of normal behavior. But usually, the defense mechanisms of the mind and the body are sufficient to handle these episodes. Only when these mechanisms are worn out, exhausted—like the athlete's stamina—do we have a failure of function, a depletion of resourcefulness, a so-called "nervous breakdown," a psychosomatic illness, or some other form of disability.

What is experienced as a stress for one person may be "easy sailing" for another. The extent to which something is felt as a stress depends not only upon one's innate physical resources and portfolio of defense mechanisms, but also upon expectations defined by oneself and by others. The degree of stress is determined not only by the intensity of the situation but also by the amount of responsibility felt by the person. It is possible, for example, for a fighter pilot to experience less stress than an executive administrator in a large corporation—depending upon their personal feelings about their jobs.

Harold G. Wolff, who spent his career investigating the relationship of bodily disease to emotions and life situations, distinguishes between *appropriate* and *inappropriate* responses to personal threat or stress. For example, if a person perceives a situation as dangerous, his heart may overwork, his blood vessels may narrow, his blood may thicken, his body chemistry may change, his head may ache, and he may develop back pain—all as ways to prepare to meet the stress. But if these changes raise the possibility of heart attack or other illness—what started out as a *protective defense* of the body against a threat then *becomes the threat itself*.

This situation is similar to fighting an infection by developing a fever, chills, diarrhea, and a cough. If these defenses tax the body to extremes, even more serious damage may result. Defenses help to a point, but they also have their limits.

Most of us know what resistance to physical disease means. We can also speak of *emotional resistance* to try to understand why, under stressful circumstances, some people "break" and others don't. Certainly, we know that when the "flu" is making the rounds, some of us get it and others don't. It is never quite clear what makes the difference.

Just as the body sometimes can fight off a cold and sometimes "gives in," so does a person develop ways to protect himself against emotional hurt. When these mechanisms fail or "give in," symptoms and illness occur.

Giving In and Giving Up

For many years, a group of researchers at the University of Rochester Medical Center have been studying how emotional distress causes physical and psychological illness. Arthur Schmale and George L. Engel of this group have found a common setting in which almost all illness develops: the person feels "It's too much," or "It's no use: I can't take it any more," or "I give up."[27] Such reactions include two different kinds of feelings: *helplessness* and *hopelessness*. Helplessness is a sense of being unable to do anything about environmental conditions. Hopelessness is a sense of failure in oneself as well as a lack of help from outside sources. In both conditions, the person feels less competent, less in control, less secure in what he can expect from others. The future may look more bleak and less rewarding than it did in the past. Such gloomy feelings may mobilize coping tech-

"It's no use: I can't take it anymore." Sometimes stress can become overwhelming. A person may feel deep despair and helplessness. Severe depression is the most common background of suicide.

niques which, nonetheless, are unable to bring satisfaction or correct the situation.

This state of affairs has been particularly noticed when an important separation or loss brings on a depression. Exactly how this condition then influences biological and physiological systems to show signs and symptoms of physical disease is not yet understood. Physical and emotional illness, therefore, can communicate the message "I give up." But the most dramatic and desperate message is conveyed in attempts at self-destruction.

Suicide: A Last Attempt to Cope

Think of all the surprises, disappointments, and chaos

you encounter every day. Generally, you take them pretty much in stride even though you may feel irritated, angry, disappointed, sad, "miffed," or disgusted. You're not inclined to give up easily because you know from experience that you will "bounce back."

A constant bombardment of such experiences, though, can weaken a person's self-confidence, make it difficult to "get over" something, or interfere with an ability to have clear perceptions about things. One may feel a nagging, persistent sense of failure—or what is described above as hopelessness and helplessness. If coping mechanisms don't work, and if the "messages" of illness are not seen or heard by others, a profound desperation may overcome a person. Sometimes a suicide attempt is a way of shouting "I can't take it any more!"

One reason that this message takes such a dramatic and frightening form is that it is so seldom discussed. Most high school textbooks do not mention it; many educators think that discussion increases the risk of suicide by "opening Pandora's box." But quite the opposite is true: risk is decreased by making possible open discussion. A retrospective review of a large number of suicides has shown that in most cases the person had tried to give clues to close friends, family members, or their family doctors.

Why do people attempt suicide? Usually there is a deep sense of worthlessness, measured against the standards of what one thinks he or she should be. There is a tendency to see oneself in a bad light, *despite the fact* that this self-image may not correspond at all to how others see the person.

This disparity shows that the person misperceives reality—about himself and about others—and this may be a sign of serious emotional disturbance. The person may

639

be so depressed that "everything looks black." This blackness and bleakness may prevent a person from recognizing that he has friends or interested parents and teachers.

Before reaching such a "low," a person may still have the energy and hope to try to find help, often through such means as a "hot line." A good example of this was a young woman who was new in town and out of work. She felt lonely and worthless. She had not yet made friends and had no local relatives. She was still feeling "homesick" and depressed since leaving home two months ago after breaking up with a boyfriend. She had been sleeping poorly and had no appetite. She thought about killing herself by taking a bottle of pills her doctor had given her some time ago for menstrual cramps.

Having seen a sign in a subway station about a "hot line," she called and spoke for a long time with a counselor who asked many questions, expressed interest and concern, but mostly listened sympathetically. After they had talked a while, the woman sensed that there *was* help available, that the city was not so lonely and uncaring, and that arrangements could be made to obtain professional advice. An appointment was made in the psychiatric clinic of a local hospital. She was seen the next day. The prospect of overcoming her distress seemed brighter.

The risk of suicide is not always so readily coped with. A person who is psychotic is unable to control impulses and unaware of what is real and what is not. Consequently, there is generally a higher degree of unpredictability, a greater risk of impulsive "acting out"—especially in response to imaginary voices giving "directions," or to frightening images (hallucinations) which suddenly bring on suicidal urges. A similar situation can occur in someone who has purposely or accidentally taken certain drugs like LSD or dexedrine or mescaline. Such suicide attempts are generally the result of disturbed perceptions which clear up once the effects of the drug have diminished. In the meantime, close attendance and supervision are essential.

Other people may attempt suicide because they are angry at someone else and have fantasies that they will make the other person feel sorry (responsible) for the hurt they have caused. This is the most common cause of all suicide attempts, and is more frequent in women than in men. A gesture by a man is usually more carefully planned, involves much more direct methods (for example, a gun as opposed to pills), and is more often successful. Many times, a suicide gesture brings about the hoped-for reconciliation and the person returns to his previous state of adaptation.

Occasionally, a person who has a terminal, painful illness will commit suicide, but surprisingly, this is much more rare than one might expect.

Usually, severe depression is the most common background of suicide. One should not hesitate to inform family members, friends, or teachers of someone who seems depressed and suicidal. You may hesitate because of reluctance to "interfere" or for fear of alienating the person, but the risks of not doing anything are much greater.

Most cities now have Suicide Prevention Centers, hot lines, counseling services, psychiatric clinics, and hospitals where help and advice can be obtained.

THE FAILURE TO COPE

1. *Is it possible for stress to be pleasurable? Can you give examples from your own experience?*

2. *What kinds of situations are apt to cause stress, and how can a person generally deal with them? What do you do to counteract negative reactions to stress?*

3. *The effects of stress can appear in the following ways:*

   Psychological

   Physical

   Social

   Can you give examples in each category?

4. *Can you think of any situations where an unexpected death occurred shortly after the loss of one's spouse? Would you account for this strictly as coincidence, or can you think of any other possible explanations?*

5. *Under what circumstances would a person be likely to think about suicide? Everyone has at one time or another in his life thought of the idea of suicide. Why is this so?*

6. *If you were really concerned about the possibility that someone you know might commit suicide or was*

planning it, what measures would you take? What people or agencies could you call on for help?

7. Invite someone in from your local hot line to tell you about his/her work.

Suggested Reading

DEATH

Grollman, Earl, *Explaining Death to Children* (Boston: Beacon Press, 1969).

Hendin, David, *Death as a Fact of Life* (New York: W.W. Norton, 1973).

Kastenbaum, Robert and Ruth Aisenberg, *The Psychology of Death* (New York: Springer, 1972).

Kavanaugh, Robert, *Facing Death* (Los Angeles: Nash, 1972).

Krant, Melvin, *Dying and Dignity* (Springfield, Ill.: C.C. Thomas, 1974).

Kübler-Ross, Elisabeth, *Death: The Final Stage of Growth* (Englewood Cliffs, N.J.: Prentice-Hall, 1975).

Kübler-Ross, Elisabeth, *On Death and Dying* (New York: Macmillan, 1969).

Kübler-Ross, Elisabeth, *Questions and Answers on Death and Dying* (New York: Macmillan, 1974).

Langone, John, *Death is a Noun* (Boston: Little, Brown, 1972).

Mitford, Jessica, *The American Way of Death* (New York: Simon and Schuster, 1963).

Weisman, Avery, *On Dying and Denying* (New York: Behavioral Pub., 1972).

PERSONAL ACCOUNTS, FICTION

Agee, James, *A Death in the Family* (New York: Bantam Books, 1971).

Alsop, Stewart, *Stay of Execution* (Philadelphia: Lippincott, 1973).

Friedman, Marcia, *The Story of Josh* (New York: Praeger, 1974).

Gunther, John, *Death Be Not Proud* (New York: Harper and Row, 1949).

Lund, Doris, *Eric* (Philadelphia: Lippincott, 1974).

Morris, Jeannie, *Brian Piccolo: A Short Season* (Chicago: Rand McNally, 1971).

Solzhenitsyn, Alexander, *Cancer Ward* (New York: Farrar, Straus and Giroux, 1969).

Tolstoy, Leo, *The Death of Ivan Ilych* (New York: New American Lib., 1960).

SUICIDE

Alvarez, A., *The Savage God* (New York: Random House, 1972).

Choron, Jacques, *Suicide* (New York: Charles Scribner's Sons, 1972).

Lester, Gene and David Lester, *Suicide: The Gamble with Death* (Englewood Cliffs: Prentice Hall, 1971).

Plath, Sylvia, *The Bell Jar* (New York: Harper and Row, 1971).

Schneidman, Edwin, *On The Nature of Suicide* (San Francisco: Jossey-Bass, 1969).

FOOTNOTES

1. George L. Engel, *Psychological Development in Health and Disease* (Philadelphia: Saunders, 1962).
2. Thomas Holmes and Richard Rahe, "Social Adjustment Raising Scale," *Journal of Psychosomatic Research*, 11:213, 1967.
3. "Abe Maslow—1908-1970," Reprinted from *Psychology Today*, August 1970, p. 16. Copyright © 1970 Ziff-Davis Publishing Company. All rights reserved.
4. Elisabeth Kübler-Ross, *On Death and Dying* (New York: Macmillan Publishing Company, Copyright © 1969 by Elisabeth Kübler-Ross), p. 7.
5. D. Dempsey, "Learning How To Die," *The New York Times Magazine*, November 14, 1971, p. 60.
6. John Gunther, *Death Be Not Proud* (New York: Harper and Row, 1949).
7. Kübler-Ross, *op. cit.*, p.34.
8. *Ibid.*, p. 35.
9. *Ibid.*, p. 44.

10. *Ibid.*, p. 73.
11. *Ibid.*, p. 77.
12. *Ibid.*, p. 78.
13. *Ibid.*, p. 78.
14. *Ibid.*, p. 104.
15. Joan Barthel, " 'I Promise You It Will Be All Right,' " Copyright Joan Barthel for *Life* Magazine, © 1972, Time Inc.
16. Harriet Harvey Coffin, "What Death Means to Children," no date p. 2.
17. *Ibid.*, p. 2.
18. J. Bowlby, *International Journal of Psychoanalysis*, 42:317, 1961.
19. Herbert Patchell, *The Facts of Death* (Boston: Massachusetts Department of Education, 1970) p. 4.
20. Erich Lindemann, *American Journal of Psychiatry*, September 1944, p. 142.
21. Coffin, *op. cit.*, p. 4.
22. *Ibid.*, p. 3.
23. *Ibid.*, p. 4.
24. Patchell, *op. cit.*, pp. 126-127.
25. "For a Time of Sorrow" in *Meditations of the Heart* by Howard Thurman. Copyright, 1953 by Harper and Row, Publishers, Inc.
26. Avery Weisman, *On Dying and Denying: A Psychiatric Study of Terminality* (New York: Behavioral Publications, 1972) p. 22.
27. G. L. Engel and A.H. Schmale, "Psychoanalytic Theory of Somatic Disorder: Conversion, Specificity and the Disease Onset Situation," *Journal of the American Psychoanalytic Association.* 15, 344-365, 1967.

15.
Darker Shades of Gray: Mental Illness

True!—nervous—very, very dreadfully nervous I had been and am; but why will you say that I am mad? The disease had sharpened my senses—not destroyed—not dulled them. Above all was the sense of hearing acute. I heard all things in the heaven and in the earth. I heard many things in hell. How, then, am I mad? Hearken! and observe how healthily— how calmly I can tell you the whole story.

EDGAR ALLAN POE, *"The Tell-Tale Heart"*

Throughout history, people have been both frightened and fascinated by strange behavior. The fear of "madness" causes some people to see it in themselves if they sense that they are different from others. More often, there is a tendency to regard the *other* person as mad or crazy. Robert Owen, an 18th-century educator, recognized how easy it is to see others as odd:

All the world is queer save thee and me, and even thou art a little queer.

The popularity of horror movies and stories can be explained by our tendency to feel safer seeing the bizarre and outlandish in fictional characters than in admitting even small eccentricities in ourselves.

Because the whole inner world of emotion seems so unpredictable and uncontrollable, it is difficult to capture in words a precise definition of mental illness. Some would like to believe that intelligence and mental illness are related, but there is no proof of this. A punch line of a popular joke, "We may be crazy, but we're not stupid," reflects the observation that one quality does not necessarily include the other. This same point is made by

Photo courtesy of Beth Nicholson

Mental health and mental illness form a spectrum of grays: lighter shades of gray ("normality") blend almost imperceptibly into darker shades (illness). Each seemingly sick condition probably represents merely an extreme form of some normal human condition.

648

Shakespeare's Hamlet—"Though this be madness, yet there is method in it."

Although "madness" is *not* caused by either too much or too little intelligence, the fact that unusual creativity is statistically "abnormal" has led people to connect it with "madness." In 1681, the poet John Dryden wrote in *Absolom and Achitophel*:

> *Great wits are sure to madness near allied,*
> *And thin partitions do their bounds divide.*

These thin partitions between madness and greatness have been, and continue to be, emphasized by professionals as well as laymen. How many great historical figures can you think of whom people at various times have considered "emotionally disturbed"? Beethoven, Van Gogh, and Dostoevsky immediately come to mind.

Unclear boundaries make it difficult to understand, describe, diagnose, accept, study, or influence behavior, whether emotional or physical. That is why we prefer to call the range of mental disorders a spectrum of grays. The lighter shades of gray ("normality?") tend to blend imperceptibly into the darker shades ("madness?").

Coping with the Fear of "Madness"

Fear of madness is often expressed in humor. For example, one way to make emotional disturbance less frightening is to speak of someone who is "out to lunch," or "off her rocker," who has "lost his buttons," or become "touched in the head." Likewise, an institution for the

649

treatment of mental illness is called the "funny farm," the "laughing academy," or the "looney bin," and the people who treat such illnesses are "shrinks" (from "head-shrinkers"), "nut-crackers," or "word surgeons." While humor may not be the most respectful way to control our own fears, it is far more civilized than some of the ways revealed to us in history—punishment, exile, or execution of the insane.

Our ideas about "madness" have gradually evolved from primitive notions of possession by evil spirits, witchcraft, and voodoo. In the medieval period, people began to believe that "madness" was a disease of the humors (fluids) of the body; this was considered a medical, scientific theory. Slowly, mental disease became a more respectable subject for scientific research. Theories arose that behavioral deviations were caused by emotional factors.

One school of thought followed a *physical* line of investigation, believing that "madness" could be accounted for as a disease of the brain. When the early physical approach failed to produce convincing results, a more psychological direction was pursued. Today, we see remnants of all these developmental threads in our understanding, definitions, and treatment of mental functioning. Important contributions have been added by new fields: biochemistry, pharmacology, endocrinology, neurophysiology, immunology, sociology, anthropology, and others.

How can we put all that is known about mental illness in perspective? To provide a basic framework for research and understanding, mental health specialists evolved a system for classifying the major mental and emotional disorders. As we study these classifications of

650

diagnoses, remember that each seemingly pathological (sick) condition probably represents an *extreme* form of some *normal* human condition. "Normal" and "abnormal" are only different "shades of gray." Think of *diagnosis* as a kind of shorthand, a labeling that permits people to exchange thoughts and ideas with a degree of common understanding. Without such a shorthand, it is hard to communicate.

Diagnosis: The Shorthand of Labeling

"Sticks and stones will break my bones, but names will never hurt me." This jingle may be comforting against jibes and taunts in childhood. But as one gets older, it is possible to see how names and labels *can* have lasting and harmful effects. The labels used to describe or diagnose the varieties of psychological problems may produce such effects. For this reason, it is important to remember that diagnostic categories of mental and emotional conditions are best used by professional people with extensive experience and education in human behavior. When students of psychology, impressed with their newly acquired knowledge and vocabulary, attempt to diagnose their friends or others, they are merely engaging in a sophisticated version of childhood name-calling.

Professional mental health workers use diagnostic labels to differentiate the degree and type of mental distress and to determine which treatments are most likely to help a particular individual. Diagnosis should *not* be regarded as criticism and should *not* be casually applied to people who seem superficially to fit a certain category. A diagnosis, by itself, does not necessarily imply anything about the seriousness or treatability of a condition. A mild psychotic reaction after a surgical operation may be more quickly and easily cured than a long-standing but less severe personality disorder or neurosis.

Imagine that a person goes to a psychiatrist because he is having "problems" and is worried about strange feelings, fears, and unusual symptoms. Before the psychiatrist can begin to help his patient, he must first learn about him—he must take a personal history, learn how the symptoms began, and how they relate to the events in the person's current and past life experiences. Using all of this information, the psychiatrist selects a tentative diagnosis.

There are four general categories of diagnosis. *psychosis, neurosis, personality disorder,* and *psychosomatic disease.* Each category has many variants within it. When the psychiatrist selects a specific diagnosis, this provides him with a way of looking at that individual's problem: how it most likely developed, the type of harm and unhappiness it brings to that person's life, and the types of treatments or therapies that are most likely to have some positive effect.

The reason for diagnosis may become clearer if we consider a "symptom" that nearly everyone has had some experience with: sadness or depression. You have not yet studied what it means to be "neurotic" or "psychotic," so these terms may puzzle you for the moment. However, a brief definition will suffice until we discuss these terms in depth. A neurosis may be said to be the repetition of self-defeating habits; a psychosis may be said to be a "derangement"or loss of touch with reality which prevents everyday functioning. The purpose of the following example is to illustrate the way a mental health worker approaches the problem of making a diagnosis.

If a person were bothered enough about "feeling blue" most of the time, he might decide to seek professional advice, much as one would go to his family doctor if he had a cold that hung on far too long. The psychiatrist or other mental health professional would want to know a lot more about the complaint:

> How long had the problem existed?
>
> How did it begin?
>
> What was happening in the person's life at the time?
>
> Has the symptom interfered very much with everyday functioning?
>
> Were there physical symptoms like loss of appetite and weight, difficulty in sleeping, constipation, physical discomfort, or other reactions?
>
> Had this happened before or was it a completely new experience?
>
> Had there been some recent losses or disappointments?
>
> What were they?
>
> Was there a family history of such symptoms?
>
> Did the person always react this way to loss or did he sometimes become excited and almost euphoric?
>
> Did the symptoms sometimes include feelings of unreality, the experience of hallucinations or delusions, or a sense of impending doom?

Using this information, the psychiatrist begins to make some important distinctions. Is there reason to suspect that this person's depression is of psychotic proportions? If there is no family history of depression, no severe mood swings from euphoria to depression, then the diagnosis of manic-depressive psychosis can be rejected. Does the depression mask an underlying schizophrenic psychosis? If there has never been a loss of contact with reality, no hallucinations or delusions, then the disorder is probably not a *psychotic* one at all.

Is this depression then, a symptom of neurosis or personality disorder? Or is the depression merely a temporary reaction to a recent unhappy event, such as the death of a close family member or friend, or the break-up of a love relationship? In this latter situation, the feelings of sadness may be perfectly normal and only require time and an opportunity to talk to someone who understands. However, if the feelings have persisted for long periods of time—even in the absence of stressful events—so that the depression has become intertwined with the individual's personality, then a diagnosis of neurosis or personality disorder may be appropriate. Diagnosing a particular depression as psychotic or neurotic influences the choice of treatment. A psychosis may require treatment with drugs, while a neurosis may respond to "talking treatment" alone.

A fourth diagnostic category to be considered is psychosomatic illness. If the depressive feelings do not appear obvious to the person or to others, but produce a physical illness instead, then a combined medical-psychiatric approach must be used in treatment.

Diagnosis, then, is an important tool for mental health workers, even though it may lack precision and may run the risk of being abused. In the remainder of this chapter, we will examine each of the major diagnostic categories in more detail, keeping in mind our "shades of gray" theme.

MENTAL ILLNESS: FIRST IMPRESSIONS

1. *Most people, at one time or another, have been concerned about their mental health. How would you decide the difference between feelings of sadness, which are normal under the circumstances, and a serious depression?*

2. *You and your class have been invited to visit a residence for mentally disturbed people. What do you think the people will be like? What are your feelings about making this visit?*

3. *Think of a movie, book, or television show which has portrayed a mentally ill person. What symptoms were depicted to convince you the person was mentally ill? How influential have these media been in forming your image of the mentally ill person?*

Neurosis: The Repetition of Self-Defeating Habits

ARNIE'S parents often had to leave him with friends or relatives for long periods of time when he was very young. This seemed like a satisfactory arrangement at first, but around the age of six, Arnie began to be extremely irritable whenever his parents would go out. He would sometimes cry for hours, finally fall asleep from exhaustion, only to be awakened by a frightening nightmare. Sometimes during the night, he would go into his parents' bedroom to see if they were there, even when they assured him they would remain at home all night. As he got older, he was afraid to be left alone, tended to cling to others, and noticed that he would have twinges of anxiety whenever he separated from anyone, including friends and teachers.

Arnie was aware of his problem, embarrassed by it, and determined to "lick it" one way or another. Sometimes he would just try to calm down by telling himself there was nothing to worry about. But at other times, it was almost as if he would intentionally set up situations where he would be left by himself—alone and disappointed. Although he thought that he would eventually overcome his problem by practicing self-control, he soon realized that his behavior was beyond voluntary correction.

All this was very puzzling to Arnie. He began feeling angry—sometimes at no one in particular, sometimes at his friends when they had to go home, sometimes at his parents, sometimes at himself. On occasion, he would become so angry that he would even have fantasies or daydreams that something terrible might happen to his mother or father. For instance, he began to sense an irresistible need to disconnect electrical plugs in his home; his behavior was accompanied by the troubling thought that if he didn't do this, the house would catch fire from an electrical spark and his father might be killed.

When Arnie behaved this way and had these thoughts, he felt guilty and ungrateful. He would feel "blue" and have trouble studying. But for most of the time, as far as anyone else could tell from just looking at Arnie, he seemed like other kids his own age. Nevertheless, a mental health professional could recognize that Arnie had developed a *neurosis*.

A person who, like Arnie, has one of the less severe neuroses can often live, work, and play without major difficulty if his life circumstances are supportive. While this "problem" may involve disturbance in all areas—thinking, feeling, and behaving—the person may be able to achieve, be creative and productive, and have meaningful relationships with others. It may be only during particularly stressful times that he or she may feel imprisoned, helpless, and unhappy about the disruptions caused by such a neurosis.

If you think of a person's personality as a fabric woven in a particular pattern, then a neurosis might be described as a minor error in the weaving—sometimes hardly visible—which may change the pattern slightly but not the basic cloth. A really severe error in weaving might result in major disorganization of the pattern, producing a "psychotic cloth." Because the process of human development is so complicated, most people probably suffer at least some degree of "misweaving" even though their basic pattern is not jeopardized.

In Arnie's case, the pattern of his neurosis was woven quite early in his life. Like all children, Arnie was born with biological needs for nourishment, elimination, sleep, and warmth. He depended upon others to fulfill his needs. The way he was treated by others and his own tolerance for pain, fear, and disappointment combined to determine just how he reacted to stress. A child's capacity to cope with both minor disruptions and major crises in life comes from the interplay of his own inner resources and the influence of parental training. Sometimes parents teach effective problem-solving; sometimes they teach their child to react with confusion, aggression, passivity, or other extreme and inappropriate behavior. This "basic

657

training" in the family teaches a child a "model" method for dealing with distress. When the child learns to master problems at this stage of development, he is equipped to handle more serious and potentially threatening situations later on. If his basic training is inadequate, incomplete, inflexible, or unresponsive, he is likely to "fall apart" or to develop "hangups" under stress. These hangups often take the form of *symptoms* such as emotional blocks, inhibitions, fears, and anxieties, which interfere with the best possible use of all his resources.

Symptoms and Defenses

Symptoms are thoughts, feelings, or actions which usually cause suffering. A trained mental health worker, hearing about or observing such suffering, understands that the person is not fulfilling some of his or her basic needs. Symptoms are the evidence that the ego and its defense mechanisms are failing in their task of moderating the "push and pull" of inner drives. As the inner drive pushes for satisfaction, the defense tries to keep it repressed; *what breaks through is the symptom.*

In Arnie's case, for example, there is a deep-seated and only partially conscious wish to have harm come to his father, because Arnie feels angry that father has gone away with mother and caused loneliness. Even though this is not an unusual thought, it is an upsetting one which stirs up Arnie's guilt. The guilt causes anxiety, and the anxiety activates his defense mechanisms to ward off the offensive thoughts and wishes. When this doesn't work effectively—either because the defenses are too weak or the wish too strong—the anxiety level soars. Under these circumstances, the id forces (wish) and the ego forces (reality) try desperately to reach a compromise.

658

Often the compromise is to *disguise* the objectionable wish. Arnie's wish to get revenge on his father, whom he blamed for his misery, is disguised by an exaggerated *opposite* wish to protect his father from accidental death. Arnie then adopts beliefs and behaviors that are consistent with this reaction. Arnie believes that his father will be in danger if a chance electrical spark burns down the house. He develops the habit of unplugging all electrical fixtures. He has no idea *why* he does this; he knows only that he *must* do it even though the need is bothersome to him and his family.

This strange behavior is a neurotic symptom. The unconscious compromise that results in Arnie's symptom accomplishes two purposes: through a reaction formation, it partly disguises the wish to hurt his father, and it also imposes some punishment on Arnie for having such a wish by compelling him to repeat an inconvenient behavior over and over. Arnie gets *some* relief from this strange neurotic symptom, but the underlying problem remains unsolved and he continues to suffer. It is the suffering caused by the *persistence* of the symptom that motivates a neurotic person to seek help.

The efficiency of defense mechanisms in regulating satisfaction of needs determines the degree and kind of neurotic symptoms. It is important to remember that neurotic symptoms occur *only when the normal function of defenses is distorted*. Under normal circumstances, defense mechanisms are an integral part of a person's coping processes. They are essential to living and growing at all stages of development. Surprisingly, many people feel accused of something "bad" or "sick" when they are told that they have defense mechanisms. This is an unfortunate mistake. Defense mechanisms are as important for successful coping with the stresses of everyday living as white blood cells are for fighting off infection. If either defense mechanisms or white blood cells are missing or defective, a person is bound to be in serious trouble sooner or later.

The defense mechanisms (described in detail in the chapter "The Push and Pull of Inner Needs") go to work unannounced, mobilized by stimuli such as fear, anxiety, or emotional pain, just as white blood cells go to work as soon as bacteria or viruses enter the body. White blood cells can keep an infection localized in the finger, with only mild redness and swelling. If they fail to "hold this line," they may find themselves struggling with a fever, chills, and a generalized infection of the blood stream. A good supply of white blood cells can control the infection so that only mild symptoms develop. Likewise, the psychological defense mechanisms are expected to protect the person from overwhelming anxiety. If the defenses function efficiently, as in repression, anxiety will be controlled at its source, with only mild symptoms like irritability and resentment. If the repression doesn't hold back the disturbing thought or wish, anxiety may break through into generalized annoyance, raised voice, unreasonable demands, uncalled-for antagonisms, headaches, and the like. It is the same with the other defense mechanisms of denial, projection, displacement, avoidance, and regression.

Ordinarily, the ways in which the defense mechanisms work are not noticeable. Only when they *fail* to ward off the anxiety of an emotional crisis or dilemma can one tell, by the symptoms that occur, which defenses are being used. It remains a puzzle as to how specific defenses or neurotic symptoms are selected. The following discussion illustrates common types of neurotic reactions.

The Variety of Neurotic Reactions

Anxiety is what you commonly experience when you are apprehensive or worried about an examination, an important date, a public speech, and so on. Usually, you know what you feel anxious about and your anxiety is no cause for alarm. You pass it off as just "nervous energy." You not only manage to do what you have to do, but sometimes you do it even better because your anxiety "keyed you up" to do a good job. In *neurotic* anxiety, however, the reason for the apprehension is not obvious—or, even if the situation is tense, the reaction is highly exaggerated. For example, a factory worker experiences overwhelming dread when his boss walks in; a mother expects an impending disaster when her child is out of sight; or a young man becomes overaware of his body, developing an unreasonable fear of physical disease (sometimes called *hypochondriasis*) even after his doctor tells him he is in good health. Talking fast, perspiring, being aware of one's heartbeat, and feeling dizzy or tired may be symptoms of an anxiety reaction. There may also be a chronic sense of tension, restlessness, and irritability.

Other situations may cause depression rather than anxiety. It is a rare person who has not been sad on the occasion of a disappointment, a loss, or even a change for the better (such as graduating from school). How many children experience homesickness or cry the first time they go off to school or camp (leaving home and mother and father behind)? To live, to grow, to have important relationships with other people is to know what it means to be sad or temporarily depressed. But these disappointments dissolve as new and gratifying experiences take their place.

The person with a neurotic depression, however, does not know why the depression exists. The depression seems to last *longer* than would be expected from those events which provoked the sadness, and it seems to be much *more intense* than the circumstances seem to warrant. For example, a woman, whose father died one year ago is gripped by feelings of disillusionment right after the birth of her baby boy who was named after the father. She experiences a sluggishness and lack of motivation, a slackening of involvement with others, tiredness and frequent sleeping, and marked feelings of inferiority that do not relate to how others see her. This painful state casts a gray gloominess over everything. A more severe depression might also be accompanied by bodily complaints such as loss of appetite, various aches and pains, a tight sensation in the head and other parts of the body, and increased sleeping difficulties.

The woman described here got over her depressive reaction when she realized that the birth of her baby triggered off an "anniversary depression" related to sadness over her father's recent death. Sometimes, what would otherwise be a normal grief reaction may develop into a neurotic depression if it persists too long.

Unreasonable fear is another type of neurotic symptom formed to relieve anxiety. Arnie had an exaggerated fear of house fires. Many people have other unreasonable fears of dark rooms, of elevators, of thunder storms, of insects, of subways, or of flying. Usually these fears are accompanied by only mild worry, so they do not interfere significantly with a person's activities. Often

662

To live, to grow, to have important relationships with other people—these are to know what it means to be sad or temporarily depressed.

these fears can be traced to a memory of a bad or painful experience.

The more severe fears are called *phobias* and are not so easily explained. They seriously limit a person's freedom of movement. Phobias may result when circumstances, events, or perceptions *seem* similar to an earlier experience that was so upsetting that it still generates enormous anxiety.

A young man entered psychotherapy with a phobia of elevators. This phobia interfered with his job because he worked in a very tall office building. If he rode in the elevator, he was overcome with fear of being trapped, attacked, and killed. He could not be talked out of this fear, even though he knew it was unreasonable. Furthermore, he noticed that the fear which was originally confined only to elevators was now beginning to spread to include buses and subways and even cars.

One day in therapy he suddenly became unexpectedly frightened of the therapist, immediately after the therapist said something which angered him. He was aware of a fleeting wish to strike his therapist which was superceded by the belief that the therapist would strike him first. Then he remembered a time on a crowded elevator when, as a little boy, two men had an argument and the boy thought they were going to hurt him. These memories had been repressed (forgotten) and his fear had been transferred to elevators. The elevator became the "scapegoat" for his unconscious fear of physical injury. As long as he *could* avoid elevators, subways, cars, and buses, he could avoid the memories and thereby keep his anxiety under control. Because such a widespread phobia seriously limited his life, he eventually sought treatment. The person with a neurotic phobia manages to unconsciously fool himself into believing there is good reason to be afraid of elevators or subways or horses or dogs in order to avoid recalling the emotional conflict that gave rise to anxiety in the first place.

Interestingly, one way people sometimes overcome their phobias is to do the very thing they most fear. This is called *counterphobic behavior*. We can all give examples of such cases—the man with a fear of heights who becomes a high-wire trapeze artist; the woman deathly afraid of water who becomes a champion swimmer; the stunt artist afraid of bodily harm who becomes a daredevil automobile driver. Counterphobic behavior is an extreme effort to master an otherwise overwhelming anxiety. Some would regard it as a form of conditioning.

We have already observed that one prominent characteristic of neurotic conditions is their tendency to be repeated over and over again. If a stimulus repeatedly elicits an ineffective response, the ego must try time and again to master the anxiety left by the unsolved problem. This is called a *repetition compulsion*.

Sometimes the repetitiveness actually becomes a fixed ritual of some kind. Can you recall rituals you developed during your childhood? Common examples are: washing up always in a certain order; or having to arrange your bedslippers just so in order to fall asleep; or brushing your teeth a certain number of times; or stepping over cracks in the sidewalk accompanied by little chants like "Step on a crack—break your mother's back"; or having to arrange everything on your desk in a certain order before you can study comfortably.

The purpose of the repetitiveness is to relieve anxiety or to keep some other thought or action out of awareness (repressed). Where the need or *compulsion* to perform

SOME TYPES OF PHOBIAS

Acrophobia . . . . Dread of high places

Claustrophobia . . . . . Dread of closed spaces

Hydrophobia . . . . Dread of water

Necrophobia . . . . Dread of dead bodies

Phobophobia . . . . Dread of fear

Xenophobia . . . . Dread of foreigners or strangers

Zoophobia . . . . Dread of animals

these rituals is so great that to omit them would paralyze the person with anxiety, we say that the person has a *neurotic compulsion or obsession*. When the ritual involves an *action*, such as washing the hands a certain number of times or not touching certain objects for fear of becoming contaminated, we refer to the ritual as a *compulsion*. Where the ritual involves thoughts, such as having to recite a certain jingle to oneself a certain number of times, or being constantly worried that your wallet is missing, we refer to the ritual as an *obsession*.

If someone is involved in either obsessive or compulsive activity a major part of the time, his functioning in other aspects of life may be seriously hampered. Such people often seem inflexible, rigid, overconscientious, strict, stubborn, or highly critical of others. The individual is often aware that he is performing a ritual, but will complain of an inability to avoid it, even though the behavior "makes no sense."

One of the most dramatic and interesting neuroses is the *conversion reaction*. This is the condition which sparked Freud's interest in searching for psychological explanations for what appeared to be serious physical disabilities like blindness, paralysis, deafness, or peculiar sensations of the skin. Through clinical experience and his psychoanalytical method of investigation, Freud found that some conditions which seemed to be physical in nature actually originated because of psychological conflicts over sex or other emotional dilemmas. A feared emotion, such as sexual excitement, is repressed and then changed (converted) unconsciously into a sensory disability such as a difficulty in seeing, hearing, tasting, smelling, or feeling. Also, the *motor* function of the arms, legs, tongue, or vocal cords may be impaired. The reluctant bride finds herself paralyzed and unable to walk down the aisle. The soldier on the battlefield is so frightened by the overwhelming destruction he sees that he becomes unable to use his trigger hand and is brought to a hospital. These symptoms "save" the person from being overwhelmed with anxiety.

People with conversion symptoms seem to have an unnatural lack of concern about their disability. It is as though the emotional feeling, having been converted into a bodily symptom, has become completely neutralized. Sometimes the benefit (*secondary gain*) to the person is so great that he or she is accused of *faking* the condition. However, these conversions are totally unconscious. Conversion symptoms are usually treated by psychotherapy, hypnosis, or a sodium amytal ("truth drug") interview.

Once the cause of a symptom is known, the conflict can often be worked out. During World War II, for example, many fighter pilots who "broke down" were discovered to have suffered severe guilt over the death of a buddy. The pilots were repressing their secret relief that they were not the ones killed. When they were helped to cope with this conflict between guilt and relief, many pilots recovered.

Another dramatic but puzzling and poorly understood neurosis is the *dissociative reaction*. In this condition, whole areas of a person's memory may be erased for long or short periods of time. In certain cases of *amnesia*, sleepwalking (*somnambulism*), or *fugue* states, for example, an individual may carry out a whole series of "reasonable" actions but have absolutely no recollection of them. In amnesia, the individual may continue his ordinary activities but forget who he is. The person *dissociates* himself from his actions. There is no reason to believe that there is any physical brain damage or that contact with reality is actually lost.

In fugue, an individual may appear to be conscious as he performs certain actions, but when asked to describe these actions even moments later, cannot. A relatively rare form of dissociative reaction—commonly but erroneously mistaken for schizophrenia—is the so-called *multiple personality* dramatized in Robert Louis Stevenson's story of Dr. Jekyll and Mr. Hyde, the movie "Three Faces of Eve," or the story of *Sybil*.

All the neurotic reactions mentioned above share certain characteristics: they cause discomfort or displeasure; they are repetitive in nature; they are recognized by the person as "foolish" or "unreasonable"; they are not accompanied by loss of contact with reality; and they do not result in a "nervous breakdown."

Treatment may take one of three general approaches:

(1) to understand and achieve insight into and control over early life experiences in a *reconstructive* way through *psychoanalysis* or *psychodynamic psychotherapy*; (2) to *desensitize* or *retrain* a person to *avoid certain habitual responses* through *behavioral techniques*; or (3) to simply and temporarily alleviate distressful symptoms through the use of *pharmacologic* substances called *psychoactive drugs* (tranquilizers and antidepressants) or other physical means, such as electroconvulsive therapy (ECT). Types of treatment are discussed more fully later on.

Troublesome Traits:
The Diagnosis of Personality Disorder

People with neuroses usually have symptoms that not only cause problems in relating to others, but also make them uncomfortable or unhappy. These feelings often motivate the neurotic person to seek psychological help. By contrast, people with *personality disorders*, who exhibit behavior patterns similar to those of neurotics, do *not* experience much personal discomfort about themselves. They may upset others a great deal, but they themselves do not get upset when others consider them to be disruptive and peculiar. Have you ever complained to someone whose behavior bothered you and had them reply, "If it bothers you, that's *your* problem"? While everyone reacts this way on some occasions, people with personality disorders employ this as their predominant response to most problems that come their way.

Before we begin to study the different types of personality disorders, it is important to note that the accuracy of this diagnosis is disputed by some psychologists. They argue that it is misleading and even dangerous to apply psychological labels based on a few unusual characteristics that are neither neurotic nor psychotic symptoms. These psychologists believe it is more accurate to say that these people have *values* different from most of us than it is to claim that they have a *psychological* disorder. A person whom some call a "drifter" or a "floater" may be said by others to be "in search of an authentic identity." Also, recalling Erikson's life-cycle concept, we should avoid the pitfall of believing that "character" is permanently formed early in life with no opportunity for changes.

To these arguments, psychologists who support the use of the personality disorder diagnosis respond that there *are* people who *do* show distinctive personality traits that stand out as extreme, inflexible, or offensive throughout their lives. They continually create problems for themselves and others, and then display the tell-tale lack of concern about their actions. Thus, even though this diagnostic label is imprecise, it does describe a psychological problem that often improves after identification and treatment. Bear this dispute in mind as you read the following descriptions of typical personality disorders.

Can you think of people who are overly fussy, neat, or critical of others? They seem to lack a sense of humor. If they seem to be rigid or perfectionists, we consider them *compulsive personalities*. This is not always such a bad thing—many such individuals become well-disciplined, enthusiastic workers who get ahead in their chosen field. (Note that if this characteristic *totally* dominates their behavior, they may become compulsive *neurotics*. However, if they function to their own satisfaction without experiencing the typical anxiety, guilt, or

SYMPTOMS OF CONFLICT

1. *You see the following letter in the advice column of your local newspaper:*

Dear Phyllis,

About a year ago I began to experience flashes of fear whenever I needed to cross a busy city street. Because traffic is so bad in this city, I felt that my fears of being run over were realistic, even if they were bothersome. These fears gradually increased until, today, I cannot even force myself across a major intersection. Even when the walk sign is on and a stream of other pedestrians is crossing, my fear is too intense to even take the first step. Needless to say, my life is severely limited by this problem, and my friends laugh at me. I don't know what to do next. Please help me.

Signed,
Desperate

If you were the columnist, how would you respond to this letter? What should the writer do?

How would a Freudian psychologist approach the treatment of someone who had this problem? How would a behaviorist psychologist be likely to deal with it?

2. *Imagine that you are a television writer who has been asked to create a character with realistic neurotic symptoms, to appear in a new series. Choose one of the neuroses presented in this section (obsessive-*

compulsive, neurotic depression, neurotic anxiety, phobia, conversion reaction), and write a one-paragraph description that summarizes how the character speaks and acts. Present your character to the class for a discussion of whether or not the neurotic symptoms are realistic and accurate.

3. *Arnie, whose case was described earlier in the chapter, began to show some unusual anxiety about his parents' departures while he was still very young. If you had been Arnie's parents, how would you have handled these first signs of trouble? Since this fear is a natural reaction, when might it become a matter of concern? Invite a local mental health professional who deals with children's psychological problems to explore the type of cases he or she treats.*

unhappiness of the neurotic, a compulsive *personality disorder* diagnosis is likely.)

Perhaps more annoying than the compulsive personality are the people who always seem to anatagonize others by blaming them, criticizing them, or acting envious or suspicious. They make mountains out of molehills and see in others their own shortcomings. They often seem to be at the center of arguments or fights. Because of this, they do not get along well with others, but are constantly irritating them. They are called *paranoid personalities*. It is important to distinguish between people with this trait in a mild form and those psychotics whose degree of mistrust puts them out of touch with reality.

672

The *hysterical personality* can be charming and attractive, with a flair for the dramatic, but he or she can also be full of surprises. How about the girl or boy who gave you the seductive "come on" only to give you "the cold shoulder" without any apparent reason? Despite their self-centeredness, such individuals seldom have trouble making friends. They may even cling to others, but suddenly change, like the familiar chameleon. They are sometimes referred to as "teasers."

There is one type of personality that seems frequently to get into more serious trouble. This is the *antisocial character*, sometimes called a *psychopath* or *sociopath*. Such people may be extremely intelligent and clever but tend to use their resources in unproductive—even harmful—ways. Their behavior seems totally uninfluenced by what others think or say about them. They may have a winning way with people, but they tend to use it to "con" them rather than to establish meaningful relationships. When they are reprimanded for misbehavior, they show no sign of remorse or guilt. In extreme situations, such individuals ultimately get into trouble with the law, sometimes through stealing, forgery, sexual "acting out," or the use of drugs or alcohol. Until they come to the attention of legal agencies, they may be thought of as resourceful or cunning. Some psychologists believe that persons with antisocial characters can be rehabilitated through treatment. Treatment may need to be carried out in secure institutions to establish the sense of control which these people usually lack. Treatment with drugs is of little use and may even increase the risk of drug addiction.

By now, it is probably apparent that the difference between neurosis and personality disorders is a subtle one.

In fact, in the next sections it will become clear that *all types of emotional conditions are differentiated from normal states according to the severity of symptoms and the extent to which they involve greater or lesser parts of the total person.* For example, a personality disorder may be more extensive than a single neurotic symptom; a psychosis is more disruptive than a neurosis; and a psychosomatic illness affects the person physically as well as mentally.

Psychosomatic Illness:
Interaction of Mind and Body

Psychological problems may be expressed through symptoms of *physical* illness as well as in the neurotic behavior pattern or character traits we previously examined. It is easy to recognize from our own experience how thinking and feeling are often intertwined with physical health. How often have we been "uptight" or "sick and tired of the whole thing"? Why do we say of someone we dislike that "he gives me a pain in the neck" or "he makes me sick to my stomach"? What do we *mean* when, if asked for our opinion about something, we say "I just have this gut reaction to it"? Have you ever "felt heartsick" about anything, such as breaking up with a friend or failing an examination?

If you are like others, you have probably used these expressions to describe *both* your feelings and your thoughts. The body responds in many ways to a whole variety of emotions. The heart pounds, the face becomes flushed, the hands sweat, the stomach has "butterflies," and the head aches when we are anxious, embarrassed, frightened, or angry. Most of the time we know what causes these feelings, but sometimes a feeling can act upon part of the body completely outside of our conscious awareness.

This common occurrence became better understood when psychoanalysts began studying certain physical illnesses which seemed especially related to emotions. In the 1930s, the following illnesses were first described as psychosomatic: stomach ulcer, migraine headaches, ulcerative colitis, asthma, rheumatoid arthritis, hypertension (high blood pressure), and neurodermatitis (itching skin). These conditions, it was believed, could be caused by intense emotional reactions in certain types of people. The term psychosomatic is a combination of "psyche" (mind) and "soma" (body).

A number of experiments clearly demonstrated how hostile feelings in a person could cause his stomach lining to become swollen and red or cause his blood pressure to rise. These discoveries became influential in American medicine, but had the disadvantage of causing physicians to think that only *some* illnesses were affected by emotions while others were entirely physical or organic. Today, all illness is believed to be influenced by psychological reactions and social conditions which are experienced as stress. Conversely, emotions and social adjustment can be influenced by physical disease.

The interaction of mind and body is now recognized as a complicated, constant process. Different emotions—rage, guilt, hate, fear, anxiety, depression—can influence the body's way of reacting with its blood, its hormones, its organs, its electrical and chemical processes (remember "The Electrical-Chemical You"). But a physical condition like thyroid disease may also have the same effects. Furthermore, a person may become depressed, frighten-

675

ed, anxious, or angry because of confinement to a hospital with a serious physical disease such as heart disease or tuberculosis. In treating the patient, the physician must carefully examine not only the physical symptoms of the condition, but also its psychological and social aspects.

The diagnoses discussed so far are all distinguished from the next category of illness in that they do not involve loss of contact with reality. We will discover that a *psychosis* differs from the previous three diagnoses in that the person *does* lose contact with reality.

Psychosis: Losing Touch with Reality

Psychosis, more than the other mental disorders, involves a mental "derangement" which can affect all aspects of thought, emotion, and behavior. A Swiss doctor named Eugen Bleuler was the first to write scientifically about the psychosis we now call schizophrenia. (Before his work in 1919, this disease, which caused intellectual deterioration for no apparent reason, was called "premature dementia" because it was thought to be a disease which made adolescents senile! This was later found to be incorrect.) Bleuler distinguished different forms of the disease by identifying the dominant symptoms.

Shattering of the Personality: The Schizophrenias

Imagine for a moment that you are visiting Bleuler's mental hospital. As you look around an open room, you see many people in a variety of moods, poses, and dress. Standing by the window, staring blankly into space and physically contorted in a very unlikely and uncomfortable manner, hardly moving at all, is a young woman who appears to be quietly thinking. She does not move or

PSYCHE AND SOMA

1. *Can you think of several ways in which thoughts or ideas can cause physical reactions? What about the reverse—physical conditions which have an effect on mental functioning?*

2. *When would the interaction between mind and body be considered an illness? After all, isn't there always a relationship between mind and body?*

3. *Have you ever heard the expression "mind over matter"? What does it mean? Can you give some examples? How would it relate to psychosomatic illness?*

4. *Every time John is about to have an exam, he develops physical symptoms: he starts to sweat, he becomes pale and nauseated, he feels weak all over. What should he do about this?*

Psychosis involves a disorder of feeling, thinking, and judgment. The person loses contact with reality, and may withdraw into a fantasy world of his own creation.

Photo courtesy of Beth Nicholson

speak when you approach, and when you try to shake hands with her, she does not vary her posture at all. Bleuler called this kind of patient a *catatonic schizophrenic*.

Another person, a slightly older man, is moving quickly about the room, gesticulating with his arms and hands, turning this way and that as though being pursued by someone. He tells you that he is being chased by people who have been instructed by God to kill him and that voices have told him to keep moving around to avoid them. Bleuler called this type of patient a *paranoid schizophrenic*.

You look around and see a rather angelic, mild-mannered woman who seems to be following you around, constantly smiling and sometimes giggling in a childlike

The paranoid person believes that people are out to get him, that he must be on guard and ready to defend himself.

way totally unrelated to any of your comments or questions. Such people, who exhibit constant inappropriate smiling or silliness, were called *hebephrenic schizophrenics*.

Another woman who looks about thirty does not appear unusual but seems preoccupied, with a dull withdrawn expression. She speaks in simple sentences when spoken to but seems uninterested in continuing the interaction. Bleuler knows more about her—that she has hallucinations and "bizarre" ideas. He called her a "*simple*" schizophrenic.

As more was learned about the schizophrenic illnesses, it became obvious that the distinct types defined by Bleuler were rare. Some people had a variety of symptoms, with some more prominent than others. Others showed different symptoms at different times. The condition might have its onset in childhood, in adolescence, after giving birth to a child (*post-partum psychosis*), or even in later life, although this is rare. *Hallucinations* (false perceptions) of hearing and vision, or *delusions* (false beliefs) were found in all types of schizophrenia. Today, not all of these people would require hospitalization, especially with the discovery of modern drugs.

It was once thought that people who could detach themselves from reality did not have any cares or worries. However, those who have experienced the condition and those who have studied it know that schizophrenia can be mental torture. A person may go to his doctor complaining of feelings of "strangeness" or "losing control," of "feeling very remote from other people and his surroundings," or "as though the parts of his body are deteriorating or don't belong to him." He may feel "frightened" and "overwhelmed" or be "without any feelings at all."

While examining the patient, the doctor may consider many alternative diagnoses, including everyday normal worries, neuroses, or the beginnings of some physical disease, like a brain tumor or even something milder like a virus. But as he talks further with the patient, the conversation may become hard to understand. The patient may invent words, start talking in a sing-song voice, or make big jumps in thinking which are unusual. He may speak about voices and sights that no one else has heard or seen and may make outlandish claims about "people coming out of air conditioners," or his "being talked about on the radio or TV." While it may be conceivable that someone is being followed by another person, the reason given for this belief is often a strange one like "because I noticed the curtain move." It is difficult for the average person to follow the speech of a schizophrenic person because it is usually full of symbolic expressions, poor logic, unconnected phrases, and nonsense words.

Many people refer to schizophrenia as a "split personality" but a more correct definition is a *disorganization of mind*. Thoughts become fragmented, disconnected, and confused. Emotions seem inappropriate, distorted, exaggerated, or altered. Behavior may be bizarre, meaningless, or purposeless. But the condition may also occur in mild form and be hardly detectable without careful examination.

Schizophrenia is the most common of the psychoses. About one in every hundred people suffer from it before reaching forty-five years of age. Those with the most severe forms are usually treated in hospitals, while the larger number with milder forms manage to live in the community, to work, to have families, and to adapt to their surroundings in ways which are sometimes called eccentric, strange, or odd. As already pointed out in the chapter on "Normality," not everyone would agree on what to call "strange." Some people, like Thomas Szasz, believe that the word "schizophrenia" is used much too frequently even though it does not have a very precise meaning. Others, like R.D. Laing, believe that what has been called "crazy" behavior is merely an attempt on the part of the person to find his or her true self.

Despite much research, schizophrenia remains poorly understood. Researchers are therefore more inclined to refer to "the schizophrenias" as a broad group of diseases with many possible contributing causes. Some scientists lean toward a biochemical explanation of the condition. The dramatic improvement in the behavior of some schizophrenic patients given drugs strengthens the idea that there is a biochemical factor. Others believe that the condition has more to do with a person's environment and early upbringing. Still others consider genetic factors important. Most likely, the cause will be found in various combinations of all three factors.

Schizophrenia is not the only form of psychosis. Severe disturbances of *feelings* are called *affective psychoses*. *Affect* or *affective* is a psychological term which means feelings. The major symptom in *psychotic depression*, for example, is a severe upheaval of feeling or affect, which is expressed as deep despair, restlessness, agitation, or even as excitement and very high spirits (*mania* or elation). Thinking may also be disturbed, but this is usually secondary to emotional changes that distort the person's perceptions. By contrast, schizophrenia involves a major disturbance of thinking and a less severe disturbance of feelings.

Emotionally Disconnected: The Affective Psychoses

The *psychotically depressed* person has a reaction which is usually far out of proportion to the situation, at least as it appears to other people. Psychotic depression is much more serious than the usual kinds of sadness or grief we all feel, or even the kind of neurotic depression described earlier. For example, if a person became totally withdrawn, stopped eating, stayed in bed, and was "convinced" that he was a very bad person who deserved to be punished for losing a wallet with ten dollars in it, we would be surprised. We would wonder why the person should change so much from an outgoing, apparently happy and talkative person to one who was slowed down in speech and physical activity, with a very sad look and maybe even tears. We would be surprised that the person could develop a bleak outlook on life—even to the extent of thinking about suicide—just because he lost his wallet and ten dollars.

Equally surprising but much harder to understand is the psychosis of *mania*. For example, after the death of his wife, a man became much *more* outgoing than usual, laughing and telling jokes, and being the "life of the party." He bought a new car, lots of clothes, and many things members of his family felt he really didn't need. Most of us would think that this man ought to be a little sad or depressed. But feeling depressed is emotionally painful, and it is the function of defense mechanisms to try to protect the person against such pain. Some defenses go to opposite extremes in trying to fight off the normal depression. Unconsciously, the person determines to "put on a happy face." In this case, the ego, which controls the defense mechanisms, tries to pretend that the distressing event does *not* cause depression. It uses the defense called *reaction formation* to keep the truth out of awareness. The extreme inappropriateness of the behavior and the loss of contact with reality makes this a psychotic rather than a neurotic reaction.

Sometimes the same person will alternate between one reaction and another—that is, become *either* depressed or *elated* in a continuous cycle—even when the situation does not change. This is called *manic-depressive psychosis*. The two opposing psychotic states of *mania* and *depression* may occur frequently and rapidly, or they may be spread out over periods of years, with emotionally stable intervals between different phases of the illness. Often there is a family history of this illness. It may even go unnoticed at times because in milder states of elation, a person may be productive, happy, talkative, and seemingly "just a normal, vigorous, lively person." But when the condition becomes a full-blown mania, the person's judgment begins to fail, he becomes very extravagant, grandiose, and overbearing, sleeps little, and eventually becomes worn out emotionally and physically. Fortunately, there are now drugs which successfully treat this condition. However, it is difficult to convince a person who feels extreme happiness that there is anything for which he should be treated.

The So-Called "Nervous Breakdown"

Not all psychotic depressions are of the manic-depressive type. Sometimes a person just "goes to pieces."

This is often called a *nervous breakdown* because it is *mistakenly* thought that conditions of great or prolonged emotional stress—such as severe physical illness and pain, poverty, torture, extreme conditions of pressure and responsibility, a life-threatening operation—cause a "deterioration of the nerves." But nerves are *physical* structures, while a psychotic reaction is an *emotional* consequence of stress. Most people are able to bounce back from even major stresses, but when stress is piled on top of stress, even the most well-adjusted person can have a depressive reaction of psychotic proportion. The person may have brief spells of hopelessness and helplessness, inactivity, and pessimism, or a sense that he is worthless, evil, dirty, and undeserving. Emotional "exhaustion" is a more accurate label than "breakdown." In more severe cases, the person may believe that others want to harm him and may become despondent enough to commit suicide. (Contrary to some people's ideas, plain hard work rarely leads to a nervous breakdown.)

In the chapter on "Adulthood and Aging," we spoke of psychological and physical adjustments which must be made as one matures. For many, a *mid-life crisis* may be accompanied by severe mood disturbance, a depression related to the many changes that occur during this phase of life. Sometimes physical or hormonal changes have been thought to cause depression as women approach menopause. Men may also experience shifts in mood during the climacteric. But depression during these years is probably caused more by psychological factors than by physical ones.

This is the time of life when a person experiences a sense of loss, and usually it is this loss which triggers depression. The man or woman in the middle years worries about the loss of youth, of attractiveness, of achievement, of ambition, of physical health. At the same time, a parent sees his or her adolescent children establish independence by leaving home for school, marriage, or a job. And the parents' *own* parents may be aging, sick, or dying in nursing homes or hospitals. The number of losses and emotional stresses at this time are sometimes too much to handle, and the person is overcome by fear, anxiety, and depression, sometimes to a psychotic degree.

If a grief reaction remains intense and prolonged after the death of a loved one, this condition may develop into a more severe or psychotic depression. It is important to seek professional help, usually from a psychiatrist who is able to give psychotherapy as well as medication and hospitalization if needed.

Other Psychotic Reactions

Besides schizophrenia and affective disorders, other psychotic reactions sometimes occur. It is possible to see the same degree of disturbance of thought, emotions, and behavior described above, although the cause is traceable to other factors.

People under the influence of certain drugs such as alcohol, LSD, STP, or dexedrine sometimes behave like schizophrenics. Frightening images (visual hallucinations) may dance before their eyes, they may think they hear messages from outer space (auditory hallucinations), or believe that they have been placed on earth for some special mission (delusions). They may become excited or agitated, and may hurt themselves or others because of a lack of judgment, or a tendency to distort everything they see, hear, or touch. In mild cases, a friend can "talk down" someone with a drug psychosis, but severe cases require medical attention and possibly hospitalization.

Psychosis also is seen in people with serious physical diseases where the chemistry of the body is substantially disturbed, either from medications, from changes in oxygen content of the blood, or from high fevers. These reactions are called *toxic psychoses*. Unlike schizophrenia, they usually are easily corrected by treating the underlying illness.

Another psychotic reaction affects memory, thinking, feeling, and behaving as a result of disease of the brain. This is called *organic psychosis*. It is caused by destruction of brain tissue, either by injury or deterioration. Some of these destructive illnesses are: long-standing syphilis, stroke, multiple sclerosis, and brain degeneration of old age (often called *senility*). Sometimes these illnesses cannot be cured. However, the symptoms can be modified with medications.

Psychosis Concluded

Words like "madness," "insanity," and "lunacy," which have been used throughout history, were more often applied to what we call psychosis than to neurosis. Poets, philosophers, and writers have generally linked insanity to a failure of reason, an inability to follow the rules of logical thinking. Actually, psychosis involves a disorder of feeling and judgment as well as thinking. This combination of disturbances often leads to a loss of contact with reality and withdrawal into fantasy, which involves a kind of creation of one's own world. Such a world may be populated by imaginary people, voices which others do not hear, and stories and beliefs which sometimes lead to loss of control over one's impulses. Psychosis, in contrast to neurosis, is much more likely to be accompanied by thrashing movements, irrational talk, and extreme distortions of relationships with other people that may lead to violence against another or against oneself.

Because of the similarities of many of the conditions described above, it is always important to have a trained professional make the distinctions. Some conditions are more treatable than others. Although we refer to psychosis as illness, it should be understood that it is not "catching" like some forms of physical illness.

Throughout our discussion of mental illness, we have seen how physical and mental characteristics often blend imperceptibly—each into the other. It is this phenomenon which makes diagnosis of mental illness so difficult and the variety of treatments so broad. In the next section, we will discuss the different kinds of therapies and the professionals who use them.

A Helping Hand (Or Ear): Therapists and Therapies

A variety of methods have at one time or another been considered appropriate treatment for the emotionally disturbed. Many of these treatments have been abandoned because they were inhumane, useless, harmful, or cumbersome. New approaches are being introduced all the time, and old ones are being questioned and sometimes discarded. The case histories described on pages 689-694 indicate the great variety of problems for which people seek help and the different ways in which that help is obtained.

MENTAL ILLNESS IN YOUR COMMUNITY

1. *Have your class plan a party for the patients of a local residence for the mentally ill. First, invite a professional mental health worker from the hospital to class to discuss what you should expect and how you can make your visit enjoyable for the patients. You may want to bring records, food, and favors. A tour of the facility may be possible before the party.*

   Often patients in mental institutions feel cut off from the real world; they have fewer visitors than patients in a hospital for the physically ill do. Some students may want to make regular visits or plan other events for these patients.

   What are your impressions of the mental health facility?

   Of the patients whom you visited?

   How do both compare with your expectations before the visit?

2. *What problems might people face when they are discharged from a mental institution?*

   In what ways does their return to the community differ from the situation facing those who have had a physical illness?

   How can a former mental patient be aided in rejoining his family and beginning work? Investigate whether there are any local voluntary groups that help patients make this transition. (Recovery, Inc. performs this function in many communities.)

3. *Should a person with obvious psychotic symptoms, who is not dangerous to himself or others, be forced to receive treatment for his condition?*

   Should a psychiatrist be able to hold that person against his will for enough time to make the determination of whether or not he is "dangerous"?

   What legal safeguards are there to protect the patient's rights and to determine the accuracy of the psychiatrist's diagnosis? Invite a local psychiatrist, judge, or attorney (or all three) to class to explain how your community deals with these issues.

4. *"Insanity" is a defense to criminal charges. Invite a local attorney to class to help you explore what this legal term means; why it prevents a criminal charge; and what alternatives it offers the defendant instead of a criminal trial.*

Case 1: George M.

GEORGE M. is a twenty-two-year-old man who has a good job working as an electrician's assistant. He is physically active, works hard, and likes his boss even though he is fairly demanding. Lately, George has had severe headaches which interfere with his ability to do his best work. Some days the headaches are so bad he even has to stay home. After a month of this, George began to worry that he might have something serious like high blood pressure or a brain tumor, so he decided to see his family doctor. The doctor asked George a lot of questions and gave him a thorough physical and neurological examination. While he did not find anything to make him concerned, he still had George see a neurologist for some special studies and further examination.

The neurologist found no physical disease to explain the headaches. George returned to his family doctor, who spent some time asking George about his personal life— his job, his habits, his home life, his family. He learned that George's headaches seemed to come on when he became concerned that he was not doing well enough on his job and was afraid his boss would be dissatisfied. The doctor also learned that George's father had always had high expectations of George and that George felt in some ways that he had really let his father down by going into the kind of work he chose. George's doctor felt that the headaches were related to emotional strain connected with his job and also with his father. He suggested a referral to a psychiatrist.

George first experiences a physical symptom and consults his doctor for an examination. Through a series of examinations, tests, and a careful history-taking, George's problem is identified as psychological. The stress of his job and the relationship with his father have triggered an old emotional problem (neurosis) for which psychotherapy is indicated. George is referred to a psychiatrist because his complaints involved physical symptoms related to emotional distress.

Case 2: Betty F.

BETTY F. is a twenty-five-year-old woman who was married three years ago to a man she had known only briefly before marriage. In the first months of their marriage, they seemed to get along very well and looked forward to having children, but as "a family" became more of an issue, Betty found herself less and less interested in sex and now had begun to worry about it. She began to have questions about her marriage and about herself. She went to her local mental health clinic and was advised to meet with a social worker, who first saw Betty for several visits and then saw Betty and her husband together for marriage counseling.

Betty's difficulties seemed clearly related to problems which grew out of her marriage. While she herself required individual consultation with a social worker, marriage counseling was important to clarify the relationship between her and her husband. It is doubtful that Betty's problems stem from any physical ailment, although a medical examination would still be important.

Case 3: Margaret Z.

MARGARET Z. is brought by her daughter to the emergency room of her local hospital because she has been showing increasingly strange behavior over the past three months. She is eighty-three years old, and at first the family thought she was becoming senile. But now, in addition to mumbling to herself and not recognizing her relatives, she suddenly has begun throwing things around the kitchen and showing peculiar movements of her face and arm. The doctor in the emergency room examined Mrs. Z. and advised the daughter that her mother should be admitted to the hospital for diagnostic studies to rule out the possibility of a brain tumor.

Because of her age, Mrs. Z. had been considered by her family to merely be showing "signs of senility." But gradually her behavior worsened and there was some question of whether she might be psychotic. Because of the sudden change to violent behavior, an emergency examination became necessary. Before a definite diagnosis could be made, it was necessary to: (1) be sure Mrs. Z. was not taking medications that might cause a toxic psychosis; (2) do neurologic studies to rule out the possibility of a brain tumor causing an organic psychosis; and (3) take a careful history to be certain that she did not have manic-depressive psychosis. Because of the need for careful observation and protection—as well as for studies and medication—hospitalization was necessary.

Case 4: Sam

SAM, a high school junior, has begun to think about applying to college next year. As he thinks about leaving home and going away to school, he begins to worry about how he will manage and notices that he is having more difficulty than usual in studying and getting his work done. He decides to see his guidance counselor, who talks with him about his concerns.

Sam's dilemma about college is a common one among

692

students who approach their final year of high school. He is concerned about his chances for getting into the school of his choice. He is not even certain which school would be best for him, given his specific interests. A school guidance counselor can provide Sam with helpful information and a sense of direction, and can assess whether his problems are more complicated than they seem.

Case 5: Andy

ANDY, a graduate student working for his Ph.D., has been having problems for a long time which he has generally been able to manage by himself. But now he begins to question his purpose in life, feels that he has sacrificed social relationships for academic success, and realizes that in general he has not been very happy for many years. As he begins to write his thesis, he finds that the words just won't come and he becomes very frustrated. He realizes that there is probably some connection between how he feels and his inability to write his thesis. He sees a college psychiatrist at the health center who suggests, after three visits, that Andy would benefit from psychoanalysis.

Andy has always been a good student, but he feels that his social life has lagged behind his academic achievements. As he continues further with his studies, he realizes that he is in the "same old rut," begins to feel depressed, finds himself losing interest in his work, and feels further demoralized because he does not even have the satisfaction of achieving academically. He recognizes that his problem is not new and that it represents many

Andy's academic success was achieved at the cost of personal happiness. Andy's problem was not new: it represented many years of a repetitive pattern. Sometimes people need help in order to break out of a rut. Andy's sense of frustration led him to seek treatment.

years of a repetitive pattern which has limited his total development as a person. In discussing his concerns with a psychiatrist at his college health center, it is suggested that psychoanalytic treatment will help him to understand his past so that he can better structure his future. He is referred to a psychoanalyst.

These examples illustrate only a few of the ways in which people obtain help. There are many different types of professionals and many places where treatment is offered. The following descriptions of therapists and therapies may help you to understand how such decisions and choices are made.

Who Treats Emotional Disturbance?

The answer to this question depends partly upon the type and severity of the problem. It also may depend in part upon how you perceive your own problem. If you feel it is mainly physical, you may go to your family doctor. If you feel it is mainly emotional, you may go to a psychologist, a counselor, a psychiatrist, a psychoanalyst, or a social worker. What are the differences among these helpers?

The *family doctor* has graduated from an accredited medical school with an M.D. degree, has had additional training as an intern, and possibly has had special training in other areas such as family practice or internal medicine. He is someone you can turn to with a general problem, and most often he can advise you about whether you should seek help from some other specialist. Some family doctors have developed counseling skills from working with many different people or from taking special courses to help people with minor psychological problems, sexual difficulties, or problems with drugs and alcohol.

The *psychiatrist* is also a doctor of medicine (M.D.) and has had special training in psychiatry, usually for three or more years. During this training, he learns general medicine, but specializes in knowledge about human behavior, which includes an understanding of emotional problems. In addition to learning about psychotherapy for individuals and groups, he also learns about the use of medication (drugs) to treat certain kinds of mental disturbances. His experience includes working with people as both inpatients (hospitalized) and outpatients.

To become a *psychoanalyst*, the physician must take additional training which includes a personal psychoanalysis to help him understand himself better, and about five years of postgraduate courses in an institute for psychoanalysis. Not all psychoanalysts are physicians. Some may have a background in psychology, social work or some other field. A non-medical psychoanalyst is fully qualified to practice psychoanalysis but cannot provide medical or pharmacologic (drug) treatment.

A *psychologist*, as distinguished from the medically oriented psychiatrist, usually has obtained a Ph.D. degree requiring three to five years of study after college. This training may emphasize clinical psychology, research, or teaching. Those who intend to practice psychotherapy usually must intern for one or two additional years in a clinical setting where their work can be supervised by more experienced practitioners. Most psychologists learn how to administer special diagnostic tests. Psychologists work in hospitals, clinics, schools, and other organizations. Those who qualify are certified by their state psychological association to treat patients in private practice.

The *social worker* has a college education, often in psychology or sociology. In addition, two years of advanced training in a graduate school of social work are required to earn the Master's Degree in Social Work (sometimes called M.S.W.). While social workers are trained to provide a number of services, many specialize in counseling and psychotherapy (or casework) and often work closely with psychiatrists and psychologists in hospitals, mental health clinics, schools, or family agencies. Their training includes intensive course work and supervision in how to diagnose, treat, or refer individuals with emotional difficulties.

Some *psychiatric nurses* are trained to provide counseling and psychotherapy, but they must have additional education beyond general nurse's training. Usually they obtain a Master's Degree in Nursing. Such professionals play a major role in general hospital work, psychiatric hospital treatment teams, and mental health clinics. Some nurses may see patients in private practice, usually with supervision by a psychiatrist.

A *counselor* may have a wide range of experience and education. Some have taken special programs in college or graduate school to prepare them for working with young people in schools and colleges. Even though many have backgrounds in teaching, they must all have experience and training in psychology. They may also work in mental health facilities which are not affiliated with schools (such as hospitals and clinics).

Another important member of the mental health team is the *occupational therapist*. Many patients, because of physical or emotional difficulties, are unable to carry on in their normal manner. This, in turn, leads to further emotional distress. The occupational therapist (O.T.) is specially trained to help these people discover new areas of interest, thus raising their psychological morale. The therapist's training cuts across the boundaries of medicine and psychiatry. He does not merely help patients to fill time by doing arts and crafts. He is trained to understand the interaction of physical skills and psychological well-being.

One can see from the list of professionals who offer counseling that help can potentially be made available for everyone who seeks it. It is true that it is expensive to have treatment with private practitioners. The fees range from fifteen to fifty dollars for a session of about fifty minutes, depending upon the therapist's training. But it is also possible to obtain help at a much lower fee at community mental health centers; at state, private, or general hospital outpatient clinics; or at family service agencies. If a person requires hospitalization as part of his treatment, there are psychiatric units in general hospitals, state psychiatric hospitals, private psychiatric hospitals, and veterans' hospitals. Health insurance usually pays for psychiatric treatment only in these facilities. Often, high schools and colleges maintain their own health services which provide counseling or treatment.

Varieties of Treatment

If you have appendicitis, there is little question about what kind of treatment is needed. But in the area of psychological adjustment and emotional problems, treatment has a much broader scope. Also, because there is disagreement about what mental illness is, diagnosis is not always clear-cut. This means that ideas about treatment will vary even more.

Treatment of any physical ailment assumes that there is something "wrong" as perceived by the individual patient or by others. In appendicitis, the person experiences *symptoms* such as pain, nausea, and fever. The physician *diagnoses* the condition by means of careful

Very often, individuals who sense that they could use help hesitate to ask for it. Whether you seek help or not depends on the extent to which you perceive something in yourself that concerns you, and on the degree to which you are interested in doing something about it.

examination, blood tests and x-rays. If the diagnosis is confirmed, the *treatment* is surgical removal of the infected appendix.

Likewise, the objectives of any kind of psychotherapy (literally "treatment of the mind") are also to relieve symptoms and to bring about a greater degree of comfort in the individual. Whether you seek help or not depends on the extent to which you perceive something in yourself that alarms you, and on the degree to which you are interested in doing something about it. If your situation is bearable, if you are not *always* unhappy with yourself, if you feel you are accomplishing what you want to, then it is

699

unlikely that you will voluntarily seek help. Sometimes you may not be dissatisfied with yourself but find that others consider your behavior to be the result of "personal problems." These people might suggest that you get some form of help, either brief counseling or long-term treatment.

Often, individuals who sense that they could use help hesitate to ask for it. Sometimes they are afraid of being ridiculed by friends or family. Sometimes they think that therapy "only concentrates on finding out your weaknesses" or that "therapy will take away characteristics in myself that I like—creativity, sensitivity, and so on." Several observations may alleviate these fears: (1) the earlier you "catch" a problem, the better it responds to treatment; (2) while treatment is certainly concerned with your "problem areas," its major focus is on the *strengths* and abilities you are not using, for psychological reasons; and (3) therapy cannot "take away" your personality, but can help you to expand your capacities so that you use everything you have. Contrary to the fear that "you have no control over your treatment," you have a great deal of control over it. How you use your treatment is up to you. Therapy is a collaborative effort, and can be a very creative experience.

If you feel you have "problems," how do you know what kind of treatment to seek? Naturally, it is as difficult for a person to diagnose his own emotional problems as it would be to diagnose some physical ailments. It is therefore important to consult one of the professionals described previously to determine the best form of help for a specific problem. Treatment may be brief or lengthy, on an individual or a group basis, with a person trained specifically in counseling techniques or with someone with a medical background.

Psychological tests can be helpful in detecting early signs of problems of which you may not even be aware. Many people equate psychological tests with measurements of intelligence, but the tests are much more than that. They can provide information to a skilled psychologist about how our defense mechanisms are functioning, whether we might be depressed and not know it, whether we are fighting internal battles with ourselves that could possibly result in psychosomatic diseases, and whether certain kinds of symptoms might be related more to physical causes than to psychological ones. Some of the tests measure understanding, judgment, and insight. Others explore our ability to make up stories which indicate the richness of our fantasy life. Tests like the famous Rorschach Ink-Blot Test and the Thematic Apperception Test (T.A.T.) can be fun to take. Making up stories to go with the ink-blots or pictures is much like creating a dream. The stories reflect our past experiences, our desires for the future, and how we perceive the world in general. Results of these tests are often helpful to a therapist in understanding our personality and behavior, and in providing the best treatment approach to specific problems.

In general, the less severe problems are usually handled adequately with some form of psychotherapy or counseling. For example, those conditions described as neurosis or personality disorders usually respond to counseling, psychotherapy, or psychoanalysis. The simpler forms of psychotherapy may consist of little more than brief guidance, reassurance, support, or some degree of re-education. The more complicated forms may require anywhere from one to five sessions per week. The goal is to understand and change one's basic patterns of behavior. Which form of psychotherapy is undertaken depends upon the training and skill of the therapist, the motivation of the person seeking treatment, and the relationship between the therapist and the patient.

Another approach to treatment of "problems" is called *behavioral therapy*. Behavioral therapists are not as concerned with the introspective aspects of the treatment, or even with the nature of the relationship between the patient and the therapist. In the behaviorist approach, problems are considered more a function of "habit" or "poor learning"; the focus is on using conditioning or "counter-conditioning" methods to help the person change his behavior. The terms which refer to such methods are *desensitization, reciprocal inhibition, conditioned avoidance, aversive conditioning,* and *positive* or *negative reinforcement.* Many have found these techniques effective and less time-consuming than the psychotherapies described above. *In some cases, a combination of the two approaches has proven extremely useful.*

For more serious emotional disorders, such as manic-depressive psychosis, schizophrenia, or severe depressive illness, a number of treatments called *somatic* (physical) *therapies* have been used for many years. Such treatments are often given in a hospital and require the skills of a medically trained psychiatrist. A number of these somatic treatments have fallen into disfavor, such as *insulin coma treatment* for certain types of schizophrenia, or *lobotomy* (cutting part of the brain) for a severe, unmanageable psychosis. The treatment called *electroconvulsive therapy* (ECT), however, has remained an important

702

emergency treatment for severe (usually suicidal) depression which does not respond to the newer drugs. While this treatment may sound extreme, its results are often dramatic and the patient rarely feels any pain or discomfort, even though the treatment produces a series of "invisible" convulsions by means of a mild electrical current passed through the nervous system. Because of occasional indiscriminate use, some states are now imposing careful regulations on the use of this form of treatment.

The chapter "The Electrical-Chemical You" mentions a remarkable new addition in the treatment of mental illness, the development of the field of *psychopharmacology* (drugs for the treatment of mental illness). Sometimes called *psychoactive agents*, these drugs—introduced in the early 1950s—have made it possible to completely change the atmosphere of psychiatric hospitals and help patients return to a useful life much sooner than ever before. Drugs to treat depression (*antidepressants)* and psychosis (*antipsychotic agents or major tranquilizers)* have had the greatest impact and are sometimes used along with psychotherapy for certain conditions. While these drugs are usually reserved for the most distressing symptoms, a group of drugs called *minor tranquilizers* are sometimes used by physicians to help patients relieve anxiety which causes sufficient distress to interfere with day-to-day functioning. *Lithium,* an old medication, has found recent use in the treatment of manic-depressive illness and has brought relief to thousands who did not respond to more traditional methods of psychotherapy or drug treatment. All these drugs must not be used carelessly because they all have potentially serious side effects.

While most individuals with emotional disorders can be treated as outpatients, some with more serious symptoms are best treated in a hospital where more continuous nursing, medical, and psychiatric care are available. Treatment in a hospital may include all the methods mentioned above, in addition to other approaches. Some hospital units emphasize the *therapeutic community*, often called *milieu treatment*. This means that the environment is regulated in a way intended to be therapeutic.

In the hospital, a *team* of psychiatrists, psychiatric nurses, occupational therapists, social workers, mental health counselors, and recreation therapists assist patients in learning to cope effectively with their problems. Sometimes patients need lesser degrees of hospitalization. This is accomplished through so-called *partial hospitalization* programs during part of a day or a night.

Group therapy, in which people with problems meet to learn more about themselves, is a method of treatment used both inside and outside hospitals. So many types of groups have developed that it is difficult for a person to know which ones are legitimate and which are not. (The chapter "Group Dynamics" offers some advice about selecting a group for therapeutic purposes.) An outgrowth of group therapy is the *family therapy* approach which involves meetings of various family members in different groupings with a therapist specially trained in this method. The objective of family therapy is to help not only the individual person with his problem but also to help other members of the family recognize how they are contributing to or aggravating the situation.

A HELPING HAND (OR EAR): THERAPISTS AND THERAPIES

1. *Invite representatives of different "schools" of therapy to your classroom and have a panel discussion about the variety of approaches to treatment. For example, invite a clinical psychologist, a behavioral therapist, a psychoanalyst, a social worker, and so on.*

2. *Try role-playing a patient and a therapist. While this may be difficult to do, it will bring up for discussion some important feelings about and reactions to "problems."*

Suggested Reading

Axline, Virginia, *Dibs: In Search of Self* (Boston: Houghton Mifflin, 1965).

Baruch, Dorothy, *One Little Boy* (New York: Julian Press, 1962).

Bettelheim, Bruno, *Love Is Not Enough* (New York: The Free Press, 1950).

Elliott, David, *Listen to the Silence* (New York: Holt, Rinehart and Winston, 1969).

Gogol, Nikolai, *The Diary of a Madman* (New York: New American Library, 1961).

Grant, Vernon, *This is Mental Illness: How It Feels and What It Means* (Boston: Beacon Press, 1963).

Green, Hannah, *I Never Promised You a Rose Garden* (New York: Holt, Rinehart and Winston, 1964).

Greenfeld, Josh, *A Child Called Noah* (New York: Holt, Rinehart and Winston, 1972).

Kaplan, Bert, *The Inner World of Mental Illness: A Series of First Person Accounts of What It was Like* (New York: Harper and Row, 1964).

Kesey, Ken, *One Flew Over the Cuckoo's Nest* (New York: Viking, 1962).

Levin, Meyer, *Compulsion* (New York: New American Library, 1968).

Lindner, Robert, *The Fifty-Minute Hour* (New York: Bantam Books, 1954).

McCullers, Carson, *Reflections in a Golden Eye* (Boston: Houghton Mifflin, n.d.).

Neufeld, John, *Lisa, Bright and Dark* (New York: New American Library, 1970).

Rogow, Arnold, *The Psychiatrists* (New York: Dell, 1971).

Rubin, Theodore, *Jordi/Lisa and David* (New York: Ballantine, 1973).

Schreiber, Flora, *Sybil* (Chicago: Regnery, 1973).

Stone, Sue and Alan Stone, *The Abnormal Personality Through Literature* (Englewood Cliffs, N.J.: Prentice-Hall, 1966).

Szasz, Thomas, *The Myth of Mental Illness* (New York: Harper and Row, 1974).

Thigpen, Corbett, and Harvey Cleckley, *Three Faces of Eve* (New York: McGraw-Hill, 1957).

Wilson, Louise, *This Stranger, My Son* (New York: G.P. Putnam's Sons, 1968).

16.

A Community Probe

The following cases illustrate realistic problems in community mental health that are difficult to resolve. Your task is to decide, first, what information you need to deal with the problem, and, second, where you can find that information in your own community. Hopefully, you will use this opportunity to invite a variety of people who make important decisions about mental health matters to join your class discussions. The "Telephone Workbook" at the end of this chapter can help you identify the range of psychological support services available.

An Unhappy Family

WANDA AND JIM married soon after graduating from high school. Their son Tad is already six years old. Yesterday, Tad's teacher told Wanda that Tad is "hyperactive" and "unmanageable" and that his parents would have to do something about his behavior. Jim and Wanda are furious but also worried. They drop by your house to let off some steam and to get a friend's advice. What do you suggest they do?

Would a medical exam be appropriate? Where can that be done in your area? What will happen if Jim and Wanda cannot afford expensive medical treatment?

If the medical exam reveals no physical problems, what do you advise then? Are there any social stresses impinging on Tad? Might he be experiencing some mental or emotional difficulties? How could you determine this by using local agencies?

If Tad's parents take him to a psychological counselor, how will that person approach Tad's problem if he has a Freudian orientation? Will it be different if he has a behaviorist orientation?

Several days later, you meet Jim in a department store. When you ask how things are with Tad, Jim looks uneasy and says that Wanda is "looking into all aspects of the problem." You hear nothing more for two weeks. Suddenly, Wanda appears on your doorstep and dissolves into tears. When she recovers her composure, she explains why Jim acted so strangely and why you haven't heard from them. "Tad is okay, at least physically speaking," she says. "The doctor definitely ruled out the 'hyperactivity' diagnosis, and I was happy about that, but then he suggested that Tad might be unhappy about something, that Tad's behavior might be connected with something happening between Jim and me. You probably don't realize it, but there's been some trouble between us for some time. Well, anyway, I told Jim what the doctor said to me. Do you know what Jim replied? He said that it was all my fault, that I'm not satisfied with being a good mother and wife, and he went on and on like that. It was terrible!"

Wanda started to cry softly. Then she continued: "I told Jim that it was time we went to see someone, for Tad's sake as well as for our own, but Jim says he refuses to have anything to do with a 'headshrinker.' And I wouldn't know how to find one, anyway. I just don't know what to do, where to go. At least I can talk to you. How can I get help? How can I make Jim *understand?*" Wanda stopped speaking and waited for you to respond.

> Do you think that professional counseling is necessary? For which people? What type of counseling? How can you go about finding psychological help, assuming that you don't know anyone who could give you a personal reference? Is there any way to get a preliminary diagnostic interview to see if there is a problem that needs psychological help? If so, what does it involve, where can you get it, and how much does it cost?
>
> Can you think of any reasons based on psychological theory why six-year-old Tad is acting "unmanageably"? What special factors might be operating at this age?
>
> Do you think Tad should be seen alone by the counselor or as part of his family? How can Wanda get Jim to agree to visit the counselor with Tad and her? What reasons can you use to reply to Jim's argument that: "Shrinks never help anybody. Why, I had an aunt who went to one for three years and only got worse. What can someone like that do for me? This is just something Tad will grow out of. I was the same way"?

Tad's problems brought to the surface some marital difficulties between Wanda and Jim. What kind of resources are available in your area to help couples who are having trouble relating to each other? How is joint therapy for couples different from individual psychotherapy? How can psychological counseling help a marriage in trouble?

As you listen to Wanda, you are reminded of a painful period in your own life. Your parents divorced when you were about eight years old. You can recall the whole ugly process in vivid detail. After a long court battle over custody, you were placed with your mother. That didn't end the trouble, however. She would constantly tell you that your father was despicable, that he didn't visit you because he didn't like his children, that he spent money that was supposed to be for you on alcohol and other women. Also, she would let comments slip out about how she couldn't really have a good time in life because she had to look after you.

The scars of that experience will stay with you forever. You would like to help Jim and Wanda avoid hurting Tad like that if they eventually decide to divorce. You wonder what should be done to protect children who are losing a parent through death or divorce. How can you help a child to cope with fear and anxiety about changes?

If you *do* have to give advice to Jim and Wanda about the problems of a child when his parents separate, what will you say? If you wanted to get advice on such matters, where could you go in your community?

"It's better not to bring the matter up with the child;

he's too young to understand the complex adult world." If someone suggests that you deal with a problem in that manner, what is your response? How can you find out what a child is thinking? How can you explain difficult matters like divorce or death to a child?

Crisis Intervention

Early one evening, you hear a pounding on your door and open it to find Debbie Dern, the seven-year-old from next door, crying hysterically about an accident in her house. You rush back with her to find Timmy, her three-year-old brother, screaming on the kitchen floor. Debbie says that her mother went in the back bedroom a long time ago and won't wake up. In the bedroom you find a half-empty bottle of pills sitting open on the night-table. Mrs. Dern appears to be unconscious.

> If you need emergency help in your community, where is the best place to call? (Police station? Fire station? Hospital? Where can you find the numbers in a hurry?)
>
> Do you know the latest first-aid techniques? If not, where can you take a refresher course in your area?

In the emergency room of the hospital, Mrs. Dern recovers consciousness after her stomach is pumped. She wants to leave the hospital, refusing the advice of a staff psychiatrist that she stay overnight to rest. "There is no one else to care for my two children until my husband returns from his latest truck run," she insists.

712

A Community Probe

A psychiatrist can usually retain someone against his or her will if there is a "danger to self or to others," or some similar standard that varies from state to state. Usually, this involuntary confinement can only last a short time before a legal commitment hearing must be held to justify further detention. Suppose you are the psychiatrist in this case. How will you go about deciding if Mrs. Dern poses a danger to herself or to others? Will you keep her in the hospital? If so, what will you do about the children? If the neighbors or friends cannot help, what public agencies can help care for the children temporarily?

Mr. Dern returns from his truck run the next day. In a conversation with the psychiatrist, he recalls how his wife's behavior had gradually deteriorated over the past months. First, she stopped visiting friends; soon she stopped going out of the house at all; then she began to neglect the house and the children, spending all her time in the bedroom crying or staring sullenly at the television. Mr. Dern regrets that he didn't take some action sooner to avoid this unfortunate event. On the psychiatrist's recommendation, Mr. Dern agrees to sign commitment papers so that Mrs. Dern can be kept in the hospital for treatment against her will. Mrs. Dern plans to contest this decision at the legal hearing, and she has contacted a local attorney to represent her.

What could Mr. Dern have done to find help for his wife earlier?

What procedures exist in your state to protect the interests of people who are being committed for psychiatric treatment against their will? If you were

713

the lawyer representing Mrs. Dern, how would you argue the issue of commitment? What if you were the lawyer representing the psychiatrist and Mr. Dern? If you were the judge, what questions would you want answered? Under what conditions would you commit Mrs. Dern for more treatment?

If Mrs. Dern stays in the hospital for prolonged treatment, how can Mr. Dern arrange for the care of the children?

Who pays the bill for extended psychiatric treatment if Mr. Dern cannot afford it?

Two weeks later, Mrs. Dern has recovered sufficiently that the psychiatrist is prepared to release her. First he wants to arrange some supportive services to help Mrs. Dern return to her home and community life.

What voluntary groups or public agencies could the psychiatrist call to help arrange such a program?

Before Mrs. Dern took the overdose of pills, the school nurse had spoken to Debbie at the request of Debbie's teachers. There were some health problems that clearly needed attention, and Debbie often missed school without an excuse. Mrs. Dern did not answer the nurse's notes about these problems, and the nurse began to worry that Debbie was being neglected by her parents.

What kind of health services are offered by your school? What can be done for a child who needs mental health services? What happens if the parents of a child refuse to cooperate? What is meant by "child abuse" and "child neglect"?

714

A Telephone Workbook

Every city and town has a telephone book. If you know how to use it properly, you can learn about the variety of counseling and psychological support services available in your community. The advantage of being able to use the telephone book to find help is that you can use this resource anywhere in the United States, even when family or friends are not available to make recommendations based on their own experience with different agencies. You will probably be surprised to find many services that you weren't aware of in your own community! Investigate what is available under these headings:

WHITE PAGES

Name of your State (e.g. Massachusetts)
Hospitals
Mental Health
Public Health Department
Public Welfare
Social Services

United States
Health, Education, & Welfare
Social & Rehabilitative Services

Children

Parents

Name of your City or Town

YELLOW PAGES

Mental Health Services

Psychologists

Physicians

Psychiatry

Marriage (or Marital) Counseling

Family

Social Service Organizations

Child Guidance

V.

Thinking About Yourself

17.

The Uses of Psychology

Man's main task in life is to give birth to himself, to become what he potentially is.

ERICH FROMM, *Man For Himself*

As we watch our lives unfold day by day, we may sometimes wonder where we are headed. It is natural to view the future with both eagerness and fear. We dream of a rich and full life still to be lived, of joys and satisfactions, growth and wisdom. At the same time we fear the unknown, that which we cannot predict and cannot control. Will all our carefully made plans come to pass?

We look for hints of the future in a variety of places. For some people, the daily horoscope may be just as much a part of their early morning routine as a cup of coffee. Others eagerly pry open Chinese fortune cookies and grin with pleasure when they are promised success. Yet when we put aside such playful self-deception, we are faced with an unknowable future. To what extent will we be able to guide the course of our lives? How much are we subject to the mysterious forces of Fate and Chance? Will the lives we have already lived prevent us from becoming what we wish to become?

719

Photo courtesy of Kenneth M. Bernstein

Life: Sometimes we move with skill and thought to reach our goals; sometimes we plunge ahead—into trouble. But we always have the potential to evaluate our mistakes, to learn from them, and to grow.

Think back to your own time line, which you charted in the "Introduction" of this book. What assumptions did you make about your future? Did you predict a smooth or uneven line of progress to your goals? Did you weave together joy and sadness, success and frustration? Would you draw your time line differently now?

While we cannot be sure what lies ahead, psychology does give us a roadmap to the future far more reliable than horoscopes and fortune cookies. Psychology teaches us to see the *patterns* in our lives, the *roles* that we play, and the *defenses* we have built. We can, in fact, look to the past to predict our futures. This is true whether we are Freudians who deal with inner thoughts and feelings, or Skinnerians who measure observable behavior shaped by learning and reinforcement.

If as children we are encouraged to try new ventures and to develop our own ideas and opinions, we are more likely to enter adolescence with the self-confidence and curiosity to do well. Yet if we were either overprotected, neglected, or discouraged from developing our own initiative and individuality in childhood, we are less likely to be independent, assertive adults. Without this self-assurance and drive, it may be difficult to achieve the goals which we seek. We also know that it is necessary to gain a basic trust in ourselves and in the world during childhood if we are to be able to give and receive love. In short, psychologists have taught us to look for the *basic building blocks of emotional, social, and intellectual development* in explaining human behavior.

Psychologists have also taught us to recognize the *complexity* of human behavior. We know that both women and men can be "socialized" into playing the roles a culture expects of them and that members of both sexes may have conflicting feelings in trying to express their *total* personalities. Women may learn to fear success; men may suppress certain emotions.

Psychologists tell us that we are different people in

721

groups than as individuals. We may be both leaders and followers, depending on the situation. Our behavior may be manipulated by social influences and pressures. Advertisers may win us over by appealing to our basic insecurities. The media may distort our world view. Authority figures may push us to abandon our moral judgment.

We have also learned that there is a wide range of *normal* behavior. Sometimes we may feel that we are "going crazy" or are "losing control" of ourselves. We have to be reminded that it is normal to feel depressed in certain situations or pressured in others. It is normal to get angry when someone insults you and to express this anger. It is normal to feel insecure and assume others are brighter or "sharper" than you are. It is not uncommon to resent a loved one's death and feel guilty about what you should have done for that person over the years. It is common to have an identity crisis in adolescence, and another in middle age; to have conflicting emotions towards the same person or situation; to want to return to the security of the past yet move on to the challenge of the future. We all share similar emotions and feelings, doubts and insecurities, even though we may express them differently.

Psychologists have taught us, then, that we continue to develop all our lives, building on our past experiences. Human behavior is complex. We are influenced by many factors: inborn aptitudes and dispositions, early learning and encouragement, cultural expectations, ethnic styles, sex-role stereotypes, and relationships with others. Yet we can *predict* many of the tasks and hurdles we face as we progress through life, and therefore we will be better able to cope with them. *We can hope to explain why we feel and act the way we do* as we unravel the "mysteries" of behavior through the study of psychology.

With this greater self-awareness, we may then be able to grow and to change, to break out of self-defeating patterns of behavior. We will no longer say, "I can't help it," or "I don't know why I do this." We will rely less on excuses, rationalizations, and Fate to explain our behavior. Psychology helps us interpret our past and gives us guidelines for the future. In appreciating our potential for growth and personal fulfillment, we may take hold of our lives and begin to actively shape them.

Psychology and Our Lives

You do not have to become a counselor or social worker to profit from the continued study of psychology. We are all amateur "psychologists" everyday of our lives. We may use a certain *strategy* to get through a difficult situation; we try to *guess at* other people's motivations; we *predict* the consequences of our actions. We *interpret* another person's mistakes; we learn to *handle* a friend's sensitivities; we try to *pinpoint* the causes of our own moodiness. In all our interactions with others, we constantly apply the principles of psychology.

Whatever job or career we choose, whatever life style we assume, whatever our goals and values, we will function better with an understanding of human behavior. Cultures and customs may differ, and what is "normal" may differ accordingly, but there will still be a rational explanation for how the people think, act, and feel. Psychology is a *universal* language.

PSYCHOLOGY AND OUR LIVES

1. *Imagine that you are the manager of a large insurance company. During the past year, one third of your salespeople resigned, and you would like to know why. You would also like your staff to make up a questionnaire to give all new applicants for these positions. To correct this situation, what kinds of information do you need to know about those who resigned, those who stayed on, and those who apply?*

2. *As a military psychologist, you have been asked to screen and test a number of candidates for a new army post in a remote section of Alaska. All candidates selected will be assigned to this post for two continuous years. Describe the type of person you feel would be most likely and least likely to succeed in this job. Explain the reasons for your choices.*

3. *The principal of the junior high school has asked you to come to the office. As the school psychologist, your advice is needed to help the principal in dealing with a new eighth-grade English teacher. The teacher's classes have been noisy, chaotic, and out of control since the opening day of school. No other teacher has such trouble.*

    What would you want to know about the teacher?

    What would you want to know about the class?

How would you help the teacher to regain control of the class?

4. *As a prison psychologist, you have been asked to analyze the recent series of riots, sit-ins, and demonstrations at the state prison.*

Whom would you question and what would you want to know about the situation?

What measures would you suggest to help return the prison to order?

5. *You are a lawyer defending a client charged with a serious crime. Since you have the right to veto potential jurors, you have to decide what types of people will be most sympathetic to your client.*

How will you decide on your choices? As the nature of the crime varies, do your jury choices change?

6. *You are a fund-raiser for a hospital. You need to raise several thousand dollars in one month or the hospital will go bankrupt.*

How will you choose your potential donors?

How will you convince them to give?

What appeal could you make to the community?

How might you advertise your plight in order to get help?

Glossary

accommodate   Piaget's term for adjusting one's perceptions to conform with the reality of a situation.

affective   Pertaining to feelings or emotions.

ambivalence   Conflicting or mixed feelings toward a person or situation.

amygdala   A part of the "old brain" which influences emotions.

anal stage   The second of Freud's psychosexual stages. The young child is ready for toilet-training; the child's struggle with parental control is dominant.

androgens   Biochemical hormones which produce and maintain male traits and characteristics.

anti-convulsant drugs   Medications which control seizures.

anxiety   A general feeling of uneasiness, apprehension, or fear.

anxiety hierarchy   A list of situations which elicit anxiety, arranged in order from least to most disturbing.

assimilate Piaget's term for viewing the world from one's own perspective; learning or absorbing information in the context of one's own experiences.

aversive conditioning A behaviorist term for the process of shaping behavior by punishment instead of by positive reinforcement. Skinner argues that this form of conditioning is ineffective.

avoidance A defense mechanism described by Freud in which anxiety is controlled by avoiding a feared person, situation, or conflict.

axon The nerve fiber that carries an electrical charge or impulse away from the nerve cell.

behaviorists Psychologists who emphasize the study of overt, measurable behavior rather than inner thoughts and feelings.

biofeedback A technological means for picking up information about physiological processes normally not accessible to our awareness and converting that information into an intelligible set of signals.

brain, new A large, complex mass with many folds that surrounds the old brain on all sides. It controls a wide range of perceptions and behaviors including speech, thought, and learning mechanisms. It is technically called the neocortex or cerebral cortex.

brain, old A part of the brain located inside the cover of the neocortex and at the top of the brain stem. It controls emotions and the general level of arousal in the body.

brain stem A part of the old brain located at the base of the brain and at the top of the spinal cord which controls basic functions like heartbeat, breathing, sleeping, and temperature.

brainstorming   Thinking up all the possible solutions to a problem.

catatonia   A psychiatric classification for describing a person who is motionless and unresponsive to what is going on around him.

catharsis   The emotional release felt when one identifies and discusses a problem which has caused anxiety and tension; figuratively, it means "getting something off one's mind," and thus feeling relieved.

chemotherapy   Therapy which involves the use of medications or chemical substances.

chromosomes   The small particles which contain genes, the transmitters of hereditary characteristics. Half of a person's chromosomes (23) come from the mother and half (23) from the father.

client-centered therapy   A "non-directive" technique of psychotherapy initiated by Carl Rogers in which an individual is encouraged to talk about his problem by a supportive, nonjudgmental, empathetic therapist. It is assumed that the person will be able to define and work out his problem in such a supportive situation.

climacteric   A period in life when the body is undergoing physiological changes; it is customarily used to describe changes occurring in men in their forties and fifties when male hormones are decreasing. It is sometimes accompanied by feelings of depression, loss of sexual interest, and loss of motivation.

cohesion   A measure of the strength of the bonds among members of a group, or of how "tightly knit" the group is.

compensation   The attempt to emphasize positive or strong traits or skills in order to make up for or disguise that which is weak, lacking, or inferior in oneself.

complementary transaction   Eric Berne's term from transactional analysis which means that two persons are following the same paths in their communications involving their "Parent," "Adult," and "Child."

compromise formation   A Freudian term referring to the attempt to achieve one's goal through an indirect, partial, or less satisfying method because direct or complete satisfaction is being frustrated or prevented.

compulsion   The need to repeatedly perform certain acts even though they are irrational and poorly understood.

concrete-operational stage   The ages between seven and eleven when, according to Piaget, a child learns, among other things, to reason, manipulate concepts mentally, follow rules, understand physical laws, and classify objects.

conditioning   A behaviorist term referring to the process of shaping behavior by influencing the consequences which follow an action. A positive consequence or reward for an action increases the likelihood that that action will be repeated. Behavior is thus learned because it brings positive results. See also *aversive conditioning*.

consensual validation   The process by which a person's

interpretation of reality is reinforced and strengthened because others share the same perception.

conservation ability Piaget's term for understanding the principle that the amount of a substance remains the same regardless of its shape or form; understanding of what is constant in a situation despite perceptual changes.

conversion neurosis A feared emotion or desire is repressed and converted into a sensory or motor disability affecting sight, movement of a limb, or other physical processes.

counter-conditioning Extinguishing a pattern of behavior that has been instilled by conditioning, and replacing it with a new pattern by a new process of conditioning.

counterphobic behavior The act of doing something that is feared, in order to master the anxiety associated with such behavior.

crossed transaction In terms of transactional analysis, it means that two people have a conversational exchange in which one person addresses someone else's "Parent," "Adult," or "Child," and the respondent addresses a *different* level (Parent, Adult, or Child) of the first speaker.

defense mechanisms A Freudian term for psychological devices used by the ego, usually *unconsciously*, to reduce one's level of anxiety. The person *distorts* reality in some way in order to feel less anxious or frustrated.

delusion A strong belief, held despite conclusive evidence that it is invalid and unrealistic.

dendrites   Nerve fibers that conduct electrical messages (or impulses) toward the nerve cell.

denial   A defense mechanism by which emotions or thoughts not acceptable to one's self-image are pushed out of consciousness, rejected, or disowned.

desensitization   A method of behavioral conditioning or retraining designed to remove strong and irrational fears by gradual degrees of exposure to that which is feared.

deviate   Someone whose attitude or actions differ from accepted group standards; as a verb, to differ or depart from the norm.

diagnosis   Identification and classification of a disease or disorder as a result of careful examination of a person.

displacement   A defense mechanism which redirects the expression of a wish or an emotion from one object to a different one which seems safer or more acceptable.

dissociative reaction   A reaction to severe stress in which an individual represses, or erases from conscious memory, episodes or periods of his life, as in amnesia.

ego   Freud's label for the thinking, reasoning part of the personality which helps to satisfy one's needs in a socially acceptable manner. The ego copes with the reality of a person's situation. Used more generally, ego means one's concept of self.

electroconvulsive therapy   See *shock therapy*.

electroencephalograph   A machine that records electrical activity in a person's brain and converts it into wave-like patterns charted on paper by means of an ink-tipped wire that oscillates between two magnets.

embryo   An organism in its initial stages of development before birth; in humans, the organism from conception up to the eighth week of pregnancy. See *fetus*.

empathy   Understanding how another person feels; being able to put oneself into another's place and share that person's feelings.

estrogens   Female hormones produced mainly by the ovaries; they influence the development of female sex characteristics.

existentialism   The philosophy that people must create their own meaning in life, that they are responsible for the kind of people they become, and that despite adverse circumstances, they have the ultimate freedom to choose their attitude and behavior. The underlying belief is that human existence is unexplainable, and every individual faces a unique and isolated experience in an indifferent and sometimes hostile world.

experimental method   A rigorous, scientific method for testing hypotheses or assumptions about behavior.

fantasy   That which is imagined or made up in one's mind, often without reference to reality; a daydream in which a wish is fulfilled.

feedback   A term coined by psychologist Kurt Lewin to describe the information people receive from others about their behavior.

fetus   The unborn human being between the eighth

week of development and birth. See *embryo*.

fixation   A situation in which a person cannot seem to progress beyond a certain stage of development because the person fears he will not be able to cope with the demands of the next stage. Also, an unusually strong attachment to something.

formal operational stage   According to Piaget, the time from adolescence on, when one can think abstractly, make judgments, and discuss political, scientific, or religious concepts.

free association   A Freudian technique of psychological investigation and psychotherapy. A person is encouraged to let his mind wander freely from one subject to another and to report all thoughts to the therapist. The aim is to eventually reconstruct significant patterns and issues in the person's life.

free-floating anxiety   Diffuse and generalized anxiety with no specific cause and out of proportion to any real threat; a gloomy, pessimistic feeling that something bad is going to happen without any definable reason to believe so.

Freudian slip   A slip of the tongue (or pen) in which a person's hidden thoughts replace or interrupt the more socially acceptable statement he had planned to make. It is believed to reveal an unresolved inner conflict.

functional theory of leadership   In this theory, a leader is defined as someone who performs an act that helps the group meet one of its needs.

game   A set of ulterior communications or transactions

which fit together and progress by steps to a predictable ending, with a pay-off, as described by Berne in *Games People Play*.

genes   Tiny units within chromosomes which carry the traits or physical characteristics one inherits.

gestalt psychology   A school of psychology which states that behavior must be understood as a *total* pattern rather than as isolated thoughts, feelings, or actions. In other words, the whole is greater than the sum of its parts.

group therapy   Psychological treatment of individuals through their interaction with each other in a group setting under the supervision of a trained therapist.

guidance counselor   A person with training in psychology and counseling who usually works with students in a school setting.

heredity   Those characteristics which are biologically passed from parents to their child and which help to shape his individuality.

homeostasis   A steady state, a balance, an equilibrium, usually of a physiological nature.

hormones   Biochemical substances produced by one of the body's organs and transmitted to different parts of the body where they influence other physiological processes.

hypochondria(sis)   The persistent but unreasonable fear that one is ill, or is likely to become so.

id   The name given by Freud to that part of the personality consisting of one's impulses, instincts, wishes, needs, and drives; the pleasure-seeking part of the personality.

idealism The desire (often unattainable) for things in their most perfect, finest, and fairest form.

identity crisis Erik Erikson's term for the time in adolescense when one struggles to define who he is, and what he wants out of life (goals, values, and the like). More generally, any time one re-evaluates his life, groping for a sense of purpose and direction.

inferiority complex A term used by Adler to describe the feeling one has that one is lacking or weak in a certain way, as compared to others; a sense of inadequacy.

innate Inborn, that with which one is born.

insanity A *legal* term referring to mental disorder. A person who is ruled insane by a court of law (after the commitment of a crime) is usually placed in a psychological treatment facility rather than a regular prison. Mental health professionals rarely use this term.

intellectualization A defense mechanism of dealing with an issue solely on an intellectual level, without allowing one's emotions to become involved.

intelligence quotient (I.Q.) A figure determined by dividing one's mental age (as measured by testing) by one's chronological age and then multiplying by 100. On most tests, an I.Q. of 100 is considered to be average. I.Q. tests measure specific academic abilities and are used to predict one's potential for success in school. Their usefulness has been questioned due to possible culture bias and other imperfections.

736

interpersonal competence A term coined by psychologist Chris Argyris to refer to (1) accurate perception and interpretation of situations, (2) ability to solve problems so that they stay solved, and (3) ability to find solutions that permit parties to work together afterwards at least as effectively as before.

intimate distance The area within 18 inches of a person, as defined by Hall.

latency The period between the ages of 5 or 6 and adolescence when a child's interest in his sexual self diminishes and the child becomes more absorbed in an expanding world of school, friends, and activities.

logotherapy Frankl's term describing a technique for helping a person to find the meaning (logo) in his life, a reason for living.

manic-depressive Psychotic behavior in which a person fluctuates between periods of extreme elation (feeling very high) and extreme depression (feeling very low).

menopause The time when a woman's capacity to bear children ends and her estrogen level decreases. Sometimes it is accompanied by depression, irritability, a changing self-image, and bothersome physical symptoms.

mid-life crisis A time during the late thirties or early forties when people question the values and priorities in their lives, feel frustrated that they are not going to accomplish all that they had hoped, and sense that time is running out on them. There is restlessness, a longing for youth, and a fear of death. It is a time for re-evaluation and redirection of their lives. It sometimes coincides with the climacteric or menopause.

moral realism   Piaget's theory that a child decides the goodness or badness of an action based on an assessment of the personal, physical consequences that the action will bring him.

narcissism   Excessive love and admiration of oneself.

neocortex   See *brain, new.*

nerve cells   The microscopic cells which specialize in transmitting impulses (electrical messages) throughout the body to integrate our perceptions, thoughts, and actions.

nervous breakdown   A severe emotional reaction to substantial, prolonged stress, characterized by feeling helpless, hopeless, unable to function, depressed, and immobilized.

neurosis   An emotional or mental state characterized by the repetition of self-defeating behavior which is inappropriate for the situation. It is usually caused by underlying anxiety. While the neurotic perceives reality correctly, he nonetheless has trouble changing his behavior.

neurotic anxiety   Fear and worry for no obvious reason or far out of proportion to the situation.

neurotic depression   Persistent and unreasonable feelings of sadness sometimes accompanied by symptoms of tiredness, withdrawal from others, lack of motivation, feelings of inferiority, and the like.

neurotic fear　An unreasonable, intense fear, often called a phobia. Closely related to neurotic anxiety.

non-directive therapy　See *client-centered therapy.*

norm　The behavioral pattern expected of members of a group; a standard or range regarded as typical for a group, against which an individual's performance can be measured; a statistical average for a certain kind of behavior or performance.

normal　Conforming to a usual, typical, or standard pattern. (Sometimes this word is used to convey a value judgment that the standard pattern is *better* than other patterns.)

obsession　A term for neurotic behavior characterized by preoccupation with a certain idea even though it may be irrational or unpleasant.

obsessive-compulsive neurosis　A neurotic reaction in which a person experiences persistent, unpleasant thoughts (obsessions) and feels the need to perform certain ritualistic acts over and over (compulsions).

occupational therapist　A person trained to help motivate people who have been physically or psychologically disabled, by enlisting them in creative or productive activity.

oedipal stage　According to Freud, the time between three and five years old when children become aware of and interested in their genitals; they masturbate, are jealous of the same-sex parent, and have fantasies of exclusively possessing the parent of the opposite sex. Also called the phallic stage.

oral stage   A Freudian term referring to the first year of life when an infant's major preoccupation is sucking, eating, taking in the world; a time when one is helpless and totally dependent on others.

organic psychosis   Mental disorder resulting from deterioration of or injury to the nervous system, or from certain physical deficiencies or abnormalities in the body. See also *toxic psychosis*.

paranoia   A system of false beliefs held by an individual that he is being persecuted, that people are against him or out to get him. Paranoid is a term for neurotic or psychotic behavior characterized by such false beliefs.

peer group   People of the same age, rank, or standing.

personal distance   The area between 1½ and 4 feet around a person as defined by Hall.

personality disorder   A mental/emotional disorder characterized by personality traits which are troublesome and persistent. The individual shows little concern or guilt over his behavior even though it bothers others.

phallic stage   See *oedipal stage*.

phobia   An exaggerated, irrational fear, such as claustrophobia (fear of being closed in or confined) or acrophobia (fear of heights).

physiological psychology   The study of the connection between behavior or sensations and biochemical processes in the body.

post-partum depression   The depression a woman may experience shortly after giving birth to a child.

740

prenatal Before birth.

preoperational stage The years from two to seven when, according to Piaget, a child learns the use of words and language, and can communicate thoughts and desires. The child's thinking is still limited, however: he assigns life to inanimate objects, is egocentric, assumes there is a purpose to everything, imitates others, and so on.

projection A defense mechanism which makes it possible for a person to deny an emotion or thought in himself by attributing it to others.

proxemics The study of the way people use space.

psychiatric nurse A nurse with specialized training in mental health and illness.

psychiatrist A medical doctor with advanced, specialized training in psychiatry. The only mental health professional licensed to prescribe drugs and certain other treatments.

psychoactive drugs Drugs used specifically to treat distressful psychological symptoms.

psychoanalysis A theory of personality and a method of psychotherapy originated by Freud which seeks to bring into awareness unconscious feelings and desires, in the hope of resolving old conflicts and inhibitions learned in one's childhood.

psychoanalyst A person trained in Freudian theories and techniques of psychotherapy. Many but not all psychoanalysts are also medical doctors.

psychologist A person with advanced training in

psychology who may be involved in teaching, testing, research, or clinical work with clients.

psychology The study of mental processes and behavior: how people think, feel, and act; more generally, the study of the behavior of organisms.

psychosis A serious mental disorder in which an individual loses some degree of contact with reality and exhibits various abnormal symptoms in his thought processes and emotional behavior.

psychosomatic Pertaining to the delicate interaction between mind (psyche) and body (soma); that which is both physiological and psychological.

psychosurgery A method of treatment in which parts of the brain causing severe mental disturbance which is otherwise untreatable are selectively destroyed.

psychotherapy A broad term which includes the treatment of personality and behavior problems by a variety of methods.

puberty The biological age of adulthood, the age when one is physically capable of sexual reproduction.

public distance The area 12 feet or more away from a person, as defined by Hall.

rationalization A defense mechanism in which the person explains his behavior by making up plausible but untrue reasons for his actions in order to maintain his social standing and self-respect.

reaction formation A defense mechanism in which unacceptable feelings and behavior are covered up by the exaggerated expression of the opposite feelings and behavior. The person's real desires and feelings have been repressed.

reality therapy   A form of psychotherapy developed by William Glasser which stresses the ability to change behavior by committing oneself to realistic and responsible programs of action.

reflex   A natural, unlearned, automatic response by a part of the body, such as a blink, sneeze, or knee jerk.

regression   A defense mechanism in which a person retreats to an earlier and more secure stage of development.

reinforce   To make a behavior more likely to occur in the future by systematically rewarding it.

repression   A psychological process described by Freud in which painful or anxiety-provoking thoughts and feelings are pushed out of awareness into one's unconscious; also regarded as a defense mechanism.

role   The expected behavior of an individual as determined by a group.

role strain   The emotional pressures an individual feels in trying to meet the expectations of others and himself concerning his role.

sanction   The punishment imposed for violation of group norms; or, in another sense, approval and support for an action.

schizophrenia   A group of psychoses characterized by a disorganization of thoughts, inappropriate or blunted emotions, bizarre or purposeless behavior. (*Catatonic form*: withdrawn, uncommunicative, motionless behavior; *paranoid form*: feelings of being persecuted; *hebephrenic form*: inappropriate smiling or silliness.)

Secondary gain   A kind of satisfaction one gets from exploiting a symptom, even though the symptom itself restricts a person's functioning or relationships.

self-actualization   Maslow's term for the process of trying to fulfill one's total potential, to make "actual" what is as yet unrealized potential.

sensorimotor stage   Piaget's term for the stage from birth to about two when a child explores the world through his senses: smelling, touching, hearing, tasting, looking.

shaping   The process of conditioning behavior step-by-step toward a desired goal (successive approximation).

shock therapy   A method of treating mental problems by use of an electric shock of strength sufficient to produce a convulsion (which is not visible because of medications given during the treatment).

sibling   A sister or brother.

Skinner box   A box used in conditioning experiments with animals. It contains a lever which, when pressed, may deliver a reward (such as a food pellet) to the animal. It was made famous by behaviorist B. F. Skinner.

social distance   The area between 4 and 12 feet around a person, as defined by Hall.

social microcosm A small group whose characteristics are representative of the larger world.

social worker A person with an advanced degree (two years of study and field work beyond the bachelor's level) who specializes in counseling, case work, and therapy.

socialization The process through which an individual learns the values, attitudes, skills, beliefs, and priorities of a particular group of people. The person incorporates these as his own.

sociogram A diagram outlining interpersonal relationships in a particular group of people.

sociometry Study of relationships of people in groups by quantifying preferences and other characteristics.

stereotype A conventional and usually oversimplified belief which does not allow for individual variations; that which conforms to a typical, unchanging pattern.

stress Any adverse, injurious, or unpleasant condition suffered by an individual, disrupting that person's equilibrium. Also used to refer to the psychological impact of the stress.

stressor A force or stimulus which produces psychological (or physical) stress or injury.

sublimation The rechanneling or redirection of an original wish or desire into an indirect but more socially acceptable outlet of expression, such as intellectual, artistic, or humanistic endeavors.

subliminal perception Absorption of information in

one's unconscious or subconscious mind which is not consciously registered.

successive approximation Shaping, or conditioning behavior step-by-step toward a desired goal.

superego A Freudian term for the "moral" part of the personality, especially one's conscience, learned from one's parents and culture—it defines what is "right" and "wrong" behavior, and makes one feel proud or guilty.

synapse The tiny gap between the inbound nerve fibers of one nerve cell and the outbound fibers of another nerve cell.

tachistoscope A film projector which flashes images or messages on a screen lasting just a fraction of a second.

token economy An environment constructed to reinforce behavior by using tokens which can be exchanged for rewards of a person's choice.

toxic psychosis Loss of touch with reality due to drugs or serious physical disease which alter the body chemistry.

transactional analysis A theoretical system for explaining behavior which evolved from Freudian ideas. Behavior is analyzed as a set of exchanges or transactions involving the "Parent," "Adult," and "Child" parts of one's personality. See Berne's *Game People Play* or Harris' *I'm O.K.—You're O.K.*.

transference The Freudian concept that previous styles of relating to others are used in present interactions. In therapy, a patient may relate to the therapist in ways the patient formerly related to someone important in his earlier life—such as a parent—and about whom the patient has conflicting and unresolved feelings.

ulterior transaction A term from transactional analysis referring to communications with double messages, one part of which is hidden or unconscious and aimed at a secret goal or "pay-off."

veil of ignorance A way of making moral decisions suggested by philosopher John Rawls. If you imagine that you will be one of the people involved in a dilemma, but you don't know *which* person you will be, you are more likely to make a decision which will be fair and just for everyone.

Index

Index

activating defense mechanisms, 658, increased, 658; normal, 661; symptoms of neurotic, 661; reaction to serious illness, 675-676; influence on body, 675; psychotic degree of, 685; minor tranquilizer used to relieve, 703; definition of, 727. *See also* free-floating anxiety

anxiety hierarchy, 283
definition of, 281, 727; example of, 281-282.

anxiety neurosis, definition of, 550.

anxiety states, definition of, 550.

Apgar test, 21.

approval, as basis for moral decisions, 509, 511.

Argyris, Chris, on "effective interpersonal competence," 411.

Asch, Solomon, and Matching Lines Experiment, 475, 484-486.

assimilate, definition of, 37, 728.

associate, definition of, 264.

asthma, as psychosomatic illness, 675.

attitudes, shaped by childhood, 13.

autonomy
as basis of second stage of emotional development, 51-52; importance of choice in developing, 51.

aversive conditioning
definition of, 271, 728; as used in behavioral therapy, 702.

avoidance, 224-226, 660
example of, 224-226; as response to aggression, 497; definition of, 728.

awareness group, *see* encounter group.

axons, 318 (diagram, 319)
definition of, 728.

B., Stephen, case history of, 258-263, **265**, **343**; Freudian approach to, 258-259, 260; behaviorist approach to, 259-260.

Bacon, Sir Francis, on beauty, 540.

balance
physical and psychological, 592-593, 597; essential for good health, 593; threatened by stress, 593, 597; maintaining, 597.

Barbara's thoughts at age seventeen, **91-93**.

Bardwick, Judith
on pressure on boys to become independent, 362; on girls' images of themselves, 363; on changing sex roles, 380; on obstacles to career women, 382-383.

Barthel, Joan
description of empathy, 617-618; on dying friend, 618.

Beaumont, and study of gastric activity and emotions, 591.

Beethoven, Ludwig van, 647.

behavior
basic patterns of, 5; study of, 8, 183, 184; child's learning of acceptable, 34, 270, 324; as product of physiology, 185, 255, 303; causes of, 185; changing, 185; towards others, 251; as product of inner states, 255; observable, 255; as product of environment, 260, 262-263, 266, 284, 292; as product of reinforcement and conditioning, 266, 292; as caused by electrical stimulation, 302, 303-304; as controlled by brain, 302, 311, 315-317, 321, 360; as product of internal chemical and physical processes, 305, 308, 309; predictions of, 341; as affected by

Browne, Sir Thomas, on death, 632.

Calley, William, 514, 520.
Cameron, Norman, on "normal" person in our society, 542-543.
Camus, Albert, 529.
cancer, 593
  as affected by stress, 593, 600.
Cannon-Bard, emergency theory of emotions, 554.
career, *see* work.
career women, 155
  negative attitudes towards, 378; and family responsibilities, 378-379, 383.
Carroll, Lewis, 541.
Casals, Pablo, 168.
case history
  on marriage, 127, 128-129, **132**, 136; on mid-life crisis, 128, 129-130, **132**, 156-157; on retirement, 128, 130-131, **132**, 170; on behaviorism, 258-263, **265**, 343; on effect of environment, 289-293; on brain surgery, 327-332, **343**; on group dynamics, 393-396, 399-401; on problems which require outside help, 689-695; on marriage and divorce, 708-712; on suicide, 712-714.
catatonia, definition of, 729.
  See also schizophrenia, catatonic.
catharsis, definition of, 190, 729.
Cervantes, Miguel, 3.
characteristic(s), personality
  under genetic control, 16; originating in oral stage, 27; originating in anal stage, 28.
characteristic(s), physical
  determination of, 15; heredity of, 16.
chemotherapy, definition of, 729.
child(ren)

personality of, 34, **35**; having, 147, 149-151; reaction of parents to, 360; perception of own sex, 360; importance of age to, 361; importance of sex to, 361; difference between adult and, 502; development of sense of worth, 560-561; development of sense of self-love, 561; transition from receiving to giving love, **562-565**; protectiveness of known fears to, 587; immobilized by fear, 587; and death, 622, 624-625, 626-630.
childbirth
  preparation of body for, 17; positive and negative aspects of, 371; stresses of, 602.
childhood
  memories of, 13, **15**, 74, 232; as most crucial period of life, 13; earliest beginnings of, 15-21, **20**; infancy period of, 21-24; Freud's theories of development, 25-36, **35**, **73**; memories recreated through psychoanalysis, 35; Piaget's theories of development, 36-49, **48-49**, **73**; Erikson's theories of development, 50-54, **73**; development of self-image in, 54-62, **61-62**; as affected by birth-order, 62-65; influence of siblings on, 65-70, **60-70**; summary on, 70-72, **74**; as beginning of career development, 135; stress experienced in, 601; effect on later life, 721.
chromosomes, definition of, 15, 729.
chronic anticipation, as result of unreleased anger, 568, 571.
"chumships," 88.
Cirino, Robert, on impact of media, 467.
classification, ability of child to

641; as symptom of mental illness, 652-654; normal, 661-662,
721; neurotic, 662; "anniversary," 662; as reaction to serious
illness, 675-676; psychotic, 681,
685; treatment for severe, 702-
703; antidepressant as treatment for, 703.
Dern Family, case history on attempted suicide, 712-714.
desensitization, 280-283
used to remove anxiety, 280-
283; used to treat neurotic reaction, 668-669; used in behavioral therapy, 702; definition
of, 732.
devaluation, as defense, 478.
development, child, 13, 26-54, **73**
beginning at conception, 21;
Freud's theories on, 25-36;
Piaget's theories on, 36-47, **48-
49**; Erikson's theories on, 50-54;
self-image in, 54-62, **61-62**; of
moral sense, 495-502.
development, human
"stages" of, 5, 27-34; as sequence of events, 13; oral stage
of, 27; anal stage of, 27-28;
phallic (Oedipal) stage of, 28-
34; infantile sexuality as normal
part of, 539; normal disappointments of, 553.
deviate, definition of, 732.
dexedrine
producing schizophrenic behavior, 685; and suicide, 741.
diagnosis, 650-654
Szasz on, 542; definition of,
650-651, 732; damaging nature
of labels, 651; four categories
of, 652; way to make, 652-654;
differing degrees among categories, 674; of schizophrenia,
680.
"difficult baby," 24.
dignity, 289.

discipline, as love- or power-oriented, 57.
disease, hereditary, 16.
displacement, 211-213, 216-217,
238-239, 599, 660; example of,
211-213; definition of, 213, 732.
dissociative reaction, 668
definition of, 668, 732.
divorce, 148-149, 708-712.
doctor, family, counseling skills
of, 695.
Dostoevsky, Fyodor, 649.
Douglas, William, 168.
dream, 191-197
and free-association, 191, 194;
as studied by Freud, 191-197,
193; and wish-fulfillment, 194-
197; in which repressed emotion is revealed, 533, 579.
See also REM period
drugs, 323-327, **325**
affecting fetal development,
19; used to alter mood, 308;
anti-convulsant, 323-326; psy-
chotherapeutic, 326-327; anti-
depressant, 326; anti-psychotic, 327; and biofeedback, 337.
Dryden, John, on wit and madness, 649.
Dubois, W. E. B., 168.

"Easy baby," 24.
Ecclesiastes, 597.
egg, 15, 16.
ego, 203-204, **210**
definition of, 25, 732; interaction with id and superego, 26,
34, 204, 206-208; as reality-oriented part of personality, 203-
204; conflicts of, 208, 210-211,
228; as employer of defense
mechanisms, 211, 213, 220, 223,
683; development of, 230;
effects of psychoanalysis on,
236; as indication of emotional

normality, 539; influence on aggression, 576; effect of stress on, 593, 658; compromising with id, 658.

"ego preoccupation," 172.

"ego transcendence," 172.

egocentric, definition of, 39.

"eight-month anxiety," 51.

Electra complex, definition of, 358.

Electric Shock Experiment, 520
description of, 469, 472-473; explanation of, 475-479.

electroconvulsive therapy, *see* shock therapy.

electroencephalograph (EEG); 304-305, 324; used to study dreams, 306-308; as biofeedback instrument, 334, 336; definition of, 732.

electrode, 302
used in brain surgery, 303, 328; in EEG, 304; in biofeedback experiment, 335, 336.

Elisabeth, Fraulein, and Freud's use of free association, 190-191.

Elkind, David, on child's confusion over names, 38.

embryo
development of, 16 (diagram, 18); definition of, 733.

Emerson, Ralph Waldo, on friends, 113.

emotional development
Erikson's eight stages of, 50; first four stages of, 50-54; painfulness of, 54; importance of self-image, 54; as affected by birth order, 62-68; based on constitutional make-up and learning experiences, 532-533; as building block of behavior, 721.

emotional exhaustion, 684
hard work alone as rare cause of, 550, 684; as more accurate

term than "nervous breakdown," 684; caused by stress, 684; symptoms of, 684.

emotional resistance, definition of, 637.

emotions, **554-555**
expressed by males, 361, 532; expressed in groups, 420; ambivalence of, 529-536, 545-546, 721; reality of, 530-531; varieties of expression, 531-536; based on constitutional make-up and learning experiences, 532, 533, 556; style of expression, 533; experiencing through feelings, 535; experiencing through thoughts, 535; experiencing through words, 535; experiencing through memories, 535; experiencing through behavior, 535-536; "connectedness" of, 550-553; basic, 553-556; love, 556-565, **567**; anger, 565-574, **577**; aggression, 574-577; humor, 577-586, **586**; fear, 586-589, **589**; interaction of emotions and body, 589-593, 597; response of body to, 674; influenced by illness, 675; in schizophrenia, 680.

empathy
used in client-centered therapy, 244; definition of, 521, 733; as important aspect of moral development, 521; when dealing with dying, 617; description of, 618; and grief, 632.

"empty-nest syndrome," 159.

encounter group(s), 420-427, 440
reliance on social microcosm, 422; use of feedback, 422; special exercises, 422, purpose of, 422, 423; harmfulness of, 423-424; precautions to take before entering, 425-427.

endurance, 635.

effects of mother's age, 18; effects of mother's medical history, 18; effects of smoking, 18-19; effects of drugs, 19; effects of emotional stress, 19; effects of Rh Factor, 19.

fetus
physical development of, 16, 18; definition of, 733.

fibers, of nerve cell (diagram, 319); inbound, 318, *see also* dendrites; outbound, 318, *see also* axons.

first-born, 63-64
tendencies of, 63-64; I.Q. of, 68.

fissure Rolandi (diagram, 317)
definition of, 315.

fixation, 599
definition of, 224, 734.

Fletcher, John, **634**.

formal operational stage, 40-41
definition of, 40, 734; child's development during, 40-41.

Frank, Anne
on self-criticism, 97; on idealism, **111**.

Frankl, Viktor, 184, 246-250, **254-255**; on need for hope for the future, 246-247; on meaning of life, 247-248; on giving meaning to life, 248-249; on freedom of choice, 249-250, 253; as his approach differs from Freud's, 253.

free association, 190-191, 205, 209
applied to everyday mistakes, 198-199; as used in psychoanalytic therapy, 235; definition of, 734.

free-floating anxiety, 209-211
definition of, 209, 734; as most distressing, 550.

freedom, 288, 289, 294
unimportance to behaviorism, 293.

Freud, Anna, on "normal" adolescence, 80.

Freud, Sigmund, 25-36, 184, 187-205, **201-202**, 208, 228, 233, 241, **254-255**, 303, 314, 315, 576, 619, 721; theory on structure of personality, 25-26, 184, 202-209, 228; theory on psychosexual stages of development, 26-36, 35, 73, 230-232, **238**; on two goals of normal person, 120-121; discovery of the unconscious by, 188-201; use of hypnosis, 188-190; use of free association, 190-191; self-analysis of, 191; study of dreams, 191-197; on dreams, 194; study of unconscious conflicts, 198-200; use of psychoanalytic therapy, 232-237; on psychoanalysis, 234, 236; influence on new theories, 237; basic approach to behavior, 253; on psychological differences between sexes, 358-359; opponents of his views, 359; ideas about normality, 538-539; Freudian psychology and aggression, 576; relation of id and unconscious and jokes and laughter, 579; on jokes, 580; on death, 608, **633**.

Freudian slip, 198-202, **201-202**
as expression of repressed emotion, 533, 579; definition of, 734.

Fried, Barbara, on "middlescent forty," 157-158.

Friedenberg, Edgar, on adolescents, **84**.

friends
as important part of adolescence, 113, 115; and mutual reinforcement, **279-280**.

Fromm, Erich
on career choice, 136; on love, 145-146; on happiness, 146; on

as response to overcrowding, 447; terminal, 612-618, **619**, *see also* illness, terminal; influenced by stress, 675; influenced by emotions and social adjustments, 675-676; producing toxic psychosis, 686.

illness, psychosomatic, 674-676, **677**; result of exhausted defense mechanisms, 636; as diagnosis, 652, 654; definition of, 674.

illness, terminal, 611-617
effect on near-relative, 611, 617; special problems of, 612; study by Ross, 612-617; importance of communication about, 614; grief and, 622; and suicide, 641.

image
of peer group, 113; from occupation, 137.

imitation
child's use during preoperational stage, 39; in Oedipal stage, 232, 359.

independence, 101-105
adolescent need for, 101-105, **106-108**, 224; encouraged by parents, 103; in early adulthood, 154; in mid-late 30s, 154-155; of boys, 361, 364; positive effect of, 362.

individuality, preserved in marriage, 147.

industry, as basis of fourth stage of emotional development, 53.

infancy, as stage of development, 24.

infant(s)
personality of, 23-24; relationship with mother, 24; difference between male and female, 354-355; need for love, 560; indication of fear in, 587.

inferiority complex, 99-101
as first step to self improve-

ment, 101; definition of, 736.

Ingham, Harry, and Johari window, 412 (diagram, 413).

initiative, 52-53
as basis of third stage of emotional development, 52-53; vs. guilt, overlapping with Oedipal stage, 53.

innate, definition of, 736.

input, as means of positive reinforcement, 275.

insanity, definition of, 736.

instinct, as part of id, 25.

insulin coma treatment, 702.

intellectual development, 36-49
shaped by early years of life, 13; potential influenced by heredity, 16; Piaget's theories on, 36-49; most decisive period of, 45-47; as building block for behavior, 721.

intellectualization
of anger, 571; definition of, 736.

intelligence, 44-47
developed through growth and experience, 38; measuring, 41-44; influenced by environment, 44-45, 46-47.
See also I.Q., test(s) of; intelligence test(s).

intelligence quotient (I.Q.), 44-45
test(s) of, 41, 45, 540; raising, 44-45; of identical twins, 44; influenced by environment, 44-45; definition of, 736.

intelligence test(s), 41-44
as measure of quality of intelligence, 41; on floating objects, 42-43; fallibility of, 45; used to test influence of "self-fulfilling prophecy," 274-275.

interaction, 449-450
of id, ego, superego, 26, 34, **35**, 204-205, 206-208, **210**, 253, 256; of mind and body, **325**, 589-593, 675-676; affected by seat-

Milgram, Stanley, 475-479
  and Electric Shock Experiment, 475-479, 520, 525; on desire to obey authority, 477, 479.
Mock Prison Experiment, description of, 473-474, 480-484.
Money, Dr. John, and study on children raised as opposite sex, 385-386.
Montaigne, on death, 607.
moral development
  Piaget's theories on child's, 495-502; Kohlberg's theories of, 502-514; six stages of, 505-506, **515-520**; Punishment-Obedience Orientation, 506-508; Instrumental Relativist Orientation, 508-509; Interpersonal Concordance Orientation, 509-511; Law and Order Orientation, 511-512; Social Contract-Legalistic Orientation, 512-513; Universal Ethical Principle Orientation, 513-514; importance of, 514, 520-521; stimulation of, 521-525; through role-taking, 521, 524-525; through discussion, 521-523; ways to discuss, 522-523.
moral dilemma, examples of, 491-492, 492-494, 498-499, 503-505; **523**.
moral issue, 494-495, **496-497, 523**
  definition of, 494; physical demonstration of conflicts involved in, 591.
moral principles, as basis for moral decision, 513-514.
moral realism
  definition of, 499-500, 738; used by child, 500-501.
moral reasoning
  three levels of Preconventional Level, 506-509; Conventional Level, 506, 509-512; Post Conventional Level, 506, 512-514.

"moratorium," definition of, 83.
Moss Howard, on maternal love, 22-23.
motivation
  physiological drives as basis for, 237; in structured environment, 287-288; study of consumer, 456-457; used by advertisers, 460; result of tamed aggression, 575.
motivational research, in advertising industry, 456.
Mussen, Paul, study on parents as role models, 365.

Namath, Joe, 460.
names, child's confusion over, 38.
Napoleon, 101.
narcissism
  and adolescent love, 564; definition of, 738.
National Institute of Child Health and Human Development, 17.
"nature vs. nurture," 47, 70.
  See also intelligence, influenced by environment
needs, general, 458.
neocortex, *see* brain, new.
nerves, as physical structure, 684.
nerve cells, 311
  definition of, 309, 310, 738; as body's messenger system, 318-321 (diagram, 319).
nervous breakdown, 683-685
  hard work alone as rare cause of, 550, 684; as result of exhausted defense mechanisms, 636; as not caused by neurotic reactions, 668; as less accurate term than emotional exhaustion, 684; definition of, 738.
nervous system, 318-321
  and emotions, 556.
Neugarten, Bernice, 168

and id in, 34; as overlap with Erikson's third stage of emotional development, 53.

Oedipus complex, 30, 358
description of, 30-33; universality of, 33-34.

old age, 165-175, **177**
conditions of, 167-168; economical difficulties in, 168-169; loneliness and boredom in, 170; habits of, 171; developmental tasks of, 171-172; literary description of, 173-175.

only child, 67-68, **70**
characteristics of, 64, 68; I.Q. of, 68.

oral stage
definition of, 27, 230, 740; and personality traits, 27.

"oral type," 27.

organic psychosis, definition of, 740.

Ornstein, Robert, 313-315
on right and left thinking, 313; on "split-brain" people, 313-314; on Freud's distinction between conscious and unconscious, 314-315.

Osmond, H. on effect of space on social relationships, 448.

output, as means of positive reinforcement, 275.

overcrowding, effect on behavior, 447.

Ovid
on pleasure and anxiety, 548; on grief, **634**.

Owen, Robert, on "oddness," 697.

Packard, Vance, 459, 461.

Paloma, Margaret M., interviews with women, 378.

parallel play, definition of, 40.

paranoia, definition of, 216, 740.

See also schizophrenia, paranoid

paranoid personality, 672.

partial hospitalization, 704.

paternal love, 150-151.

pathological, definition of, 550.

"Peanuts," 562.

Peck, Robert, and developmental tasks for old age, 171-172.

peer group, 110-115, **116-117**
pressure, 115, 533; values, 533; definition of, 740.

"penis envy," affecting female personality, 358.

perception, 445-451, **452-454**
influenced by space and communication patterns, 450; influenced by sensory factors, 451; as studied by advertising researchers, 457; definition of selective, 469.

Persius, on death, **633**.

personal decisions 88-90, **94-96**.

personal distance, definition of, 447, 740.

personal growth group, *see* encounter group.

personality, 342-343
changing, 4, 119, 244-245; basic, 4, 233; molded by childhood, 13, 35, 72, 228; Freud's structure of, 25-26, 184, 202-209, 228; interaction of id, ego and superego in, 26, 34, 35, 206-208, **210**, 253, 256; continuous development of, 50, 239; affected by birth order, 62-65; and career choice, 136-137; as outward expression of inner needs, 184; shaped by environment, 184-185; as product of physical and chemical processes, 185; influenced by hormones, 358, 360; affected by anatomy, 358-359, 360; affected by feelings about body,

by over-permissiveness, 57; fading away in adolescence, 93; and career choice, 136; from marriage, 146-147; from maternal love, 151.

self-actualization, **245**
definition of, 242, 744; in studies by Maslow, 243.

self-esteem
sense of, 93-99, **100**; achieved in adolescence, 93; description of achievement of, 97-99; in old age, 171; as affected by feelings toward body, 360; based on achievement, 362, 364; of women based on acceptance, 378; following participation in encounter group, 424; maintained through healthy expression of anger, 574; as result of tamed aggression, 575.

self-fulfilling prophecy
definition of, 274; experiment to test influence of, 274-275.

self-image, 37, 54-62, **61-62**
development of child's, 54-62, **61-62**; dependent on acceptance of others, 115; adolescence as time to consolidate, 371; as factor in styles of emotional expression, 533; of person attempting suicide, 639.

self-reliance, development of healthy, 560.

"self-sabotage," as mask of anger, 571.

self, sense of
definition of, 119; awareness of, 411-413, 415, 560; assessment of, 425; in baby, 560.

senses
of newborn, 21; used by child to explore world, 37.

sensitivity training, *see* encounter group.

sensorimotor stage, 37-38

definition of, 37, 744; child's development during, 37-38.

sensory factor, 450-453, **452-453**
as environmental factor, 450-451, stress caused by deprivation of, 598-599.

Separate Peace, A, on initiation test, 115.

separation anxiety
example of, 221-224; definition of, 223.

sex
as submerged issue during latency, 34; fantasies about, 86; discussions about, 86-87; viewed by boys, 370; as "double message" for girls, 371; and love, 564-565.

sex differences, **353, 366-367, 372-375, 384-385,** 386; influence of anatomy, 354-360, **361;** as basis for treatment by parents, 360; in independence and aggression, 361-362; in learning and achievement, 363-365; in verbal and social sophistication, 363, 364; in intelligence, 364; stereotyped, 367-369; in viewing sexual relationships, 370-371; psychological, 383; importance of social conditioning in shaping, 385, **372-375.**

sexual desires, 86-87, 90, 358
expressed in dreams, 197; expressed in jokes, 579-580.

sexual development
stimulated in adolescence, 85; of girls, 85; of boys, 85; and masturbation, 86; influenced by hormones, 359.

sexual intercourse, 89
before marriage, 89-90.

sexual relationships, **94-96**
viewed by girls and boys, 370-371.

sexual tension, released through

Miriam S. Grace is a counselor and psychology teacher at Brookline High School (Massachusetts). She is a graduate of Brown University, with a Masters degree in counseling from Boston University. This book evolved from the curriculum she developed and tested with high-school students over a four-year period.

Philip T. Nicholson is an educational film producer and a Research Associate in Psychiatry (Law and Public Health) at the Mental Health Training Film Program of Harvard Medical School. He is also a member of the California State Bar.

Don R. Lipsitt is Chief of Psychiatry of the Mount Auburn Hospital, Associate Professor at Harvard Medical School, and Editor of the International Journal of Psychiatry in Medicine. His wife and two sons keep him in touch with reality.